D0567279

Louisiana State University Pres
3 3029 00566 8363

973.918
T867zh

Haynes   1295
   The awesome power,
Harry S. Truman as Com-
mander in Chief
                    c.1

CENTRAL

SACRAMENTO CITY-COUNTY LIBRARY
SACRAMENTO, CALIFORNIA

THE
AWESOME
POWER

Richard F. Haynes

THE AWESOME POWER

Harry S. Truman as Commander in Chief

LOUISIANA STATE UNIVERSITY PRESS / BATON ROUGE

To Carol

ISBN 0–8071–0054–4
Library of Congress Catalog Card Number 73–81847
Copyright © 1973 by Louisiana State University Press
All rights reserved
Manufactured in the United States of America
Printed by The TJM Corporation, Baton Rouge, Louisiana
Designed by Albert Crochet

CENTRAL

c . /

Contents

Acknowledgments

The author wishes to express his deep gratitude to T. Harry Williams for his wise counsel over the years. He also desires to thank the staff of the Harry S. Truman Library for their cooperation. Thomas Hohmann and Hazel Ward of the Modern Military Records Division of the National Archives went far beyond the call of duty in guiding this researcher through the labyrinth of government documents. For varied kinds of assistance to me in producing this book I am grateful to my editor, Martha Hall, at the Louisiana State University Press, Dianne Green of Sandel Library, Eugene and Camille Schroeder, Ewing and Louise Cook, and Betty Stanley. My wife, Carol Cook Haynes, has contributed more to this work through her advice, encouragement and secretarial efforts than words can say. Lastly, the author would be remiss if he did not acknowledge the patience of his daughters, Allison and Melissa, while their father was preoccupied.

THE
AWESOME
POWER

1 / The Clause

He's the absolute commander of the armed forces of the United States in time of war. He's the commander of the armed forces when they're called out for any purpose, if he wants to take control of them. Nobody else can do it.[1]

—HARRY S. TRUMAN

Early one summer morning in 1950 Harry Truman, over his bedside telephone, ordered army combat units into Korea. This was the beginning of American military involvement in the Korean War. At no time did Truman seek the advice or approval of the Congress or the American people. His successors involved America in a far more costly war in the Far East in much the same manner. American presidents exercise an almost exclusive control over the military might of the nation. They can, for example, without consent from anyone, order a nuclear missile attack that could end civilization. On a less drastic level, they can order the military into combat action for any reason they personally and solely deem sufficient. Congressional checks, judicial restraints, and majority opinions have yet to effectively diminish this authority.

This awesome power of the presidency is predicated upon one brief clause of the Constitution: "The President shall be Commander-in-Chief of the Army and Navy of the United States, and of the militia of the several states, when called into the actual service of the United States." This vaguely worded sentence provides the power resources of the presidency.

The broad spectrum of discretionary command authority available to the presidents evolved through custom, judicial interpretations, legislative action or inaction, and the obvious exigencies imposed by modern military technology. The drafters of the Constitution had not anticipated that the clause meant any more than that the president was to have a general, final authority over the military. In the *Federalist Papers* (No. 69), Alexander Hamilton wrote that the title of com-

3

mander in chief "would amount to nothing more than the supreme command and direction of the military and naval forces, as first general and admiral of the Confederacy." Discussing this military function again (in No. 74), Hamilton argued that it must be vested exclusively in the president. He also felt that the division between civilian and military powers of the executive office should disappear, particularly in time of war.[2] Most of the Founding Fathers believed that the primary purpose of the commander-in-chief clause was to insure that the president, in the exercise of his war (emergency) powers, would be unmistakably superior to any of his military or civilian subordinates. They conceived of a clearly established path of authority, all emanating from a single source—the civilian head of the executive branch of the national government.[3]

Civilian control over the conduct of military operations was accepted as a fundamental tenet. It was felt that the democratic process would be under constant threat if a military commander were to be granted ultimate authority for the conduct of the armed forces of the nation. In the ratifying conventions the only objection to this clause, as Joseph Story explained in his *Commentaries*, was that "It would be dangerous to let him [the president] command in person." But Story added, "The proprietary of admitting the President to be Commander-in-Chief, so far as to give orders and have a general superintendency, was admitted." [4]

Numerous court tests of the war and emergency powers have worked their way through the judicial system. The general principle which has emerged is that the courts accept the president's supremacy over the military without significant limitations. After studying hundreds of court cases involving tests of the president's military powers, Clinton Rossiter has concluded that the commander in chief enjoys "a peculiar degree of freedom from the review and restraints of the judicial process." [5]

There seems little doubt that, so far as the courts are concerned, the president's control over the armed forces of the nation is complete. The judiciary, when confronted with tests of the war powers, has generally accepted Hamilton's view that "there can be no limitation of that authority which is to provide for the defense and protection of the community . . . in any matter essential to the formation, direction, or support of the national forces." Rossiter's study of this subject has led him to conclude that not only do the courts accept Hamilton's view, but that the Constitution *encourages* exercise of the war powers, and the restraint on presidential use of these powers is a "moral limitation" alone.[6]

The Constitution specifically delegates to Congress the power to declare war, to raise and support an army and navy, and "to make rules for the government and regulation of the land and naval forces." The language of these clauses would seem to indicate that the drafters intended that the legislative branch have coextensive powers over the armed forces in order to offset the possibility of a military dictatorship. While permanent military dictatorships have not resulted, Congress has failed to exercise an effective check on presidential control over military policy.[7]

Not only has the Congress been generally ineffective in limiting the president's use of military powers, but it has also often been unable to protect its own delegated military authority from executive usurpation. This is particularly true of the post–World War II era. The congressional role in the formulation of military policy is peripheral at best, ordinarily being confined to lobbying for certain defense programs, the development of particular weapons systems, and the creation, expansion, or continuation of various military bases for political reasons.[8]

Aside from these considerations, in the normal course of events, Congress provides the force levels and military budgets requested by the president. It is difficult for Congress to challenge the validity of presidential requests in these two areas where the president must have legislative sanction. The only solid ground for attack would be that the troop or budget requests are not consonant with the broad objectives of the nation's military policies. As often as not, these goals are established by the president (as a popular leader) in the first place. To attack these goals, or their proposed legislative implementation, would require substantial proof often not available to Congress. The president's advantage lies in the fact that through control of the executive agencies, he monopolizes the available information. The Congress obtains its knowledge of military policy matters through hearings conducted by the various committees concerned with military and foreign affairs. Of necessity, the witnesses are high-ranking civil and military officials of the Pentagon, directly responsible to the commander in chief.

The other great military check held by the Congress, the exclusive power to declare war, has seldom been employed, simply because the United States has been in a formally declared state of war on only a few occasions. Yet, in the period 1789–1956, there are more than one hundred separate instances of American military forces engaging in hostile actions on foreign soil at the order of the president, without a declaration of war or other form of prior approval on the part of the Congress.[9] In most cases the president's action was based on his judgment that an "emergency" situation existed, necessitating immediate decision. Often the Congress has subsequently approved the president's action by a resolution or war declaration. Congress has never declared war on its own initiative, nor has it ever refused a president's request for a war declaration.[10] The problem is, of course, that Congress is confronted with a *fait accompli*: It can endorse or condemn; it cannot undo, the spilling of blood being an irrevocable action by its very nature. A distinguished senator, Arthur H. Vandenberg, writing in 1947, expressed the congressional dilemma this way: "The trouble is that these 'crises' never reach Congress until they have developed to a point where Congressional discretion is pathetically restricted. When things finally reach a point where a President asks us to 'declare war' there usually is nothing left except to 'declare war.' " [11]

In practice, if not in law, once war or a national emergency has been declared, total military authority is assumed by the president. This power of command given to the president is not effectively limited by the Congress, nor willingly shared with that body by the commander in chief.[12] A staff study by lawyers attached to the White House, Justice, Defense, and State departments in 1948 offered the opinion that "it seems doubtful whether Congress has the Constitutional power to limit the President's freedom of action in disposing of the forces under his command." It is a fair generalization to conclude that the constitutional separation of military powers is ignored in practice.[13]

The expansion of the military powers of the presidency has been an evolutionary process that began with the office. Prior to Truman, the presidents most responsible for enlarging the role of the commander in chief were James Polk, Abraham Lincoln, and Franklin Roosevelt. It is instructive to note that all served in time of war when Congress is less likely to insist upon its prerogatives.

Polk had indicated to the cabinet on his very first day in office that he would insist on the Rio Grande River as the southern border of Texas and that he considered acquisition of California a major objective of his presidency. His offer to purchase the California territory was a sham exercise, for he would accept only his own terms. And when Mexico refused to treat with the minister bearing his demands, the president ordered Zachary Taylor to move his forces south from the Nueces River to the Rio Grande, "an order that altered the situation by making war a probability rather than a mere possibility." There can be little doubt that Polk precipitated hostilities with Mexico. His objective in doing so was to take by military conquest all Mexican land north of the Gila and Rio Grande rivers and from Texas westward to the Pacific.[14]

> When war broke out he made it . . . clear that he intended to be *the commander in chief*. The president, Polk declared, was held responsible for the conduct of the war; he intended to be responsible, and he exercised that responsibility to the limit of his endurance. He determined the general strategy of military and naval operations; he chose commanding officers; he gave personal attention to supply problems; he energized so far as he could the General Staff; he controlled the military and naval estimates; and he used the cabinet as a major coordinating agency. . . . The president was the center on which all else depended; Hamilton's doctrine of the unity of the executive power was seldom more truly exemplified.[15]

Polk clearly interpreted his function as commander in chief as including not only military policy-making and supreme command, but leadership in determining overall campaign strategy as well. Although devoid of any military training, as were the majority of his cabinet and other advisers, the President did a sound job of administering the war effort.[16]

Polk also established a precedent for future commanders in chief with respect to the war powers of the Congress. In the first place, it was his ordering of Taylor's army into disputed territory between the Nueces and the Rio Grande that led inevitably to bloodletting on both sides. Then, Polk asked the Congress to declare war on the basis of the hostilities which were engendered by his decisions. The Congress exercised its constitutional power to declare war, but, in reality, it merely acknowledged an existing condition created by the president.

With respect to the other military controls granted specifically to the Congress by the Constitution, Polk also had his way. He demonstrated that in this area, the principle of separation of powers simply was not operable. Congress, being a large, deliberative body with an inherent inertia, showed that it was structurally incapable of exercising coordinate authority over the conduct of war. Polk led the Congress in the establishment and financing of the military and the disposition of these forces. In the first real test of its military authority, the Congress had—more by default, than design—relinquished its powers to the commander in chief.

During the Mexican War an effective unity of the military command structure was established, with James Polk as the single, ultimate source of all military decisions. The president had clearly shown in his conduct of the war, as Leonard White concluded in his study of Polk, that "A president could be a commander in chief. A president could run a war." [17]

It is ironic that a Whig representative from Illinois, who was highly critical of Polk's extraordinary war powers, was to become the next wartime commander in chief. Abraham Lincoln first gained national attention by his "Spot Resolutions" which attacked the president for ordering Taylor down to the Rio Grande and justifying his demand for war on the resultant fighting. Lincoln consistently maintained that the Mexican War "was unnecessarily and unconstitutionally commenced by the President." [18]

Lincoln not only attacked Polk for unlawfully initiating the war with Mexico, he also condemned the methods exercised by the president in his conduct of the war. For example, in a speech at Wilmington, Delaware, in June, 1841, a newspaper recorded that Lincoln denounced Polk's administration as despotic, unresponsive to the will of the people, and one characterized by an abusive use of power. The article, apparently paraphrasing Lincoln, continued: "The manner in which the present Executive had carried on the Mexican war should condemn it . . . before the whole people. . . . It was a war of conquest brought into existence to catch votes." [19]

There is little reason to doubt that at least part of Lincoln's attack on Polk's application of the war powers was motivated by partisan political considerations. In addition, Lincoln found himself in the awkward position of denouncing the autocratic powers of the commander in chief, but voting in the House for war legislation that had the effect of continuing and extending these powers. Lincoln voted his approval of the administration's requests because he recognized the need to fully support the armed forces in what, in the final analysis, he believed to be a just war.[20] Certainly many congressmen during Lincoln's presidency, finding themselves in the same quandary, could sympathize with the representative from Illinois.

Even granting that Lincoln was influenced by partisanship and the limited perspective of a back-row seat in the House, it must still be acknowledged that he sincerely deplored in principle this erosion of congressional authority. He revealed this genuine concern in a letter written in February, 1848:

> Allow the President to invade a neighboring nation, whenever *he* shall deem it necessary to repel an invasion, and you will allow him to do so, *whenever he may choose to say* he deems it necessary for such purpose—and you allow him to make war at pleasure. Study to see if you can fix *any limit* to his power in this respect. . . .
> The provision of the Constitution giving the warmaking powers to Congress, was dictated, as I understand it, by the following reasons. Kings had always been involving their people in wars, pretending generally, if not always, that the good of the people was the object. This, our Convention understood to be the most oppressive of all Kingly oppressions; and they resolved to so frame the Constitution that *no one man* should hold the power of bringing this oppression upon us.[21]

It fell to Lincoln to act as commander in chief in the first modern total war, a war involving all of the people and a complete commitment of all the nation's resources; a war without compromise or any limitation on its objectives. In the end, Lincoln, having tested many of the outer reaches of his constitutional grants of authority, emerged in the role of "emergency dictator," in effective control of a mighty military arsenal.[22]

With the fall of Fort Sumter on April 14, 1861, Lincoln began immediately to employ his emergency powers. He called for a special session of the Congress to convene on July 4, 1861. But in the ten-week interim, Lincoln took steps that represent "perhaps the widest use of unilateral Presidential power without prior congresional sanction." [23] Basing his actions on the commander-in-chief clause of the Constitution as well as the clause instructing him "to take care that the laws be faithfully executed," he began by issuing a presidential proclamation on April 15, 1861, calling the militia into federal service and demanding an end to insurrection. In the weeks remaining before Congress convened, Lincoln ordered several extraordinary measures which he deemed necessary:

During this period of ten weeks Lincoln amalgamated the available state militias into a ninety days' volunteer force, called 40,000 volunteers for three years' service, added 23,000 men to the Regular Army and 18,000 to the Navy, paid out two millions from unappropriated funds in the Treasury to persons unauthorized to receive it, closed the Post Office to "treasonable correspondence," subjected passengers to and from foreign countries to new passport regulations, proclaimed a blockade of the Southern ports, suspended the writ of *habeas corpus* in various places, and caused the arrest and military detention of persons "who were represented to him" as being engaged in or contemplating "treasonable practices"—and all this for the most part without the least statutory authorization.[24]

When Congress was assembled on July 4 it heard Lincoln's powerful defense of his conduct, and it soon after passed a series of statutes authorizing the emergency actions taken by the president.[25] But this does not diminish the fact that Lincoln had acted unilaterally and boldly, establishing a number of precedents to guide future chief executives. The belated congressional sanction of these steps was little more than a gesture of approval, albeit significant for the future. It is not really noteworthy that Lincoln—or the other wartime presidents—did not face any considerable opposition to the use, or usurpation, of the war powers. During times of national emergency the Congress has quite freely transferred its war powers to the commander in chief, either for a fixed period of time, or the duration of the emergency. "Congress too, likes to win wars," Clinton Rossiter has pointed out, "and Congressmen are more likely to needle the President for inactivity and timidity than to accuse him of acting too swiftly and arbitrarily." [26]

Lincoln apparently believed and acted on the assumption that his emergency powers as commander in chief were sufficient for all situations produced by the Civil War. While he did work with and through the Congress as a general rule, he apparently felt no impelling obligation to wait for congressional authorization or for the judiciary's blessings, if he believed conditions dictated otherwise. This fundamental assumption of power was the underlying policy upon which Lincoln's war administration was predicated.[27] Lincoln's own words can be used to support this contention. The most obvious example is his oft-quoted remark to the Congress in defense of his suspension of habeas corpus: "Are all the laws, *but one*, to go unexecuted, and the government itself to go to pieces, lest that one be violated?" [28] Again, in August, 1863, Lincoln replied to a critic who demanded retraction of the Emancipation Proclamation by saying, "You say it is unconstitutional—I think differently. I think the constitution invests its commander-in-chief with the law of war, in time of war." [29] Finally, in an explicit statement on his concept of his role, Lincoln wrote: "I did understand . . . that my oath to preserve the constitution to the best of my ability, imposed upon me the duty of preserving by every indispensable means, that government—that nation—of which that constitution was the organic law. . . . I felt that measures, otherwise unconstitutional, might become lawful, by becoming indispensable to the preservation of the nation. Right or wrong, I assume this ground, and now avow it." [30]

In his preparedness moves prior to American involvement in World War II, Franklin Roosevelt expanded the historical definition of the commander in chief's function. On September 8, 1939, the president issued a proclamation declaring the country to be in a state of "limited national emergency." Under the authority of this proclamation Roosevelt increased the National Guard by thirty-five thousand and the army by seventeen thousand over prior limits. This cautious early step was, Roosevelt felt, about all he could do in view of the prevailing isolationist sentiment. As this isolationist spirit withered in the face of Axis advances into Scandanavia and the Low Countries of Europe in early 1940, Roosevelt was able to move more boldly.[31]

In June, 1940, on Prime Minister Churchill's request, Roosevelt ordered the War Department to release to Great Britain "surplus or outdated" rifles, planes, and other military hardware. In this busy summer of 1940 FDR also dispatched American technicians and military advisers to England. He allowed British pilots to be trained and British warships to be repaired in the United States. And on September 2, 1940, the administration concluded an executive agreement with England called the "destroyer-bases" deal. By its terms, fifty "outdated" (but recently reconditioned) naval warships were transferred to English control in return for the leasing to the United States of sites for military bases on British possessions. "The deal was an abandonment of any pretense of neutrality. It was an act of war." [32]

Roosevelt further compromised the quasi-neutral posture of the United States in securing the enactment of H. R. 1776, the Lend-Lease Act of March, 1941. By its terms the president could, whenever he believed "national defense" to be involved, authorize his administrators to procure and "sell, transfer, exchange, lease, lend or otherwise dispose of the same to any government whose defense the President deemed vital" to United States security, on whatever terms he cared to set.[33] The commander in chief now had the power over and control of the dispersal of all arms and munitions manufactured in the United States as well as control over all its armed forces. He was the most powerful single human being in the world. Edward S. Corwin rightly states, with respect to the Lend-Lease Act, that "No more sweeping delegation of legislative power has ever been made to an American president." [34]

A good case can be made that American participation in World War II was inevitable. But such an argument does not justify the propriety of the destroyer-bases deal and the Lend-Lease Act. The former was an executive caveat, exercising the commander-in-chief powers to determine future foreign relations and military alignments. The latter represented a sweeping abdication of military responsibility by the Congress, giving the commander in chief extremely broad controls over an America still (technically) at peace. The opponents of Lend-Lease recognized this and argued in vain that the act changed and distorted the traditional commander-in-chief theory. As Senator Burton Wheeler expressed it, "The proponents of this bill . . . are proclaiming a new constitutional theory which places the actual power to involve our country in war at the uncontrolled discretion of the Executive." [35]

Roosevelt's direct command of the military during World War II was effected by his issuance of a formal military order in July, 1939. The order removed from the service departments the Joint Army-Navy Board and a number of procurement agencies and placed them in the executive office of the president. Among other things, this order had the effect of placing the chief of naval operations and the chief of staff of the army, directly under the command and supervision of the commander in chief:

> The immediate results of this new arrangement were modest but significant. The principal war agencies in both the strategic and the production fields were clearly established as presidential, not departmental, agencies. . . . The Military Order of 1939 had the effect of raising the Joint Board above the departmental level. By placing the chiefs in a special relationship to the President, it made them in some way inde-

pendent of their immediate civilian superiors. . . . Increasingly after 1939 the Joint Board, under the control of the President, concerned itself with questions of national rather than service strategy. . . .

By this little-noticed Military Order of 1939, Franklin Roosevelt laid the institutional foundations of his powers as commander in chief. The new arrangements were not a model of administrative symmetry. . . . In particular the service secretaries were placed in an anomalous position; they retained control over, and responsibility for, their departments but *not* their military chieftains, who, with their advisers, operated directly beneath the President. If the service secretaries were indeed the principal agents of civilian control over the military, it would seem that in strategic matters the chiefs, as Admiral Leahy was to remark at the end of the war, were "under no civilian control whatever," apart, of course, from that exercised by the President himself.[36]

Despite FDR's own unsystematic and often haphazard style of leadership, he found his command authority highly institutionalized by the very vastness of the military structure he had to command. Roosevelt discovered that even the commander in chief could have little direct effect on the machinery of command in such a vast undertaking. Nor was there much need to. He set the grand strategy of the war with his joint chiefs, with whom he maintained a personal, amiable relationship, and they implemented it throughout the command structure. Because the system worked, Roosevelt did not involve himself in operational planning; nor did he attempt to dictate tactics to the theater commanders. For a time in the midst of the war FDR doubted the strategic advice of his joint chiefs, leaning more toward politically oriented Allied proposals, but he soon relented, relying generally upon his military planners to determine strategy. William R. Emerson, in an essay on Roosevelt as war leader, came to this fitting conclusion: "He performed truly the function of the American commander in chief, which is to bind together the varied political and military strands which make up war, keeping each in its proper relation to the whole." [37]

On April 12, 1945, with victory in Europe a certainty, but the war in the Pacific still far from over, Franklin Roosevelt died of a massive cerebral hemorrhage. And so, with brutal suddenness, the vice-president found himself in full command of the most powerful military apparatus the earth has ever known.

2/ The Apprentice

One thing I am certain about, there's nothing in our history ... that shows that a man can be trained to be President of the United States, or that we could ensure that he would ever become President even if trained for the job, because there are so many factors that enter into the making of a President.[1]

—HARRY S. TRUMAN

Harry S. Truman's life lends credibility to the myth that any boy born in America can be president. He was born in Lamar, Missouri, in 1884, of solid, rural, Protestant stock. His youth was spent on a six-hundred-acre farm and in Independence, an unexceptional small town near Kansas City. His early life was uneventful—the ordinary progression of minor tribulations and small triumphs which characterize the background of most Americans. If Harry Truman was anything, he was "average," showing no particular abilities or special promise.[2]

Truman's family could not afford to send him to college. He had hoped to apply to the United States Military Academy but gave up the idea when told his poor eyesight could not meet the minimal standards required for admission. He remained an avid student of history and government, but his formal education ended with graduation from high school: "I've always been sorry I did not get a university education. But I got it in the Army the hard way—and it stuck." [3] His first job after high school was as a timekeeper for a railroad construction crew. He went from that to bank clerking and, in 1906, honored his father's request to return and work the six-hundred-acre family farm at Grandview. For the next decade farming remained Truman's principal occupation, although he also served at various times as a road overseer and postmaster. Looking for the main chance, in 1916, he acquired a one-third interest in a wildcat drilling company, but the firm never returned him any appreciable profits, one reason being the disruption caused by American participation in World War I.[4]

The future commander in chief got his first taste of military life in

14

1905. As he wrote, "having been something of a student of military history, I decided to join the 'militia' referred to in Washington's message of 1790." [5] So he enlisted in Battery B of the National Guard at Kansas City in the year it was organized. Shortly afterward, in his first guard encampment at Cape Girardeau, Missouri, Truman was a private, serving as "number two man" on a three-inch gun. With United States entry into World War I, the Kansas City–Independence guard batteries were expanded into a full regiment. In the custom of the time, officers were chosen by the members of the regiment; Truman was elected a first lieutenant of light artillery in Battery F of the Second Missouri Field Artillery. Three months later, in August, 1917, his unit was sworn into federal service as the 129th Field Artillery of the Thirty-fifth Division. The unit was activated and ordered to Camp Doniphan, Fort Sill, Oklahoma, on September 26, 1917.[6]

After training in Oklahoma, Truman was shipped to France in March, 1918. There he received additional instruction at two separate artillery schools, and on July 11, by now a captain, he was given command of Battery D, 129th Field Artillery, in the Vosges Mountains. He fired his first combat barrage there on September 6, 1918. From then until the armistice in November, Captain Truman commanded his unit at St. Mihiel, the Meuse-Argonne, Varennes, Verdun, and Metz.[7]

Truman referred to these brief months of combat often during his political career, always with a mixture of pride and romantic nostalgia, as, for example, in a radio address he broadcast to the armed forces following FDR's death:

> I have done as you would do in the field when the Commander falls. My duties and responsibilities are clear. I have assumed them. These duties will be carried on in keeping with our American tradition.
> As a veteran of the First World War, I have seen death on the battlefield. When I fought in France with the 35th Division, I saw good officers and men fall, and be replaced. . . .
> I know the strain, the mud, the misery, the utter weariness of the soldier in the field. And I know too his courage, his stamina, his faith in his comrades, his country, and himself.
> We are depending on every one of you.[8]

Among men who have known the mud and misery of warfare, there often exists a mystic bond; a tribal sense that leads them into postwar quasi-military organizations wherein they can continue their wartime associations and (presumably) relive past glories. So it was with Truman. Following his return to Missouri after the war, he continued his contact with the military world, most notably by becoming active in the field artillery reserve. In addition, he was instrumental in creating Missouri's first chapter of the Reserve Officers Association, at Kansas City in 1921. Later, when the organization had spread across Missouri, Truman became the first president of the statewide association.[9]

"My whole political career," Truman would say many years later, "[was] based upon my war service and war associates." This was certainly true of its beginnings. He opened a clothing store at Kansas City in 1919 in partnership with a friend from the war days, former sergeant Eddie Jacobson. Following a successful initial year, the business went downhill because, as Truman explained it, the Republicans gained control of the nation. In the spring of 1922, with his business at the point of bankruptcy, he was urged by Jim Pendergast to seek election as county judge. Pendergast had served with Truman as an officer in the 129th, later commanding his own battery in the 130th Field Artillery. His father was Michael J. Pendergast, who, with his brother Tom, ruled the powerful political machine that controlled Kansas City and Jackson County. According to Truman, he won the endorsement of the machine in a meeting in which Mike Pendergast praised him as a veteran of World War I and one of the few officers "whose men didn't want to shoot him." [10]

Truman won the race for county judge in 1922 but lost his bid for reelection in 1924, the only defeat of his political career. In 1926 he ran for "presiding judge" of Jackson County and won by the substantial margin of sixteen thousand votes. Four years later, by a far wider margin of fifty-eight thousand votes, Truman was reelected to his judgeship. His enthusiastic program of road building, hospital and courthouse construction had apparently won him the support of the voters as well as the Pendergast machine. [11]

As his term ended in 1934, Truman considered running for county collector, governor, or congressman from the newly created Fourth Congressional District in eastern Jackson County. But Boss Pendergast, for political reasons of his own, insisted that Truman run for the Senate. Although his chances appeared very slim, Truman agreed. It would probably have been a futile exercise for a Democrat to seek any of the posts Truman had considered without the blessing of the Kansas City machine.[12]

In the Democratic primary Truman defeated two experienced congressmen by a plurality of some 44,000 votes. In the general election he opposed the incumbent, Roscoe C. Patterson, a conservative Republican from Springfield. Truman campaigned on a pro-New Deal platform and took the Senate seat from Patterson with a 254,000-vote majority.[13]

During his senatorial campaigns and in his first months in office, Truman was vilified as a "messenger boy" for Pendergast and as "the Senator from Pendergast." The Kansas City machine was nationally infamous for its brazen election frauds and use of brutality and intimidation. Yet Truman was able to shake the onus of this association, for —confounding his political opponents—he was apparently above reproach in his personal and public conduct. Despite intensive digging by many, no substantive evidence has yet been unearthed to discredit his conduct in office.[14]

Biographers of Truman, notably Cabell Phillips, have been inclined to explain this contradiction—the straight man in the crooked machine—as political pragmatism. For Truman to aspire to political office, he had to come to terms with the realities of hard-nosed urban machine organization. The picture that emerges from such defense of what was at best an unholy alliance is that of an ethical bankrupt, not a Don Quixote fighting hopeless odds in a righteous cause. For example, Phillips writes:

> Moralists will find it difficult to exculpate Harry Truman while condemning the machine of which he was a part. To Truman himself there was no paradox in his relationship with the Pendergasts. He understood the nature of organization politics and the code of loyalty by which it survives. . . . So he did what many another smart political comer has done: He rode the machine as far as it would take him but kept his hands clean along the way. That is a pragmatic rather than a moralistic philosophy, but under the rules of our political system it is what pays off.[15]

Truman did subscribe to a "code of loyalty" where his friends and political comrades were concerned. For example, although it would have been politically expedient to disavow his connections with Pendergast once in the Senate, particularly after the machine was crushed in the late thirties, he remained loyal to the man although he voted his own way. As he put it: "Tom Pendergast never asked me to do a dishonest deed. . . . He was always my friend. He was always honest with me, and when he made a promise he kept it." [16]

Truman's first term in the Senate was unmarked by any singular contribution. He was assigned to the Interstate Commerce and Appropriations committees. He regretted not being assigned to Military Affairs: "Ever since World War I, I had maintained an active interest in the Army and its administration, and I would have welcomed an assignment to the Military Affairs Committee." As a freshman he accepted the unwritten rules of the club, remaining quietly in the background, voting generally with the administration. In his *Coming of the New Deal*, historian Arthur Schlesinger, Jr., has described Senator Truman as a typical New Deal Democrat, "who combined the party regularity of the older Democrats with the liberal fervor of the older progressives." [17]

Truman's faithfulness to the Roosevelt administration was not reciprocated. FDR ignored him, giving all the patronage for Missouri to the senior senator, Bennett Champ Clark, who often voted against New Deal measures. Without the support of the president or any substantial power bloc back in Missouri, and the Pendergast machine in ruins, Truman's prospects for reelection in 1940 were extremely gloomy. The campaign was made no easier by his having to face two impressive challengers for his seat, the incumbent governor, Lloyd C. Stark, and Maurice Milligan, the district attorney for Kansas City, who had led the investigation that exposed and destroyed the Pendergast machine. In addition to these difficulties, the only sizable Missouri newspaper to endorse the candidacy of Harry Truman was the Kansas City *Journal*.[18]

Despite these impressive odds, Truman won the 1940 Democratic primary by a margin of less than eight thousand votes in a triumph as surprising and unpredictable as his presidential victory eight years later. In the general election he had a relatively easy time of it, defeating Manvelle Davis, the Republican nominee. Now he could return to the Senate free of any labels, for he had unquestionably won in his own right.

The Roosevelt administration was pushing its military preparedness program in earnest as Truman's second term in the Senate began in January, 1941. Through his membership on the Appropriations Committee, Truman was intimately aware that billions were being expended under contract to private manufacturers for the production of military items. Besides these defense expenditures, the administration requested an additional $4 billion to expand the army and $7 billion for aid to England. The total additional appropriations for the first few months of 1941 exceeded $25 billion.

During his campaign Truman had heard many tales of gross inefficiency and mismanagement of government contracts. As a politician he particularly bridled at reports that plants in Missouri were not getting their fair share of these lucrative defense contracts. As the rumors of waste, corruption, and favoritism to major producers continued to pile up, Truman decided to conduct his own investigation. Traveling in his own car, he drove down the eastern seaboard from Maryland to Florida, across the Gulf Coast to Texas, northward through Oklahoma and Nebraska to Wisconsin and Michigan, and back to Washington. He visited numerous defense plants and war camps and related military projects without—as Truman remembers it—identifying himself as a United States senator.[19] Security questions aside, his personal odyssey confirmed the rumors and convinced him of the need for a congressional watchdog over these expenditures.

In February, 1941, Truman made a speech in the Senate denouncing the methods used for awarding defense contracts, condemning the concentration of these awards among a few large manufacturers and citing several abuses by corporations, particularly in "cost-plus" contracts. He proposed a resolution calling for a five-member committee to investigate the national defense program on a budget of twenty-five thousand dollars.[20] Truman's timing, although accidental, was excellent: A similar resolution had just been offered in the House by Eugene Cox of Georgia, who was bitterly hostile to the administration.

Roosevelt, with the encouragement of Senator James F. Byrnes, his close confidant and a power in the Congress, decided to support the Senate resolution, with Truman, a consistent loyalist, as committee chairman. After considerable infighting, Truman was named to head the Special Committee to Investigate the National Defense Program. The bipartisan membership was raised to seven from the five originally proposed and the appropriation reduced from twenty-five thousand to fifteen thousand dollars. Both changes were forced on Truman by Byrnes, who wanted to prevent the committee from becoming powerful enough to hamper or embarrass the administration.[21]

Truman was concerned about the role his committee was to play. He had been granted a broad franchise by the Senate to investigate every phase of military spending. However, he was determined to avoid interfering in policy or strategy matters, which he firmly believed were the sole province of the chief executive. "The Special Committee never discussed military strategy, although we took testimony from many generals and admirals," Truman wrote in his *Memoirs*, adding, "The military policy of the United States was entrusted to the President and the Joint Chiefs of Staff and not to any congressional committee." He recalled too, resisting other senators, usually Republicans like Robert Taft, Owen Brewster, and Arthur Vandenberg, who encouraged the committee to take actions similar to those of the Committee on the Conduct of the War that bedeviled Abraham Lincoln in his exercise of the war powers.[22] "Thank goodness," Truman said, "I knew my history and I wouldn't do it." [23]

The history of congressional/presidential relations during the Civil War was known to Truman long before from his avid reading of military history. However, when he became head of the Special Committee, he borrowed the *Reports of the Joint Committee on the Conduct of the War* from the Library of Congress, studied them, and came to this conclusion: "These historic records constitute a most interesting set of documents. That committee of the Union Congress was said by Douglas Southall Freeman, the biographer of Robert E. Lee, to have been of material assistance to the Confederacy. I became familiar with its mistakes and was determined to avoid the same errors in the conduct of my special committee. Here, as in many other instances, I found the teachings of history to be valuable in my own approach to current problems." [24]

Truman established rigid guidelines within which his committee operated. He functioned as a "chief of staff," firmly directing the committee, but freely delegating responsibility. By insisting that all reports to Congress had to be unanimous, he made this bipartisan committee apolitical. The committee concerned itself almost exclusively with fact-finding relative to military procurement, construction, types and terms of government contracts, and the method of awarding such contracts. Through the committee, Truman also made certain that small manufacturers and suppliers received an equitable percentage of the government's business, chiefly through subcontracting with the principal contractual agents.[25]

In the four years it existed, the Truman Committee—for so it was called—accomplished much with very little money: Truman estimated that his committee saved the nation $15 billion while spending about $400 thousand for expenses. Through the countless investigations, endless hearings, special reports, and annual reports to the Senate, the committee generated a great deal of nationwide publicity that must have had a strong deterrent effect on those who might otherwise have been tempted to misuse government funds. As the committee grew in stature the White House and the Pentagon became less wary and more amenable to suggestions. According to Truman, Roosevelt gave him "wholehearted cooperation" once he realized the senator was not out to smear him.[26]

The military services were not always to cooperate with the Truman Committee. The best example of military opposition concerned planning for industrial reconversion. Following the lead of others like the distinguished Bernard Baruch and Donald M. Nelson, head of the War Production Board, the committee urged in March, 1944, that an immediate start be made on plans for reconversion of industry to peacetime production. The War Department somehow feared that such planning would jeopardize full military strength prior to the war's conclusion. The army responded to Truman's appeal with a forceful propaganda campaign that garnered public and administration support by playing up a patriotic theme and making dire predictions about troops in the field without guns or ammunition because of production lags. The end result of this campaign was a failure on the part of the government to adequately prepare or initiate any important reconversion steps prior to Harry Truman's taking office. The chaotic demobilization process was one of the most serious problems of his first year as president.[27]

Truman had a lifelong love affair with the military. He wrote and spoke of America's wars with obvious pride and a romantic view of soldiering. His struggles with the services in his committee investigations qualified his romanticism with the realization that there were areas of national life that should be free of military influence. As early as 1942 (in an interview) he expressed concern over what President Eisenhower would describe eighteen years later as the "military-industrial complex." Truman said:

> The function of generals and admirals is to fight battles. . . . They have no experience in business or industry, and the job of producing what they ask for should be left to businessmen under the direction of ex-

perienced civilians. I am firmly convinced that any attempt on the part of these ambitious generals and admirals to take complete control over the nation's economy would not only place vital functions in inexperienced hands, but would present a definite threat to our post war political and economic structure.[28]

Truman steadfastly maintained that his committee functioned only as an investigative body "trying to remove obstructions to the success of the production program and to prevent the repetition of costly errors." [29] However, the committee had, in fact, begun to influence the way the services, defense agencies, and the Roosevelt administration itself conducted the military production efforts of the nation. This was so because of the prestige the committee had acquired and because Truman was seldom at cross-purposes with the White House.

On those few occasions when Truman thought it necessary to challenge the president, he found FDR willing to accomodate him. For example, in January, 1942, Truman told Roosevelt that his committee was going to recommend that wartime production be concentrated under a single person for greater efficiency. The following day, the White House announced that Donald Nelson was to coordinate all defense production as director of the Office of Production Management. A short time later, when Truman became critical of OPM and called for a drastic reorganization, the president responded by establishing the War Production Board. Although Truman greatly admired FDR, he was not intimidated by him: "Mr. President," he told him during one exchange, "the White House and Capitol are not connected by a one-way street." [30]

The conflicts between the senator and the president were few and far between. For Truman recognized that whatever influence he and the committee enjoyed was tied to the fact that the president approved of their activities. Truman was surprisingly candid about his lack of any real authority. Typical is this reply to a correspondent in 1943: "The Congress is only a legislative body. . . . There is not very much a Senator or Congressman can do but publicly discuss the shortcomings of those who are supposed to administer the law."[31] Particularly, Truman might have added, when the Congress is confronted by a chief executive armed with extraordinary war powers. But with FDR in sympathy with Truman's objectives, this was never a problem. In fact, FDR used Truman to help keep members of his own executive department in line. As Truman recalled in 1959, the president frequently summoned him to the White House to make the same request: "I'd go down and talk to him [Roosevelt], and he'd say, 'So-and-so over here, I can't do anything with him, and he's causing me trouble. I wish you'd give him a poke or two.' I'd do it and the thing would straighten out. That got me into a lot of trouble. He finally decided that maybe I'd make a good Vice-President." [32]

Viewed in that light, the special committee was his passport to the vice-presidency. It was also a good training ground for a man destined to become a wartime president. In a profile on Senator Truman in 1945, one journalist described him as the civilian (aside from FDR) who contributed most to the war effort. Similar views were expressed by the majority of correspondents covering Washington during this period.[33]

The committee did make mistakes, usually minor, often involving faulty data or the misuse of sweeping critical generalities, but it is very difficult to find criticism of its total effort during World War II. The reverse is true. For example, James Forrestal, then under secretary of the navy, told Truman that the committee "served a useful purpose in providing a medium for the exploration of criticism of the war effort. . . . The Navy . . . welcomes the kind of additional outside scrutiny which your Committee provides. Testifying in 1942, Under Secretary of War Robert Patterson spoke of "constructive assistance" Truman had provided: "Some of the very best features of our war program have their origins from the investigations made by this Committee." In a similar vein, the chairman of the War Production Board wrote of the "high purpose" comprehended by the special committee.[34]

Many journalists appeared equally impressed. Luther Huston, in a 1945 profile of Truman for the New York *Times*, wrote that the special committee had probably averted numerous national scandals and saved the country billions of dollars. An editorial in the same newspaper, following Truman's swearing-in after the death of FDR, found reassurance in "the ability which Mr. Truman has shown, and of which the work of the Truman Committee is sufficient proof, to grow in stature with the assumption of increased responsibility." About the same time, the *New Republic* editoralized on the "excellent series of reports" that the committee produced on the defense effort.[35] In a cover story on Truman in 1943, *Time* magazine called the special committee the most useful agency of the government in World War II. The article, describing this group as "the closest thing yet to a domestic high command," went on to say:

> Its members had no power to act or order. But using Congress's old prerogative to look, criticize and recommend, they had focused the strength of public opinion on the men who had the power. . . . With battle-royal impartiality, they had given thick ears and red faces to Cabinet members, war agency heads, generals, admirals, big business-men, little businessmen, labor leaders. . . . For a Congressional com-mittee to be considered the first line of defense . . . is encouraging to believers in democracy. So is the sudden emergence of Harry Truman, whose presence in the Senate is a queer accident of democracy.[36]

There is little reason to doubt that the Truman Committee served the nation well. It also served its chairman well. Harry Truman would most surely have remained an obscure senator, a footnote in the political history of the times, had he not chaired the special committee. His chairmanship brought him a large, deserved degree of favorable national recognition. It earned for him a reputation for dedication and incorruptibility which dispelled the shade of Tom Pendergast and the attendant fumes of rotten politics from automatic association with his name. And while there is no position that can fully prepare a man for the singular office of the presidency, Truman's committee work had given him invaluable experience in leadership and administrative organization, along with a unique insight into the myriad complexities of commanding a nation involved in total war.[37]

On August 3, 1944, Truman submitted a letter to the president of the Senate, resigning from the special committee. He was now the vice-presidential nominee of the Democratic party and feared that con-tinued association would lead to attacks on the bipartisan nature of its work. Members of the special committee urged him to stay but respected the reasons for his resignation. The members unanimously adopted a resolution on the occasion of his departure. The language was lauda-tory, these closing lines being typical of the whole: "The accomplish-ments of the Committee reflect . . . its great Chairman, and its members say to their colleague from Missouri, Colonel Harry S. Truman, Field Artillery, Officers Reserve Corps, 'Well done, soldier!' "[38]

The "Second Missouri Compromise" was the term used by some to describe Roosevelt's surprise selection of Truman to replace the controversial Henry Wallace on the ticket. Truman's presence probably made little difference since FDR carried thirty-six states in his victory over Thomas E. Dewey. Truman spent only eighty-two days as an understudy. During that time he saw the president far less frequently than he had as chairman of the special committee. The new vice-president found himself at loose ends with little to do aside from presiding occasionally over the Senate, a task more ceremonial than exacting. Truman had anticipated this. His reading of history, he said, familiarized him with the "incongruities and inadequacies" of the office.[39]

Late in the afternoon of April 12, 1945, Truman received a message at the Capitol asking that he come to the White House immediately. Upon his arrival he was taken to Eleanor Roosevelt's study where she met him with the words, "Harry, the President is dead." After a pause, he asked if there was anything he could do for her. Truman recalled being quite moved by the grace and consideration of her reply: "Is there anything we can do for you?" Mrs. Roosevelt asked. "For you are the one in trouble now." [40]

3/ The Steward

I had hurried to the White House to see the President, and when I arrived, I found I was the President.[1]

—HARRY S. TRUMAN

Some two hours after being called to the White House, Harry Truman was sworn in as the thirty-second president by Chief Justice Harlan Stone. In his brisk but polite manner, Truman completed the oath-taking ceremony in little more than a minute, made a few announcements, and told reporters he was going home.[2]

Before leaving the White House, Truman asked all of FDR's cabinet to remain in their positions, at least temporarily.[3] He tried to allay fears of any great changes by stating that he intended to carry on as Roosevelt would have. He underscored this with an announcement that the organizational meeting of the United Nations, due to open in San Francisco on April 25, would convene as scheduled by FDR. Truman's final announcement on this fateful evening also struck a note of assurance, although it hardly seemed necessary under the circumstances: "The world," he said, "may be sure that we will prosecute the war on both fronts, east and west, with all the vigor we possess to a successful conclusion."[4]

Looking back on these crowded days of April some four years later, Truman offered his belief that no American in history had ever to assume a greater responsibility.[5] Overnight, he departed the comfortable obscurity of the vice-presidency and became commander in chief of the largest military force ever assembled on earth. He had little more knowledge of existing military policy and global strategy than any citizen could obtain from the censored accounts appearing in the newspapers. Roosevelt had not confided in the man who was to be his immediate successor. It was as if the understudy in a drama had

26

not been allowed to see the script. Truman later acknowledged that he was "inadequately informed" on matters of policy. He had not been told of the atomic bomb, for example; nor had he ever been allowed inside the "super secret map room" of the White House, which contained detailed maps of current troop dispositions and battle situations throughout the world. Given the poor condition of Roosevelt's health and the complexities of the massive war effort, FDR must be faulted for not keeping Truman apprised of major planning and developments. While such a procedure seems dictated by common sense, it was not required by law and would have been precedential. Winston Churchill, then British prime minister, considered the failure to keep Truman informed extraordinary and believed it worked a "grave disadvantage" in Allied affairs for the first few months.[6]

Although it is certain that Truman could have benefited from being taken into Roosevelt's confidence, it appears equally certain that few men in the nation were better prepared to assume civilian direction of the military. It was a fortunate accident of fate that his work on the Truman Committee had provided the new president with an unparalleled knowledge of military organization. This did not go unnoticed by the press, which seemed eager to emphasize anything positive about Truman, so as to assure their readers that all hope did not die with FDR. An editorial in the New York *Times* noted: "No member of the Senate, no elected official of the Government of the United States, has had a better and more intimate view of the whole war machine than the man who directed the activities of the Truman Committee." [7] To become informed of current policies, Truman summoned his military leaders and the head of the State Department to meet with him on April 13, 1945, his first full day in the presidency.

President Truman's first official caller was Secretary of State Edward R. Stettinius, who briefed him on all current diplomatic matters. Truman asked the secretary to continue the practice begun under Roosevelt whereby the State Department prepared a two-page summary of diplomatic developments for daily presentation to the president. He found these summaries, along with the daily reports from the Joint Chiefs of Staff, "immensely helpful in filling gaps in my information" and "indispensable as aids in dealing with many issues." [8] Truman asked Stettinius to have a report for him before the day was out on the background and status of all international problems confronting the administration. That part of the report analyzing relations with the Soviet Union gave a chilling hint of the Cold War attitude that was developing. "Since the Yalta Conference the Soviet Government has taken a firm and uncompromising position on nearly every major question that has arisen in our relations." [9]

The military leaders of the nation came to the White House to acquaint their new commander in chief with the military situation and strategic planning. At the time of their meeting on April 13, some units of the Ninth Army had crossed the Elbe River and were moving eastward. The "Ruhr Pocket"—last major German resistance west of the Elbe—was crumbling rapidly. In the east, Soviet forces had crossed the Oder and were moving against Berlin. It was obvious that Germany was beaten, that the tide was irreversible. The military chiefs told Truman that it would take at least six more months to completely defeat Germany. This very pessimistic estimate (Germany capitulated in less than a month) was based in part on Allied intelligence reports of a heavily fortified "National Redoubt" in which the Germans planned to resist to the last man. This redoubt did not exist.[10]

As to the Pacific, the military reported that Japan had now been driven out of most of the conquered islands, with the major fighting being concentrated on Okinawa. The bitter struggle for Iwo Jima in March had provided the Army Air Force with fields within fighter escort range from which to strike at mainland Japan using the B–29 "superfortresses" based in the Mariana Islands. These massive bomber strikes at heavy industries later failed to substantially lower production. General Curtis LeMay, leader of the Twentieth Bomber Command, received approval for a change in tactics to the use of incendiary bombs on urban population centers. The new targets were, as A. Russell Buchanan has written in his history of World War II, "the congested inflammable cities and the people in them." Buchanan has vividly depicted the first massive demonstration of the "fire-bombing" technique.

> On March 8, counting on the surprise of low-altitude night attack, General LeMay ordered a mass fire bomb raid on Tokyo. On the following day 334 bombers, carrying about two thousand tons of bombs, left bases in the Marianas. . . . The result was one of the worst holocausts of all time. The target was a part of Tokyo into which people were crammed on an average of 103,000 to the square mile. The conflagration gutted about a fourth of the city's buildings and rendered homeless more than a million persons. Casualty lists were terrific; 83,793 persons died

and 40,918 were injured. People caught in the bombed area were helpless for there was no place to go, and the fire-fighting equipment was utterly inadequate. Water boiled in some of the smaller canals running through the flaming city. Not excepting later raids, the Tokyo fire raid on March 9–10, 1945, was the most destructive air raid in history.[11]

Truman approved these new air tactics against nonmilitary objectives on the Japanese mainland, and on his authority the Joint Chiefs of Staff approved a list of thirty-three other cities in Japan that the Army Air Force could attack with incendiary devices. Although LeMay and the air force hoped that these attacks would be a substitute for invasion, most of the military planners were convinced that only by invasion would the Japanese be conquered. Their estimated time for the final conquest of Japan was as conservative as it was for Germany; they told Truman it would take about a year and a half.[12]

As the military chiefs were leaving the meeting on April 13, Truman asked Admiral Leahy to remain behind. He asked Leahy to continue in his unique post as chief of staff to the commander in chief. FDR had created the post; it consisted simply of meeting with the president each morning and briefing him on all military events of the preceding twenty-four hours, along with any other factors—political events, economic or production problems, and the like—which might have a bearing on the conduct of the war. Truman noted in his *Memoirs* that he asked Leahy to stay on because he found in the admiral a blunt and direct man who would not equivocate in his presentations.[13]

Truman apparently decided on his first day in office that the nation and the Allies needed pointed reassurance that the change of chief executives did not mean a change in American policy. Accordingly, he asked the leaders in the House and Senate to convoke a joint session of Congress on Monday, April 16, that he might address them. Underlining the concern felt by the Allies toward changes in United States policy was a meeting between Truman and Anthony Eden, the British foreign secretary, the morning of the president's address to the Congress. During the course of their discussion Truman assured Eden that it was his intention to pursue "exactly the same lines of foreign policy" established by his predecessor.[14]

In his address to Congress, which was broadcast live by the major radio networks, Truman began by eulogizing Roosevelt as "a great man who loved, and was beloved by, all humanity." He pledged himself to carry out the military plans and peace proposals of FDR. The president warmly endorsed the existing military leadership and promised they would remain "unchanged and unhampered." In a warning to Germany and Japan, he said that they should not misunderstand, "that America will continue the fight for freedom until no vestige of resistance remains!" Truman said that anything short of total victory would endanger a future peace. Thus, "Our demand has been, and it remains—Unconditional Surrender!" In counterpoint, the remainder of the speech (about half) was devoted to an earnest plea for all Americans to support the efforts about to begin at San Francisco to form the United Nations organization as the one great hope for enduring peace.[15] Apparently he never seriously considered that a demand for unconditional surrender was not a step toward everlasting peace.

It was quite clear after just a few days in office that Truman's ideas on the role of the chief executive and his relationship with the war cabinet and military chiefs were not the same as FDR's. For example, Roosevelt met individually with cabinet officers to discuss the problems of their departments. Seldom was there any contention or open discussion in FDR's cabinet meetings, which were largely cut-and-dried affairs. Truman felt that Roosevelt expended much time and energy unnecessarily doing those things that should have been the delegated responsibility of cabinet members. The Truman style was quite different and more direct: All matters were normally discussed in open cabinet sessions. Personal leadership now gave way to an institutional approach to administrative matters that was more efficient but less colorful than the flamboyant style of the Roosevelt era.[16]

The joint chiefs and the service secretaries found that they, too, were dealing with a very different leader. Although Truman did have to be brought up to date on current operations, he was not dependent upon the military for command decisions. In fact, the new commander in chief "acted as a full-fledged master of the guild from the day he took office." It was Truman's conviction that the president must be the absolute commander of the country's armed forces. He believed he should set guidelines for the military, approve their strategic and major tactical recommendations when proper, and see to it that they implemented the policies of the administration. The most obvious immediate change that Truman made with respect to the command function was that, unlike Roosevelt, he insisted that all military decisions above the very routine receive his approval prior to their implementation. He has given his reasons for this: "I took the position that the President, as the Commander in Chief, had to know everything that was going on. I had had just enough experience to know that if you are not careful the military will hedge you in." [17]

Truman's relationship with his military chieftains began well and, with few exceptions, continued harmoniously throughout the five months remaining in World War II. Secretary of War Stimson said that he was encouraged from the very beginning "by the calm, decisive demeanor of Harry S. Truman, the new Commander in Chief." [18] All seemed impressed with his energy and ability to absorb and retain lengthy technical reports. The relationship was also smoothed by Truman's sincere admiration for men like Admiral Leahy and General George C. Marshall. For their part, the military leaders were grateful for Truman's frankness and full acceptance of command responsibility. Because of these factors he was able to write: "My meetings with the Chiefs of Staff were always highly informative and productive." But he hastened to add the qualification that "the policy of the government determines the policy of the military. The military is always subordinate to the government." [19] At a later date, in another war, this same commander in chief was compelled to make a very unpopular decision in defense of this principle.

In Europe, as April drew to an end, the remaining German forces found themselves pressed into an increasingly narrow and deadly corridor between the Russians advancing from the east and the Allied troops driving forward from the west. The Allied advance had been halted generally along the Elbe River line in the first days of May where they were joined by advance units of the Soviet army. As the jaws of this martial vise were drawing together, and European victory became a certainty, a struggle went on within the Allied camp over military objectives. [20]

The original plans for the conquest of Germany had called for the major push of the Allies to be directed against Berlin. But the unanticipated speed with which the advance proceeded on both fronts in March changed the strategic situation. Toward the end of March, General Dwight Eisenhower, the Allied supreme commander, determined that concentration of his forces in movement against Berlin was no longer worthwhile. The bulk of major German strength was south of Berlin.

Eisenhower shifted the thrust of his advance southward, deciding that his proper objective was the elimination of enemy resistance. This decision was clearly consonant with a basic principle of warfare: The object of military activity is the destruction of enemy forces, not the capture of areas of limited military significance. Although there were political and diplomatic factors involved, from Eisenhower's viewpoint the decision to abandon a futile race with Soviet forces for the capture of a place—Berlin—was based primarily on military considerations.[21]

Truman accepted Eisenhower's decision which had been previously approved by the American Joint Chiefs of Staff and President Roosevelt just prior to his death. However, the British chiefs of staff and Prime Minister Churchill took strong exception to this decision to leave the capture of Berlin to the Russians. On April 18, 1945, Churchill sent a message to Truman asking that Eisenhower extend his advance as far eastward as possible. The areas thus occupied would be held as "tactical zones" pending final settlement on the permanent zone of occupation with the Russians. The prime minister's arguments for the extension of the Allied advance, which he hoped would include Berlin, were politically motivated. Truman did not accept the British proposal. He later indicated that he had recognized the political nature of the British request: "Churchill was worried over Russian intentions and wanted all the territory we could get for bargaining purposes after the war. . . . For him, Berlin was not just a military matter but a matter of state." [22]

By the end of April the success of Eisenhower's troops in southern Germany added a new dimension to the controversy over military and political objectives. The British urged an advance into Czechoslovakia at least as far as Prague, the capital. On April 28, army Chief of Staff George C. Marshall communicated the British suggestion to Eisenhower, indicating that if military gains would not ensue, he opposed the loss of lives to obtain political advantage. Eisenhower replied that he agreed with Marshall and that he still considered his primary mission to be the capture of Linz (Austria) and the "National Redoubt." [23]

Churchill appealed this decision of the generals to their commander in chief on April 30. The prime minister told Truman that Allied liberation of Prague and western Czechoslovakia could well determine the postwar political environment of that country as well as many neighboring nations. Although this movement toward Prague must be secondary to Eisenhower's drive against remaining resistance, Churchill concluded, "The highly important political considerations mentioned above should be brought to his attention." [24]

While Truman worried over what response to make to the British, he received a memorandum from Acting Secretary of State Joseph Grew indicating that the State Department felt the proposal had merit. The note argued that an American occupation to the Moldau River line (Prague) would significantly enhance the bargaining relationship vis-à-vis the Russians. Truman was urged to ask the joint chiefs to give the proposal serious consideration. [25]

Truman did submit the proposal to the joint chiefs, and he also cabled Eisenhower asking for his views. The president's military advisers were all agreed. On May 1, 1945, Truman replied to Churchill. He explained in a few curt lines that the proposal necessitated high casualties for questionable results and that he was in full accord with Eisenhower's latest recommendation. The latter called for concentration on the destruction of all remaining organized German forces and then a movement into Czechoslovakia, if it was still desirable. [26]

The dispute between Truman and Churchill involved a prior agreement between the Allied powers respecting eventual zones of occupation to be established following the defeat of Germany. The operational lines of the Allies had already passed these boundaries of late April, and they were fighting for land they would eventually have to surrender to the USSR. The troops were sent into these areas for sound military reasons; they were pursuing a force in retreat in hope of ending all armed resistance. But Churchill encouraged still deeper penetrations (toward Berlin and Prague) to capture geographic trophies of psychological and political importance in postwar negotiations. Truman and his military leadership demurred because the price in casualties would be too high. Truman further disagreed because he was not inclined to dictate a change in strategy to a general who was carrying out such an eminently successful military operation. "The only practical thing to do," Truman recalled in his *Memoirs*, "was to stick carefully to our agreement and to try our best to make the Russians carry out their agreements." [27] The zonal agreements on Germany were drafted at the Quebec Conference in September of 1944. In the Crimean (Yalta) Conference of February, 1945, the Quebec Plan was accepted by Stalin. In a message to Truman on April 18, Churchill admitted with obvious regret, that these zones were decided upon "rather hastily at Quebec . . . when it was not foreseen that General Eisenhower's armies would make such a mighty inroad into Germany." [28]

The "mighty inroad" made by Eisenhower's forces had a telling effect by the end of April. On the twenty-fifth, the British informed Truman that the Swedish government had been contacted by Heinrich Himmler, head of the Gestapo, proposing to surrender all German troops on the western front. The Germans would continue to oppose the Russian advance on the eastern front. In an exchange with Churchill, Truman agreed that the offer, even if valid, was unacceptable. The Allies had previously agreed to an unconditional surrender on all fronts, simultaneously. The president informed Stalin of the offer and his response to it. [29] Truman clung to insistence on unconditional surrender because of the Yalta Pact.

With their lines bisected and the military pressures upon them intensifying, the ability of the remaining German armies to resist gradually crumbled. On April 27 Eisenhower reported that American and British troops had met a Russian force advancing from the east at Torgau, south of Berlin. [30] Less than a week later (May 2) the German forces in Italy, along with their Fascist divisions, ended their resistance. Truman sent a message of congratulations to General Mark Clark, the American commander in Italy, and issued a public statement on the surrender heavy with the leaden phrases he favored on such occasions: "The Allied Armies in Italy have won the unconditional surrender of German forces on the first European soil to which, from the West, we carried our arms and our determination. Let Japan as well as Germany understand the meaning of these events. Unless they are lost in fanaticism or determined upon suicide, they must recognize the meaning of the increasing, swifter-moving power now ready for the capitulation or the destruction of the so-recently arrogant enemies of mankind." [31]

The last days of the fighting in Europe were characterized by the desperate flight of German units away from the Russian front toward the American and British lines, where they hoped to surrender to more forgiving enemies. On May 5 Admiral Karl Doenitz, now ruling Germany, ordered Admiral Hans von Friedeburg to go to Eisenhower's headquarters, then located at Rheims, to attempt to surrender on just the western front. Backed by Truman's express position that only a total capitulation on both fronts was acceptable, Eisenhower rejected the offer. The next day, Friedeburg was joined by General Alfred Jodl, apparently with orders from Doenitz to stall the negotiations, thus allowing more Germans to move westward and surrender to non-Russian forces. Eisenhower ordered the negotiations ended unless the Germans ceased these delaying tactics. Informed of this, Doenitz gave up. A surrender document was drafted and approved, and the lethal machines fell silent in Europe at 11:45 P.M., May 8, 1945.[32]

"In recognition of the unconditional and abject surrender of the Nazi barbarians," the president cabled Eisenhower, "please accept the fervent congratulations and appreciation of myself and of the American people." The general responded in kind: "Permit me to assure you of my personal gratification that my Commander-in-Chief has found my efforts worthy of special commendation." [33] This exchange marks the beginning of a friendship between the general and the president that endured until the campaign of 1952. Truman did, in fact, greatly admire practically all of the military leaders who commanded in World War II and was not reluctant to publicly note his admiration for them. However, he always reserved his most lavish praise for General Marshall. He has said that Marshall was the "brains" that made the military organization function properly: "General Marshall . . . was in every sense the chief architect of the grand strategy of the war for the Allies." [34]

When the fighting ended, western Allied armies occupied Germany to the Elbe River, a small portion of western Czechoslovakia and most of Austria. Churchill attempted once again (on May 6) to get Truman to hold the farthermost line of advance rather than retiring about one hundred miles westward to the prearranged zones. The prime minister desired to use the occupied territory to force Russian concessions. Truman wavered as to the pace of his withdrawal, but as for the eventual retirement to the agreed-upon zones, he fully intended to keep Roosevelt's promises. Probably anticipating Truman's attitude, Churchill asked for an immediate meeting of the Big Three to settle the postwar status of Europe and to complete plans for the defeat of Japan. Truman accepted this call for what became the Potsdam Conference, but in his reply to Churchill he emphasized that "In the meantime it is my present intention to adhere to our interpretation of the Yalta agreements, and to stand firmly on our present announced attitude." [35]

On May 11 Churchill repeated his earlier request, asking Truman not to order his troops out of the Russian zones. In fact, he asked Truman to issue a freeze order on all troops in the European theater of operations. The president rejected these requests after consultation with his military leadership, although he acknowledged that he, like Churchill, was concerned over Soviet intentions in Europe. Truman had sound reasons for pulling the troops back: His interpretation of the Quebec and Yalta agreements; a desired redeployment of forces into the war in the Pacific; and an unwillingness to antagonize the Soviet Union, whose promised aid against Japan appeared necessary at the time. Churchill's urgent pleadings were purely political, whereas Truman's chief advisers, General Marshall and Secretary Stimson, had their minds fixed on concentrating maximum military force against the Japanese. Their advice quite naturally reflected their orientation and their primary objective, victory in the Pacific.[36]

Despite Churchill's pleas, on June 3 Truman had the Joint Chiefs of Staff inform Eisenhower that the removal of his forces from the Russian zones was essentially a military matter. Five days later, Truman met with Harry Hopkins, then a presidential adviser, who had just returned from talks with Stalin. Hopkins advised the president to set a positive date for withdrawal from the Russian zones. Fixing a date of June 21, Truman so advised Churchill on the twelfth, explaining that he could not further delay withdrawal in order to pressure the Russians into solving other problems, as the prime minister desired.[37]

At a Columbia University symposium in 1959, a student asked Truman what his role as commander in chief had been with respect to the diversion from Berlin and subsequent events. His reply was that an agreement had been reached at Yalta "that certain lines would be drawn in Germany. . . . I simply carried out the agreement, by ordering the troops to the lines which had been agreed upon. That's all there was to it." A revisionist scholar, Gar Alperovitz, argues that the delay in withdrawal was brought about by Truman's decision in late April to go along with Churchill in applying diplomatic pressure on Stalin with regard to zonal boundary questions in Austria. His argument, although lacking primary documentation, is not without merit.[38]

The agreement to which Truman seemed to be committed had been worked out at Yalta, in the Crimea, between Churchill, Roosevelt, and Stalin in February, 1945. Agreement was reached on the convoking of a conference at San Francisco to establish the United Nations. The

Yalta protocol also prescribed the voting formula for the UN Security
Council and other procedural matters. The signatories also reaffirmed
the principles of the Atlantic Charter: the right of all peoples to select
their own form of government and the restoration of sovereignty and
self-government to those being forcibly deprived of them. The USSR
also agreed to enter the war against Japan within two or three months
following the surrender of Germany. The tripartite administrative division of Germany was accepted, with the details to be worked out by
the Allied Control Council. Several territorial concessions were made
to the Soviet Union in eastern Europe and the Far East. These latter
were in return for Stalin's agreement to bring his nation into the war
with Japan.[39]

Truman had said that the most pressing reason for his meeting Stalin
and Churchill at Potsdam was to secure immediate involvement of the
Soviet Union in the war with Japan. The service chiefs' plan for the
defeat of Japan was based on the assumption that the Russians would
enter the fight as Stalin had promised. Pentagon planners were urging
Truman to secure a specific date from the Russians.[40] The meaning of
Russian entry had been stressed by the joint chiefs in a memorandum
to Roosevelt early in 1945: "Russia's entry at as early a date as possible
consistent with her ability to engage in offensive operations is necessary to provide maximum assistance to our Pacific operations. . . .
The objective of Russia's military effort against Japan in the Far
East should be the defeat of the Japanese forces in Manchuria, air
operations against Japan proper in collaboration with United States
air forces based in eastern Siberia, and maximum interference with
Japanese sea traffic between Japan and the mainland of Asia." [41]
Like Roosevelt before him, Truman seemingly accepted the military arguments for the desirability of involving the Soviet Union in the
war against Japan.[42] However, in doing so, he rejected political objections to Russian involvement. Churchill, for one, saw no genuine need
to include the Russians, and at some point prior to Potsdam, he became convinced that the United States did not desire Soviet participation. Averell Harriman, wartime ambassador to Russia, was generally
distrustful of Soviet intentions and felt that they had compelling reasons to enter the war without American encouragement. Harriman
had acquainted the president with his doubts on several occasions.
George F. Kennan, then minister-counselor of the Moscow embassy,

cabled a message to Harriman (in April, 1945) that eventually reached Truman's desk. Kennan warned that the Soviet Union would undoubtedly use intervention to secure "maximum power with minimum responsibility" in areas of Asia beyond its own borders. "It would be tragic," Kennan believed, "if our natural anxiety for the support of the Soviet Union at this juncture . . . were to lead us into an undue reliance on Soviet aid." [43] Truman concluded that military considerations outweighed the possible political disadvantages that might accrue with Russian entry. His decision was not altered when—just before Potsdam—code intercepts indicated that the Japanese were actively seeking to end the fighting, although slightly short of total unconditional surrender.

The Potsdam Conference opened July 17 with Stalin reaffirming his commitment to declare war upon Japan. In a meeting of the American, British, and Russian chiefs of staff, the latter indicated they were concentrating forces along the Manchurian border as rapidly as possible and would be ready to attack by the latter part of August. The exact date of Soviet entry would be dependent upon concurrence of the government of China with the Yalta concessions. [44]

At the outset of the Potsdam meetings, Stalin had confirmed what Truman already knew from American intelligence activities: The Japanese were seeking terms of peace through Moscow. [45] Discussing these peace feelers privately with Churchill on July 18, Truman balked at the prime minister's suggestion that they might consider accepting a Japanese offer short of unconditional surrender. "I had in mind saving their military honour and giving them some assurance of their national existence," Churchill recalled telling Truman. But Truman's response was to the effect that "The Japs had no longer any military honour after Pearl Harbour." [46] Truman insisted upon such a surrender regarding Germany and—when announcing the German surrender—he called for the Japanese to lay down their arms unconditionally, promising only that they would not be enslaved or exterminated. [47]

At the July 28 meeting at Potsdam, Stalin announced that his government had received another peace overture from Japan. The gist of the message was that the emperor wished to send Prince Konoye to Moscow to present the Japanese position on ending the war and to obtain the services of the Soviet Union as intermediary. Stalin told Truman that he intended to send a negative reply. Truman thanked him

and the matter was dropped. The Japanese efforts to secure a negotiated settlement were futile for two reasons. First, their request to have
the Soviet government act as mediator was in vain, for, as one student
of the war has noted, "The leaders in the Kremlin had secured advantages at Yalta which they could insure only by entering the war against
Japan, not by interceding on the latter's behalf to terminate the war." [48]
Second, two days prior to this last request the governments of Great
Britain, the United States, and China had jointly issued a policy statement that precluded Japanese efforts to obtain an end to the hostilities
short of abject surrender.

The ultimatum to Japan (called the Potsdam Declaration) had its
genesis in late May, 1945. Acting Secretary of State Grew, a former
ambassador to Japan, suggested to Truman that he consider issuing a
proclamation calling on the Japanese to surrender, with the express assurance that the emperor could be retained as head of state. Truman
asked Grew to submit this proposal to the State-War-Navy Coordinating Committee (SWNCC) and the Joint Chiefs of Staff for
their views. The president felt the idea had merit. Grew reported back
to Truman on June 18 that all involved were agreed that such a statement should be made, but though Grew favored immediate issuance,
the majority favored delaying publication until a "more appropriate"
time. The military chiefs wanted to wait until such time as they could
answer a refusal of the surrender demand with invasion of Japan.[49]

The president accepted the idea but rejected the proposed timing of
both Grew and the military. He decided to issue the surrender ultimatum during the Potsdam Conference, which was then a few weeks
away. Truman's reasoning was that such a statement, coming from
Potsdam, would demonstrate Allied unity. He also would know by
then the two factors that could change the military equation and effect
the terms of surrender: Soviet intentions on entering the war and the
results of the atomic bomb test.[50]

Secretary of War Stimson, who, at Truman's request, had been
working on a memorandum concerning the ultimatum to Japan, submitted his efforts to the president on July 2, and discussed it with him
at Potsdam on the sixteenth. Truman and his new secretary of state,
James F. Byrnes, also reviewed Stimson's memorandum. It advocated
immediate notification to the Japanese of the unconditional surrender
demand, guaranteeing their internal polity, not excluding "a constitu-

tional monarchy under her present dynasty." [51] On the seventeenth, the joint chiefs sent the president their views on the draft warning. They indicated their objection to the lines which told the Japanese that with the coming of peace a new monarchial government could be formed. The military advisers favored a more general statement on a postwar government that would appeal to all elements in Japan and—they felt—be more likely to achieve the desired result. Stimson told Truman that he accepted this reasoning of the joint chiefs, with which Secretary Byrnes also concurred.[52] The position taken by the military advisers runs counter to an army G–2 (Intelligence Division) report dated June 30, which indicated Japan might accept a modified surrender demand that assured retention of the imperial system.[53]

The Potsdam Declaration was drafted without any mention of the fate of Emperor Hirohito or the monarchial institution, the very factors that had impelled Grew to initiate the discussions that led to this document. In accepting a purposely ambiguous statement, Truman did nothing to improve the possibilities for a prompt surrender. It should be noted that he acted upon the advice of his secretaries of war and state and chiefs of staff.[54] However, in the light of subsequent events—preservation of the imperial order being the condition that the Japanese would make and that Truman would accept—the decision was most unfortunate. This is particularly true in consideration of the fact that by the twenty-fourth, two days prior to the issuance of the ultimatum, Stimson had returned to his original position on including an assurance to the Japanese that the imperial dynasty would be preserved. Barring this, the secretary told Truman, he hoped that the president would at least keep his mind open on the subject and if the Japanese made this a condition of surrender, grant it to them. Truman said he would if those circumstances arose, as they did.[55]

A decade after his presidency, Truman was asked, "Would it have been better to have made it clear in the Potsdam Declaration that the Japanese would be permitted to retain the Emperor?" Truman's reply was couched in the earthy phrases typical of his response to sensitive questions: "How could you do it? When we asked them to surrender at Potsdam, they gave us a very snotty answer. That is what I got. They didn't ask about the Emperor. I said, if they don't surrender, they would be completely, totally destroyed. They told me to go to hell, words to that effect." [56]

Churchill approved the draft of the declaration that Truman showed him at Potsdam. Both agreed that China should be invited to become a signatory to the ultimatum. The text was transmitted to Chiang Kai-shek by radio, and he sent Truman his approval. The USSR, still technically at peace with Japan, was not invited to sign. The president issued the Potsdam Declaration at Berlin on July 26, at the same time ordering the Office of War Information to inform the Japanese of its provisions as fully and rapidly as possible.[57]

Powerful radio transmitters located on Saipan began beaming a continual broadcast to the Japanese home islands. On July 28 American bombers dropped about twenty-seven million leaflets over Japan. The leaflets summarized the terms of the Potsdam ultimatum. They also contained a list of eleven cities, indicating that soon four of them would be utterly destroyed from the air. What the leaflets did not mention and what the Potsdam Declaration did not note, was that plans called for these cities to be destroyed not by massive fire bombings which were then becoming commonplace, but by individual nuclear devices.[58]

The reaction within the Japanese government to the ultimatum bears out the Stimson-Grew position that Truman had rejected, for the pivotal issue in the Supreme War Direction Council concerned the fate of the imperial house. The Japanese determined that they must fight on through an invasion if necessary and win concessions from the Allies that would assure national existence and the imperial order. On the afternoon of July 28, Prime Minister Kantara Suzuki told a press conference that his government found little that was new or of any value in the Potsdam Declaration. He concluded with the fateful remark, "There is no other recourse but to ignore it entirely and resolutely fight for the successful conclusion of this war." [59] This statement set in motion the events that brought the war to a swift, dramatic end.

The Potsdam Conference ended officially on August 2, 1945. Truman felt that the Russians had been "pig-headed" and he expressed the hope that he would "never have to hold another conference with them." By the time the meeting ended, so had most of the ground fighting in the Pacific theater, except on the Asian mainland. What turned out to be the last major land battle of the war had been won in late June, with the capture of Okinawa, largest island of the Ryukyus group. Located only 350 miles from Kyushu, one of the four main islands of Japan, Okinawa was considered an essential target by American strategists. The island would provide air bases within medium bomber range of Japan and would serve as a major staging area for the planned invasion of the Japanese home islands.[60]

The aerial bombardment of Japanese cities had been gradually intensified. By mid-June the destruction planned for the five principal cities of Japan had been achieved. In Tokyo alone, an estimated 3,100,000 persons had lost their homes to the fires generated by the incendiary bombs. The bombers were ordered to attack other cities of Japan. By late July and early August, the Strategic Air Force B–29s based in the Marianas were meeting only limited resistance from enemy fighter planes. Several hundred bombers were striking Japan nightly. For example, on the night prior to the atomic bombing of Hiroshima, six hundred B–29s attacked Japan, with the returning pilots reporting results from "good" to "excellent." [61]

As the fighting in Europe drew to an end, Truman consulted several times with his military chiefs and the cabinet about the best method of concentrating military force against Japan. The president accepted their suggestion that there be a rapid redeployment of troops to the Pacific, with the units that had seen the least combat being the first to go. American troop strength in Europe was to be reduced to a number sufficient for occupational duty only.[62]

The burden of the war in the Pacific theater was borne chiefly by the United States, with some assistance from Britain and the Commonwealth nations. Exclusive command over these forces was exercised by the American Joint Chiefs of Staff, unlike Europe, where Eisenhower was under the authority of the Combined (British and American) Chiefs of Staff. In July, 1945, Truman went along with a Joint Chiefs of Staff recommendation that he reject a British request that a similar combined chiefs arrangement be adopted for the Pacific. But he overrode the joint chiefs' recommendation that all military Lend-Lease to Britain's occupation forces in Europe be terminated.[63] Truman's general policy toward further expenditure of Lend-Lease military equipment was that it be limited to that which would be used directly against Japan. Following the Japanese surrender he did cancel all Lend-Lease operations.[64]

Commenting on his struggles with Congress over Lend-Lease appropriations, Truman revealed that he believed the president's war powers should not be limited by the Congress:

> A great many of the war powers that are delegated to the President when a war is actually going on are made for the duration of the war. But Congress is very jealous of its authority to keep the purse strings tight, as in the case of appropriations for Lend-Lease. That is all right in a republic when the republic is not in danger, but it always seemed to me that matters such as Lend-Lease should have been authorized for the duration of hostilities. . . .
>
> I made a fundamental distinction between powers that I requested during wartime and those that I expected during peacetime . . . in connection with Lend-Lease appropriations, I felt all along that Congress should have given the President authority there for the duration of hostilities instead of renewing the legislation periodically.
>
> *When a nation is at war, its leader, who has the responsibility of winning the war, ought to have all the tools available for that purpose.*[65]

In planning for the conquest of Japan, the president's military advisers were generally agreed that this could only be accomplished by a massive amphibious invasion of the Japanese home islands. The strategic use of atomic weapons was never a major factor in their deliberations since less than a month elapsed between the successful testing of the nuclear bomb and its operational use.*

At the Quebec Conference in September, 1944, FDR and Churchill, on the advice of their military staffs, agreed in principle that the unconditional surrender of Japan necessitated an invasion of the home islands. The first strategic proposal for this invasion was presented to Roosevelt by the Joint Chiefs of Staff in a memorandum dated January 22, 1945. The chiefs stated that the overall objective of the war against Japan was to achieve unconditional surrender by establishing air and sea blockades, an intensive aerial bombardment, and eventual invasion of Japan. This would be accomplished, the joint chiefs' memorandum stated, by first capturing additional island bases nearer Japan so as to be able to intensify the blockade and bombardment. The next tactical step was to be an attack on the major Japanese island of Kyushu, to be followed by "the decisive invasion of the industrial heart of Japan through the Tokyo Plain." [66]

* The development of the atomic bomb, Truman's decision to employ it, and the postwar policies he established for nuclear weaponry are the subjects of the following chapters.

With the success of operations by April of 1945 the navy was arguing that the joint chiefs' plans should be amended. Admirals Leahy and King were now convinced that an expanded naval blockade and an intensified bombardment by air would force Japan to surrender. General Marshall took the lead in opposing this idea. The army chief of staff argued that an invasion would be faster and less costly. He also noted that massive aerial bombardments had failed to bring about Germany's surrender. In his position Marshall had the support of Admiral Chester Nimitz and—most importantly—of General Douglas MacArthur, the Far Eastern commander.[67]

MacArthur disagreed with the joint chiefs' plan with respect to the assault against Kyushu. He thought the major initial landing should be directed against the Tokyo Plain in concert with a Russian move against Manchuria. MacArthur did agree that there was little possibility of a blockade and bombardment strategy being effective in bringing about surrender.[68] Bolstered by such arguments, the plan to force unconditional surrender by invasion remained unchanged.

In May, Truman was approached by T. V. Soong, China's foreign minister, who said that his government hoped that the showdown battle against Japan would be fought by the United States on the Asian mainland. Secretary of War Stimson was openly opposed to this strategy, believing—with Marshall—that a direct invasion of Japan would be the least costly plan in the long run. Meeting with the president on May 16, shortly after Soong's visit, Stimson argued against the Chinese proposal and outlined the grand strategy advocated by the military planners. He told Truman that the War Department strongly favored attacking Japan itself, and not involving American ground forces in China. While deferring an immediate decision. Truman clearly leaned toward the joint chiefs' plan since it would cost less in American lives than a major engagement on the Chinese mainland.[69]

Truman postponed any decision on the invasion plan because there was no pressing need to decide. He was undoubtedly hoping that the two unknown factors at the time, Russian entry into the war in the Far East and a workable atomic bomb, would be settled before he had to decide. The joint chiefs continued to refine their plans, and, increasingly, what they proposed was an exclusively American operation. They did not want the proffered British assistance, and they were coming to feel that the Russian invasion of Manchuria, while desirable, was probably not essential. In a meeting on May 25 the Joint Chiefs of Staff issued a directive setting the date for the invasion of Kyushu by the Sixth Army (Operation Olympic) to be November 1, 1945. The invasion plans for the attack on Honshu (Operation Coronet), the major island of the Japanese group, set the assault on the Kanto (Tokyo) Plain for about March 1, 1946.[70]

These were the plans formally presented to Truman for his approval by the joint chiefs and the service secretaries on June 18, 1945. In defending the plan General Marshall told the president that he was certain that the Japanese would not surrender until they had actually been invaded. This, he said, combined with a Russian attack in Manchuria and the havoc being inflicted by aerial bombardment of the cities and naval blockade of its sea-lanes, should bring about Japan's capitulation. The general estimated that the first month of fighting on Kyushu would involve thirty-one thousand casualties. Truman asked each of the others present for their views on the proposed invasion. No one disagreed.[71] He then ordered the War Council to make final preparations for the invasion of Kyushu. As for Coronet, the operation against the heavily industrialized central plain of Honshu, Truman told the military to continue to make preparations, but that he was withholding final approval until it was essential for him to decide.[72]

At Potsdam (July 17, 1945), Truman called together his principal advisers to reexamine military planning in view of the successful testing of the atomic bomb the previous day. The potential of the new weapon was clearly not comprehended from the test reports, for the advice Truman received was to continue with the invasion plans as drafted. As Truman later recalled: "We reviewed our military strategy in the light of this revolutionary development. We were not [*sic*, "now"] ready to make use of this weapon against the Japanese, although we did not know as yet what effect the weapon might have, physically or psychologically, when used against the enemy. For that reason the military advised that we go ahead with the existing military plans for the invasion of the Japanese home islands." [73]

A few days after this meeting with his war council, the new commander in chief ordered the use of the new weapon, and, suddenly, the invasion plans, along with most contemporary military strategy, became obsolete. Truman had inaugurated an entirely new age in the history of mankind.

4/ The Decision-Maker

To me, it was a weapon of war, an artillery weapon. We faced half a million casualties trying to take Japan by land. It was either that or the atom bomb, and I didn't hesitate a minute, and I've never lost any sleep over it since.[1]

—HARRY S. TRUMAN

Secretary of War Stimson had his last meeting with Franklin Roosevelt on March 15, 1945. They discussed the project to develop an atomic weapon. Roosevelt was concerned with criticism he had received to the effect that the Manhattan Project was a multibillion-dollar "lemon" that scientists had sold him. Stimson calmed FDR's fears by pointing out that every physicist of note, four Nobel laureates included, was working on the bomb. The remainder of this meeting dealt with future control of atomic secrets, postwar policy, and a statement to be issued following the first detonation of the bomb. Implied throughout the conversation, but never explicitly stated, was that Roosevelt would use the bomb against Japan once it was ready.[2] Upon his death the decision was left to Harry Truman.

Following the swearing-in on April 12, 1945, Stimson told Truman only that an immense project was underway to perfect a new explosive of enormous destructive force. This was the second time that Stimson had discussed the subject with Truman. In June, 1943, the Truman Committee had become curious about several secret military plants and the budgetary masking of vast expenditures for these installations. Stimson called Truman and explained to him that the project was of the utmost secrecy and asked him to call off his investigation. Truman had complied immediately, without demanding further explanation.[3]

As secretary of war, Stimson was charged with overall supervision of the Manhattan Project, and he was senior adviser to the president on the military applications of atomic energy. On April 24, he wrote to Truman requesting a meeting at the earliest possible time. The secre-

46

tary, in whom Truman had total confidence, wanted to brief him on atomic developments and to determine what the president's policy would be. The meeting was scheduled for the next day, the twenty-fifth. Stimson remembered his curious feelings that day: two years earlier Senator Truman had accepted his assurances that the project was too important a secret to be revealed to him. "Now he was President and Commander in Chief, and the final responsibility in this as in so many other matters must be his." [4]

Stimson began the briefing by saying that it was imperative that the president understand that this new weapon would not only affect future foreign policy, but would also revolutionize military thinking. If used, the bomb would undoubtedly shorten the war; but whether such an awesome device should be used remained for Truman to determine. Stimson also told him that he must consider the postwar implications of American possession of the secrets of atomic energy. Scientists involved in the project were convinced that the United States could not maintain exclusive knowledge of the atomic process indefinitely. Perhaps, Stimson suggested, international control through the United Nations might be the best course to follow. [5]

General Leslie Groves, chief administrative officer of the Manhattan District, accompanied Stimson to this meeting with the president. Groves brought Truman up to date on the entire project, indicating its status, and offered approximate completion dates on the bombs. The general anticipated a test in mid-July at the proving grounds near Los Alamos, New Mexico. If the test proved successful, an operational bomb could be ready in August. A special air group was already in training to deliver the bomb. [6]

Before the meeting ended, Stimson suggested that a committee be created to advise the president on all the ramifications of the new weapon, particularly, whether it should be used against Japan or not. Truman agreed and the interim committee was established. Later, various panels were created to advise the committee on particular aspects (scientific, military, political) of their task. [7] The interim committee met for the first time in the Pentagon on May 9, 1945, chiefly to define the major problem areas. They dwelt at length on what the president should tell the nation about the bomb test, what other nations should be told about the process, and how long it would take the Soviet Union to develop their own bomb (estimates varying from three to twenty years). The other question explored by this meeting had been raised by several scientists working on the bomb's development: Should it be used at all, especially considering that Japan's defeat seemed certain? On that same day, in another office of the Pentagon, General Groves, who had already answered that question in his own mind, met with another committee to select the Japanese city that would be the target of the first bomb.[8]

The decisive meetings of the interim committee occurred on May 31, and June 1, 1945. The recommendations to the president which emerged from these sessions can be stated briefly: (1) The atomic bomb should be used directly against Japan as soon as it was operational. (2) The target should be a war plant or military installation surrounded by buildings of light construction. (3) No advance warning as to the nature of the weapon should be given to the Japanese.[9]

James Byrnes informed Truman of the recommendations soon after the second meeting ended. It is his recollection that Truman said that although it was regrettable, the "only reasonable conclusion" he could see was to employ the bomb against Japan. The reasoning behind the committee's recommendations to Truman is obscured by conflicting accounts of the participants and security restrictions on the records of the interim committee. However, it is possible to make some general observations: There was only limited discussion of whether or not the bomb should be used at all.[10] The question of a nonmilitary demonstration of the weapon—upon a deserted island, for example—was deliberated. Objections were made that such a test might not be a strong enough argument to convince the militarists in control of Japan. It was also proposed that an uninhabited area of Japan be destroyed. The consensus seemed to be that, like the island test, such a demonstration might not be convincing, would be a waste of fissionable materials, American prisoners might be moved to the site, and it could be costly and embarrassing, should the bomb fail to detonate.[11]

The interim committee did not absolutely reject the idea of a technical demonstration to the Japanese of the power of the atom. Instead, they asked their scientific advisory panel to consider the subject and make recommendations. The scientists submitted their report on June 16. The key statement of their report read: "We can propose no technical demonstration likely to bring an end to the war; we see no acceptable alternative to direct military use." [12] It should be noted that the interim committee did not wait for this study, which confirmed its judgment. The committee recommendation to Truman that a Japanese city be bombed had been submitted two weeks earlier.

The reports and recommendations of the interim committee and scientific panel were well known to all the participants in the meeting of the War Council held by Truman on June 18, 1945 (discussed in preceding chapter). The meeting was taken up with presentation of the joint chiefs' plans for the invasion of Japan. The atomic bomb was not even mentioned until—just as the meeting was breaking up—Truman asked Assistant Secretary of War John J. McCloy to express his views on the planning. McCloy, who had not spoken before because his superior, Stimson, was present, suggested to Truman that some consideration should be given to the likelihood that the bomb would bring about unconditional surrender. McCloy favored telling the Japanese that the United States had the bomb and would use it unless they surrendered. Truman was interested in the idea of including this warning in the ultimatum to be issued at Potsdam. However, every member of the War Council present disliked the idea of a warning to Japan, chiefly because they were not at all certain the bomb was going to work. McCloy's proposal was put aside, only to be reconsidered and rejected at Potsdam.[13]

In the weeks just prior to the testing and use of the bomb, many atomic scientists tried to persuade the administration not to use it against Japan. A seven-member committee at the University of Chicago's Metallurgical Laboratory, chaired by Nobel laureate James O. Franck, was the first to dissent from the interim committee recommendations to Truman. In a report drafted for submission to Stimson they argued postwar implications for obtaining a ban on atomic warfare and the shock to public opinion if America were first to use such an "indiscriminate method of wholesale destruction of civilian life." The basic recommendation of the Franck Committee was for a test demonstration in a deserted area. If the Japanese subsequently rejected an ultimatum specifically warning that the bomb would be used, then perhaps it should be employed (with the specific sanction of the American public and the Allied powers). On June 12, unable to see Stimson, or George Harrison, who was alternate chairman of the interim committee, Franck left the report with an aide in Harrison's office.[14]

The report submitted by the scientific advisory panel to the interim committee on June 16 (discussed earlier) noted that there was dissension: "The opinions of our scientific colleagues on the initial use of these weapons are not unanimous," the panel reported. They described the alternatives suggested as ranging from a technical demonstration to direct military application. The panel rejected anything less than a direct attack on Japan as unlikely to bring about surrender.[15]

In late June, Ralph Bard, a member of the interim committee, reversed his opinion with respect to bombing Japan without warning. In a memorandum on June 27 Bard said that Japan should be given a few days' notice, ascribing his changed views to a consideration of America's spirit of fair play and humanitarianism. Bard also believed that Japan was seeking the opportunity to surrender that such a warning could provide, especially if accompanied by assurances from Truman with respect to the treatment of the emperor and the Japanese nation following surrender.[16]

These early dissenters from the interim committee policy recommendations to Truman were joined by a substantial number of atomic scientists in July. Leo Szilard, one of the members of the Franck Committee, drafted and circulated a petition addressed to Truman directly. On July 17 Szilard submitted the petition—bearing the signatures of sixty-nine colleagues at the Metallurgical Laboratory—to Washington. The Szilard petition argued the moral and political implications of using the bomb, particularly without advance warning to Japan, and began and ended with pleas to Truman to use his military powers with prudence and in consideration of the future: "The liberation of atomic power . . . places in your hands, as Commander-in-Chief, the fateful decision whether or not to sanction the use of such bombs in the present phase of the war against Japan." [17]

Other atomic scientists began to question the wisdom of using the monster they had helped to create. For example, on July 12 a poll taken among 150 scientists at the Metallurgical Laboratory revealed that a significant percentage of them favored options other than the bombing of Japan without warning that had been recommended by the interim committee. In this same period a petition from the atomic plant at Oak Ridge, Tennessee, carrying sixty-eight names and another from Chicago bearing eighteen names, were submitted through channels, indicating strong degrees of reluctance about military use of the bomb.[18]

From all indications, few, if any, of these dissenting views ever reached Truman. At least one petition was held up on a decision made by General Groves. A memorandum from his office attached to the petition explained that since the scientists had an opportunity to express themselves through the scientific advisory panel, "no useful purpose would be served by transmitting . . . [the petition] to the White House, particularly since the President was not in the country." [19] Truman was, in fact, at the Potsdam Conference, having left the United States on July 6, but he was not incommunicado. The momentous decision Truman made to use the bomb was based on military advisories and the interim committee recommendations. Many (if not all) of the substantial number of objections to this line of reasoning were not made known to the president.

At 7:30 P.M., July 16, the day following Truman's arrival at Potsdam, a cable was received with the information that an implosion-type atomic fission bomb had been successfully detonated at the Alamogordo test site in New Mexico. Subsequent messages indicated the force of the bomb exceeded expectations. The blast yielded a force equivalent to twenty thousand tons of TNT; its light could be seen for 250 miles from the epicenter of the explosion. [20]

This was the news Truman had been waiting for. The bomb strengthened his position, for it meant that Soviet participation in the Far Eastern war was no longer as essential as it had been. Almost certainly Truman pushed back the date of the Potsdam meeting to await the test results. He knew the test was scheduled for mid-July when he asked for the postponement from July 1. [21] The scientists preparing the experiment at Alamogordo were definitely pushed to test around July 16. J. Robert Oppenheimer, a key figure in the project, recalled (in 1954) being told by Stimson that it was very important that he test before the Potsdam meeting. Truman said that "preparations were being rushed for the test . . . at the time I had to leave for Europe [July 6], and on the voyage over I had been anxiously awaiting word on the results." At Potsdam, prior to receiving the test results, Truman purportedly remarked, with respect to the test and negotiations with the Russians: "If it explodes as I think it will, I'll certainly have a hammer on those boys." [22]

At a Pentagon meeting in the first week of July, the British had agreed that the bomb should be used against Japan. However, they noted that one problem existed in that Russia was officially ignorant of the bomb. If Truman said nothing about the weapon to Stalin at Potsdam, relations between the Big Three would be jeopardized when the bomb was used a short time later. The general feeling was that Truman should inform Stalin of the bomb sometime during the conference. The recommendation of the interim committee, made to Truman at about the same time, was in agreement with this position. The committee had also suggested to the president that he might invite further talks with the Soviet Union relative to a postwar policy on atomic energy, but they did not think Truman (if asked) should divulge any particulars yet.[23]

At lunch with Churchill on July 18, Truman discussed with the prime minister what Stalin should be told about the bomb. Churchill had been informed on the previous day of the successful testing of the device he would later refer to as "the Second Coming in Wrath." Since it was settled that Stalin had to be informed, the discussion dealt only with how much he should be told and when to tell him. Truman said he would simply disclose to the Soviet premier the fact of the weapon's existence without going into any detail. "I think," Churchill recalled Truman saying, "I had best just tell him after one of our meetings that we have an entirely novel form of bomb . . . which we think will have decisive effects upon the Japanese will to continue the war." Churchill agreed.[24]

As the evening session ended at Potsdam on July 24, Truman approached the Soviet premier privately: "I casually mentioned to Stalin that we had a new weapon of unusual destructiveness." The president was quite surprised by the reaction he received: "The Russian Premier showed no special interest. All he said was that he was glad to hear it and hoped we would make good use of it against the Japanese!"[25] Churchill, watching the scene from a few yards away, but out of earshot, remembers that Stalin's face remained "gay and genial" and that "he seemed to be delighted." As they waited together for their cars a few moments later, Churchill asked the president, "How did it go?"

"He never asked a question," Truman replied.[26] There was no further discussion with the Soviet Union at Potsdam regarding atomic energy.

Once the reports were in confirming the success of the bomb test, Truman called together his chief military advisers on July 17. All present were conversant with the mid-July status reports prepared by the intelligence branch of the War Department General Staff. These reports estimated Japanese strength in the home islands at 2 million; a like number on the Asian mainland and Formosa; with another 600 thousand scattered about in small groupings for a total of just under 5 million. The intelligence reports, while taking cognizance of the Japanese mediation feelers to Russia, came to the curious conclusion that no discernible, genuine weakening in Japanese determination to continue the war existed.[27]

The invasion plans the president had approved in June were reviewed at this meeting. They called for a combined American military and naval attack force of 5 million men. Truman asked everyone present for their views on use of the atomic bomb. General Marshall opposed a surprise attack, but he told Truman that if the bomb could bring about surrender without an invasion, it would save a quarter of a million American lives and also the lives of millions of Japanese.[28] Apparently there was little discussion of a specific warning to the Japanese that this new weapon was to be used against them. "The consensus of opinion," Truman said in summarizing this meeting, "was that the bomb should be used." [29] It should be noted that although the participants in this meeting agreed that the bomb should be used without specific warning, the decision was also made to continue preparations for the invasion. The military advisers to the president were by no means convinced that the bomb would end the war.

The last two weeks of July were hectic and pressure-packed for Truman. He was engaged in daily complex negotiations over the conference table with Great Britain and the Soviet Union, determining the structure of the postwar world; he was meeting often with Stimson, Byrnes, and Churchill regarding the language of the Potsdam ultimatum; and he was pressed from the seventeenth to the twenty-fourth to make a decision whether to order the atomic-bombing of Japan. He had been informed that the bomb could be used on or after August 1, but that the technical preparations involved made it necessary that his authorization to proceed be given prior to July 25.[30]

As he moved toward a decision on the bomb, Truman continued to consult with his military and civilian advisers, contending that he "wanted to weigh all the possibilities and implications." He also met with Churchill to discuss the bomb, with Leahy and Marshall present.

Churchill later recalled that there was not a "moment's discussion" of whether the bomb should be used. He described their agreement on the subject as "unanimous, automatic, unquestioned." [31]

The president not only had to come to a final decision to bomb Japan, he also had to choose which cities to use as targets. He wanted to be sure, he said, that the bomb was used against an area with military significance. That way, Truman reasoned, he would be employing "a weapon of war in the manner prescribed by the laws of war." He had earlier instructed Stimson to tell the War Department Target Committee to propose only cities of "prime military importance." Essentially, this meant a city with industrial plants producing military equipment. All of this was in conformance with the interim committee's recommendations with which the joint chiefs had concurred. Stimson brought the target recommendations to Truman, and, along with Marshall and General H. H. Arnold, they compiled a list of four cities. Listed in order of their military importance, they were Hiroshima, Kokura, Niigata, and Nagasaki.[32]

In the preface to his *Memoirs*, Truman commented from his own experience on the decision-making process of the presidency: "No one can make decisions for him. . . . To be President of the United States is to be lonely, very lonely at times of great decisions." [33] Although surrounded by his advisers as they chose the target cities in Japan, Harry Truman must have felt very lonely. He recalled that after the target selection was completed, "I then agreed to the use of the atomic bomb." [34]

With the long-awaited authorization from the commander in chief secured, orders, dated July 24, 1945, were dispatched by the War Department to General Carl Spaatz, commanding general of the Army Strategic Air Force. The orders authorized the 509th Composite Group of the Twentieth Air Force—a special unit trained for this mission— to "deliver its first special bomb as soon as weather will permit visual bombing after about 3 August 1945 on one of the targets: Hiroshima, Kokura, Niigata and Nagasaki." The orders also stated that additional bombs were to be dropped on the designated targets as soon as they were available. Copies of Spaatz's orders were also to be personally delivered by him to General MacArthur and Admiral Nimitz for their information.[35]

Since Truman's order to use the atomic bomb was given two days prior to promulgation of the Potsdam Declaration of July 26, it could be assumed that the document was a cynical gesture. The assumption is unwarranted. If the bomb was to be used as soon as it was operational (as advocated by the interim committee) then technical necessity and the structure of the command system required that Truman initiate the order when he did. The order was not irrevocable, but no further commands were required from the commander in chief, or anyone else in the military hierarchy, for the bomb to be used on or after August 3. Truman's instructions to the secretary of war were clear on this: "The order would stand unless I notified him that the Japanese reply to our ultimatum was acceptable." [36]

The Potsdam ultimatum, which said nothing about the emperor and nothing about the atomic bomb, was not wholly rejected by the Japanese. Rather, Premier Suzuki told the press that since the document did not seem to propose anything new, his government chose to "ignore" it for the present. This, to Truman, was unacceptable. He felt that there was no longer an alternative course. While the Japanese still vainly placed their hopes for a negotiated settlement on the Russians, American technicians assembled an atomic weapon on Tinian Island in the Marianas. Since he believed that the Japanese response gave him no cause to, Truman did not countermand his decision, one he said he reached after long and careful study: "It was not an easy decision to make. I did not like the weapon. But I had no qualms if in the long run millions of lives could be saved. The rest is history." [37]

History records that 60 percent of the city of Hiroshima, Japan, was destroyed at 8:15 A.M., August 6, 1945. The B–29 crewmen returning to their base reported that the results exceeded expectations.[88] They did indeed. The predicted twenty thousand that would be killed by the bomb became, in fact, more than seventy-eight thousand men, women, and children. At least thirty-seven thousand others were injured; thirteen thousand were missing. One single bomb in one apocalyptic minute had transformed Hiroshima from the eighth-largest city in Japan into a village. "This is the greatest thing in history," Truman told a group aboard the U.S.S. *Augusta* en route back from Potsdam, when he received news of the bombing.[89]

In a prepared statement released from Washington the same day, the president told the nation of the bomb and warned the Japanese that more would follow:

We are now prepared to obliterate more rapidly and completely every productive enterprise the Japanese have above ground in any city. . . .

It was to spare the Japanese people from utter destruction that the ultimatum of July 26 was issued at Potsdam. Their leaders promptly rejected that ultimatum. If they do not now accept our terms they may expect a rain of ruin from the air, the like of which has never been seen on this earth.[40]

Seventy-five hours after the attack on Hiroshima, the seaport of Nagasaki was atom-bombed. The casualties numbered above 100,000. A one-square-mile area was instantaneously cratered by the force of the blast which detonated some two thousand feet above the city. The bomb, much more powerful than the device used on Hiroshima, left a pall of radioactive dust over Nagasaki that did not dissipate for several days.[41]

Questions must inevitably arise about the time span between the dropping of the first and second bombs. The second bomb was originally scheduled to be dropped on August 11, not the ninth. However, the schedule was advanced because meteorologists indicated that the targets would not be visible by the eleventh. Truman should have waited longer; Nagasaki was destroyed before the Japanese government could reasonably be expected to react to the delayed, confused reports from Hiroshima. Truman, of course, thought the time was sufficient. He gave them three days to surrender, he said, and would have given them two more were it not for the unfavorable weather forecasts.[42]

Although there is no apparent *military* reason for advancing rather than delaying the second attack, the seemingly unwarranted haste in employing the second bomb may have been occasioned by strategic considerations. A "second-bomb strategy"—the idea of dropping two bombs, rather than dropping one and waiting a substantial interval for Japanese reaction—was developed by military planners in December, 1944. The reasoning was that the first bomb would demonstrate the magnitude of the weapon; the second would be proof to the Japanese that the first was not an experimental fluke and that the United States had the capacity to continue these attacks. General Groves liked the second-bomb strategy and described the concept to Truman, who neither accepted nor rejected it. But it must be remembered that the president had placed no limitations on the number of bombs to be used.[43]

When, as commander in chief, Truman put his name to the order to General Spaatz to use atomic weapons on Japan—an order which General Groves had drafted—he was tacitly accepting a multiple-bomb strategy. In part, the order reads: "Additional bombs will be delivered on the above targets as soon as made ready by the project staff." Additionally, Truman had a message sent to General Spaatz on August 7, telling him to continue the bombing as ordered unless advised to the contrary by the president.[44]

As Truman had ordered the situation, the atomic attacks were to continue unabated, with the frequency of the attacks to be determined by field commanders, subject only to the availability of fissionable material and proper weather conditions over Japan. The process would continue until Japan accepted unconditional surrender.

In the course of a discussion with Columbia University students in 1959, Truman was asked about the timing of the second bomb. From his remarks it can be reasonably inferred that he did endorse the second- (or multiple-) bomb strategy:

> Student: Mr. President, would you be willing to explain to us what led you to believe that the first atomic bomb had failed to achieve peace with Japan and made it necessary to drop the second one?
> Truman: It was a military procedure, under which the armed forces decided that it would be necessary to destroy both towns . . . and the objective was, as nearly as we possibly could determine, to shut off the supplies to the Japanese. . . .
> Student: The reason I asked this was that it seemed to me the second bomb came pretty soon after the first one, two or three days.
> Truman: That is right. We were destroying the centers, the factories that were making munitions. Just a military maneuver, that is all. . . . I was there. I did it. I would do it again.[45]

● Was it necessary to use the atom bomb in order to defeat Japan without a costly invasion? It is almost impossible to judge such an immeasurably emotional event objectively. The maimed, disfigured children of Hiroshima live; a new generation of children breathe air polluted by radioactive fallout from the testing of bombs over one thousand times more powerful than those which scarred Japan; the threat of nuclear annihilation faces every living being; and the urge to damn those who advocated and initiated atomic warface is overwhelming. But examination of the complex of circumstances involved in the atomic decision reveals that any judgment demands severe qualifications.

● Japan would have conditionally surrendered without the atomic bomb being used and prior to the invasion of Kyushu in November.[46] Several high-ranking military officials have said (after the fact), that there was no *military* need to drop the bomb; among them, Generals Arnold and MacArthur and Admirals Halsey and Leahy. Eisenhower was opposed before the fact, and Marshall had serious reservations.[47] Thus, neither invasion nor atomic bombing of Japan was essential to obtaining a conditional surrender.

Truman and all his military and civil advisers were fully aware through intelligence reports that Japan was actively seeking a negotiated end to the war for some time prior to the decision to use the bomb. There was little effort made, aside from the ambiguously worded Potsdam Declaration, to follow up on the possibility of a political settlement. Obviously Truman did not energetically seek nonmilitary solutions; why he did not is the subject of continuing controversy among diplomatic historians. The basic revisionist argument is that the atomic bombs were used against Japan to gain an advantage in the developing European diplomatic confrontation with the Soviet Union and to prevent the Russians from having a voice in the Far Eastern peace settlement.[48]

If the first bomb was unnecessary, then it follows that the second was doubly so, particularly given the brief interval between them. Had the Japanese been told after the first bomb that the attacks were to be suspended temporarily, but would be resumed at some specific date if they had not by then surrendered, there is little reason to doubt that they would have submitted. Even if the second-bomb strategy was valid when it was proposed in 1944, by August, 1945, Nagasaki was not needed to convince the Japanese their cause was doomed. "It was my responsibility as President," Truman said, "to force the Japanese warlords to come to terms as quickly as possible with the minimum loss of lives." And again, in a radio message to the nation, the president said, "We have used it [the atomic bomb] in order to shorten the agony of war." [49] Quite the contrary, more lives were lost and great agony brought to the people of Nagasaki because of excessive haste in employing the second atomic bomb.

The distinction between military and civilian targets had disappeared on both sides at some point during World War II. In Europe, the German rocket attacks on London and the Allied destruction of Dresden are notable examples. In the Pacific, the Japanese had shown little concern for the sparing of noncombatants. At the same time, American fire bombing of Japanese cities had killed over one quarter of a million civilians and left over nine million more homeless. The belligerent nations were all engaged in research and development of more efficient and sophisticated war machines, the prevailing view being that a nation could use any weapon not explicitly barred by international agreement. In that regard, the atomic bomb was just a bigger, more effective device for destroying enemy cities. Thus, although Truman showed no particular concern over this subject, the historical precedents did exist for using the bomb. The only effective deterrent to the use of such insidious weapons thus far discovered has been the fear of retaliation in kind, as the absence of poison gas in World War II aptly demonstrates.[50]

The initial response in America to the atomic bombings was overwhelmingly favorable.[51] Truman was subjected to severe criticism from several Allied nations as the horrendous effects of the blasts became public knowledge. And as the years passed and the nuclear arms race accelerated, many Americans have looked back ruefully to the initial act and bitterly condemned the commander in chief who ordered the bombings. Truman never attempted to shift responsibility for the use of the bomb or deny that the decision was his alone to make: "The final decision of where and when to use the atomic bomb was up to me. Let there be no mistake about it." [52]

Although the American political system does accord ultimate military authority to the commander in chief, in this instance, there is ample reason to believe that it would have been difficult for Truman to have decided otherwise. He was new to command, overawed by the reputations of Stimson and Marshall, and untutored in international relations. The flow of information about extant conditions which would determine how he would decide demonstrated a type of tunnel vision which admitted no feasible alternative. The military intelligence he received created a false syllogism, by providing him with almost exclusively military premises, leading to an inevitable acceptance of a military conclusion: Use the bomb.[53]

Harry Truman did not so much decide to use the atomic bomb as he decided to acquiesce in the completion of a vast project that had cost billions of dollars and hundreds of thousands of man-hours and that promised a speedy, life-saving, dramatic finale to the most costly struggle in the history of international warfare. The project had developed an irresistible momentum of its own, with the implication always present that once the bomb was perfected, it would be used against America's enemies. Had Truman desired to stop this process, he would have had to justify his decision to the bomb's makers, the generals, and, eventually, the people. This would have meant arguing from the uncertain ground of future implications of the bomb's use; arguments that, as one scholar wrote, "posed such huge imponderables and contingencies that they defied easy calculation." [54] The proposed military solution, on the other hand, offering an immediate, direct, readily calculable result, was bound to have appeal to the president. For Truman was a practical politician, used to direct action and not given to abstract reasoning. And so, taken together, the system, circumstances, and his own predisposition led Truman to accept a military conclusion. It will be recalled that Truman said, after discussing with his advisers the Japanese cities to be marked as targets, "I then *agreed* to use of the atomic bomb." [55]

It would be unreasonable to fault Truman for not having the vision to see what the passage of decades revealed. Nor is it at all probable that any other decision he made on the bomb would have prevented the subsequent nuclear arms race. But his acceptance of the specious arguments against a test demonstration and against a specific warning in the Potsdam Declaration can be greatly regretted, if not condemned. The wisdom of his open-ended order to General Spaatz to continue the bombing until otherwise informed may also be questioned. What is beyond question is that when Truman did act—however wrong that action may have been—he was convinced that this was the only available course: "I could not worry about what history would say about my personal morality, I made the only decision I ever knew how to make. I did what I thought was right." [56]

In his public utterances regarding his decision to use the bomb, Truman seldom varied from the position that he had no regrets over using this "purely military" weapon against what were "essentially military" targets. But privately he did have his doubts. For example, a few weeks after the war he was discussing military problems with his director of the budget, who reminded the president that he now had the atomic bomb to fall back on. Truman replied, "Yes, but I am not sure it can ever be used again." [57] Three years later, in a White House meeting he spoke of his decision in quite troubled terms.

David Lilienthal, then director of the Atomic Energy Commission, recorded in his journal these recollections of Truman's words: "It is a terrible thing to order the use of something that . . . is so terribly destructive, destructive beyond anything we have ever had. You have got to understand that this isn't a military weapon. . . . It is used to wipe out women and children and unarmed people, and not for military uses." [58]

This uniquely destructive device had the desired effect on the Japanese government. On August 10, 1945, Radio Tokyo broadcast a message accepting the terms of the Potsdam Declaration, with the understanding that the surrender must not prejudice the sovereign rule of the emperor. Truman called a meeting that morning with Admiral Leahy and Secretaries Byrnes, Forrestal, and Stimson to discuss a response. The discussion centered around the reservation expressed by the Japanese with regard to Emperor Hirohito. Stimson, who had long advocated retention of the imperial order, told the president that allowing Hirohito to govern under American supervision would greatly facilitate both the surrender of all Japanese forces and the postwar administration of the country. Leahy agreed with Stimson, but Secretary Byrnes was against such a suggestion. He wanted to hold to the unconditional surrender formula; anything less would represent a reversal of policy. Truman seemed inclined to agree with Byrnes when Navy Secretary Forrestal settled the dilemma by proposing that the reply be drafted to reaffirm the Potsdam Declaration but reassure the Japanese that the emperor would be retained. In other words, he proposed that the response accept the Japanese condition though continuing to insist upon unconditional surrender. Truman liked the idea and ordered Byrnes to prepare a draft statement along those lines. He further ordered that the war effort against Japan was to continue at existing levels, except that atomic bombs were to be employed now only with his express consent.[59]

The secretary of state's draft response to Japan, since referred to as the Byrnes Note, was ready for a cabinet meeting that afternoon (August 10), its apt phrases walking the thin line of Forrestal's suggestion. Truman approved the note, and its text was radioed to the Allied capitals of London, Moscow, and Chungking for approval. The Soviet Union, having declared war on August 8, accepted the text of the Byrnes Note after some half-hearted struggling with Ambassador Harriman over the Soviet desire to share military control of Japan with the United States. England and China readily agreed to the text which was then forwarded to the Japanese by the Swiss on August 11, 1945.[60] On the fourteenth, having received Japan's acceptance of the Allied terms, the president told a news conference: "I deem this reply a full acceptance of the Potsdam Declaration which specifies the unconditional surrender of Japan." [61] While Truman spoke, his message ordering a cease-fire was being transmitted to all operational forces in the Pacific.

The president ordered the Joint Chiefs of Staff to give maximum publicity to the surrender ceremonies, which, with obvious personal pleasure, he directed take place aboard the battleship U.S.S. *Missouri.* Another obvious choice for Truman, although one that would not remain a constant source of pleasure, was the designation of Douglas MacArthur as supreme commander in Japan. Through the terms of the surrender document and the various directives Truman caused to be issued to MacArthur, the general became the virtual ruler of the Japanese nation, as well as supreme commander of all American military forces operating in the Far East.[62]

The fateful days of August finally ended, and September began with the formal surrender ceremonies held in Tokyo Harbor on the first. The war was over, or at least the killing had stopped; but a peace treaty with Japan would wait another decade. In fact, Truman did not even officially declare an end to hostilities with Japan until December 31, 1946, in order to retain several of the emergency war powers Congress had granted to the commander in chief.[63] But legal technicalities aside, peace had come by mid-August, 1945.

Columnist Walter Lippman, writing shortly after Roosevelt's death, said, "The genius of a good leader is to leave behind him a situation which common sense, without the grace of genius, can deal with successfully." [64] Truman, untouched by genius, but with a goodly measure of common sense, did precisely as Lippman hoped; he managed to deal with the situation of total war successfully. However, Truman was not truly commander in chief during the final months of the war, but a steward implementing a predetermined process.[65] He said as much in a letter to the secretary of the navy: "I deserve no credit for the victory except the little I contributed as United States Senator. It was already won when I became President and all I had to do was carry out the program." [66]

5/ The Guardian

*We have got to treat this differently from rifles and cannon and
ordinary things like that.*[1]

—HARRY S. TRUMAN

Whatever Truman's role was in the closing scenes of World
War II, postwar nuclear weapons policy was his alone
to determine. Initially he tried to suppress all information regarding the bombings that ended the war. Ironi-
cally, at the same time he freely disclosed information about the bombings that began World War II.

Late in August, Truman released to the press the army and navy
fact-finding reports on the Pearl Harbor attack. The president told the
press that there was nothing that had to be covered up—an apparent
effort to end widespread speculation on the subject which was then
current.[2] When Congress created a joint committee to investigate Pearl
Harbor, Truman proved his sincerity by ordering the heads of the War,
Navy, and State departments, the joint chiefs, and others involved to
make full disclosure of information to the committee.[3] Conversely,
Truman muzzled these same military policy advisers concerning information on the atomic bomb, telling them that nothing regarding the
design, production, or use of nuclear weapons in warfare was to be
released without his specific authorization. The president defended this
silencing directive by explaining that Hiroshima and Nagasaki were
"lesson enough" to him that the world could not afford atomic warfare. Until effective international control could be implemented, the
bomb secrets were to be preserved. But a world hungry for news of
this doomsday weapon could not be completely denied; Truman relented to the extent of allowing release of general-interest information
which, in the opinion of the War Department, would not endanger
national security.[4]

Concerning postwar nuclear weapons policy, three developments stand out in the Truman period. First, as the only national leader with control over atomic energy, Truman made an effort to turn over this control to the United Nations, but on his terms. Second, as the first commander in chief to have control over atomic bombs, he denied to the military services any direct authority over the very weapon that became the bulwark of American diplomatic and military thinking on strategy and policy. Last, Truman ordered continued testing and development of nuclear weapons, and when the Soviet Union detonated their first test bomb, he ordered a massive program which led to the perfecting of a device far more powerful than the Hiroshima bomb.

The possibilities and problems contemplated in international control of atomic energy were first brought to the president by Secretary of War Stimson in his discussion with Truman on April 25, 1945. One of the reasons for the creation of the interim committee (out of this meeting) was to advise the president on postwar atomic controls policy. Truman said that the frightful implications of Hiroshima made him aware that the bomb had the capacity to destroy civilization unless placed under effective control.[5]

In a presidential statement released on August 6, 1945, to announce the attack on Hiroshima, Truman had said he would make prompt recommendation to the Congress for the establishment of a commission that would control the production and use of atomic energy within the United States. Three days later, in a radio report on the Potsdam Conference, he reiterated his plans to go to Congress to seek cooperation in finding effective control methods. Since this new weapon was "too dangerous to be loose in a lawless world," atomic technology was to remain secret until workable controls were found. "We must," Truman said, "constitute ourselves trustees of this new force. . . . It is an awful responsibility which has come to us." [6]

Secretary Stimson, charged with making recommendations to the president on future policy, spent a great deal of time going over the interim committee reports and reconsidering his own views toward international atomic control. The problem was multifaceted, but every recourse seemed to lead back to the Soviet Union, the reason being that all the other major nations of the world either knew the secrets of atomic fission, or were in no position to capitalize on such information. Great Britain, Canada, and the United States had cooperated in producing the weapon; France and China were too fragmented by the war to organize the massive effort needed to produce the weapon in the foreseeable future; Germany and Japan were under Allied military control and could be prevented from attempting such experiments. The Soviet Union was the only nation with the resources, technological capability, and the opportunity to make immediate use of the information. The crux of the problem of international control, as Stimson viewed it, was whether the Russians could be trusted and if they should be approached directly, or through the offices of the United Nations, which was still in the formative stage. Stimson's recommendations were presented to President Truman in a memorandum dated September 11, 1945.

This memorandum began with an accurate anticipation of Cold War developments. The secretary pointed out to the president that the bomb clearly gave the United States an effective, temporary counter to Soviet influence and expansionism. However, the Russians realized this too, and, "Unless the Soviets are voluntarily invited into the (nuclear) partnership upon a basis of co-operation and trust," Stimson warned, they would certainly be impelled to "feverish activity . . . toward the development of this bomb in what will in effect be a secret armament race of a rather desperate character." Two pivotal passages in this lengthy document merit direct quotation:

> I consider the problem of our satisfactory relations with Russia as not merely connected with but as virtually dominated by the problem of the atomic bomb. . . . Those relations may be perhaps irretrievably embittered by the way in which we approach the solution of the bomb with Russia. For if we fail to approach them now and merely continue to negotiate with them, having this weapon rather ostentatiously on our hip, their suspicions and their distrust of our purposes and motives will increase. . . .
>
> I emphasize perhaps beyond all other considerations the importance of taking this action with Russia as a proposal of the United States. . . . Action of any international group of nations, including many small nations who have not demonstrated their potential power or responsibility in this war would not, in my opinion, be taken seriously by the Soviets.[7]

Meeting with Truman on September 12, Stimson went over the memorandum with him, line by line. What he was proposing, the secretary explained, was direct negotiations with the USSR by the United States (with England's assent) looking toward an agreement by which this nation would impound its present weapons and agree to end further development and ban their use in war, if the British and Russians agreed to do likewise. Stimson did not propose giving the Soviet Union the technological data necessary for manufacturing the weapon, for the president had already determined that this would not be done. But Stimson did suggest that Truman offer to exchange knowledge with the Russians leading to further development of atomic energy for peaceful applications. Truman agreed with this approach and asked Stimson, who had already resigned, to remain until the cabinet meeting on September 21, at which this memorandum would be the sole topic of discussion.[8]

The cabinet meeting on the twenty-first began with Truman asking Stimson to summarize the position stated in his memorandum. In brief, the secretary told them that maintenance of secrecy on the basic principles of atomic energy was impossible. He advocated a scientific exchange and collaboration with the Soviet Union, in seeking the development of atomic power and a properly safeguarded mutual renunciation of atomic weapons development. The discussion that followed, to use Dean Acheson's phrase, "was unworthy of the subject." [9] Truman confessed to enjoying the heated exchange but apparently got little from it, since he asked those present to submit written opinions to him.

The cabinet's memoranda to the president, although varying widely in detail, generally favored either an approach similar to Stimson's or maintenance of an American monopoly on all facets of atomic energy. The new secretary of war, Robert Patterson, the Joint Chiefs of Staff and Acting Secretary of State Acheson all advocated following Stimson's recommendations. The only major presidential *military* policy adviser to oppose this proposition was Secretary of the Navy Forrestal. The attorney general and secretary of the treasury agreed with Forrestal, but the postmaster general and commerce secretary generally followed Stimson's reasoning. However, given the division and qualifications made, no clear consensus emerged among the president's advisers. Truman was recognizing more than just a constitutional truth when he told a reporter a few days later that whatever decision was made on the subject, he alone would have to make that decision.[10]

In a special message to Congress on October 3, the president revealed his initial decision on control. He told the Congress that the fate of civilization might well be determined by the success or failure of an international ban on the use and development of atomic weapons. Echoing Stimson's memorandum, Truman said that, although there were great difficulties involved in such a ban, the alternative was a disastrous arms race. The president assured Congress that the secrets of the manufacturing process to produce bombs would not be divulged. His proposal was to initiate discussions, first with the nuclear partners, Canada and Great Britain, "and then with other nations, in an effort to effect agreement on the conditions under which cooperation might replace rivalry in the field of atomic power." [11]

The initial step in atomic control discussions was taken in November when the British and Canadian prime ministers met with Truman in Washington. Their talks concluded on November 15 with a joint statement from the White House. The sense of the statement was that the three nations possessing the knowledge necessary to generate atomic energy had decided that the most effective means of preventing its use for destructive purposes was through the United Nations. They recommended that a commission be established on atomic energy that would submit recommendations to the UN on means to ban military use and facilitate the exchange of scientific information on peaceful uses of atomic power. [12]

On the following day Truman asked his cabinet for their comments on the agreement. Secretary Wallace expressed reservations about the effectiveness of a commission-type approach. However, "all agreed," as Truman recalled, that handing the problem of controls policy over to the newly created United Nations would give that body a chance to prove its worth. Those present at this meeting, including Truman, had approved of exactly the opposite approach less than two months earlier. Stimson had emphasized in his memorandum "beyond all other considerations" that the United States must approach Russia on the controls question singly and directly, not through the United Nations, since such action would not be taken seriously by the Soviet government. [13] Nevertheless, on January 24, 1946, the United Nations Atomic Energy Commission was created.

The president charged the State Department with responsibility for drafting a plan for international control of atomic energy. Secretary Byrnes delegated the task to a committee chaired by Undersecretary of State Acheson which submitted a proposal to Byrnes and Truman on March 16, 1946. This working paper had, as the heart of its recommendations, a proposal that an international authority be created with a complete monopoly over all destructive uses of atomic energy. On Byrnes's recommendation, Truman appointed Bernard M. Baruch as American representative on the United Nations Atomic Energy Commission. Following some controversy with Acheson and Truman over provisions of the proposed American policy statement, Baruch received permission to revise the terms somewhat. The president approved these changes and gave the revision to Baruch as his official policy directive early in June, 1946.[14]

The American proposal for international control was submitted to the commission by Baruch on June 14, 1946. The essential points are succinctly detailed in the following newspaper account:

> As soon as a satisfactory international agency can be set up; as soon as other powers have joined with us to guarantee that agency and give it the scope and authority it needs; as soon as we are assured that no other nation will or can use atomic bombs against us, the United States will cease the manufacture of atomic weapons, will destroy the bombs now in its possession, will give to the new agency, by stages as required, all pertinent information, and finally will turn over to this agency control of its own uranium and thorium deposits, its own primary production plants and the output of these plants.[15]

The plan, perhaps sincere in intent, was not acceptable to the Soviet Union. The Russians were being asked to cease all efforts at developing atomic weapons, while the United States continued to hold a stockpile of these devices. The Soviet government would be required to perform a supreme act of diplomatic faith: They were to accept the American promise to destroy the existing atomic stockpile at such time as (by an exclusively American decision) it was determined that the UN Commission control procedures were sufficient to safeguard the security of the United States. It may well have been that no proposal, however phrased and selfless, would have caused the Soviets to halt before they achieved atomic parity. But that can never be known with any certainty.

Aside from the requirement that the United States was to enjoy an atomic monopoly for an indeterminate period, the American plan contained other features onerous to the Soviet Union: surrender of the veto power on all matters respecting control of atomic energy; a thorough "on-site" system of inspection and control; and by implication, a partial subjugation of national sovereignty to an international body. A Russian counterproposal agreed to banning the production and use of atomic weapons, but called upon the United States to first cease bomb production and destroy all existing weapons *before* any discussion of international inspection and controls. Truman found the Soviet proposals equally unacceptable. He wrote to Baruch: "It is my opinion that we should stand pat on our program." [16]

During the years that followed, both the United States and the Soviet Union did "stand pat" in their initial positions, making only minor concessions to the other's views. The welter of proposals, counterproposals, and artful rephrasings of essentially the same posture continued for years. [17] Truman's determination that there must be effective international inspection and control prior to elimination of the United States atomic stockpile remained constant. He demonstrated this in a campaign speech at Milwaukee in October of 1948. After restating his controls position, Truman went on to tell his audience that the United States was still willing to sacrifice some of its national sovereignty and destroy its bombs as originally proposed in the Baruch plan. "There has been no change in the American position," Truman said. "But the Soviet Union rejected such a plan as an intrusion upon its national sovereignty." [18] And there the matter of international control has stood, made more complex and urgent by Soviet acquisition of atomic weapons in 1949. [19]

One by-product of the early stages of weapons control discussion was that it precipitated a painful conflict within the administration, centering on the policy views of Secretary of Commerce Henry Wallace. On July 23, 1946, Wallace had written a twelve-page single-spaced letter to Truman in which he condemned the military buildup, atomic policy, and the administration's attitude toward international controls. Truman thanked Wallace for the letter and promptly forgot it. On September 12 Wallace spoke in New York, delivering "an all-out attack" on American foreign policy, according to Truman, who publicly disavowed the secretary's statements. Five days later, evidently deciding that he would rather be right than secretary of commerce, Wallace released to the press a copy of his letter of July 23. [20]

The Wallace letter generated a great deal of commentary in both the American and international press. The State Department received numerous queries from ambassadors anxious to learn if the former vice-president's statements represented a change of policy. Secretary of State Byrnes wired from a Council of Foreign Ministers meeting in Paris that Wallace's comments were making his position difficult.[21] Truman's first reaction was to order the secretaries of war and navy to write him a joint letter, immediately released by the White House, repudiating Wallace's contentions about military policy. In the letter, the secretaries denied that they or anyone in their respective departments were advocating a "preventative" war before the Soviet Union acquired the atomic bomb, as Wallace had charged. Baruch also joined the group assailing Wallace with a lengthy memorandum to the president containing a detailed refutation of Wallace's statements respecting the American position on controls. Truman wrote to his mother on September 20: "Well I had to fire Henry today, and of course I hated to do it." [22]

In Truman's message to the Congress of October 3, 1945 (cited earlier), in which he called for international control of atomic energy, he also told the Congress that there was need for legislation providing for domestic control. He proposed that the Congress establish an Atomic Energy Commission, its members appointed by the president, with authority to regulate all activities related to atomic energy.[23]

The president's message did not detail the structure and operational policy of the Atomic Energy Commission (AEC), but merely suggested its functions in the broadest terms. However, shortly after the message was sent up, the leadership in both the House and the Senate received twenty-one-page drafts detailing the proposed legislation. Reporters were aware of the draft bill, but were mystified as to where it originated.[24] The source was undoubtedly the secretary of war. A letter in Patterson's files, addressed to the Speaker of the House, dated the same day as Truman's message, reads: "There is inclosed herewith a draft of a bill 'For the development and control of atomic energy.' This bill is offered pursuant to the President's message to Congress today and is consistent with this message and with the policies announced by the President therein. The bill was prepared by the Interim Committee appointed by the Secretary of War with the approval of the President." [25]

The following day (October 4), the May-Johnson bill was introduced. It received strong backing from the Pentagon, with Secretary Patterson continually referring to the proposed legislation as representative of the views of the War Department and the White House. This was not correct. Although Truman knew that Patterson was submitting draft legislation, he was not aware of the specific nature of the proposals. When asked about the May-Johnson bill in a press conference two weeks after it was submitted, Truman said it seemed satisfactory, but added, "I don't know, because I haven't studied it carefully." [26]

In his message to Congress the president had emphasized the peaceful applications of the power of the atom. He was quite opposed to military control of the AEC. He came to realize that the May-Johnson bill favored a military approach: "Its aim was to set up a kind of permanent 'Manhattan District' under military control." [27] With the War Department earnestly urging adoption of a bill to which Truman became increasingly opposed, a struggle inevitably erupted between the commander in chief and the nation's military leadership over control of the most powerful instrument of destruction ever known.

During October and November the president was made aware of the deficiencies in the proposed AEC legislation through memoranda received from several individuals in the administration and through criticism from outside the government, notably from nuclear scientists. Truman was also aware that military leaders were energetically lobbying for May-Johnson: "The military services felt very strongly that the control of atomic development should be under their auspices, if not under their immediate jurisdiction, and they were making strong representations to that effect to the Congress." [28]

The president wrote a memorandum to the secretaries of war and navy late in November to indicate his dissatisfaction with their proposed legislation. Truman told them that the receipt of numerous objections had caused him to reexamine the bill in detail. He found it had several undesirable features and would require extensive changes. He listed ten specific amendments to the bill which he considered essential. Among them were several having direct bearing on presidential authority over atomic policies. Truman also told the secretaries that the provision allowing members of the AEC or its administrator to be military officers would have to be eliminated before the bill would be acceptable to him. He ended by asking that the interim committee be reconvened for their views on these changes and that May-Johnson be recommitted in the House for the purpose of making these amendments.[29]

The War Department did not reply to Truman's memorandum until late in December. In the meantime the military chiefs continued to aggressively lobby for congressional approval of May-Johnson. At the suggestion of Brien McMahon, chairman of the Senate Special Committee on Atomic Energy, Truman decided to air the controversy in a White House meeting which he called for December 4. Among those present were Forrestal, Patterson, and Groves, all of whom were publicly on record as favoring military control of atomic energy. Following his normal routine when dealing with crucial or controversial questions, Truman asked each person present to express his views. The consensus apparently favored strong military influence over all atomic matters. Truman was a strong dissenter, insisting that the entire AEC program should be under civilian control and operation.[30]

Senator McMahon, taking his cue from Truman, introduced legislation in the Senate December 20, incorporating the president's concepts of total civilian control. A week later, the secretary of war sent a long memorandum to Truman that replied to his earlier ten-point critique, but ignored the McMahon bill. In this note, Patterson took exception to six of Truman's ten points. His strongest objections were, of course, to the president's insistence that no member of the military could serve on the Atomic Energy Commission. Patterson told Truman that military control over atomic energy would be of paramount importance in time of war or similar emergencies. The secretary further argued that preventing military men from holding positions pivotal to determining the development, storage, and use of atomic weapons was "contrary to the philosophy of unified military direction." Patterson closed by telling Truman that it might be difficult to get May-Johnson recommitted and that it would be better to try to amend the bill on the floor of the House or in the Senate.[31]

An exasperated Truman terminated any further overt Pentagon opposition to civilian control of atomic weaponry on January 23, the language of his note leaving no doubt that he considered the matter closed:

> After careful consideration, it is my judgment that the recommendations contained in my memorandum of November 30th [*sic.*, 28th] should be adhered to without modification. . . . I deem adherence to all the recommendations in that memorandum to be essential.
> The Chairman of the Military Affairs Committee of the House and

the leaders in the House should be advised that the Administration desires recommitment of the May-Johnson bill for purposes of amendment or, failing this, that no steps be taken to alter the present status of the bill in the House.

It is my wish, furthermore, that in appearing before Congressional committees or in discussions with Members of Congress relative to atomic energy legislation officials of the Administration present views not inconsistent with the points given in my memorandum of November 30th and reaffirmed herein.[32]

Although the memorandum ended the War and Navy departments' advocacy of May-Johnson, the concept of military control of the atomic energy program had strong congressional support, as Senator McMahon reported to the president. To help encourage support for McMahon's bill, Truman wrote the senator a long letter of endorsement which was released to the press, February 1, 1946.[33] With open White House support the McMahon bill began attracting more backers, but lost one final skirmish to the supporters of military control.

In March, 1946, Senator Arthur Vandenberg introduced an amendment to the McMahon bill, calling for the establishment of the Military Liaison Committee to the Atomic Energy Commission, the committee to be composed of representatives of the War and Navy departments. Vandenberg's proposed committee would be authorized to advise and consult with the AEC on all military applications of atomic energy. The Military Liaison Committee would also be able to appeal any action or proposal of the AEC directly to the secretaries of war and navy, and if either agreed, the matter would be referred to the president for a final decision. Vandenberg, who generally endorsed a civilian AEC, said that the idea was his alone, that he had not consulted with the military at all, a claim disputed by Forrestal's biographer.[34]

Writing later, Truman attacked the Vandenberg amendment as being destructive of the civil supremacy principle; he described it as representing a military veto over AEC activities.[35] Asked about the proposal in a press conference following its introduction, Truman said that many erred in believing that only the military services could safeguard the nation's security. He acknowledged that the military had a major role to play and should be consulted by the AEC. However, the Military Liaison Committee, Truman implied, would be an unwarranted intrusion upon presidential command prerogatives: "The President is the Commander in Chief of the Armed Forces of the United

States, and the civilian board under him would in no way hamper the military in their proper function." [36]

The McMahon bill, after considerable give-and-take in the Congress, became law as the Atomic Energy Act on August 1, 1946. Civilian control predominated through the five-member Atomic Energy Commission, serving at the pleasure of the president. The Vandenberg amendment remained in the final act without substantive change, meaning that the Military Liaison Committee remained in a strong advisory position. The act also established the Division of Military Application within the AEC, stipulating that its director must be a military officer.[37]

Despite Truman's hyperbole and the actual concessions made to military influence on the Atomic Energy Commission, the president had prevailed. For what was permanently established in the course of this struggle was the principle that authority over the most destructive weapon of war ever devised rested with a body of civilians, acting under a mandate from another civilian, the commander in chief. The Atomic Energy Act not only excluded the military services from exercising direct control over nuclear weaponry, it also strengthened the president's military powers at the expense of the Congress. Dorothy James observed regarding this legislation in her study of the presidency, that it "gives a dimension to the President's function as Commander in Chief that it never had in peacetime, providing a further means for erosion of Congressional power in matters of defense." [38]

Although Truman had firmly established the principle of civilian control of nuclear weaponry, he failed to provide any guidelines for ever using the bomb or under what conditions such use might be authorized. This presented a very obvious difficulty for military planners. The services were not even allowed physical control over these devices which had revolutionized strategic and tactical thinking.[39] Certainly there were long-range complications in contingency planning resulting from Truman's failure to establish specific atomic guidelines.

The War Department did not entirely give up its efforts to secure direct authority over the atomic bomb stockpile; intermittent struggles continued throughout the remainder of Truman's administration. In fact, he had anticipated this. The president told the members of the Atomic Energy Commission just prior to their taking over that "the Army will never give up without a fight, and they will fight you on this from here on out, and be working at it in all sorts of places. But you can count on it, I am your advocate." [40]

The Atomic Energy Act provided that the new commission would take complete control of all facets of atomic energy on January 1, 1947. Until that time, responsibility for maintaining atomic secrecy for research and development, and for the first postwar testing of nuclear weapons rested with the War Department.[41]

In a news conference just after the Japanese surrender, a reporter asked the president what was to be done with the Manhattan Project facilities since the war was over. Truman replied that, Congress willing, the project would continue with experiments in the peaceful uses of the atom. At another meeting with the press some three months later, Truman was asked if the United States was still manufacturing atomic bombs. When he replied affirmatively and was asked why, he explained that they were for "experimental purposes." [42]

Truman's press conference remarks in November, 1945, were the first public acknowledgment of a decision he had made earlier to continue research in the decidedly nonpeaceful uses of atomic energy. Truman had granted the joint chiefs' request to test-detonate nuclear devices. They had told the president that they needed the tests to determine the effect of such a bomb against naval vessels and to ascertain what the consequences would be regarding the size, structure, and use of the armed forces.[43]

The first of the Pacific tests was performed upon a fleet of seventy-three surplus ships anchored off Bikini Atoll on July 1, 1946. The device, dropped from a B–29, sank five vessels and damaged fifty-four others. A second test, detonated underwater, proved more successful, sinking twelve ships. However, the latter test created a severe problem with radioactivity: "Five days after the bomb exploded, vessels near the center of the target area were so hot with continuing radioactivity that even damage control parties were not permitted to board them." In May, 1948, the White House announced that a second series of nuclear tests had been undertaken on Eniwetok Atoll in mid-April. Three different devices of an improved design had been tested with results, according to one press source, "that transcended all other developments in nuclear energy since the dawn of the atomic age." [44]

In authorizing the initial postwar atomic tests, the president began an enormous, expensive continuing process of research and development into the destructive powers of the atom. His decision was doubtless influenced by intelligence estimates that the Soviet Union had begun a crash program to produce their own atomic weapons. He may also have been swayed by the Soviet refusal to accept the American proposals for banning atomic weapons. In beginning their crash program the Russians seemed willing victims of the same destructive logic expressed by General Thomas Farrell, deputy director of the Manhattan Project (in 1945): "There is no conceivable defense at present against the atomic bomb, except to have more than your enemy or to stop him from using them against you by hitting him first." [45]

In February, 1949, Truman met with AEC Chairman Lilienthal, who projected the United States nuclear weapons capacity as of January 1, 1951. Truman's eyes widened at the figures and he said, "Boy, we could blow a hole clean through the earth!" The discussion continued in a more serious vein about the incredible power of the bomb, with the president assuring Lilienthal that he would never order its use again if he could avoid it, "But I know the Russians would use it on us if they had it." Less than seven months later, on September 3, 1949, an air force B–29 collected a radioactive air sample over the North Pacific. Truman's intelligence advisers, who had been estimating a Soviet nuclear test no earlier than 1952, now had to inform the president that an atomic device had been exploded somewhere on the Asiatic mainland in the last week of August.[46]

The most significant result of the Russian atomic test news was to accelerate nuclear bomb research in the United States, and to give a sense of urgency to the decision on whether or not to proceed with a crash program to speed development of the proposed, thermonuclear "superbomb." The question of beginning an intensive effort to produce the so-called hydrogen bomb was first submitted to the General Advisory Committee, the major scientific advisory body of the Atomic Energy Commission. The committee reported back to the AEC on October 30, indicating unanimous opposition from a scientific standpoint, but acknowledging that the question involved decisions on foreign and defense policy not within its purview. The AEC reported to Truman in substantially the same vein on November 9; the question of a crash program could not be decided "without reference to political and military as well as technical considerations." [47]

To resolve the hydrogen bomb development question Truman created a special committee on November 10 composed of the secretaries of state and defense and the chairman of the Atomic Energy Commission.* On January 31, 1950, the special committee submitted the following recommendations to President Truman:

>(a) That the President direct the Atomic Energy Commission to proceed to determine the technical feasibility of a thermonuclear weapon, the scale and rate of effort to be determined jointly by the Atomic Energy Commission and the Department of Defense; and that the necessary ordnance developments and carrier program be undertaken concurrently;
>
>(b) That the President defer decision pending the reexamination referred to in (c) as to whether thermonuclear weapons should be produced beyond the number required for a test of feasibility;
>
>(c) That the President direct the Secretary of State and the Secretary of Defense to undertake a reexamination of our objectives in peace and war and of the effect of these objectives on our strategic plans, in the light of the probable fission bomb capability and the possible thermonuclear bomb capability of the Soviet Union.
>
>(d) That the President indicate publicly the intention of this Government to continue work to determine the feasibility of a thermonuclear weapon, and that no further official information on it be made public without the approval of the President.[48]

The members of the special committee were not actually in agreement. Lilienthal was definitely opposed to the idea of a crash program, but he ended up signing the memorandum to Truman for want of an alternative. The secretary of defense objected to recommendation (b), and with the backing of the Joint Chiefs of Staff, was eventually able to get Truman to direct the AEC to plan full hydrogen bomb production. The final recommendation was necessitated by Senator Edwin C. Johnson, a Democrat of Colorado, who revealed on a television program that the United States was developing a superbomb with one thousand times the destructive power of the Nagasaki bomb. Long after the fact, Lilienthal said he deeply regretted that security regulations forced him to fight against the hydrogen bomb development proposals in secret. He said (in 1969) that the decision should have been openly and publicly debated, as the Nixon administration's proposal for an antiballistic missile system was then being openly aired, for the simple reason that it had direct bearing on the fate of every living being.[49]

* Dean Acheson, Louis Johnson, and David Lilienthal, respectively.

At the time, when Truman was handed these proposals of the special committee, Lilienthal began a statement by which he intended to indicate to the president that he had serious reservations about the recommendations made. However, Truman cut the AEC chairman off, saying that with all the talk in Congress and the press about a super-bomb, he had no alternative but to approve the crash program. There was, he said, no time for quiet reexamination of the proposals. It was Lilienthal's impression that Truman's mind was made up before they entered his office.[50]

If Lilienthal's impression is correct, Truman decided to accelerate the nuclear arms race when he learned of the Soviet atomic test. His explanation that congressional and newspaper clamor left him without recourse sounds contrived and represents (for him) an uncharacteristic reaction to pressure. The entire meeting in which the special committee presented its hydrogen bomb policy recommendations to Truman lasted only seven minutes. A few hours later, the White House released a presidential statement in which the decision to produce the hydrogen bomb was announced. In this release, Truman explained that the decision was based on his conception that part of his responsibility as commander in chief included providing adequate protection for the United States against any potential aggressor.[51] The first hydrogen bomb was successfully tested on November 1, 1952, just days before the election to choose Truman's successor.

As the first commander in chief to bear responsibility for nuclear weapons, Truman established precedents and policies the eventual consequence of which cannot yet be determined. As chief of the military in World War II, he ordered the dropping of atomic bombs upon strategic, nonmilitary targets. After the war, in form, if not entirely in fact, he took away from the military control over the production and deployment of these weapons. He made sincere, but naïve and uncompromising, attempts at an international ban on nuclear weaponry; and, failing in this, he spent the remainder of his tenure stockpiling evermore strategic bombs and superbombs and developing an arsenal of new tactical weapons employing nuclear warheads. And if the nuclear race Truman was unable to prevent ends in the cataclysm every human dreads, no doubt the survivors will begin again, fashioning crude weapons out of stone.

6/ The Reformer I

There should be a place into which every young American can fit in the service of our country.[1]

—HARRY S. TRUMAN

In his struggle to create an atomic energy commission that would be under complete civilian control, Truman had successfully contended against stiff opposition from the War Department and a large bloc in Congress. The establishment of AEC was but one of the innovations Truman proposed within the military and in the civil-military relationship. Briefly stated, the major reforms Truman attempted were: (1) the establishment of a system of universal military training; (2) the elimination of racial segregation in the military services; (3) a massive restructuring of organizational and command relationships to achieve unification of the armed forces.

As with civilian control of AEC, these reform efforts were not clear-cut victories for the administration, nor did they bring about the best of all possible military organizations. However, it can be reasonably argued that Truman's reforms left the American military more efficient, less biased, and more powerful than in all history. Universal military training and desegregation of the services—the first a total failure, the other a moderate success—are discussed below. Unification of the armed services, which Truman considered one of his most significant achievements, will be the subject of Chapter 7.

Preceding World War II there were two basic concepts for national military organizations in time of peace: a large standing army, commanded by an elite class of professional soldiers, its ranks stocked by ordinary citizens conscripted for varying lengths of service; and secondly, a minimal peacetime force of professional volunteers (in all ranks) which depended upon the creation of massive armies of citizen soldiers to meet any military emergency. Nontotalitarian governments, such as the United States, depended upon the latter form of organization.

Toward the end of World War II, military planners, anticipating the postwar period, envisioned a new kind of "citizen army" that would require far less mobilization and training in the event of another war. These planners were, of course, anticipating a total war similar to the one the nation was then fighting. They did not anticipate an American policy of containment of Communist expansionism which necessitated fighting limited wars by conventional means with relatively small armies. The governing assumption in postwar planning was that Congress would be willing to enact legislation requiring that every young, able-bodied, male citizen receive military training and be made a member of a ready reserve following such training. The War Department rationale behind this proposal for a massive peacetime reserve force was that it was "merely a proposal for perfecting a traditional national institution to meet modern requirements which no longer permit extemporization after the outbreak of war." [2] This concept is commonly called universal military training (UMT).

When a former citizen-soldier entered the White House—in the person of "Captain Harry," formerly of the Second Missouri Field Artillery—the advocates of universal military training acquired a powerful ally. Truman's pride in his own service in World War I and in that of his fellow guardsmen rings clearly throughout the volumes of his *Memoirs*. At one point in that work he said that ever since World War I he had believed that the only recourse to America's distaste for a large standing army was a trained soldier-citizenry. He once told a reporter that he had been for UMT since 1905, the year he became eligible and joined the National Guard. During his years in the Senate, Truman recalled, he vainly supported a bill to make permanent the Civilian Conservation Corps in the hope that it could eventually be converted into a universal training program. Truman's first chief of staff of the army was General George C. Marshall, the leading military advocate of UMT and a man for whom the president had a profound respect. Given these factors, it was natural for Truman to publicly back such a training program from the very outset of his presidency.[3]

Truman's first public statement, as president, on UMT occurred in a press conference in June, 1945. He told reporters that he had already conferred with some congressmen on the subject and did not want to comment further. However, he did add; "I have got a few views on universal military training of my own, which don't agree with the Army, and don't agree with the Navy, and don't agree with the House or Senate." [4]

On June 4 the House Postwar Military Policy Committee began hearings on universal military training legislation. The military leadership was convinced that their best hope for a satisfactory compulsory training bill was to obtain passage prior to the end of the war. They were fearful that postwar apathy would set in quickly so they presented to the committee "a glittering array of military witnesses in favor of the proposal." They included Secretary of War Stimson, Secretary of the Navy Forrestal, Admiral Ernest J. King, and General Marshall.[5] General Eisenhower and Admirals Nimitz and Halsey, all of whom were unable to attend the hearings, sent statements endorsing universal military training.[6] The gist of their statements, taken collectively, was that the concept of a large standing army was repugnant to American tradition and prevailing public opinion, in addition to being very expensive. Universal military training, they argued, was much less expensive, would provide the nation with a deterrent to possible aggressors, provide peace through strength, and, besides, would be good for the boys. In their report of the hearing to the House, the Postwar Military Policy Committee recommended immediate legislative action on such a program of universal military training.[7]

The policy committee report sparked increased comment—both for and against compulsory postwar training—in the news media during the next several months. Truman kept his own views on UMT planning to himself. In mid-August he told a reporter: "I am going to make recommendations to Congress on a universal military program which is not a peacetime conscription." [8] He refused to elaborate as to details and timing. The president presented a preliminary draft of his training plan to a cabinet meeting on August 31, and found their overall response to be favorable. He told the cabinet that this was the beginning of a new military policy that was required if the United States was to continue international leadership.[9]

One of the points in Truman's twenty-one-point message to the Congress on September 6 called for legislation extending conscription into the postwar period. The president explained that this was only a stopgap measure for the immediate war-to-peace transitional period.

Conversant with his statement to the cabinet a week earlier, Truman told the Congress that he would soon send them recommendations for "a comprehensive and continuous program of national security, including a universal training program, unification of the armed forces, and the use and control of atomic energy." The president had already put his chief speechwriters, Judge Samuel Rosenman and Clark Clifford, to work drafting an address on universal training. On October 9 Rosenman sent a memorandum to the president in which he urged him to accept the army position on one continuous year of training, rather than breaking the training into four periods totaling one year, which Truman favored. Rosenman also urged the president to give the plan to Congress as soon as he approved it: "The longer we get away from war . . . the smaller are the chances of favorable reception in the Congress." [10] Truman accepted both suggestions.

On October 23, 1945, the president presented his universal military training plan to a joint session of Congress. In his address he outlined what he considered to be the prime elements of a modern military structure. He would maintain a relatively small regular army, navy, and Marine Corps, but greatly expand the National Guard and the organized reserves of the army, navy, and marines. The innovative element in this military structure which Truman envisioned was a General Reserve, comprising all male American citizens who had received military training. To establish this General Reserve, of course, would require the enactment of his UMT system. [11]

In explaining the plan to Congress, Truman said that critics erred in calling this type of training "conscription." He defined conscription as compulsory membership in a branch of the armed forces, whereas those involved in a UMT program would simply be civilians receiving training. Truman emphasized this by saying that the program would not replace selective service, which would continue in its function of furnishing replacements for the services. [12] His argument that the training would not be conscriptive strains the definition, since it would be compulsory and under the control of the military.

The specifics of Truman's UMT plan called for one continuous year of training to be commenced at age eighteen or upon completion of high school, whichever was later. All the selective service exemptions and deferments usually granted for dependents, occupations, illiteracy, and medical disabilities, excepting the most grievous physical impairments, would be disallowed. The year of training would be followed by six years of General Reserve membership, then would come transfer to a secondary reserve status.

The president acknowledged that the fundamental reason for universal training was to provide full military preparedness for any potential aggression against the United States. But he also believed that numerous useful by-products of great benefit to the individual trainee could also be derived from his UMT proposal. The training would, he felt, lower the national illiteracy rate, improve the general physical condition, and remove minor medical disabilities. Truman also assured Congress that the trainees would receive ample opportunity for self-improvement, instruction in useful civilian skills, and proper care for their moral and spiritual well-being.[13]

There were several UMT bills in the Congress at the time of Truman's speech, none of which quite matched the administration proposal. Congress, which was generally unsympathetic to the idea, took no action on UMT in 1945. Truman reminded the Congress of its inactivity—on what he now preferred to call "universal training"—in his State of the Union Message, released January 21, 1946.[14] In a conference with Budget Director Harold Smith on the material to be included in this message to Congress, the president had explained his preference for the phrase "universal training." He told Smith that he did not want a military program as such, but one which emphasized physical and educational improvement. Truman said he chose the army to run the program simply because it alone had sufficient resources. He also believed that the program would democratize the army and "overthrow the West Point and Annapolis cliques" of the services by "recruiting commissioned officers from the rank and file." [15] The commander in chief—who, as a young man, was rejected in his application to West Point, and who, entering as a "rank-and-filer," rose to a captaincy in World War I—may not have been entirely motivated by pure, democratic considerations.

The one universal training proposal receiving congressional attention early in 1946 was H.R. 4774, a bill "to provide for military training of youths in peacetime." But the administration and the military would not support the bill because it varied sharply in its particulars from their proposals. Secretary of War Patterson made this clear to the chairman of the House Military Affairs Committee late in February. "This bill," Patterson wrote, "which is not in accord with the President's message and War Department policy with reference to universal military training, cannot be favorably looked upon by the War Department." A week later Truman told a reporter that he had done all he could to get a UMT bill through Congress. Except for a brief reference in a speech in April, Truman seemed reconciled to letting universal training languish in the Congress until later in the year.[16]

On October 2, 1946, the War Department issued a new plan of universal military training. The basic principle remained unchanged—one continuous, compulsory year of training for all male citizens, eighteen to twenty years old. The difference was an emphasis now placed on a civilian board that would control the nonmilitary phases of the training program.[17] The president was ready to try anything to sell the new plan. In a memorandum to Patterson a few days after the new UMT plan was made public, Truman enclosed copies of two letters written by Thomas Jefferson, which spoke of a need for a prepared citizenry. "It seems to me," Truman wrote, "that these letters . . . could be used effectively in our proposed campaign for Universal Military Training, as these letters show Jefferson was not quite the pacifist he was supposed to be." [18]

One phase of the "proposed campaign" mentioned in the note to Patterson was Truman's announcement on December 19 that he had created a nine-member President's Advisory Commission on Universal Training. Although the group was ostensibly an impartial body created to examine objectively the question of universal military training, it was, in fact, composed of nine persons presold on the UMT concept. The suggestion that such a committee be created had been made by Patterson to the president in November, 1945. Truman liked the idea and told the secretary of war to choose prospective members, in conjunction with the navy and Coast Guard. Following his approval and the appointees' acceptances, Truman said he would announce the new commission from the White House, thus drawing the attention of the country to the civilian aspects of the program.[19]

The president brought the advisory commission to the White House the day following announcement of the appointment of its members. In remarks to the commissioners, later released to the press, Truman made it clear that he conceived the purpose of such training to be the molding in young men of a sense of obligation to serve the state. He told the commission members that he did not think of it as universal military training: "I want that word *military* left out. The military phase is incidental to what I have in mind." While the president consistently held that there was no relationship between UMT and the draft, the War Department did not agree. When queried for reaction to the new commission, a War Department spokesman said that the army would not request further continuation of selective service, which was due to expire in March, 1947, until congressional intentions on universal training were clear. The spokesman added that if UMT was not forthcoming, then a continuation of the draft would be inevitable.[20] The expectation was that enough volunteers would emerge from the UMT program.

The Advisory Commission on Universal Training did not submit its recommendations to the president until the end of May, 1947. However, on March 3 Truman asked Congress to allow selective service to lapse on March 31. He said that after consulting with Secretaries Forrestal and Patterson, he had decided to take the gamble on an all-volunteer force. He did not mention that selective service director Lewis Hershey and the army's chief of personnel, General W. S. Paul, were adamantly opposed.[21] Congress did allow the draft to expire, and the nation was without peacetime conscription for fifteen months.

The report of Truman's advisory commission, 445 pages long, was submitted May 29, 1947. The report was unique only in its length and the explicitness of its procedural recommendations. In general principles it differed little from the Truman/War Department proposals. The idea was totalitarian in concept, with strong emphasis placed on the responsibility of each individual male to serve the state, a proposition unprecedented in the American experience. "The universal service advocated by the Presidential Commission," historian Arthur Ekirch wrote, "not only contradicted this tradition, but it also envisaged a type of service that, no matter how disguised, was basically for military purposes." [22]

The impact of the advisory commission report was nugatory. A Republican Congress was not receptive to an administration measure with an estimated cost of two billion dollars annually, particularly one that was freighted with overtones of militarism and totalitarianism. However, Truman continued urging UMT legislation throughout 1947, making only occasional allusions to the stillborn report of his Advisory Commission on Universal Training. The report had at least one staunch advocate in Forrestal, then secretary of defense, who urged every officer in the military services to read the complete report and have a thorough knowledge of its content.[23]

The president began 1948 as he had begun the two preceding years, offering up his—by then—traditional plea to the Congress for enactment of universal military training. Congress was now ready to consider such legislation, motivated by a growing tension in international affairs. The House Armed Services Committee favorably reported out a universal training bill, designated H.R. 4278, which was in general accord with administration desires. For three weeks in March the Senate Armed Services Committee held extensive hearings on UMT and selective service.[24]

On March 17, 1948, the president spoke to a joint session on the threat to world peace and the independence of European states, caused by expansionist activities of the Soviet Union. Truman recommended to Congress three measures which he felt were needed to improve the nation's strength and to maintain the free, democratic character of the nations of Europe. The three measures Truman described were passage of the program for economic assistance for Europe, enactment of universal training legislation, and temporary reenactment of selective service legislation. (The Joint Chiefs of Staff had just advised him that voluntary enlistment had failed and that restoration of the draft was essential.)[25]

The administration's draft of a bill that would have provided both renewal of selective service (Title I) and establishment of UMT (Title II) was submitted to the House by Secretary Forrestal early in April. After much struggle Congress passed the Selective Service Act in June, providing for its termination in two years. However, the universal training proposal failed again. It failed for the same reasons it had in the past and, also, because 1948 was an election year.[26]

Truman's and the Pentagon's faith in the value of universal military training never flagged in the years that followed.[27] Efforts to obtain legislation eventually ceased, only to be revived during the Korean War. On August 29, 1950, Truman found himself in the peculiar position of asking the Congress not to take action creating a UMT program. His reason, as he explained in identical letters to the chairmen of the Senate and House Armed Services committees, was that the demands of the Korean conflict would make it impossible for the military to provide the installations and personnel necessary to implement the program. Truman asked that action on UMT be deferred until 1951.[28]

The secretary of defense, on January 17, 1951, transmitted to Lyndon B. Johnson, then chairman of the Senate Armed Services Preparedness Subcommittee, a draft of legislation authorizing "universal military service and training." The bill finally passed in altered form on June 19, 1951, as an amendment redesignating the Selective Service Act of 1948 as the Universal Military Training and Service Act. As amended, the act extended the life of the Selective Service System until 1955 and authorized the establishment of a universal military training system at some time in the future. But UMT could not be implemented until it received further specific approval from the Congress.[29] Such approval has never been forthcoming; the United States remains the only major power without a system of UMT. The spartan concept of universal military training and service has died.

There should be no mourners at the bier of UMT. The concept is antithetical to democratic principles. Truman's resort to peacetime conscription as a means of replenishing the military, while not as undesirable, did result in a disproportionate obligation for service falling upon the poor, the black, and the uneducated. General Marshall recognized this when he wrote, "In fairness it must be stated that the Selective Service system has imposed on too few the entire burden of military service." [30]

Truman erred in his belief that universal military training was the answer to the obvious inequities in selective service. He erred, not out of meanness of heart, but from an oversimplified view which failed to recognize that a sense of dedication to public service must come from within, as his had; it cannot be compelled by governmental ordinances.

The prevailing racial attitudes in the United States were traditionally mirrored by the military services. Until the manpower demands of World War II made necessary the calling of men regardless of color, the services had enlisted a limited number of Negroes. Those who were accepted were assigned to the more menial ratings and found themselves segregated from Caucasian servicemen. According to a War Department public statement in October, 1940, separation of the races had proven "satisfactory over a long period of years"; any change might hamper national defense preparations and be detrimental to morale.[31] The Navy Department was blunter: "The policy of not enlisting men of the colored race for any branch of the naval service but the messman's branch was adopted to meet the best interests of general ship efficiency." [32] During the war, although the number of black persons in all of the services increased, they were normally assigned to all-Negro units. These units were often given insignificant duties or ignored altogether unless pressure was applied. An example of this attitude was the experience of several Negro air units that were in training for well over a year; they were not considered for combat service until black congressmen began to complain that these units were not being utilized. At the request of the War Department, General MacArthur agreed to accept an all-black group made up of two medium bombardment squadrons and one P–47 fighter squadron if he could be assured that they were well trained, well organized, and well led.[33]

Improvement in the postwar period was slight. The navy had begun integrating Negroes into numerous branches and departments during the war and in February, 1946, officially lifted all racial restrictions on the assignment of Negro personnel. But the implementation of this nondiscriminatory policy was very slow. The great majority of enlisted blacks continued to serve as messmen, and there were only two Negro officers in the entire navy in April of 1946. In early 1947 the marines gave every enlisted Negro the option of transferring to the steward's branch or being discharged from the corps. Army integration in the postwar period, as with the navy, existed almost exclusively as a recommendation on paper.[34]

With regard to civil rights, although his rhetoric far exceeded his record, Truman was a sincere, if cautious, advocate of equality of opportunity throughout his political career. The demography of the border state of Missouri and his own inclinations were such that he was a centrist in the Democratic party.[35] As such, Truman tended to pursue the least divisive pathway. It would be just to characterize him as a moderate reformer, particularly in the civil rights question.

During the first two years of his presidency, Truman spoke regularly about equal justice, but he did not act. In October, 1946, Attorney General Tom Clark suggested that the president create a committee on civil rights. Staff members at the Justice Department and the White

House were working, with Truman's approval, on an order implementing this proposal when the election results in November revealed a stunning general defeat of the Democratic party in Congress. A discernible trend away from the Democrats by black voters occurred because of legislative inaction and the prominence in the party of southerners like Theodore Bilbo, James Byrnes, Will Clayton, John W. Snyder, and Eugene Talmadge.[36]

On December 5, 1946, by Executive Order 9808, Truman created the President's Committee on Civil Rights with instructions to investigate and make recommendations to him on all areas of religious and racial discrimination in the United States.[37] The committee took the president at his word. The report to Truman, entitled "To Secure These Rights" was submitted in October, 1947. It was a stinging condemnation of bias in America; it made numerous recommendations with regard to voting rights, antilynch laws, fair employment practices for federal employees, naturalization procedures, and discrimination in the armed forces. One writer has called the committee's report, "one of the great documents in the tradition of our free society." [38]

To implement the report, the president sent a special message to Congress on February 2, 1948. In it Truman went down the line in asking for legislation suggested in the committee's basic recommendations. He also announced that he had already taken steps (for which he did not need legislative sanction): He had created the Civil Rights Division within the Department of Justice, ordering the FBI to closely assist the new division. Truman also informed the Congress that he had "instructed the Secretary of Defense to take steps to have the remaining instances of discrimination in the armed services eliminated as rapidly as possible." [39] As he might have expected, the Congress took no action.

Political controversy clouded the civil rights question. In May, 1948, Truman's request for selective service legislation faced opposition from southern Democrats because of his order to Forrestal to eliminate discrimination in the military forces. But Truman told reporters that his order to the secretary of defense remained unchanged.[40] Political considerations may have caused Truman to postpone executive action to end racial discrimination in federal agencies and in the military departments. A Washington correspondent reported that on the advice of

Senator J. Howard McGrath, chairman of the Democratic National Committee, Truman had decided to delay any action until after he had received the presidential nomination of his party.[41]

Ten days after winning the nomination and the day before Congress was to reconvene in a special session, Truman issued two presidential decrees. The first, Executive Order 9980, established fair employment policies for all departments of the executive branch of the national government. The second, Executive Order 9981, was the pivotal step in reforming the racial policies of the American military. The major provisions of the order are quoted below:

> WHEREAS it is essential that there be maintained in the armed services of the United States the highest standards of democracy, with equality of treatment and opportunity for all those who serve in our country's defense:
>
> NOW, THEREFORE, by virtue of the authority vested in me as President of the United States . . . and as Commander in Chief of the armed services, it is hereby ordered as follows:
>
> 1. It is hereby declared to be the policy of the President that there shall be equality of treatment and opportunity for all persons in the armed services without regard to race, color, religion or national origin. This policy shall be put into effect as rapidly as possible, having due regard to the time required to effectuate any necessary changes without impairing efficiency or morale.
>
> 2. There shall be created in the National Military Establishment an advisory committee to be known as the President's Committee on Equality of Treatment and Opportunity in the Armed Services, which shall be composed of seven members to be designated by the President.
>
> 3. The Committee is authorized on behalf of the President to examine into the rules, procedures, and practices of the armed services in order to determine in what respect such rules, procedures and practices may be altered or improved with a view to carrying out the policy of this order.[42]

Prodded by the secretary of defense and the president's committee, the military departments began to initiate new policies designed to end discrimination. The army and navy were relatively slow in implementing these policies, while the air force set the pace under the leadership of Stuart Symington. The relative slowness of change in the Navy Department would appear to come from an inherent traditionalism that was slow to accept change, rather than any specific intent to subvert Truman's orders.

However, the army was not encouraged to move toward desegregation because of the position taken by Secretary Kenneth Royall and army Chief of Staff Omar Bradley. In April, 1948, Forrestal had assembled a conference of fifteen Negro leaders to get their views on how best to improve race relations in the military. During the meeting Royall held firm to the army policy of keeping black soldiers in segregated units, a view he knew was shared by General Bradley. Royall told the conferees that this segregation did not represent discrimination.[43] In a bitter memorandum to the secretary of defense several months later, Royall complained that the army was taking an unfair "rap" from "the Negro and the liberal press in the matter of race relations." The army secretary recognized that the attacks stemmed from his remarks at the April meeting, but he told Forrestal that since neither the president nor the secretary of defense had disapproved of the army policy, Forrestal should now publicly endorse it. If not, Royall continued, he would feel it necessary to make public "the facts showing the tacit approval of the Army's position and demonstrating the fact that our own treatment of the Negro is equal to that of the Air Force and superior to that of the Navy." [44]

Despite Royall's comments, it seems clear that the air force had adopted a much more enlightened policy. In January, 1949, Symington approved an air force policy that, except for allowing the continuation of a few all-Negro units, proposed a complete end to any racial reference as a factor in determining personnel policies.[45] One other qualification was made in a memorandum to commanding officers describing implementation of the order: "Care should be taken to insure that a reasonably small number of Negro personnel is assigned to any individual white organization." Symington was clearly in earnest when he told the secretary of defense and later the president that he planned "to completely eliminate segregation in the Air Force." [46]

Louis Johnson, who replaced Forrestal as secretary of defense at the end of March, issued a directive to the service secretaries in early April, 1949, establishing "supplemental policies" to Truman's Executive Order 9981. Johnson insisted that there must be uniform application of the racial equality policy throughout the armed services.[47] The substance and some of the language of the Johnson directive were quite similar to the statement of policy that Symington had issued to the air force in January.

The final report of the President's Committee on Equality of Treatment and Opportunity in the Armed Services, entitled "Freedom to Serve," was submitted to Truman on May 22, 1950. The committee was able to report that important strides had been made. The navy had eliminated *de jure* segregation and opened all jobs, ratings, and technical schools without regard to race and was slowly beginning to implement these policies. The Marine Corps had eliminated segregation in basic training, but still assigned many black marines to all-Negro units. The air force had established its policy of equality in the spring of 1949 and at the time of the report was phasing out the few segregated units remaining. By January, 1950, the army had removed racial restrictions from all jobs and technical schools and discontinued the practice of assigning Negroes exclusively to overhead (housekeeping) units. An army policy change of March 27, 1950, ended the 10-percent limit on Negro strength in the army, and the racial quotas on enlistments were discontinued.[48] The Korean War began soon after the report was submitted to Truman. During the course of the Korean emergency, the military services, particularly the army, were impelled to eliminate the majority of segregated units and discriminatory practices.[49]

Truman was frustrated by Congress in his efforts to guarantee equal rights to all citizens, but his success in eliminating discrimination in the military services is worthy of recognition. Executive Order 9981 was a significant breakthrough in the civil rights movement. The example set by the military establishment in ending all *de jure* and much *de facto* bias undoubtedly gave a strong impetus to the movement in the civilian community. If this nation can one day stand free at last of bigotry, it can well reflect that Harry Truman's desegregation of the military was an early step on the road to that utopia.

7/ The Reformer II

You know, what we are trying to do—what I am trying to do is set up an organization on the experience that we have had in the greatest war in history, so that organization will be ready to operate in case of an emergency—which we hope will never come.[1]
—HARRY S. TRUMAN

James Forrestal once confided to his diary a belief that President Truman urged unification of the armed services not so much for the greater economy and efficiency which might result, but more as a means of selling universal military training to the Congress as part of a unification package. The navy secretary added that the president's thinking on both subjects was clearly based on his World War I and National Guard experiences only. It was his impression, however, that Truman was not "closeminded" on the subject and would not "hold rigidly to his own views." [2] This patronizing remark, written in mid-1945, serves as an apt example of the attitude Truman encountered in his long struggle to unify the military services.

Harry Truman was not the father of the unification concept, but the present-day military command structure in the United States is uniquely his progeny. In the early years of World War II, Truman served as a member of the Military Affairs and Appropriations committees of the Senate, as well as chairman of the Special Committee to Investigate the National Defense Program. These functions afforded him a sweeping view of the waste, inefficiency, and duplication that redounded from having two separate military departments.[3]

Truman became an active civilian proponent of service unification when an article appeared under his name in a popular national magazine during his vice-presidential campaign. The senator wrote that he had not just lately embraced the issue, but had helped draft an American Legion policy that had been advocating integration of forces for years. The basic thesis of his article was that the Pearl Harbor disaster and subsequent bitter experiences during the war years had made evident the danger of dividing military responsibilities between the services. He proposed that the military be coordinated under a single civilian secretary, administratively assisted by three undersecretaries for the ground, sea, and air forces. Truman's plan envisioned a General Staff replacing the Joint Chiefs of Staff. His General Staff would be concerned solely with tactical and strategic control of all armed forces.[4]

Less than nine months after the article appeared, the author was commander in chief, in a position to implement these beliefs. He later recalled that when he entered the presidency one of his strongest convictions was that the military structure was antiquated. America's future security and the preservation of world peace, he believed, depended upon military strength. So from the outset he pushed for unification because "It was my opinion that the Commander in Chief ought to have a co-ordinated and co-operative defense department that would work in peace and war." [5]

The conduct of vast operations in World War II had revealed flaws in the military organization that generated planning for a unified postwar command structure. This planning had begun more than a year before Truman took office.[6] In April, 1944, the House Select Committee on Postwar Military Policy opened hearings on a War Department plan for unification. The army proposed the establishment of an Armed Forces Department administered by a secretary, who would be the principal adviser to the Congress and the president on all defense subjects relevant to politics and administration. The joint chiefs would advise the president on funds allocation and other budgetary matters.[7]

The Navy Department, represented by Secretary Forrestal, opposed the army plan. In fact, the navy opposed any thought of merger out of fear that it might lose control of its air units and the Marine Corps. Forrestal argued that such a unitary system might be too cumbersome for efficient management and that duplication was not always undesirable. He urged considerable further study prior to any action. The secretary also told the committee, in what became a recurrent theme of his, that the job of administering such an organization would be too much for any one man. (Truman appointed Forrestal the first secretary of defense, and the pressures of the job eventually brought on a general breakdown in his mental health, forcing his resignation.) The Select Committee report to the House (June, 1944) agreed with the navy argument that the time was not right for legislation and urged the services to make further studies into the means for implementing unification.[8]

In a meeting with Truman, June 13, 1945, Forrestal asked for his opinions on the army proposal to consolidate the War and Navy departments. Truman told him that he had some definite views on the subject and intended to work with his staff on a legislative proposal as soon as he was finished with the Potsdam Conference. With this warning, Forrestal hurriedly created his own committee, headed by Ferdinand Eberstadt, a trusted adviser. The Eberstadt Committee was charged with recommending to the navy the most effective structure for interservice coordination. Forrestal intended that the navy should have its own unification plan as a counter to the army proposal and the one Truman contemplated. He was wary of what the president's stand would be, since he knew, too, that Truman's latest comments were similar to the plan being advanced by the army.[9]

The Eberstadt Committee submitted its report to the navy secretary in September, 1945. It discounted an army-navy merger and proposed instead that there be three separate departments of war, navy, and air. Each department would have a civilian secretary with cabinet rank, aided by an undersecretary and an assistant secretary. Administrative coordination would be achieved through numerous interdepartmental committees and agencies. The Joint Chiefs of Staff, then existing only by executive order, would be made permanent on a statutory basis and would have responsibility for military coordination of the armed services. To solve the obvious need for a closer conjunction of military with foreign policy, the report recommended the establishment of a national security council.[10]

Forrestal was pleased with Eberstadt's efforts, since the emphasis was on coordination and cooperation, rather than unification, which the navy saw as a threat. The Senate Military Affairs Committee convoked unification hearings beginning on October 17, 1945. Forrestal immediately presented the Eberstadt Report—slightly modified—as the navy plan for unification. Not to be outdone, General J. Lawton Collins presented another, more detailed, War Department merger proposal.[11]

The widely divergent proposals provided the *causus belli*, and the senate hearings provided the arena for what reporters were soon calling "the Battle of the Potomac." Secretary of War Patterson opened the hearings by asserting his conviction that a single department of armed forces would enhance future national security. General Marshall followed, going a step further in holding that without unification "there can be little hope that we will be able to maintain through the years a military posture that will secure for us a lasting peace." [12]

The Army Air Force was particularly enthusiastic over the War Department plan, since it proposed establishing the air force as a separate military department. General officers of the Army Air Force in the Pentagon were asked to write personal letters to key field commanders, keeping them briefed on the status of unification legislation. The generals (Lauris Norstad, Hoyt Vandenberg and others) were even given a model letter and a list of the commanders with whom they would correspond. However, the "individual touch" was emphasized, "in order to prevent an inference that there is a concerted effort in Hq AAF to force field commanders to hew to the party line." [13] As presented in the hearings, the Army Air Force party line simply endorsed the army plan of unification. Their spokesman, General Arnold, told the committee that the services confronted each national crisis ineffectively, inefficiently, and uneconomically organized and that unification could solve these problems. [14]

Truman chose not to interfere as the navy counterattacked. Admiral King, chief of naval operations, told the Senate committee that the army proposal was revolutionary. King also offered the observation that "Any step that is not good for the Navy is not good for the country." One of the basic contentions of Admirals Sherman and Leahy in their testimony was that there was no real need for unification since a unified command already existed under the president, functioning as commander in chief. Just as the Army Air Force supported the army plan for selfish reasons, the Marine Corps defended the navy plan, fearful that any subordination of the navy would ultimately affect the corps. Marine Commandant Alexander Vandegrift accused the proponents of unification of having a blind faith in something they did not understand. [15]

Forrestal, who always knew he was fighting a delaying action against some form of unification, wrote to the president and secretary of war early in November, suggesting still further study of unification by a presidential commission and an end to the "injurious acrimony" of the interservice bickering then going on.[16] No immediate action was forthcoming on Forrestal's proposal. With each service adamantly holding to its own position, the rhetoric became repetitious and the dialogue embittered throughout the fall of 1945.

Until mid-December, Truman remained an interested observer of the army-navy struggle, not interfering publicly or privately, although by the end of October he realized that Forrestal and the navy had "double-crossed" him on unification. The president was concerned, not about the dispute, but about the timing of his own message. At a news conference on November 20, a reporter asked if Truman had a view on military reorganization. He replied, "Yes, the Commander in Chief has a point of view, and he will express it at the proper time." Earlier, the president had told Budget Director Harold Smith that he wanted to wait until early in 1946, when the Congress had cleared up other legislative matters. He planned, Truman told Smith, to tie in unification with universal training, which he had already proposed.[17]

Truman was compelled to change his timing on the unification message by circumstances. His universal military training proposal was not being well received in Congress; the struggle between the services had reached extremes and was generating unfavorable press commentary; and the Military Affairs Committee adjourned December 17 with the army and navy no closer to agreement. Although there is no real evidence, a suspicion lingers that Truman deliberately allowed the services to pick at each other in public. Whether or not he did, the effect of their internecine skirmishing was to strengthen the president's case for unification of the services. It was at this juncture that Truman recalled "seeing the need for presidential intervention." [18]

Truman's chief speechwriter, Samuel Rosenman, had begun working on a unification message in mid-November, based on preliminary drafts submitted by the Army and the Bureau of the Budget.[19] After several revisions, Rosenman followed the usual practice during Truman's administration of sending the proposed presidential message around to all concerned agency and department heads, asking for their suggestions and criticism. In this instance, he probably wished he had not asked. For example, Admiral Leahy, who was against the merger in the first place, told Rosenman that he was particularly opposed to the proposed chief of staff of the Department of National Defense: "It is wrong and dangerous in that it effectively takes away from the President his constitutional responsibility as Commander in Chief." [20] The War Department and the air force expressed concern about the implications that the Joint Chiefs of Staff was to be discontinued. Although the budget director disapproved, Truman insisted there be a civilian secretary in control of each of the component parts of the military establishment. The frankest comments came from Secretary Forrestal: "As the President knows, I am so opposed to the fundamental concept expressed in the message that I do not believe there is any very helpful observation that I could make on the draft you referred to me." Forrestal felt that the president should not send the message up to Congress and should take no position on unification until more hearings had been held.[21]

Despite Forrestal's advice, Truman sent the military reorganization message to Congress on December 19, 1945. In it, he laid down broad guidelines that he hoped would be followed; he detailed nine reasons why unification was necessary, stressing greater efficiency and economy and a more effective civilian control over the military. His one major break with the War Department proposals involved the Joint Chiefs of Staff, which he suggested replacing with a chief of staff for the Defense Department, who, along with the military commanders of each service, would form an advisory body to the secretary of defense and the president. He said that the Joint Chiefs of Staff and the other agencies that sought to coordinate the services during the war had not provided the necessary unity of command and had been just slightly better than no coordination at all.[22]

Upon delivery of the president's message to Congress, the conjecture over his position on the various aspects of reorganization ended for the services. They now had fixed points to rally around or to develop arguments against. Truman also made it clear to Forrestal that the navy was still free to discuss and attempt to amend the plan and that it was not his intention to muzzle anyone. The day following this conversation, December 19, the secretary called Clark Clifford at the White House to get a clarification. Clifford explained that the president felt that civil and naval personnel of the Navy Department should no longer publicly attack unification, since it was administration policy. However, if called to testify before Congress, these individuals should feel free to express their opinions, after first explaining to the committee that they were expressing personal views under leave to do so granted by the commander in chief. On the same day the navy released to the press a memorandum to all navy and marine officers ordering them to refrain from all public criticism of unification except when testifying before Congress. At a press conference on December 20, Truman explained to reporters that it was not his intention to prevent further discussion of unification, as long as those discussing the subject made it clear they were expressing only their personal views.[23]

The public controversy abated in the next few months, and sincere efforts were made to reconcile differences. As an example, late in January, 1946, General Eisenhower, who had replaced Marshall as army chief of staff in November, 1945, reported to Patterson on the progress being made toward coordination of activities with the navy. Eisenhower said that he had discussed the reorganization of several joint boards and committees with Forrestal on at least two occasions.[24] In March, 1946, the protagonists of the interservice controversy, Forrestal and Patterson, met together in another effort to reach an accommodation consonant with Truman's guidelines. The navy secretary said he would accept a secretary of defense with authority to coordinate the services, but with no authority over administration, which was to reside exclusively in the army, navy, and air secretaries. The navy seemed willing, apparently, to accept the form, while rejecting the substance of unification. Patterson made it clear that the army would not accept the navy's scheme. Patterson personally favored a complete consolidation into one military department, presided over by a single secretary.[25]

Forrestal had come around closer to Truman's view in his new willingness to accept a "supersecretary," albeit one without administrative functions. The polarity of the army-navy views, which could be characterized as consolidation *versus* coordination, was diminished somewhat by Forrestal's concession in the direction of unification. In the White House on March 18, Truman talked at length with Forrestal about their differences. The conversation revealed that they were not too far apart on many points. Several of Eberstadt's original recommendations on the method for civil-military coordination were attractive to the president. Forrestal explained at length to Truman the navy concept of the coordinative secretary of defense.[26]

Following the president's message on unification in December of 1945, the Senate Military Affairs Committee had created a special subcommittee to draft legislation responsive to Truman's request. In the first three months of 1946 the subcommittee drafted eight separate bills that were rejected by the parent committee for a variety of reasons. Finally, on April 9, 1946, the subcommittee reported out a ninth bill, the Thomas-Hill-Austin bill (S. 2044), which received a favorable vote in the Military Affairs Committee. The Thomas bill closely followed Truman's recommendations. Although most of those involved considered the proposed legislation an acceptable compromise, the navy did not. In the subsequent congressional hearings on S. 2044, all navy witnesses were unanimous in their opposition.[27]

Although Forrestal was taking a much more conciliatory tack, naval officers were still adamantly opposed. They were convinced that, given the greater size of the army and the greater glamour of the air force, the navy would be submerged and subordinated in any reorganization such as that proposed in the Thomas bill. They sincerely believed that this unification would mean loss of the Marine Corps to the army and loss of naval aviation to the air force as a first step. The admirals' reactions to the Thomas bill caused a sharp counterreaction from Truman at a press conference on April 11. A reporter asked if the navy was justified in still fighting unification. The president said he did not think the navy should oppose unification now that it was his announced policy. Asked whether or not he had authorized the military to express their opposition if they chose to do so, Truman said he granted leave to express "honest opinions." But, he said, naval officers were instead engaged in propagandizing and lobbying. Truman said they were still free to express their honest views, "but when the President of the United States, the Commander in Chief of the Army and Navy, sets out a policy, that policy should be supported by the Army—and War Department—and by the Navy Department." [28]

Truman called in the secretary of the navy on April 17 for another conference on reorganization. The meeting was quite friendly, despite Truman's chagrin at the admirals. In fact, both Forrestal and the president agreed that all such activity should cease. In the course of his talk with Truman, Forrestal again expounded his views on a single secretary of defense. Forrestal came away from the meeting satisfied that Truman had not shut his mind to the navy plan and announced (to his diary) his own conversion: "Speaking personally, I am for unification." The secretary undoubtedly believed that he had moved Truman closer to his position on unification, but Eisenhower met with the president ten days later and came away with the impression (as he wrote to the secretary of war) that Truman "was not weakening in the slightest degree in his stand on the matter." [29] Truman, an accomplished poker player, was keeping his next move to himself.

On the day (May 13) that the Military Affairs Committee favorably reported the Thomas bill to the Senate, Truman summoned Patterson and Forrestal to his White House office. He reminded them of the necessity to reconcile their areas of dispute on unification. The president told Patterson that the idea for a single chief of staff recommended in the army plan was "dangerous" and that he had decided against it. He told the two to meet together and by the end of the month submit to him a list of the areas of agreement and disagreement between the services. [30]

Forrestal and Patterson worked on their problems, but were unable to report full agreement in their letter submitted to Truman on the deadline, May 31, 1946. They were able to list eight major points of agreement: (1) establishment of the National Security Council (NSC); (2) establishment of the National Security Resources Board (NSRB); (3) continuation of the Joint Chiefs of Staff; (4) no single military chief of staff; (5) a Central Intelligence Agency (under NSC); (6) coordination of military procurement and supply; (7) establishment of an agency to coordinate scientific research and development for the services; (8) establishment of an agency to review and adjust all military education and training. The areas of disagreement were also listed: (1) single military department; (2) three coordinate service branches; (3) the role of aviation; (4) future functions of the Marine Corps. [31]

"I was deeply disappointed," Truman wrote later, "that no substantial progress had been made toward resolving this traditional conflict." Although he may have been disappointed, he was not surprised. Nine days before the deadline he told the budget director privately that he really did not expect Patterson and Forrestal to come up with a satisfactory plan. The president agreed with Smith's observation that there was little possibility of getting the unification measure through Congress before adjournment, in any event. Truman had determined that whatever proposals were submitted, he was not going to compromise very much with the fundamentals of his own unification plan. Since the joint letter of May 31 acknowledged the impasse existing between the army and navy, Truman elected to personally settle the differences between them.[32]

Resolution of the interservice dispute over unification came with identical letters to Forrestal and Patterson from Truman, dated June 15, 1946. He informed them of his decisions on the four areas of controversy. First, there was to be one single military department, directed by a civilian with cabinet rank. Each service would be directed by a civilian with the title of secretary, subordinate to the secretary of national defense. Secondly, there were to be three coordinate services, army, navy and air force. Thirdly, the air force was to have control over the military air resources of the nation, except for the missions previously assigned to naval aviation, which would continue. Lastly, the Marine Corps, along with supporting air units, was to continue as a part of the navy.[33]

In letters to the key congressional chairmen on June 15, Truman listed the twelve elements for a plan of unification that had his "unqualified endorsement." The twelve were made up, of course, from the eight areas of agreement between the services and the four areas that Truman had decided for them. He concluded his message with a futile plea: "It is my hope that the Congress will pass legislation as soon as possible effecting a unification based upon these twelve principles." [34] The Congress adjourned early in August, without having taken action.

With the basis of reorganization defined, Truman left the working out of the details to Forrestal, Patterson, and their staffs. The secretary of war had replied to Truman's letter of June 15 immediately, promising his and the War Department's wholehearted support of the implementation of the new military command structure. The president summoned the secretary of the navy on the nineteenth to inquire why he had not responded in kind. Forrestal explained that he wanted to discuss a reply with Nimitz and that both had several pronounced reservations. He also obliquely suggested to Truman that he was ready to resign if it would facilitate unification. Truman ignored the offer, but told him that he wanted a reply before Forrestal departed to observe the atomic bomb tests at Bikini. The letter to Truman was dated June 24, the day of the secretary's departure. In it, he accepted the president's decisions of the fifteenth, noting that there were difficulties ahead in drafting legislation, but that he felt they were surmountable. The

War Department was not reassured that the navy would now be co-operative, since all were aware that Forrestal had been compelled to reply. Stuart Symington, then assistant secretary of war for air, was informed by the War Department's legislative liaison officer that the publicity campaign for the Thomas bill would continue throughout the congressional recess.[35]

The War Department continued to campaign and so did Forrestal. On September 7 he wrote to Clark Clifford describing a meeting he had with Secretary Patterson in late August for the purpose of implementing the unification agreements, as ordered by the president. Forrestal charged that the army still held to a single military establishment headed by a secretary with total administrative control. Despite Truman's orders, Forrestal believed the army was still out to curtail the Marine Corps. Truman talked with the unhappy secretary of the navy on September 9. Forrestal told the president that he intended to introduce his own unification bill into the new congressional session. The bill which Forrestal described was contrary to many of the principles previously "agreed" to by the army and navy. Truman was no doubt surprised. Forrestal, ordinarily a meticulous diarist, did not record the president's reaction.[36] Truman must have realized that his directive of June 15 had not had the desired effect. He ordered all of his top-level military advisers to meet with him at the White House the next day, September 10.

Truman opened the meeting by saying its purpose was to consider what legislative proposals were to be submitted to the upcoming session of Congress. He told those assembled that he was going to have Clark Clifford and Admiral Leahy draft a new unification bill. After all of them had had a chance to mull over the new bill, it would become administration doctrine and he would expect complete support for it in Congress. Truman then followed his practice of asking all present to express their views candidly. None of the opinions expressed reflected any important change of position, particularly with regard to the powers of the secretary of defense.[37] The meeting adjourned and there the matter rested, unresolved, until early in 1947.

With White House pressure clearly on them to agree, Patterson and Forrestal finally produced a mutually acceptable formula for unification, which they transmitted to Truman on January 16, 1947. He replied to them on the same date, expressing his pleasure at the plan and his recognition that each of the services had made some concessions to achieve this "thoroughly practical and workable plan of unification." The New York *Times* headlined the White House announcement as, "A Truman Victory—Patterson and Forrestal Compromise at Last on Unification Idea." [38] It was less a victory than a long-delayed step that Truman should have forced through sooner; there was no reason to allow protracted debate after his directive of June 15, 1946. But Truman had no intention of delaying any longer; he released the secretaries' joint letter and his reply immediately, and the following day sent communications to the Speaker of the House and the president pro tempore of the Senate. The letter to the congressional leaders transmitted copies of the Forrestal-Patterson letter of January 16 and Truman's reply, by way of announcing that an agreement had been reached. Truman also assured the two leaders that members of his staff and the military were drafting the bill, which the president would submit to Congress for consideration as soon as possible. [39]

The military leadership, having taken almost a year and a half to agree on the principles of unification, now found it difficult to agree on the text of the unification bill. The chairman of the Senate Armed Services Committee wrote to Secretary Patterson on February 21 asking why the bill was not ready. The senator complained that he was being hounded daily by his colleagues and reporters wanting to know why the army and navy could not agree on a bill. The secretary of war was apparently not the cause of the delay, since he forwarded Senator Chan Gurney's letter to Clark Clifford the same day, asking if he could help in any way to expedite submission of the bill to the Congress. [40]

Truman, tired of the bickering over details of the bill, ordered Clifford to expedite it. The following memorandum from Clifford to the secretaries of war and navy gives some indication of the president's mood: "Enclosed herewith find three copies of the 8th draft of the bill entitled 'National Security Act of 1947.' The President asks that you kindly initial one copy indicating your approval and return the copy to him. Because of the urgency of this matter, it is hoped that you will be able to approve this draft today. If this is not feasible, you are requested to return a copy at the very latest by noon tomorrow." [41]

Both Forrestal and Patterson sent pledges of their full support of the draft on February 25; the president transmitted the bill to Congress the following day. [42] Hearings on the unification bill, designated S. 758, were held before the Senate Armed Services Committee from March 18 to May 9, 1947. As anticipated, in light of Truman's express order, the testimony given by the hierarchy of the military departments was strong in endorsement of the draft bill. Forrestal's testimony was characterized by a cautious optimism. He restated his fear that the secretary of defense post was too much of a job for any one man. The navy secretary also warned the senators that, "If any single item were withdrawn or modified to the advantage of any one service the mutual accommodation would be thrown out of balance." With only minor qualifications, those who followed—Secretary Patterson, Generals Eisenhower, Norstad, Vandenberg, and Spaatz; Admirals Nimitz and Sherman—gave their support to the proposed bill. Even former Secretary of War Henry Stimson sent a long letter to Senator Gurney strongly supporting S. 758.[43]

After some small modifications in the Congress, the National Security Act of 1947 passed on July 25 and was signed into law by Truman the next day, along with Executive Order 9877, which defined the roles and missions of each branch of the armed forces. As finally passed, the act established the army, navy, and air force as equal departments, each with its own civilian administrator, under the supervision and control of a single, civilian secretary of defense. The act provided for a major reorganization of the military, as well as for a more effective coordination of all the agencies and departments of the national government—both civilian and military—that were concerned with national security.[44]

Title I of the National Security Act established three bodies divorced from the military establishment: (1) National Security Council; (2) Central Intelligence Agency; (3) National Security Resources Board.

The National Security Council was composed of the president, the secretaries of defense, state, army, navy, and air force, the chairman of the National Security Resources Board and other officers of the government as the president might choose to designate. The council was specifically charged with the function of advising the president regarding integration of foreign and military policies relating to the security of the United States. The establishment of the National Security Council was statutory recognition that the foreign and military policies of the nation are inextricably involved and must be coordinated. Although

Marshall declared that the council is the most significant policy-making body in the United States, the group has served only in an advisory capacity to the commander in chief, who alone can make national policy.[45]

In operation under Truman, the National Security Council functioned, to use Forrestal's description, "not as a place to make policies, but certainly as a place to identify for the President those things upon which policy needs to be made." Up until the time of the Korean War, Truman did not attend council meetings regularly, because his presence tended to inhibit debate. When he did attend sessions, Truman seldom offered his opinion or accepted or rejected a recommendation during the course of a meeting.[46]

Title I of the National Security Act also established the Central Intelligence Agency (CIA) under the National Security Council. The Administrative structure of this agency already existed as the "Central Intelligence Group" which Truman had created by a presidential directive in January, 1946.[47] The CIA was assigned the task of coordinating the intelligence-gathering activities of numerous government departments, evaluating the information received, and distributing this material to government officials with a "need to know." The director of the agency was routinely one of the president's first appointments each morning, briefing him on intelligence developments in the preceding twenty-four hours.[48]

The third coordination body established by the National Security Act was the National Security Resources Board (NSRB). The board was to be directed by a civilian chairman, with the membership to come from various departments and agencies of the federal government, as designated by the president. The NSRB was designed to coordinate all civilian, military and industrial factors necessary for an emergency mobilization.[49]

Title II, the other major section of the National Security Act, created the National Military Establishment (NME), headed by a civilian designated as secretary of defense. The new structure was to consist of the departments of the army, navy, and air force, each directed by a civilian secretary, the Joint Chiefs of Staff, a joint staff under the Joint Chiefs of Staff, and War Council, Munitions Board, and the Research and Development Board.

Under the direction of the commander in chief, the secretary of defense was charged by the bill with the following duties:

(1) Establish general policies and programs for the National Military Establishment and for all of the departments and agencies therein;
(2) Exercise general direction, authority, and control over such departments and agencies;
(3) Take appropriate steps to eliminate unnecessary duplication or overlapping in the fields of procurement, supply, transportation, storage, health, and research;
(4) Supervise and coordinate the preparation of the budget estimates of the departments and agencies comprising the National Military Establishment.[50]

The Joint Chiefs of Staff took on increased prominence under the reorganization. This body was made responsible for formulating strategic plans and issuing military directives to the field commanders. Thus, the joint chiefs recommended military policy—as advisers to the secretary of defense, National Security Council, and the president—and also executed military policy through its directives to the unified field commands. In operation under Truman, all joint chiefs' directives, except for the most routine, were cleared by the secretary of defense and had to receive final approval from the president before being dispatched to the field commands. The organizational structure of the National Military Establishment removed the individual chiefs of staff from direct contact with the commander in chief, but Truman made it clear to all members that they were to have direct, individual access to him, bypassing all the civilian hierarchal structure above them, whenever they felt it necessary. Truman was once asked if the existence of the Joint Chiefs of Staff caused the commander in chief to rely less upon his own judgment and more on the advice of his generals. "Those professional military men are supposed to know the military situation as it is in the world," Truman replied, "and they're supposed to inform the President, so that he can make up his mind on what he ought to do in case of an emergency." [51]

The changes made in the military departments necessitated that Truman make several new appointments. He asked Robert Patterson, then secretary of war, to become secretary of defense. Patterson, explaining that his strained financial condition would not permit his staying in government, refused the post and insisted upon resigning as secretary of war (army). The president asked Forrestal to take the post and he accepted. Thus the man who had consistently believed that the job was too much of a burden for any man to bear, became secretary of defense, and his suicide two years later marked an ironic fulfillment of his own prophecy. With Forrestal's concurrence, Truman appointed Undersecretary of War Kenneth C. Royall secretary of the army; Assistant Secretary of the Navy John L. Sullivan secretary of the navy; and Assistant Secretary of War for Air Stuart Symington became the first secretary of the air force.[52] Forrestal was sworn in as secretary of defense of September 17, 1947, and the new military establishment became operational the following day.

The organization which Truman had created through patience, persistance, and compromise eventually revealed major flaws that required reform legislation. But since it did centralize, streamline, and clarify some of the command system, it served to aid the president in formulating military policy and getting that policy implemented. Truman was usually sure of what he wanted to do in a given situation; the National Military Establishment told him how best to accomplish his objective. The newly established agencies, particularly the National Security Council, performed a valuable function in recognizing that the formulation of military and foreign policies had to be considered as an integral process, particularly in the Cold War environment of the postwar period. The removal of the joint chiefs from direct access to the president, while not practical during time of war, provided a desirable dilution of strictly military viewpoints before they reached the commander in chief's desk. The National Security Act also, as one writer said, "sharpened the weapons at the President's disposal and added a new dimension to his command of American foreign policy." [53]

Full unification was not achieved in 1947. This is true largely because of compromises and accommodations made by zealots concerned more with preserving the traditional powers of a particular service than with the requirements of an effective national defense structure. As one critical Republican newspaper put it:

> President Truman has produced what he calls a merger plan for the army and navy. It is not a merger plan, it is in most respects a sham, and in some respects will contribute to the disintegration rather than the integration of our defense forces.

The question of unification of the forces is a difficult one. It requires the most serious consideration. . . . Instead of a solution, Mr. Truman offers an evasion. . . .

The attempt to relieve the President of the responsibility for conduct of national defense, by creating a secretary charged with that task . . . is futile because the President constitutionally is the commander in chief of the army and navy. He can delegate authority but he cannot delegate ultimate responsibility.[54]

While the editorialist wrongly assumed that Truman intended to divest himself of decision-making responsibility, he correctly identified the act as something less than what the president said it was. For example, the administration had often emphasized the economy that would be realized by unification when, in fact, the merger act was not designed to save money, nor did it do so. Also, in its aim (as summarized by Walter Millis) "to provide the United States with a coherent and self-consistent system of military-political direction, fully informed by the best intelligence available," the unification act failed.[55]

The office of secretary of defense proved to be too weak under the 1947 statute. Although the defense secretary was nominally the immediate superior of the three department secretaries, all four served equally on the National Security Council. In addition, the three secretaries were permitted to bypass their superior and bring their concerns directly to the president. As constituted, the office of defense secretary suffered from divided responsibility and a severe lack of authority. The Joint Chiefs of Staff, while obliged to advise the secretary of defense, were not controlled by him to any appreciable extent.[56]

The National Security Council was too vaguely defined to be effective. It was supposed to advise the president on the coordination of all factors affecting the security of the nation, but it was not made clear whether the council should initiate the consideration of policies or deliberate only when told to consider a subject by the president. The council would be of value in working out long-range policy recommendations but proved of little worth for the resolution of emergency situations. Also, a disproportionate number of its members (four), although civilians themselves, represented military departments. In operation under Truman, a representative of the Joint Chiefs of Staff also attended each meeting and was heard, so that five of the seven or eight usually present at Security Council meetings approached each problem with a military orientation.[57]

Whether the navy-Forrestal struggle against unification was justified is a moot question. All the key participants were responsible to some degree for the untoward delays, including Truman. The military leadership of the country spent over two years absorbed in what was often petty haggling over bureaucratic politics. In the end, Truman accepted an inferior structure that was not at all consonant with his own ideas on unification, primarily because the struggle had intensified to a point where imposition of a thorough unification would have been destructive of military morale and politically explosive.[58]

In the final analysis, Forrestal had prevailed. The National Security Council, Central Intelligence Agency, and National Security Resources Board were all originally proposed in the plan that Eberstadt's committee had drafted for Forrestal. He had lost out with the establishment of the air force as a coequal to the army and navy departments. But Forrestal succeeded in blocking the army proposal for a single chief of staff for all the services. He had preserved the Marine Corps intact and kept most of naval aviation against the wishes of War Department planners. Most important of all, from Forrestal's point of view, he had managed to have the authority of the secretary of defense limited to coordination and an overall generally powerless supervision of the three service departments. The irony, of course, is that Forrestal had unwittingly performed an act of self-emasculation.

As Forrestal attempted to make a functioning office from the rigid statutory edifice he had built, he became increasingly aware that changes would be necessary; hence the secretary asked for major revisions in both the National Security Act and the accompanying executive order defining the roles and missions of the services. Forrestal took action on the executive order first, in January, 1948, by asking the service secretaries and the joint chiefs to send him recommendations on a redraft of the order. The defense secretary received the service secretaries' recommendations and, finding them so diverse as to make coordination impossible, postponed any immediate proposal to the president.[59]

Late in February, 1948, Forrestal told Truman that he had not yet been able to get any agreement from the joint chiefs on the definition of functions of the services, but had instructed them to inform him on March 8 concerning the areas of disagreement between them, on which he would then make his own decisions. The problem required decision because Forrestal had to have a definition of the specific roles and missions of each service before he could make budgetary allocations for carrying them out.[60] Whether the participants appreciated it at the time is unknown, but Forrestal was precisely in the same position he and Patterson had placed the president in earlier, of pressuring his subordinates for an agreement by threatening to decide the matter arbitrarily.

The joint chiefs reported their disagreements over service functions to the secretary of defense on March 8. To settle the matter, Forrestal assembled a conference with the Joint Chiefs of Staff in Key West, Florida, from the eleventh to the fourteenth. The agreement finally reached was that each service would be assigned both primary and collateral functions. The primary functions were those for which a service would have clear-cut responsibility. Collateral functions were defined as instances where a service force acted to support or supplement another service in carrying out a primary function. The secretary of defense submitted the new draft of armed services functions to the president, asking that it be approved and requesting that Executive Order 9877 be rescinded.[61]

Truman turned the draft over to Clark Clifford for study. Clifford recommended to him after consultation with Admiral Leahy, General Harry Vaughan, the Bureau of the Budget, and others, that Forrestal's proposals be approved, subject to the addition of a phrase making it clear that Forrestal was issuing the statement "by direction of the President." On April 21, 1948, the president revoked Executive Order 9877 and informed the secretary of defense of his approval of the new statement on roles and missions of the services. On the same day Forrestal issued the new statement to the joint chiefs and the service secretaries, formally completing the first revisions in the military reorganization of 1947.[62]

It was obvious to Truman and Forrestal that the National Security Act had to be amended, particularly with a view towards increasing the authority of the secretary of defense. In June, 1948, Forrestal had ordered all of the leadership within the National Military Establishment to cooperate with the committee of the Hoover Commission that was studying the organizational problems of NME. The defense secretary also sought recommendations from the departmental secretaries and the military chiefs, asking that they report to him by September 1.[63]

The reports submitted to Forrestal showed the usual divergence of views existing between the services. For example, Secretary of the Navy John L. Sullivan advised "that no amendments to the National Security Act of 1947 be made at this time." [64] An opposite view was expressed by Air Force Secretary Symington. He proposed strengthening the office of secretary of defense by changing the language of the unification act to eliminate divided responsibility and centralize authority. Symington also proposed the appointment of an undersecretary to assist Forrestal along with a single chief of staff of the armed forces, responsible only to the secretary of defense. He also recommended that the law be changed to eliminate the secretaries of army, navy, and air force from membership in the National Security Council, leaving the secretary of defense as the sole representative of the National Military Establishment. Symington's views, which were consonant with those held by both Forrestal and Truman, eventually became part of the amended act.

Forrestal, as he received these reports, was also cognizant of a report to the president on the status of national preparedness made by the National Security Council. The report informed Truman that the country was not internally secure nor was it ready in the event of a conflict with other large nations, a declaration of war by or upon this nation, or a normal or unconventional surprise attack. It was with these several reports on his mind that Forrestal drafted a long memorandum to Truman on September 16, 1948. The secretary reviewed the subject of national defense, which was his immediate responsibility under the president, and urged upon Truman his conviction that little could be done until the authority and responsibility were centralized in one officer of the government. Forrestal had in Truman a sympathetic audience.[66]

The secretary of defense sent his first draft of revisions in the National Security Act to the White House early in December. Truman apparently asked Forrestal to revise his recommendations in cooperation with the budget director and his White House counsel, for two subsequent draft proposals—January 24 and February 10, 1949—bear the signatures of Frank Pace, Jr., and Clark Clifford.[67] The president could derive some satisfaction from these recommendations, since, to a quite appreciable extent, they proposed the kind of unification that Truman has asked for in his original message to Congress of December 19, 1945.

The president sent a special message to Congress on March 5, 1949, requesting changes in the National Military Establishment. He based his request on the experience gained under the National Security Act and on the Hoover Commission Report on the National Security Organization, which had recently been submitted to the Congress. The message followed very closely the recommendations made in the February 10 memorandum from Forrestal, Pace, and Clifford.[68]

After following the normal legislative process, without the interservice struggles that characterized the original reorganization, save for continued *pro forma* opposition from the Navy Department, Truman's proposals became law on August 10 as the National Security Act Amendments of 1949. At the bill-signing ceremony, Truman said that he was pleased that the act had passed embodying most of the recommendations he had made, as well as several suggestions made by the Hoover Commission: "These provisions afford sound basis for further progress toward the unification of our Armed Forces and the unified management of our military affairs.[69]

Under the terms of the act, the National Military Establishment became the Department of Defense, an executive department of the government. The army, navy and air force became military departments within the Defense Department, rather than executive agencies in their own right. The powers of the secretary of defense were significantly expanded giving him a far more effective control over the entire military. He was also provided with an undersecretary of defense and three assistant secretaries, all civilians. The chiefs of staff lost their individual influence with the commander in chief, but the Joint Chiefs of Staff gained a chairman who, as military adviser to the secretary of defense and the president, represented the views of the military to these officials and in the National Security Council. The post of chief of staff to the president was abolished, although the chairman of the joint chiefs, in practice, would function in approximately the same capacity. A fourth title was amended into the National Security Act providing for uniform budgetary and fiscal procedures and the appointment of comptrollers for the Department of Defense as well as the army, navy, and air force.[70]

James Forrestal never enjoyed the newly obtained powers and prestige of the office. His mental health had deteriorated under the pressures of the job, and press attacks upon him were building, so Truman forced him to resign. In a "Dear Jim" letter dated March 2 and made public the next day, Truman wrote of his reluctance to accept the resignation made necessary by "those urgent personal considerations about which you have spoken to me so many times." The president indicated he was reassured to know that Forrestal would be "standing by to give advice and counsel as we go forward in the work of enhancing the national security." [71] Forrestal would not be "standing by" very long; he was dead by suicide before the amendments passed.

There can be little doubt that Truman was right in urging unification. The reorganization brought many desirable changes and ended much of the duplication and interservice bickering that was undesirable. Truman established a modern military structure capable of immediate and effective response to any threat to the security of the nation. However, in their unity the military services found greater strength in making budgetary requests, in obtaining legislation in Congress and in influencing the foreign policy of the United States.

Although recognizing that he had not obtained the full, true unification he wanted, Truman was proud of what had been accomplished in that direction. He described passage of the National Security Act and its corrective amendments as one of the "outstanding achievements" of his administration.[72] Some time after his presidency, Truman was asked if the unification process should continue so that there could be an even tighter amalgamation of the armed forces. He replied:

> There isn't a doubt in the world but that the whole thing ought to be tightened up so that the President, as commander-in-chief, could deal through a Secretary of Defense who should have direct control of the defense of the nation. . . . We need to get the idea over that the Defense Department of the Government of the United States is of vital importance and must not be tampered with by conflicting forces. It ought to operate under direct control of a man who knows where he's going and why. He should be the Secretary of Defense in complete control of all the services, ground, sea and air, under the direction of the Commander-in-Chief—the President of the United States.[73]

Truman was right. The structure of the Defense Department does need tightening up periodically, as does any similar massive bureaucracy. This was made evident in mid-1970 when a Blue Ribbon Panel reported the results of one year's study of the Defense Department to President Richard Nixon. The panel noted numerous examples of gross inefficiency and recommended major reforms. Gilbert Fitzhugh, who headed this study, described the Pentagon as, "just an amorphous lump with nobody in charge of anything." [74] So Truman's effort to produce an efficient, responsive military organization has not been an unalloyed success. But nothing ever is in the dynamics of the body politic.

8/ The Cold Warrior I

While the cruel lessons of war are fresh in every mind, it is fitting that we now undertake appropriate measures for the future security of the United States.[1]

—HARRY S. TRUMAN

The years between World War II and the Korean War were crowded with changes in foreign policy that compelled changes in military policy and strategic thinking. The interrelationship between military capabilities and diplomatic decisions became so complex and inextricably woven together in this period as to defy efforts at separation for purposes of analysis. However, so much as this may still be possible, this and the following chapter will attempt to isolate the military factor in selected events of the last half of the roaring forties. Such problems as demobilization, struggles between Truman and the navy over ships, and the air force over planes, and the decision to send military aid to Greece and Turkey will be examined below. The following chapter will examine Truman's response to the Berlin crisis, the creation of North Atlantic Treaty Organization (NATO) and the expansion of the containment philosophy to the point where the decision to involve the American military in Korea seemed logical and quite necessary.

The most immediate military problem facing Truman at the end of World War II was demobilization. At war's end the United States faced the problem of an orderly disassemblage of the mightiest war machine this nation had ever known. There were over 12 million men and women in uniform in mid-1945, over 7 million stationed outside of the United States. Planning for the eventual release of these personnel began during the war, and, in September, 1944, the War Department announced that releases would be by a point system on an individual basis. A serviceman accumulated points for length of service, number of children, overseas service, and combat experience, as well as a set scale of points for various military decorations.[2]

The president approved a plan which provided for an orderly, gradual demobilization of forces. The postwar army strength was set at 1.5 million; the navy expected a 600,000-man force; and the Army Air Force was hopeful of becoming a separate service with about 400,000 members. Truman and the military planners were to find that their orderly demobilization schedules would become irrelevant in the face of concerted pressure for the immediate release of all servicemen. Truman told an August 23 press conference that talks with his military leaders had led him to the conclusion that the armed services were doing all that they possibly could to expedite the demobilization process.[3]

In his special message on September 6, 1945, the president asked Congress to continue conscription, since enlistments would not fill the anticipated gap created by discharging those who served during the war. Truman told Congress that to suspend inductions would be "an unforgivable discrimination . . . requiring continued sacrifice from those who have already done their part." [4] The president already knew that retention of some veterans was inevitable. He gave some indication of that in his message, when he asked that continuation of the war powers be granted to the executive branch and asked Congress not to pass a resolution declaring the war had ended. The war statute stipulated that those inducted could not be retained beyond six months of the war's termination.[5]

What Truman was trying to make clear in his several statements on demobilization was that the postwar military posture of the United States was to be far different from any past experience. The president envisioned a new military and foreign policy that rejected traditional isolationism and projected the United States into the role of defender of the peace. "We are committed now," Truman told Congress, "to an armed occupation of the lands of our defeated enemies. . . . To meet these . . . obligations will require the maintenance for some time of a real measure of our present land, sea, and air power." [6] Much of what Truman said with regard to the postwar military reflected the views of General Marshall.[7]

Global military policy considerations did not concern the servicemen who had fought the good fight and wanted to return to their homes and families. Neither they nor their relatives and congressmen could understand why the mustering-out process should take so long. As the clamor rose, Truman tried to stem it with a statement issued on September 19, telling the nation that the army assured him they would have two million released before Christmas and that there was no padding of the size of the postwar forces. The country would maintain only those numbers necessary to meet national commitments; he had ordered that all other military personnel be discharged as rapidly as possible.[8]

The original form of protest to the pace of demobilization was a letter-writing campaign directed at Congress by parents and wives of servicemen, and, eventually, letters from the servicemen themselves. The letters were followed by petitions and cables to the president and Congress. The army responded by reducing the total points required for discharge eligibility some five times in the closing months of 1945. This rapid reduction in requirements overtaxed the available transport, which the navy tried to offset by temporarily converting over forty cruisers, battleships, and carriers into troop transports. Demobilization succeeded to the extent that a War Department announcement in early 1946 stated that inductions were not high enough to meet overseas troop requirements, so that the 1.5 million servicemen then eligible for discharge would be released gradually over a six-month period, rather than the planned three-month span.

The resentment and frustration which had been accumulating among troops idled by victory for six months and more was ignited by the War Department announcement. The protests now took the form of nonviolent mass marches and demonstrations, the first by 20,000 soldiers in Manila on January 6. Similar protests occurred in France, England, Guam, China, Japan, Germany, Hawaii, Austria, India, and the United States.[9] Two days after the initial mass demonstration at Manila, the White House released a presidential statement on demobilization. In the message Truman said that in consideration of the shipping involved, as well as the clerical mountains that had to be moved, the processing was going as fast as possible. About 8.5 million had been separated from the service in the months since the fighting ended in Europe. He had personally reviewed the army and navy procedures and was fully convinced that demobilization was being carried out with "commendable efficiency" and fairness to all.[10]

Patterson and Forrestal had met with Truman on October 26, 1945, and warned him that the continuous acceleration of the demobilization process was endangering the strategic military posture of the United

States in its worldwide commitments. Truman was of a like mind: "I agreed entirely with this view and stated at the meeting that . . . the program we were following was no longer demobilization—it was disintegration of our armed forces." [11] Thus, although he privately recognized that the system was chaotic, Truman allowed it to continue because of political pressure, and he publicly praised demobilization's "commendable efficiency." It is upon such rocks that the credibility of presidential statements run aground.

The demobilization process—which, combining Truman's public and private utterances, could be styled "efficient disintegration"— continued throughout 1946 and into 1947. By June 30, 1947, there were just over 1.5 million under arms. The army ground forces numbered just under 700,000. For this same date, the army had projected a 2-million-man force, but the pressure for accelerated demobilization, budget cuts by Truman, and further cuts by Congress had altered these plans. By July, 1946, Army Chief of Staff Eisenhower was vainly hopeful of getting a ceiling of 1.7 million officers and men. An army spokesmen said that of these numbers, only about two and one-third divisions were available for immediate deployment in a national security emergency. By mid-1947, the American army ranked sixth in size among the nations of the world.[12]

Numerous factors were converging in the early postwar period, and these of their own mass and momentum changed American strategic thinking. The hurried demobilization, combined with a traditional American distaste for a large standing armed force, the defeat of Truman's universal military training proposal and the forced budgetary economies sharply reduced the size of the military establishment. Roughly half of the forces-in-being were employed as policemen, *i.e.*, enforcing occupation policies in Germany, Japan, and Korea. With the portents of war with the Soviet Union an increasingly insistent theme of the early Cold War years, the United States, for the first time in its history, was impelled to prepare for war in time of peace. The final factor in the evolving equation was the existence of nuclear weapons.

These imperatives brought to the forefront a growing reliance on a strategic air force armed with atomic bombs. The concept of employing conventional, ready forces as a deterrent to aggression received lipservice, but was gradually losing out to the "air-atomic reaction" school of thought. This type of planning did not prepare the United

States for the conventional, limited warfare that it eventually became involved with in Korea and Indochina.[13]

Truman came to the presidency convinced from his Truman Committee experience that the military services had "unquestionably squandered billions of dollars." [14] In planning for the 1946 budget during the closing days of World War II, he developed a "remainder method" of determining military allocations; he would continue to employ this standard until the advent of the Korean War. The method involved subtracting all anticipated expenditures of the civilian government from anticipated revenues, the remainder determining the dollar ceiling on military appropriations.[15]

The navy fought hardest against the cancellation of shipbuilding contracts and the reduced spending levels in the first postwar budget. Truman had cut back on all ship construction that was less than 50 percent completed. With little success, Forrestal struggled with the president, in the first of several appropriation fights, to reinstate five heavy cruisers. But the navy, as well as the other services, found that Truman was very difficult to move on budget questions. He instructed the budget director in February, 1946, in the midst of a naval personnel dispute, to ignore the navy and hold the budget line. Forrestal told the president in August that it would jeopardize the security of the nation to meet the budget reductions he had ordered for the navy. In a crisp reply, Truman instructed the secretary of the navy to reduce expenditures to the levels called for. He also informed Forrestal that in the future he wanted a monthly report submitted to him through the Bureau of the Budget, detailing actual and projected expenditures of the Navy Department. Truman later wrote that he found the military always made excessive budgetary demands, "but the Navy was the worst offender." [16] However, the most extensive and acrimonious dispute over the military budget arose out of the air force's demand for seventy air groups.

Because of rapid developments in civilian and military aviation, which dated most aviation policy and procedures, Truman appointed a temporary Air Policy Commission in July, 1947. He charged the commission, chaired by Thomas K. Finletter, with the task of making an objective analysis and submitting recommendations to him on an integrated national aviation policy.[17] At the same time a similar review was being carried out by the Joint Congressional Aviation Policy

Board. Upon completion, the separate studies were found to be in agreement on one important military recommendation: the establishment of seventy regular air groups within the air force. However, in his budget message to Congress on January 12, 1948, the president said, "The plans for the Air Force contemplate operation of 55 combat groups." [18]

The air force had apparently set a seventy-air-group goal for itself late in 1945. How they arrived at that precise figure has never been made clear. Walter Millis has made the credible suggestion that it was probably based "more on a deduction as to what the taxpayer would stand for and the air industry could reasonably supply than on a calculation of the probable military requirements." For the next four years and more the air force's spokesmen would argue that the seventy air groups they were proposing represented an irreducible minimum. As Air Secretary Symington wrote in December, 1947, "The Air Force has consistently advocated its 70 Group Program as the minimum force adequate to the requirements imposed by the position of the United States in the modern world." But with the fluid military situation in the period 1945–1950 and the technological advancements in nuclear weaponry and jet propulsion, the consistent advocacy of seventy groups had more of a symbolic than specific meaning.[19]

Secretary Symington, who saw the budget message before it was sent to Congress, informed Secretary of Defense Forrestal and White House aide Clifford that he was going to protest. He did so in a letter to James Webb, director of the Bureau of the Budget. Symington warned of the grave implications of not meeting the seventy-group figure.[20] Although he was really attacking the budget that Truman wanted and had approved, he ended up in a public fight with Forrestal, who, though opposed to the low ceilings himself, was obliged to defend them as secretary of defense.

The issue came to a head late in March, 1948, with Forrestal's testimony before the Senate Armed Services Committee in support of supplemental rearmament appropriations requested by Truman in a special message on March 17. The defense secretary was cognizant of congressional sympathy for the seventy-group air force and openly expressed to the committee his agreement in principle with the concept of a powerful air arm. But, Forrestal said, air force requirements had to be obtained within the framework of a balanced military force. As a compromise, he proposed a supplemental appropriation of $775 million for aircraft procurement and research. He also asked for additional funds for increasing the size of the army and Marine Corps. In all, his requests would add $3 billion to the president's budget proposal of $11 billion for defense in fiscal-year 1949. A few days later Forrestal wrote a letter to Senator Gurney, chairman of the Armed Services Committee, clarifying the remarks he had made in his testimony on the twenty-fifth of March. He explained to the senator that the air force program, if approved and balanced out by concomitant increases in land, sea, and merchant marine elements, would mean a dramatic increase in the total military budget annually. To bolster his position that such increments would be necessary if the expanded program were initiated, Forrestal ordered the Joint Chiefs of Staff to study and report the probable costs of a military establishment balanced against the requested increase in the strength of the air force.[21]

While the dispute continued in the press and congressional hearings, Truman kept silent. Forrestal was carrying the burden of defending a budget that was not his in any sense. Most of the fuel for the attacks was coming from Symington, who, like Forrestal, was obliged to support Truman's budget, but refused to do so. Symington told the Senate Armed Services Committee that expansion to seventy air groups had been his position for years and he did not propose to change. General Spaatz, air force chief of staff, added his testimony to Symington's; together they constituted a refutation of their nominal superior's testimony.[22] By this time, Forrestal must have been fully aware of his great error during the unification struggle in insisting that the secretary of defense be a powerless "coordinator" rather than a true executive officer.

Truman was unable to stifle air force resistance to the proposed budget and ended up making a deal. The Joint Chiefs of Staff, which had reported to Forrestal that their review showed that a military establishment balanced against a seventy-group air force would cost an additional $9 billion annually, agreed to back a $3.5 billion supplement instead. The air force agreed to support the request, since they would get sixty-six air groups and most of the additional appropriation.[23]

With Truman's approval Forrestal went back to Congress on April 1 with the compromise. Forrestal emphasized the unanimity of the president, the joint chiefs, and the service secretaries on this revised proposal.[24] However, Truman made a review of the supplemental request by the Bureau of the Budget a condition of his approval.

The president had apparently had his fill of opposition from his own military leadership to the administration's budget. Shortly after Budget Director Webb and he agreed on the limits, Truman called for a White House session (May 13, 1948) with the secretary of defense, the service secretaries, and the Joint Chiefs of Staff. He began the meeting by reading to them a ten-page statement in which he explained that the Budget Bureau review was completed. The study had recommended a cut from the April compromise figure of $3.48 billion to $3.17 billion. Truman said he was willing to submit a request for $3.19 billion, a figure suggested by Forrestal, provided the armed forces did not try to spend it all. His reasons for this rather unique solution were described as "the uncertainty of world conditions" and "other factors." Truman also set a ceiling of $15 billion for the defense budget for fiscal-years 1949 and 1950, explaining that to exceed it would drive the total national budget several billion dollars above anticipated revenues. In an extraordinary move, he concluded with an emphatic warning to all present:

> Therefore, as Commander in Chief, I am issuing in writing instructions as outlined in the memoranda delivered to you today. I expect these orders to be carried out wholeheartedly, in good spirit, and without mental reservation.
>
> If anyone present has any questions or misgivings concerning the program I have outlined, make your views known now—for once this program goes forward officially, it will be the Administration program and I expect every member of the Administration to support it fully, both in public and in private.
>
> The statement I have just read will form part of my record of this meeting. This paper will be on file for your examination.[25]

On the same date, Truman also sent a lengthy memorandum to Forrestal, reiterating much of what he said in his statement.[26] His troubles, of course, were not with Forrestal. In fact, the statement Truman had read to the meeting had been drafted in the Pentagon by William McNeil, Forrestal's assistant, according to specifications provided by the president.[27] But Truman sent identical memoranda to the air force, army, and navy secretaries, the army and air force chiefs of staff, and the chief of naval operations. In these memoranda, Truman informed the military leaders that he was also sending them copies of his letter to the secretary of defense in order to eliminate any misunderstanding as to the policies he had approved. He told them they must subordinate their private and service biases to the established national policies.[28] In military vernacular, Truman was issuing a "shape up or ship out" notice. They shaped up.

As the bill finally passed in April, it provided for a total defense budget for fiscal 1949 of $13.8 billion. Against the express wishes of Truman and Forrestal, the Congress voted an extra $822 million appropriation to bring the air force up to a full seventy air groups. The vote for the budget supplements in Congress—which was understood to be an affirmation of the seventy-group concept—was an overwhelming 343 to 3 in the House and 74 to 2 in the Senate.[29] The air force had clearly won out over the secretary of defense and the commander in chief. But it was a hollow victory; Truman signed the supplemental appropriation act, but, as promised, refused to spend the extra funds voted by Congress. The air force was allowed only fifty-nine air groups by Truman for fiscal-year 1949.[30] Most of the Congress and a majority of the public were convinced that "the next war would be fought in the air," but the commander in chief seemed more inclined to Forrestal's "balanced forces" concept, for fiscal rather than strategic reasons.

The president's decision to freeze appropriated air force funds was repeated in the next budget.[31] Truman's action represented a new dimension of the commander in chief's function. The Congress, which exercises a constitutional check on the executive powers through its annual appropriations for the budget, now found that it could not force the president to increase the size of the military establishment against his will. And the ability of Congress to argue against any requested increase was hampered by a lack of information and military intelligence which, by the terms of the National Security Act, they were not privy to, except at the discretion of the president.

One more serious struggle erupted within the Defense Department which eventually required presidential intervention. The navy had received authorization from Truman in the fiscal 1949 budget to construct a prototype, flush-deck aircraft carrier, on condition that it halt construction on thirteen smaller vessels then under construction. Although this was a heavy price to pay, the navy agreed, since such a carrier would be capable of participating in strategic atomic warfare.

At the time, the air force objected strenuously, but to no avail, since Forrestal considered the project sound. However, Louis Johnson, Forrestal's sucessor as secretary of defense, was determined to cut defense spending.[32]

On April 23, 1949, five days after the keel of the carrier had been laid, Johnson ordered the construction to halt. In his decision the secretary of defense was backed by the Joint Chiefs of Staff (Admiral Louis Denfeld dissenting) and the president. John L. Sullivan, secretary of the navy, who had not been consulted on this decision and was in Texas when Johnson made his announcement, immediately informed Johnson that under provision of Section 202 of the National Security Act of 1947, he was exercising his right to appeal the decision directly to the commander in chief.[33] Truman, however, decided against Sullivan.

The navy secretary resigned on April 26, but not before delivering a bitter attack on the secretary of defense. In a letter to Johnson, Sullivan accused the secretary of killing the one weapon upon which the navy placed the highest priority without even the courtesy of consulting with the chief of naval operations or the secretary of the navy. Sullivan was "very deeply disturbed" by this unprecedented action blocking the development of a new, powerful weapon, he told Johnson. He also added his conviction that "this will result in a renewed effort to abolish the Marine Corps and to transfer all Naval and Marine Aviation elsewhere." The navy secretary talked with Truman on April 25, and the president agreed to make Sullivan's letter to the secretary of defense public. Sullivan apparently felt no ill will toward the president over cancellation of the carrier, since his letter of resignation was quite friendly, as was Truman's acceptance.[34]

Secretary Sullivan's fears for the future of the Marine Corps and naval aviation were a surface indication of deep-seated interservice bickering that had not ended with unification. The navy was particularly resentful of the growing power of the air force. Not only had the romantic and heroic legend of the grizzled seadog been replaced in the public mind by the glamorous image of a dashing jet pilot, but the navy's prestigious role as the first line of the nation's defense had also been lost to the continent-spanning, nuclear weapons delivery vehicle, the B-36 bomber. Soon after canceling the navy's supercarrier, Secretary of Defense Johnson, who was emerging as a strong advocate of strategic air power, allowed the air force to order seventy-five additional B-36's. The result was a rebellion within the Navy Department called the "Revolt of the Admirals." [35]

Charging corruption and favoritism in the B-36 contract awards, a representative from Pennsylvania, James E. VanZandt, demanded an investigation.[36] The resulting hearings before the House Armed Services Committee constituted a complete examination of the national military posture, for it broadened into an inquiry on unification, military strategy, the B-36, and other matters. During the course of the hearings, a host of high-ranking navy and marine officers attacked the prevailing air force policy of long-distance, nuclear airborne retaliation as dangerous, deceptive, and not based on sound military principles. Admiral Louis E. Denfeld, chief of naval operations, summarized the navy's position in an attack leveled principally at the secretary of defense. Denfeld accused Johnson of violating the spirit of unification, criticized him for canceling the supercarrier, and said that "uninformed and arbitrary decisions" had grievously weakened the navy. The chief rebuttal witnesses were Air Secretary Symington and General Omar Bradley, then chairman of the Joint Chiefs of Staff. Generals Eisenhower and Marshall, Secretary Johnson, and former President Hoover also testified, generally asking for unity and cooperation and an end to interservice politicking. One thing that clearly emerged from the contentious testimony was that the integrated strategic viewpoint which unification promised had not been achieved.[37]

Secretary of the Navy Francis P. Matthews, Sullivan's successor, wrote to Truman saying that "for the good of the country, I respectfully request you as President and Commander in Chief to authorize the transfer of Admiral Denfeld to other important duties." Matthews had the support of the secretary of defense in asking Truman to remove Denfeld as chief of naval operations. Following some deliberation in the White House over the extent of the commander in chief's authority to remove Denfeld, who had just been confirmed by the Senate for reappointment for another two-year term, Truman ordered his removal on October 27.[38] Other officers were eventually transferred to less sensitive assignments, or they retired, ending the "Revolt of the Admirals."

The revolt had revealed not only a fundamental failing of unification, it also had pointed up a lack of a fixed overall military strategy.

The president and the Bureau of the Budget still held (in principle) to the balanced-force concept of national defense, to which the military leadership paid at least a grudging lip service. However, Truman's hard-money policy of fixing a $15-billion ceiling on the military budget dictated, as Paul Hammond has written, "increasing reliance solely on the most 'efficient' weapons system, strategic air atomic retaliation, which was a military capability designed for a showdown war with the Soviet Union." [39] The value of this controversy, along with concern over Russian atomic capability, was that it led to a study by the National Security Council of global military strategy. Their recommendations, contained in a very important policy paper submitted to Truman (discussed later), were implemented during the Korean War. In the interim between World War II and Korea, despite the inefficiencies and the lack of a coherent strategic policy, the American military establishment was adequate to the demands made upon it by the events of the Cold War. The first serious demand it met in the postwar era concerned Soviet pressure on Turkey.

It takes no more than an elemental knowledge of geography to comprehend the intense concern of the Soviet Union with the Dardanelles Strait. The strait is a direct warm-water gateway to Soviet commerce with the oil-rich Middle East. Premier Stalin had received at Potsdam the concurrence of the United States and Great Britain to a revision of the Montreaux Convention of 1936, which was an international agreement regarding control of the strait. The Soviet Union desired a more favorable agreement. The United States, although not a signatory to the original convention, indicated it would be a willing party to any new international accord for controlling the use of the Dardanelles. [40]

On August 7, 1946, the Russians sent a diplomatic note to Turkey insisting, among other things, on replacing the Montreaux Convention with a bilateral pact which would eliminate British influence in Turkey and provide for joint Russo-Turkish control and the establishment of Russian military bases along the strait. Dean Acheson, then undersecretary of state, considered the Soviet proposal merely a euphemism for the occupation of Turkey. [41] Acheson was ordered by Truman to prepare recommendations for him in consultation with the secretaries of war and navy and the joint chiefs.

The committee had its report ready on August 15, and they met with Truman in the White House. Acheson told the president that the committee was recommending that a strong diplomatic note be sent to the Soviet government acknowledging the need for a revision of the Treaty of Montreaux, but insisting that there be no interference with the exclusive rights of Turkey to defend the strait. To impress the Russians that the United States was in "deadly earnest" on the matter, Truman's advisers also felt that a strong naval force should be sent to the area. They recommended that the battleship *Missouri*, already at Istanbul on an unrelated mission, be held there and joined by the Mediterranean fleet, led by the newly commissioned aircraft carrier *Franklin D. Roosevelt*. Truman immediately approved the recommendations and asked that the diplomatic notes and orders be drafted at once.[42] General Eisenhower, who was present at the meeting as army chief of staff, apparently taken aback by the abruptness of the president's decision, asked if Truman was cognizant of all the implications; the recommended course could lead to war with the Soviet Union. Acheson has recorded Truman's response: "The President took from a drawer of his desk a large map of the Middle East and eastern Mediterranean and asked us to gather around behind him. He then gave us a brief lecture on the strategic importance of the area and the extent to which we must be prepared to go to keep it free from Soviet domination. When he finished, none of us doubted he understood fully all the implications of our recommendations." [43]

The American fleet moved into Turkish waters as soon as it was assembled. This naval pressure was sufficient enough to cause the Soviet Union to ease its pressure on Turkey. The Turkish government felt it necessary to continue a full mobilization of its armed forces, a constant strain on the economy that sapped resources. The Soviet Union switched its offensive pressures to the Balkan peninsula in hope of toppling the monarchial government of Greece.

Following the German withdrawal in late 1944, the Greek government-in-exile returned to power. The Greek leadership was soon confronted by a Communist-inspired guerrilla revolt against its authority. As a result of this struggle, the United States urged an international commission to supervise an election in Greece to determine majority will. The electorate, voting in March, 1946, chose the monarchial party of King George II. The Greek Communists, united under the banner of the National Liberation Front, resumed guerrilla warfare following their electoral defeat. These Greek insurrectionaries received substantial military equipment and supplies from the bordering Communist nations of Yugoslavia, Albania, and Bulgaria. The Greek conservative leaders, or "monarcho-fascists," as the Soviet press styled them, were sustained in their struggles by the presence of British troops and by a great deal of economic assistance from Great Britain.

The British, facing grievous financial conditions at home, informed the United States in February, 1947, that their financial and military support of Greece (and financial assistance to Turkey as well) would have to cease by March 31. The British expressed hope that the United States would be able to assume the burden of sustaining Greece and Turkey. The message from England underscored what American envoys in the field had been reporting: Because of inflation, corruption in the right-wing government, strikes and the effectiveness of the guerrilla forces, Greece was near collapse even with British aid. Without it, a Communist takeover was inevitable, unless the United States, the only nation then capable of such large-scale largesse, was willing to intervene.[45]

The secretary of state, George Marshall, was away on a speaking engagement when the British note arrived on February 21, so undersecretary Acheson informed the president of its substance. Truman ordered Acheson to convene the State-War-Navy Coordinating Committee for preparation of a detailed policy memorandum. Acheson reported to Truman on the committee's progress as of the twenty-fourth. The basic recommendation was that Greece should receive whatever funds and military equipment the president could provide under existing legislative authority as soon as possible. Truman approved. On February 25 Truman met with the congressional leadership. Flustered by the glaring, but accidental, omission of the powerful Senator Robert Taft from the list of those invited, Truman allowed Dean Acheson to brief the congressmen on the situation and urge their support of an American aid program for Greece and Turkey. Acheson made a very effective presentation of the case. None of the congressional leadership present saw fit to question the propriety of the nation's extending a protective shield over Greece and Turkey.[46] The executive and legislative leadership agreed then, at least in principle, that the United States should assume the traditional British role of containing Russian expansionism in the eastern Mediterranean.

Secretary Marshall, accompanied by Acheson, brought Truman the policy recommendations on February 26. Their report carried the endorsement of the coordinating committee, the secretaries of war and navy and the Joint Chiefs of Staff. Greece needed immediate and substantial assistance, the report stated, aid which only the United States was capable of providing. Turkey, while not in danger of immediate collapse from Russian pressure, could not long sustain its full mobilization without economic disaster. If either nation fell, the other would be seriously endangered. The choice was to abandon both countries to Communist ambition, or intervene directly and immediately. The report recommended the latter course to Truman and urged him to request an appropriation from Congress for economic and military aid for Greece and Turkey.[47] The President approved and ordered the State Department to draft an address to Congress.

When Truman finally received a satisfactory draft of his message, he arranged to appear before a joint session of the Congress on March 12, 1947. The president knew that what he was going to ask of the nation represented a dramatic reversal of traditional American peacetime isolationism. He knew, he said, that the names of Washington and Clay and "the other patron saints of isolationists" would be invoked against his stand. But he was thoroughly convinced that this action was essential to continue free-world leadership by the United States.[48]

Truman began his speech by telling the Congress that a grave situation had arisen that involved the foreign policy and the national security of the United States. Truman then reviewed the desperate condition of Greece, repeatedly referring to Greece's "democratic" government, but acknowledging that that government had made some mistakes. He briefly summarized Turkey's need for financial support. The president then said that a primary objective of the foreign policy of the United States was to establish conditions whereby other nations "will be able to work out a way of life free from coercion." Free people could not maintain free institutions and national integrity against totalitarian aggressors unless other nations were willing to help them. "I believe," Truman said, "that it must be the policy of the United States to support free peoples who are resisting attempted subjugation by armed minorities or by outside pressures." This was the essential statement of what has come to be known as the Truman Doctrine. It represented a significant alteration of American policy, since it proposed that the

United States stand as guarantor and protector, not just of Greece and Turkey, but of all "free, democratic nations" which were confronted by internal or external threats to the existing regime. While emphasizing that "our help should be primarily through economic and financial aid," Truman did not preclude direct American military intervention.[49]

Specifically, Truman asked the Congress for $400 million for assistance to Greece and Turkey for the current fiscal year. He also requested permission to send civilian and military personnel as financial, political, and military advisers, with the latter also serving as instructors in the use of American weapons. In addition, the president asked Congress to provide him with the authority to implement this assistance in the fastest and most efficient manner possible. Implicit throughout the message was the identification of the Soviet Union as the malefactor and the recognition that the United Nations organization was too weak to perform its primal function.

News media reaction to the address was mixed, but all seemed to recognize that the implications of Truman's proposal went well beyond simply aiding Greece and Turkey. The New York *Times* endorsed the speech as signaling an end to the era of "isolation and occasional intervention" and the beginning of "an epoch of American responsibility." The Baltimore *Sun* editorial writer lamented the shift in thinking with respect to the Russians reflected in this address, "from the possibility, and the necessity, of finding a formula for living together to emphasis on the differences which divide us." The Philadelphia *Inquirer* called the assistance program, "a task we must not shirk." A New York writer urged the use of American troops if necessary, because "to rule out any possibility of military support in advance removes any possibility of success. We would in that case merely be throwing our money away." The Chicago *Tribune* felt that "the outcome will inevitably be war. . . . We are to have the 'commander in chief' back with us again." "He was asking America to be Atlas," according to a Washington *Post* editorial, "offering to lead his country in that tremendous role, yet his flat voice carried no significance of his fateful recommendation." *Izvestia* described the Truman Doctrine as "a fresh intrusion of the U.S.A. into the affairs of other states," which was designed to place Turkey and Greece under American control.[50]

A Gallup poll on the Truman Doctrine proposal found the people, like the newspapers, divided, with a majority favoring assistance. For example, 83 percent were in favor of sending civilian advisers to Greece, but only 56 percent approved of financial aid. The same questions with respect to Turkey found 77 percent endorsing civilian advisers, but only 49 percent backing the financial assistance. Only 30 percent of those surveyed felt that lending the money to both nations would lead the United States into war, but less than one third supported the sending of military advisers to either country.[51]

The president had hoped that Congress would act on his proposals before March 31, 1947, the deadline Great Britain had set for the cutoff of their assistance to Turkey and Greece. But the public hearings on the bill and the floor debate continued through March and late into April. Finally, the Greek-Turkish aid bill passed the Senate by a vote of 67 to 23 and the House, 287 to 107.[52] In signing ceremonies on May 22 Truman called the bill "an important step in the building of the peace." He also said that the "overwhelming majorities" it received in both houses of Congress were "proof that the United States earnestly desires peace and is willing to make a vigorous effort to help create conditions of peace." On May 22 Truman also issued Executive Order 9857, which contained the regulations for carrying out the provisions of the bill. The order delegated the authority conferred on the president by the act to the secretary of state, George Marshall. It also allowed Marshall to subdelegate his authority to "Chiefs of Mission" for Greece and Turkey. Marshall actually wrote the order for the president which facilitated his carrying out the task of Greek-Turkish aid Truman had entrusted to him.[53]

The Communist-led Greek rebels intensified their attacks after Truman announced his intention to aid the government of Greece in opposing them. Their success, particularly in northern Greece, led the American embassy to report on June 9 that there was a "marked deterioration" in the government's position. A week later, the Greek government sent an urgent appeal for an acceleration in the delivery of critical materials and for a greater portion of American aid to be allocated to weapons and other military supplies. Secretary Marshall, agreeing with the first part of their message, asked Truman to indicate to the agencies involved the urgent necessity of their hastening the procurement and shipment of materials destined for Greece. Truman complied with Marshall's request, asking Army Secretary Royall, for example, to spare no effort in employing the full power and facilities of his office in expediting, as efficiently as possible, the Greek aid program.[54] Eventually, by the fall of 1949, American aid brought about a shift in the balance of power that led to the triumph of the government over the guerrillas. This was accomplished with some difficulty because the Greek leadership continually attempted to use all American aid for military purposes, to suppress opposition, rather than to stabilize the economy and broaden their base of popular support. Turkey, not facing a massive internal revolt, was a far less serious problem. United States financial aid was sufficient to continue the Turkish mobilization without endangering the economy.[55]

Truman considered the decision to take over Britain's commitment to aid Greece and Turkey one of the most important of his acts, because it set an entirely new pattern in foreign policy. He later said that it was incorrect to call this decision the Truman Doctrine since he had obtained the consent of the leaders in Congress before implementing this policy.[56] But the idea that the United States should shore up the endangered economies and political structures of Greece and Turkey led to the proposition that other nations should get the same aid before they collapsed from Communist pressure. The end product of this thinking was the Marshall Plan of American assistance to Europe, which became law as the European Recovery Act of April, 1948.

The Marshall Plan, working on the "belly reform" premise that communism appeals particularly to hungry and desperate people, went a long way toward restoring European prosperity and equalizing trade imbalances. The motivation of the United States in pursuing this recovery program was justified by Truman's administration in economic and humanitarian terms. However, beyond these considerations was the growing East-West schism that caused a high strategic importance to be placed on bolstering the economies of nations that might otherwise fall into the Soviet camp.

The commitment of the United States to the political status quo in the Balkans and western Europe was more than an economic tie; it carried with it the strong implication that America would resort to military intervention to sustain these governments and its own substantial investments. However, the United States did not have sufficient forces-in-being to back up this implied commitment. For while the services argued for a buildup of their force levels to meet any challenges on the European continent, they generally faced budgetary cutbacks in the late forties. The Marshall plan and Greek-Turkish Aid were "measures short of war," designed to prevent the spread of the Communist philosophy of government. They have succeeded to the extent that the nations involved remained more or less democratic in their governmental organization. The Marshall Plan was a natural outgrowth of the Truman Doctrine. At the same time, however, the Truman Doctrine was hardening into a policy called containment.[57]

9 / The Cold Warrior II

*We must not at any time falter in maintaining our strong position,
no matter what it costs, since we are the principal discouraging
force to Communist imperialism—and to war.*[1]

—HARRY S. TRUMAN

The thinking underlying the attitude toward communism in the containment policy is similar to that of the Republicans toward slavery in the pre–Civil War period. Although they would have been happiest if slavery were to disappear, they were at least determined that this pernicious institution be prevented from expanding beyond the boundaries of the region where it already existed. So, too, were the advocates of containment, who maintained that "the main element of any United States policy toward the Soviet Union must be that of a long-term patient but firm and vigilant containment of Russian expansive tendencies. . . . The Soviet pressure against the free institutions of the Western world is something that can be contained by the adroit and vigilant application of counter-force at a series of constantly shifting geographical and political points."[2]

Truman said that it is a mistake to call his foreign policy a policy of containment: "This is not true. Our purpose was much broader. We were working for a united, free, and prosperous world."[3] Euphemisms aside, the application of American policy has fit the pattern called containment. Since 1947 the United States has become party to regional military alliances having the effect of encirclement of the Communist-bloc nations; has met the threat of Soviet force with the threat of counterforce; and has met Communist "wars of national liberation" in Korea and Indochina with military intervention.

Truman believed that the Marshall Plan, promising hope and assistance to the peoples of Europe, seriously upset Soviet attempts at gaining hegemony over all of Europe. Soviet reaction to the Marshall Plan precipitated a serious military confrontation in 1948. Because the plan

135

blocked the communization of western Europe (so Truman believed), it caused the Russians to retaliate by two moves. The first was the creation of a counterpart system for Soviet-bloc nations. The second and more provocative move was to test America's determination by risking a military incident in Berlin.[4]

The Allied "Big Three" conferences at Teheran, Yalta, and Potsdam had defined the status of postwar Germany. The city of Berlin, deep within the Russian zone of Germany, was divided into zones of occupation itself, just as the German nation had been. For the immediate postwar period, Germany was to be governed by an Allied Control Council, sitting at Berlin, whose membership was to be made up of the Allied military commanders in chief. In practice, these military leaders acted as a supreme authority for Germany, but they operated under a regrettable rule that required unanimity for action. The general principles that guided their deliberations had been established at Potsdam and provided that, in most matters, Germany was to be regarded as an entity, with uniform treatment for all citizens, and to whatever extent feasible, freedom of the press, speech, and religion were to be restored. Further, Germany was to be treated as a single economic unit, with common operational policies established on such matters as trade, industrial production, agriculture, currency and banking, transportation, communications, wages, prices, and rationing.[5]

What had been agreed to in principle with respect to Germany, did not often occur in actual practice. In the American zone, steps were taken to implement the Potsdam agreement, with Eisenhower moving rapidly to turn governmental administration over to civilian authority. As the general wrote to Truman in November of 1945, "Separation of occupational and governmental responsibility is sound . . . if for no other reason than because of its conformity to the American principle of keeping the army as such out of the civil government." [6] The Russians, however, began to intensify control over their zone and eliminate contacts with other parts of Germany. It became increasingly difficult to treat Germany as a single economic unit because of conflicting policies. Eventually, the British and American governments, later joined by the French, created machinery to deal with their combined zones as a unit, to the exclusion of the Soviet zone of occupation. However, the access of the western powers to their zones of occupation in Berlin was by narrow corridors through the Soviet-controlled zone.[7]

The access corridors through the Soviet zone of Germany were not guaranteed by any written agreement. The western powers had agreed that Germany should be governed from Berlin, deep in the Soviet sector, but their right of access to their respective enclaves in Berlin was not formally stipulated. The Soviet governor for Germany, Marshal Zhukov, had orally assured General Lucius Clay, Eisenhower's deputy, that the simple presence of American and other forces in Berlin presumed the right of access. The Russians initially provided ample access by a railroad line, highway, and an air corridor.[8] The absence of a bilaterally guaranteed permanent access route to Berlin became a serious issue in 1949 when the Soviets chose to block the land corridors. As journalist Arthur Krock wrote, "We can't throw the book at them because there is no book." [9]

On March 5, 1948, a few days after the Communist coup in Czechoslovakia, General Clay, military governor of the American zone, dispatched a message to the army's director of intelligence. Clay said that while he had no concrete evidence to offer, he had detected a subtle change in the attitude of the Russians that made him feel that war might come with "dramatic suddenness." [10]

Walter Millis says that Clay's cable had a "cataclysmic" effect on the Pentagon and the White House. The Central Intelligence Agency was set to work studying the possibility of war. On March 16 they reported to Truman that "major war was not probable within sixty days." [11] The following day the president spoke to a joint session of Congress on "The Threat to the Freedom of Europe." He directly attacked the Soviet Union for obstructionism in the United Nations and the destruction of "the independence and democratic character of a whole series of nations in Eastern and Central Europe." He spoke of the "ruthless course" and "growing menace" of Soviet imperialism and summed up with a call for additional action, saying, "There are times in world history when it is far wiser to act than to hesitate." Considering the tone of his speech, Truman's requests were relatively mild. He asked for passage of two stalled programs: universal military training and the Marshall Plan, as well as the temporary reinstitution of selective service.[12]

General Clay was notified by the Russians on March 31, 1948, that they intended henceforth to check the identification papers of all American personnel and check all freight shipments traveling through the Soviet zone. Clay informed the Pentagon that he proposed to order his troop trains to continue their normal runs and to "prevent the Russians from coming aboard and shoot if necessary." [13] Forrestal met immediately with the service secretaries and the Joint Chiefs of Staff. They recommended an order to Clay, which Truman subsequently approved, telling the general that his troops were not to open fire, except in self-defense. The trains went through to the East German border, where they were stopped. When the Americans refused to allow a search by Soviet personnel, the trains were turned back. There was no shooting. Had fighting begun, the United States Army could have bolstered the occupation forces by only one division (approximately fifteen thousand) without reverting to mobilization.[14]

Throughout April, May, and June, the Soviet military authorities made it increasingly difficult to get into or out of Berlin. On June 18, 1948, Britain, France, and the United States, in a move to halt an inflationary spiral, announced that they were to immediately establish a new type of currency for the three western zones of Germany. The Soviets opposed this change, according to Truman, because it would reveal that their own currency was unsound. That the Russians considered this important is illustrated by Truman's statement that "They offered to reopen the approaches to the city of Berlin if the Western powers would call off the currency change-over." [15] The three nations refused the Soviet offer, although this meant violation of the part of the original agreement which provided for a single economic and financial policy for all of Germany. The Soviet Union, of course, had violated both the spirit and letter of the agreement on numerous occasions.

As an apparent reaction to the announced currency reforms, all rail traffic to the three western zones of Berlin was cut off completely by Soviet officials on June 21. At six o'clock on the morning of the twenty-fourth, all highway, river, and canal traffic was also halted. Air Force C–47 transport planes, on orders of General Clay, had begun a small-scale airlift of foodstuffs into Berlin on the twenty-first. But the western sector of Berlin, with two million residents, became an island totally devoid of any surface contact outside its boundaries. The only way to enter or leave Berlin was by air. A written agreement existed, dated November 30, 1945, establishing three 20-mile-wide air corridors over the Soviet zone.[16]

Despite the three months of increasing pressure and restrictions on access to Berlin, apparently there was no contingency plan in force at the time the blockade was established. The planners in Washington would have to improvise a solution. The basic decision the president had to make involved three alternatives: order American forces to abandon the city; postpone any positive measures; or force a military confrontation by sending an armed column down the blockaded highway to Berlin, as General Clay suggested. Truman decided to defer any irrevocable decision until the situation was clarified. He met with the secretary of defense, secretary of the army, and Undersecretary of State Robert Lovett on June 25, but the conference was inconclusive, dealing only with the legality of the American position in Berlin. On June 26 Truman ordered that Clay's improvised airlift be continued and stepped up to meet the immediate needs of the Berliners, as well as those of American military personnel.[17]

Truman's order of June 26 to continue the airlift did not anticipate that the planes were to be anything more than a stopgap measure, a way to temporize until diplomatic means could be found to settle the Berlin crisis. The following day General Curtis LeMay, air force commander at Wiesbaden, European headquarters of the U.S. Air Force, cabled Washington a request for forty-five C–54 heavy transport planes. The C–47s available to LeMay had only a three-ton load capacity, whereas the newer and larger C–54 could lift ten tons. To meet the need for transports in Germany, fifty-four C–54 aircraft were eventually moved from bases in Alaska, Hawaii, the Caribbean, and the United States. General Hoyt Vandenberg, air force chief of staff, protested to Truman that this concentration of aircraft in one region seriously endangered national security, but the president overruled him.[18]

Secretary of Defense Forrestal met with top Pentagon officials on Sunday, June 27, 1948, to discuss what recommendations they should make to Truman in a meeting he had called for the following day. Those present were agreed that the existing supplies in Berlin, plus additional material that could be brought in by air, would suffice approximately sixty days before the logistical situation became critical. The group spent considerable time on the alternatives of abandonment, the difficulty of remaining under extant circumstances, and the odds of war if they opted to force their way into Berlin. According to Forrestal's diary record of the meeting, there was no consideration given to the possibility that the airlift provided another choice. The planners may have been influenced by General Clay's initial estimate that the airlift could bring in a maximum of five hundred to seven hundred tons a day, whereas the food requirements alone for West Berlin were estimated at eleven hundred tons a day. The meeting adjourned after deciding that Forrestal, Lovett, and Royall should meet with the president the following day, apprise him of the alternatives and the arguments for and against each. They were also to discuss sending two squadrons of B–29 bombers to Germany or England. The advantage of negotiating while nuclear weapon carriers were within striking distance of the Soviet Union was not to be ignored.[19]

Secretary Lovett began the meeting with the president on June 28 by reciting the options derived from the Pentagon meeting the previous day. Truman interrupted him to say that there was no need to discuss staying in Berlin; he had no intention of pulling out. This major decision represents one of the infrequent instances of Truman making a command decision without benefit of considerable deliberation and recommendations by his staff of military advisers. The latter were still busily trying to decide *if* the United States should attempt to remain in Berlin.[20]

In addition to the pivotal decision to stay in Berlin, the president made two other command decisions in the meeting on the twenty-eighth. He agreed to send more B–29 bombers to Germany, a decision with which Clay heartily concurred, since he did not have sufficient conventional land forces in Germany to confront the Russians. (Nor was he to obtain such a force: On the basis of existing army manpower and global requirements, no additional troops could be made available for Germany.) Truman also instructed the National Military Establishment to take whatever steps were necessary to make the airlift sufficient to the immediate needs of West Berlin.[21] Writing later in his *Memoirs*, Truman said he reasoned at the time that staying in Berlin required a show of strength even though this confrontation might precipitate war with the Soviet Union.[22]

Truman's actions and decisions as commander in chief during the early days of the Berlin crisis are unusual and revealing. What seems most obvious is that he bypassed the very institutional framework he had labored to create. One of the prime purposes of the armed forces unification that he had brought into being was to establish an efficient, clear line of communication in the command system. The National Security Council recommendations to the president were not yet before him when he acted. The Central Intelligence Agency had failed to anticipate the Soviet move. The Joint Chiefs of Staff were still debating alternatives, but were at least certain that the airlift Truman endorsed could not work for any extended period. In the normal, institutionalized process Truman had established, policy recommendations would have come up to the commander in chief from the military advisers represented in these bodies. In this instance, Truman decided on a course of action—to stay in Berlin and supply the city by air—and he then convinced his military advisers that it would work. In the hectic days of the Korean decision the president would again bypass part of the staff process which he otherwise placed great faith in.[23]

By early July the airlift, which someone in the air force with a singular lack of imagination had code-named "Operation Vittles," was beginning to show signs that it could succeed against all odds. Much of the burden had been eased by the arrival in late June of the four-engine C–54 Skymaster transports, which had more than triple the capacity of the smaller C–47s. The British Royal Air Force soon joined in the airlift, taking approximately one third of the burden. To make the operation more efficient, the British and American air elements were joined in October, 1948, into the Combined Airlift Task Force. In the 324 days of the airlift, well over a quarter million flights were made, delivering a total of over two million tons of food and other supplies necessary to the survival of the people of Berlin.[24]

The National Security Council had studied at length the proposal to send B–29 bombers to bases in Great Britain, which the British were willing to accept, although (supposedly) they would be armed with nuclear weapons. In a report to Truman, July 15, 1948, the council recommended this move and the president approved. The Security Council reasoned that it would underscore the seriousness of the current crisis to the public, provide experience for the air force and accustom the British people to having the atomic weapons carriers around as a permanent fixture.

Putting the weapons and bombers in Germany, and now in England, was obviously designed to intimidate the Russians. At the same time the Berlin crisis provided the perfect cover for a permanent long-range decision to extend the "atomic perimeter" around the Soviet Union.

The first American Strategic Air Command base in Great Britain was established as a direct result of the Berlin blockade. However, it is not at all certain that these planes were carrying atomic weapons. Whether they were or not remains classified.[25]

Beginning in the spring of 1948, as the Berlin crisis developed, Secretary of Defense Forrestal tried to get the president to formulate a specific atomic policy for American use of the bomb. The secretary also wanted Truman to transfer custody of the atomic devices from the Atomic Energy Commission to the air force, arguing that those responsible for using the weapon when ordered to do so, should possess it physically.[26] During the next few months Truman displayed an unusual reluctance to decide the issues on nuclear policy that Forrestal had raised. In a meeting on July 15, 1948, the defense secretary informally broached the subject of atom bomb custody again. The president told Forrestal that he wanted to keep the decision on use of the bomb "in his own hands." According to Forrestal's diary entry for this date, Truman said that he did not intend "to have some dashing lieutenant colonel decide when would be the proper time to drop one." [27] Six days later, the National Military Establishment formally requested an executive order transferring the bombs to its custody. Truman reserved decision on the transfer, but commented that since the responsibility was his, he proposed to keep that power intact. Two days later (June 23), he privately told Forrestal he was going to reject the proposed transfer of bomb custody to the military. Forrestal claimed the president admitted that his decision was politically inspired and that after the presidential race was over he would be willing to reconsider his position.[28] In fact, the issue of civilian or military custody—presuming proper fail-safe systems—is of only passing importance, since only a civilian, the commander in chief, can order the employment of nuclear weapons. Of far more significance is the question of whether they should be used. And on this, Truman either wanted to keep his options open, or did not wish to decide.

The president's reluctance to fix conditions under which he would approve nuclear warfare, while understandable, created problems in military contingency planning. This was particularly true in the bellicose atmosphere of 1948 when available conventional forces were at their lowest levels. The reduction in military appropriations, except for strategic bombers, indicated a reliance on massive nuclear retaliation in the event of total war. A conventional military response in a limited conflict could not be planned for, since, in lieu of a stipulated nuclear policy, the guiding assumption prescribed that the American response to pressure would be strategic atom-bombing of the aggressor.

The nuclear-weapons planes went to European stations without an established policy as to the use of the bombs which were—theoretically at least—nestled in their bellies. The B–29s were atomic guns pointed at the Soviet heartland. Russian intelligence was reasonably sure Truman would not pull the nuclear trigger over Berlin. However, neither they, nor Truman's military advisers, really knew. Forrestal discussed this policy vacuum with the president several times in July and August, without receiving a conclusive response. The defense secretary persisted in pressing Truman for a nuclear-use policy and was rewarded with an answer, of sorts, in September: "The President prayed that he would never have to make such a decision, but that if it became necessary, no one need have a misgiving but what he should do so." Forrestal must have considered the answer satisfactory for he never again raised the question.[29]

Whether or not they carried atomic bombs, with or without a clearly defined policy, the B–29s Truman ordered to Europe gradually changed the military and diplomatic policies of the United States. In a brilliant passage from his *Arms and Men*, Walter Millis has analyzed the effect on policy of the B–29s. Millis sees the Berlin conflict as marking a major divide in American military thought. The appearance of the atomic weapons in Europe in 1948 made it plain "that the atomic arsenal had entered American thought as an appropriate instrument of policy for the future." [30]

The secretaries of state and defense met with Truman on July 19 to review the Berlin situation. General Marshall emphasized to him that if he did not hold to a firm policy there, then the remainder of American European policy would also fail. Secretary Forrestal added a note of caution, telling the president that the United States had just slightly more than two army divisions in reserve, only one of which could be in Europe quickly. Truman concluded the discussion by saying, according to Forrestal, "our policy would remain fixed . . . we would stay in Berlin until all diplomatic means had been exhausted in order to come to some kind of an accommodation to avoid war." [31] Truman's statement seems firm, but much depends on what he meant by "until all diplomatic means had been exhausted." There is no such ambiguity in a diary-type note Truman wrote to himself the evening of the meeting with Forrestal and Marshall. In it, he clearly stated that the United States would stay in Berlin, whatever happened. The strain of these days on him is evident in the note:

> Have quite a day. See some politicos. A meeting with General Marshall and Jim Forrestal on Berlin and the Russian situation. Marshall states the facts and the conditions with which we are faced. I made the decision ten days ago to *stay in Berlin*. Jim wants to hedge. . . . I insist we will stay in Berlin—come what may.
>
> Royall, Draper and Jim Forrestal came in later. I have to listen to a rehash of what I know already and reiterate my "Stay in Berlin" decision. I do not pass the buck, nor do I alibi out of any decision I make.
>
> Went to Pershing's funeral in the marble amphitheatre. An impressive ceremony. . . .
>
> Bess and Margaret went to Missouri at 7:30 EDT 6:30 God's time. I sure hated to see them go. Came back and read the papers, some history and then wrote this. It is hot and humid and lonely. . . .[32]

Truman felt a need to talk to his field commander face-to-face about Berlin. He ordered General Clay to return to Washington for consultation. The president invited the general to attend the National Security Council meeting on July 22 with him, so that Clay might brief them on the German situation. Clay told the Security Council that the airlift was working well, averaging twenty-five hundred tons of goods per day, but that additional aircraft would be required to bring in the coal necessary for the coming winter. He said the morale of the German people was high and they were determined to wait out the Soviet blockade. Clay then returned to the possibility of sending an armored convoy up the highway to Berlin. It was his opinion that it would be met by armed Soviet resistance. But the general was not quite consistent, for he had dined with Forrestal the previous evening and told him that he believed that three weeks earlier he could have put through an armored convoy without difficulty and that he still believed it could be done. Clay had, on July 10, cabled Washington a request for authority to force his way through the blockade, convinced that the Russians would not forcefully resist such a passage.[33]

The air force chief, General Vandenberg, objected in the National Security Council meeting of July 22 to any further concentration of forces in Germany. Truman asked the general if he thought it better to send an armed force down the highway, thus precipitating World War III. Without giving Vandenberg a chance to answer, Truman said that the airlift was working and involved less risk than a convoy. He ordered the air force to "furnish the fullest support possible to the problem of supplying Berlin." [34]

By September the Berlin airlift had expanded to the point where it could provide foodstuffs and most other necessities of life without difficulty. However, bulk commodities, like coal, which would be needed in great quantities in the coming winter, would require additional aircraft. A review on Berlin in the National Security Council on September 9 disclosed that the diplomatic negotiations to end the blockade had broken down because of Soviet intransigence on all key points. In addition, the Russians announced they planned to hold ground and aerial training maneuvers in an area of East Germany that included the airlift corridors.[35] A meeting with the secretary of defense and other Pentagon leaders four days later left Truman despondent: "Berlin is a mess," he confided in a diary note that evening (September 13). "I have a terrible feeling . . . that we are very close to war. I hope not." [36]

Truman's somber estimates of the threat of war may have been colored by his own political problems; he was in the midst of a campaign for reelection which few thought he had a chance of winning. In any event, the Russians continued to make hostile gestures, but they always stopped short of actual armed contact.

The success of the airlift was an ever-increasing embarrassment to the Soviet government. The airlift project, Clay reported to the Security Council, was no longer an experiment, but a success which could be continued indefinitely. On October 22 General Clay received the authorization of the National Security Council and the commander in chief to add sixty-six more C–54 transports to his airlift. Truman and the Security Council also approved appropriations to the air force for expansion of maintenance facilities and the procurement of new aircraft to offset the attrition caused by the airlift.[37]

Early in 1949 the Soviet Union began sending out diplomatic signals indicating a willingness to discuss an end to the Berlin blockade. Talks began between Philip Jessup and Jacob Malik, the American and Soviet representatives to the United Nations, in March of 1949. The end result was an agreement made public on May 4, announcing that the blockade would end as of May 12. The détente had been made possible by Truman's resort to the only peaceful and reasonable course left open to him, the dramatic and amazingly effective airlift. The air force could well boast, as Secretary Symington did, that "The Berlin airlift is one of the great transportation achievements of all time." [38]

Truman's conduct in the Berlin blockade crisis showed him at his best; resolute but restrained. He rejected the direct military solution of testing the blockade with an armed convoy in favor of the airlift, which, for a time, only he seemed to believe could work. Although Berlin, like Greece and Turkey and other lesser confrontations with the Soviet Union could be counted as victories for Truman's containment doctrine, it should be noted that all were achieved while the United States enjoyed a monopoly on nuclear weapons.[39] This monopoly ended four months after the Berlin blockade. Which is not to gainsay what Truman accomplished: He had taken a peaceful path and obtained his objective without appreciable compromise. That West Berlin still stands as a republican enclave in the center of a Soviet satellite is due largely to the firm leadership of Harry Truman. That Berlin still stands unnaturally divided is a mocking reminder in microcosm of the politico-military dichotomy of the world which began with Truman and his Soviet counterpart.

The Berlin blockade offers an excellent illustration of the great power inherent in the accepted modern concept of the commander in chief. At no time during the days of decision in the Berlin crisis, nor in the long months of tense confrontation with the Soviet Union, did the president consult with the legislative leaders. Not once did he ask authority from Congress to take action, nor request that they give legislative sanction to decisions he had made.[40] Truman was virtually without check. He could just as easily have ordered General Clay to send an armed convoy to Berlin and to meet force with force. The resulting bloodshed would have confronted the nation with a state of war, albeit undeclared. The exclusive power of the Congress to declare war is a largely illusory constitutional check on the sweeping military power of the modern presidency.

In March, 1948, Great Britain, France, the Netherlands, Belgium, and Luxembourg signed a collective self-defense treaty, called the Brussels Pact. This was a purely military agreement predicated on the principle that an attack on one was an attack on all. The reasons for it, of course, were the events of the Cold War in Europe in 1947 and early 1948, particularly the Soviet-sponsored Communist takeover of the governments of Hungary and Czechoslovakia. Finland was under extreme pressure to enter into a "pact of friendship" with the Soviet Union. A general malaise existed in western Europe occasioned by Communist pressure on the "free nations" which led directly to the formation of the Brussels Pact.[41]

In a message to Congress at the time of the pact's signing, Truman called it "a notable step in the direction of unity in Europe for the protection and preservation of its civilization." The president told the Congress that the Brussels Pact deserved the full support of the United States. Then, in what was probably a trial balloon regarding American association with the pact, Truman said: "I am sure that the determination of the free countries of Europe to protect themselves will be matched by an equal determination on our part to help them to protect themselves." [42] The president was aware that the military alliance between France, Britain, and the Benelux nations did not constitute any genuine deterrent to Soviet ambition. Any effective military alliance for Europe was only possible with American participation. But here Truman was wary of American tradition: "I always kept in mind the lesson of Wilson's failure in 1920. I meant to have legislative co-operation." [43]

What Truman hoped to do was to enlarge the Brussels alliance by the inclusion of the United States and the nations of western Europe who were not yet members. This meant, of course, that he would eventually have to ask a generally hostile Republican Senate to ratify American participation in an international military alliance. He was fortunate to have Arthur Vandenberg, a staunch believer in bipartisan foreign policy, as chairman of the Senate Foreign Relations Committee. Vandenberg, with the encouragement of Undersecretary of State Robert Lovett, agreed to try to obtain the prior consent of the Senate to the principle of such an alliance.[44]

The result of Vandenberg's efforts, Senate Resolution 239, was artfully led through the legislative process by the senator to passage on a final roll-call vote in which only four votes were recorded against it. Thus on June 11, 1948, the Senate went on record as endorsing the participation of the United States in a regional collective security arrangement.[45]

With the resolution as security, Truman then initiated talks with other nations and they resulted, on April 4, 1949, in a pact establishing the North Atlantic Treaty Organization (NATO).[46] The president submitted the treaty to the Senate for approval on April 12, reminding them that the document was in accord with their resolution of the previous June, and rehashing the venerable argument that the way to lasting peace was through military might.[47] Lengthy hearings and floor debate followed. The most persistent question dealt with the power of the commander in chief to send troops abroad without congressional sanction in compliance with a military alliance. Administration leaders blocked an attempt by the Senate to stipulate on the matter.[48] The ratification vote came on July 21 with the treaty passing 82 o 13. The ratification process was completed on August 24, 1949, and NATO began its formal existence.[49]

The American commitment to a peacetime military alliance was a unique and significant departure from established practice. It was an obvious extension and militarization of the Truman Doctrine. However, its value, particularly in the first years of its operation, was largely symbolic since it lacked sufficient arms, forces and, coordination. The establishment of NATO recognized the obvious: military power had become a fixed adjunct of foreign policy.

Standing alone, the North Atlantic Treaty was, in historian Richard Leopold's words, "a diplomatic gesture rather than a military bulwark." [50] These European nations could act as little more than a trip wire in the face of an all-out Soviet movement westward. They could not meet even a conventional probe by Communist forces without significant military assistance from the United States. A program of military aid was an essential concomitant if NATO were to be anything more than a wall of paper.

The National Security Council recommended to the president that the request for military assistance appropriations for the NATO nations be combined with similar existing aid programs into one package for presentation to the Congress. The programs already in operation provided for the military equipment and troop-training assistance for Iran, Greece, Turkey, the Philippines, China, Korea, and several Latin American republics. There was an obvious efficiency to combining all military aid into a unified program, but the administration was also concerned about the resistance in Congress to military aid for the NATO bloc. Accordingly, the tactic was to divorce the request for military assistance from the NATO treaty and tie it to a unified military aid request.[51]

Four days after the Senate advised favorably on the NATO pact, Truman sent to Congress a request for a Mutual Defense Assistance Program (MDAP). The principal purpose of the bill was to provide the requisite military implementation of the NATO alliance. The president asked the Congress for $1.45 billion. In his message to Congress, Truman said the assistance program was intended to provide compact, mobile defensive forces for nations whose security was vital to the security of the United States. He acknowledged that the aid envisioned by his program would give the nations involved only sufficient arms and equipment to resist internal disorder and provide the initial resistance to external aggression. Truman said that the only genuine "deterrent to aggression" was the military might of the United States, and that no nation need fear that he would not use this power to prevent its being overrun. The president told the Congress that the requirements for military aid had been unified under one program so that the distribution of American arms and equipment could be adapted to United States foreign policy and changing conditions.[52]

Many members of the Congress, appalled by the amount of the Mutual Defense Assistance Program request, joined with the neo-isolationists, led by Senator Robert Taft, in opposition to the president's request. One of Taft's strongest allies was Senator Vandenberg, a key figure in making NATO a reality. Vandenberg believed, as did Taft, that the bill was too costly and that it was "almost unbelievable in its grant of unlimited power to the Chief Executive." The president assigned Dean Acheson, who had replaced Marshall as secretary of state in January, the task of steering the defense assistance bill through Congress.[53] The Congress battled over the bill the rest of the summer months and well into September; it seemed clear that Truman would have to accept major amendments in the amount and conditions for military aid in order to secure passage. But Truman's program and Acheson's task were both simplified by the Soviet Union. On September 23, 1949, the president made public the information that the USSR had successfully tested a nuclear device. Impelled by the loss of nuclear monopoly, solid majorities in both legislative houses approved the bill in less than a week, cutting the original request by only $100 million.[54]

The president signed the Mutual Defense Assistance Act of 1949 on October 6, describing it as "a notable contribution to the collective security of the free nations of the world." In an obvious reference to the Soviet atomic explosion, Truman also said at the bill-signing: "Recent developments in the field of armaments have strengthened the free nations in their adherence to the principle of a common defense . . . that underlies this act." [55] Truman made implementation of the act the responsibility of the secretary of state.[56] However, the Department of the Army was given the duty of administering the Mutual Defense Program. In operation, each country that received MDAP-authorized arms and equipment was assigned an American "Military Assistance Advisory Group." Each group was composed of army, air force, and navy sections. The functions assigned to these groups were described in the army's official history: "Each advisory group assisted its host government in determining the amount and type of aid needed and helped train the armed forces . . . in the use and tactical employment of material received from the United States." [57]

It took more than a year for the NATO countries to come to agreement on the precise implementation of the principles they had approved in the North Atlantic Treaty. The difficulties centered on reaching accord on each nation's contribution to the common effort, the participation of West Germany in the alliance, and the amalgamation of national forces into a common balanced force for mutual defense. The outbreak of the Korean War impressed upon the NATO signatories the need for a functioning body to prevent a similar attack in Europe. A general agreement was finally hammered out by Secretary Acheson and the allied representatives on September 26, 1950, which established SHAPE (Supreme Headquarters Allied Powers Europe).[58] One understanding reached by the NATO countries was that the supreme commander of the NATO forces was to be an American. And Truman knew just the American he wanted for the job.

To a note for General Eisenhower on October 19, 1950, Truman had added a handwritten postscript: "First time you're in town I wish you'd come see me. If I send for you we'll start the 'speculators' to work." Eisenhower saw the president on October 28. Truman asked him to take supreme command of the NATO armies and the general accepted. Eisenhower's formal appointment was made by the president on December 19, 1950. The order gave the general full operational command of all American army, air force and naval forces in the European theater, as well as designating him as supreme allied commander in Europe. "You are undertaking a tremendous responsibility," Truman concluded in his order to Eisenhower. "As President and Commander-in-Chief of the Armed Forces of the United States, I know that our entire country is wholeheartedly behind you." [59] Truman might have thought twice about this prestigious appointment had he had any way of knowing that in less than two years Eisenhower would be the Republican nominee, publicly damning the Korean military policies of his former commander in chief.

Six years after he left office, Truman told an interviewer that the conclusion of the NATO treaty gave him the greatest sense of personal satisfaction. The former president wrote in his *Memoirs* that western Europe was secure largely because the United States was able to break with tradition during his administration and join a peacetime military alliance. Subsequent events did not shake his conviction that NATO is an important deterrent shield against a third world war. [60]

The test detonation of an atomic device by the Soviet Union had encouraged the Congress to pass the Mutual Defense Assistance Act substantially in the form Truman requested. The Soviet test had also been a major factor in Truman's decision to authorize a crash program to develop the thermonuclear (hydrogen) bomb. There was another major development attributable to the successful Russian experiment: The drafting of a policy paper for Truman that would come to have a major influence on the military and foreign policy thinking of the American government. The paper had its beginnings in a report dated January 31, 1950, dealing with recommendations to the president in light of the end of the American atomic monopoly. [61] One of the recommendations made then was that the president order the State and Defense departments to make a detailed examination of American objectives in both war and peace. They should also assess the effect that those objectives have on strategic planning now that the Soviet Union had a "probable fission bomb capability and possible thermonuclear bomb capability." [62] The president accepted this recommendation and when he signed the directive ordering the acceleration of the hydrogen

bomb program on January 30, 1950, he appended to it a letter ordering the secretaries of state and defense to make this reassessment of
defense and foreign policy.[63]

The staff studies that followed eventually produced a "white paper"
titled NSC–68 (National Security Council Policy Paper No. 68). The
paper began by recognizing that events since World War II had brought
about a basic realignment among nations, with the United States and
the Soviet Union forming the terminals of an international polariza-
tion. NSC–68 discounted the existence of a Communist "master plan,"
but did conclude that the Soviet government had three major objectives: (1) to preserve the internal power position of the regime and
develop the USSR as the base for that power; (2) to consolidate control over the Soviet satellites and add them as support for that base;
(3) to weaken any opposing centers of power and aspire to world
hegemony.[64]

America's stated objectives of individual freedom and self-determi-
nation constituted a threat to the three objectives of the Soviet Union.
There existed a basic incompatibility between the two systems of government. The assumption was then made that a continuous assault
upon the United States and other democratic nations was in prospect,
since force was an accepted means of obtaining Communist political
objectives. America must be willing to preserve its avowed principles
both at home and abroad, no matter what the cost. This should be accomplished by peaceful means, but should these means fail, the nation
should be willing and prepared to wage war to preserve those conditions under which this form of government can survive and prosper.

The paper next analyzed the relative military capabilities of both
nations and their respective allies in the event of war. The Russians
would have sufficient atomic weapons and an adequate delivery system
by 1954. The effect of this would be to negate the deterrent value of
American nuclear weapons, bringing about an atomic stalemate. In a
recourse to conventional warfare, the Soviet Union had substantial
superiority. The United States and its western allies were inadequately
prepared for limited warfare because of low troop levels, weakness in
the military and economic structure of western European nations, and
a lack of strength in the western alliance system.

The document described for the president four possible courses of
action: (1) a continuation of the present policy course of limited de-

fense budgets with the same commitments and military capabilities; (2) a preventive war against the Soviet Union; (3) withdrawal from international commitments and acceptance of the "fortress America" strategy; (4) development of the conventional war deterrent potential of the free world by a massive buildup of the American military forces as well as those of the allied nations to the point where they were capable of responding to each new Communist challenge quickly and decisively.[65] The NSC–68 drafters, who obviously endorsed the fourth option, deliberately avoided making any cost estimates in the paper itself, but in their discussions estimates had ranged from $3 billion to $35 billion over Truman's existing ceiling of $15 billion. But the paper did indicate a belief that even in time of peace a military budget totaling up to 20 percent of the gross national product was possible without bringing about national bankruptcy.[66]

The secretaries of defense and state signed the document and submitted it to Truman on April 7, 1950. Five days later the president sent the policy paper to the National Security Council (where it acquired the designation "NSC–68"). The president instructed the council to work out a program based on the fourth option and present him with cost estimates for its implementation. Truman had not approved NSC–68 as the new national military policy; he simply committed it to his staff for further study.[67] Before the difficult task of translating the generalized principles of NSC–68 was completed, war broke out in Korea.

The value of NSC–68 was that it eventually provided a framework within which the buildup of strength to meet the demands of the Korean conflict were considered. It provided the rationale which rejected the strategy of those who urged total war in Korea. NSC–68 was an important milestone for overall military defense planning because it established, as one scholar phrased it, "some kind of order of priority and magnitude between economy and military means, American and allied strength, and short and long-run national interests." [68] But while it did clarify the policies employed in fighting that war, NSC–68's warning that the nation must be prepared to fight limited, conventional wars came too late to prevent the initial military defeat suffered by the United States in the opening months of the Korean War.

10/ The Intervener

Dean, we've got to stop the sons-of-bitches, no matter what. And that's all there is to it.[1]

—HARRY S. TRUMAN

The decision to intervene in Korea was made by Harry S. Truman alone. He did not seek the consent of Congress or of the American people. An examination of his actions during these days of decision can be illuminating both to Truman's concept of his role as commander in chief and to the vast military powers incumbent on the modern presidency.

Korea is a mountainous peninsula jutting out from the land mass of Asia. The Sea of Japan to the east, the Yellow Sea to the west, and the Korea Strait to the south wash against its more than fifty-four hundred miles of coastline. To the north, the Yalu and Tumen rivers form the natural boundaries shared with China (500 miles) and Russia (only 11 miles). The Korean peninsula, encompassing some 85,000 square miles, varies from 90 to 200 miles in width and from 525 to 600 miles in length.[2]

America first extended military assistance to Korea in 1888, in the form of army personnel sent to train the Korean forces.[3] This aid was a result of a "treaty of friendship" signed at Tien Tsin in 1882 between the United States and Korea, then under the suzerainty of China. The peninsula was a focal point in power struggles among Russia, Japan, and China throughout the next quarter century which culminated in Japanese dominion over Korea by 1905. The Taft-Katsura "agreed memorandum" of July 27, 1905, put the United States on record as accepting Japanese suzerainty. When Japan formally annexed Korea in August, 1910, the United States offered no objection.[4]

From 1910 until 1945 Japan retained its control over Korea. That control was imperiled by the Cairo Declaration of December, 1943, in

154

which China, the United States, and the United Kingdom pledged that "in due course" Korea would become a free, independent nation. A reaffirmation of this promise was made in the Potsdam Declaration, issued on July 26, 1945. When the Soviet Union declared war on Japan on August 8, it became a party to this guarantee. The atomic bombings on the sixth and the ninth, coupled with the entry of Russia into the war, forced Japan to sue for peace. While the negotiations were being carried out, armies of the Soviet Union prepared to enter the Korean peninsula.[5]

The president received a good deal of encouragement from numerous sources, urging him to order American forces into all of Korea, to accept the surrender of the Japanese army, and to act as an occupation force. The State Department urged this action on Truman. He also received separate cables from Ambassadors Averell Harriman and Edwin O. Pauley advising him to block Soviet intentions by having the United States Army occupy as much of Korea and Manchuria as possible.[6] However, physical conditions dictated otherwise. The Soviet forces were already in Manchuria and nearing the Korean border which they would cross on August 12. There were no American forces in Korea, the closest units being on Okinawa, with very little shipping available to transport them to the peninsula. The Joint Chiefs of Staff informed the president that any attempt to race the Russian army for territory in Korea was doomed from the outset by the logistics of the situation. The War Department recommended that an arbitrary dividing line, the 38th parallel of north latitude, should be suggested to the Soviet Union as an operational and occupational division between the Russian and American forces. The army planners reasoned that acceptance of this line would operate to the advantage of the United States. The Russians were in a position to take all of Korea if they chose to, since the Twenty-fourth Corps assigned to occupy Korea was at Okinawa, six hundred miles away. On August 14 the joint chiefs accepted this recommendation, as did the State Department, and it was forwarded to Truman, who also approved it.[7]

While the status of Korea remained questionable, the State-War-Navy Coordinating Committee (SWNCC) began drafting a directive on August 11 for General Douglas MacArthur, prescribing the procedures to be followed in accepting the surrender of all Japanese forces in the Far East. MacArthur, who was commander in chief, U.S. Army

Forces, Pacific, had been designated by Truman as supreme commander, Allied powers, Japan (SCAP), a selection endorsed on August 12 by all the Allied powers. By August 15, the coordinating committee had completed the drafting of the orders to MacArthur, and they had received the president's approval. The orders included the proposal to establish the 38th parallel as a line of demarcation.[8]

The directive to MacArthur, known officially as General Order No. 1, was transmitted to him on August 15. The text of the order was also submitted to Premier Stalin for his approval on the fifteenth. The following day, August 16, the Soviet leader cabled his approval, without taking exception to the provisions regarding Korea. These provisions stipulated that the Japanese troops in Korea north of the 38th parallel should surrender to the Soviet army and those south of that line to the American army. The United States did not intend to create fixed zones of occupation, as in Germany, by asking that the 38th parallel be used as a divider. The line was considered temporary, a military expedient made necessary by extant conditions.[9]

General MacArthur caused General Order No. 1 to be promulgated on September 2, 1945. Six days later, the twenty-fourth Corps arrived in Korea, and the following day Japanese forces south of the parallel formally surrendered to Lieutenant General John R. Hodge, who was designated as U.S. commander for (South) Korea. The Soviet army, which had advanced beyond the 38th parallel, occupying the cities of Seoul and Inchon, retired to the dividing line without incident.[10]

The demarcation line quickly became a permanent border. General Hodge and his Russian counterpart became *de facto* military rulers of their respective halves of the peninsula. Hodge started off on the wrong foot with the Korean people by announcing on September 9 that the Japanese civilian officials controlling the government would be temporarily retained in their posts. The clamor in the United States and Korea was immediate. Truman had to order the Joint Chiefs of Staff to send Hodge a countermanding directive and issue a public statement assuring that the "Japanese warlords are being removed," but cautioning that full independence for Korea would require "time and patience."[11]

A growing resentment of the United States arose among the Koreans during the latter months of 1945. The Korean people were beginning to realize that the dividing line was a permanent partition of their land, for which they blamed the United States. Soviet authorities vigorously patrolled the 38th parallel, severely restricting passage between the zones. Hodge was frustrated in his persistent efforts to negotiate with his Russian counterpart on arrangements for reestablishing Korean unity. The general sent a message to the joint chiefs in December which was forwarded to Truman, reporting on the first three months in his command. Hodge said that the dual occupation "imposed an impossible condition" on any sincere efforts at achieving the assigned missions of stabilizing the economy and preparing Korea for full independence. Hodge recommended that the Allied governments reiterate their promise of complete independence for Korea and demonstrate sincerity by removing the barrier imposed by the 38th parallel. As an alternative, Hodge suggested that the United States and the Soviet Union remove their forces simultaneously, "and leave Korea to its own devices and an inevitable internal upheaval for its self-purification." [12]

As an alternative to Hodge's recommendations, the president instructed Secretary of State Byrnes to take up the independence of Korea in a meeting of the foreign ministers of the United Kingdom, the United States, and the Soviet Union, held at Moscow in December, 1945. Out of these negotiations came the Moscow Agreement which provided that the American and Soviet commands in Korea should establish a Joint Commission. This body was to be charged with making recommendations for the establishment of a provisional government for all of Korea, following consultation with the leadership of the various political parties and social organizations. The Moscow Agreement was never put into effect. The United States and the Soviet Union were unable or unwilling to make mutually acceptable accommodations that would have made the reunification and full independence of Korea possible.[13] The result of this impasse was that an artificial and illogical line became a permanent international boundary, cruelly dividing a racially and ethnically homogenous people into separate, hostile nations.

The political stalemate regarding Korea continued throughout 1946. In June of that year the president received an informative report from Ambassador Pauley, who as Truman's personal representative, was one of the few Americans allowed to visit North Korea by Soviet officials. Pauley reported that the Soviet armies displayed no immediate intention of pulling out of North Korea. The Soviets were, in the ambassador's view, clearly stalling on creating a provisional government for a united Korea, while at the same time engaging in an intensive propaganda campaign extolling the Soviet form of government and promoting the interests of the Korean Communist party. Pauley recommended to Truman that the United States resort to similar tactics, propagandizing "to sell democracy and the four freedoms." He also recommended that the United States publicly condemn the Soviet Union for its failure to implement the Moscow Agreement and that the question be taken to the United Nations or a Big Four summit conference.[14]

In responding to Pauley's letter, Truman outlined his basic thinking on postwar Korean policy:

> I have given further consideration to your informative letter of June 22, 1946, on the Korean situation. I agree with you that Korea is, as you so aptly phrase it, "an ideological battleground upon which our entire success in Asia may depend." Korea has been for many decades the focus of international rivalries and I consider one of the principal objectives of our policy there to be to prevent Korea from again becoming the source of future conflict.
>
> . . . I believe that the most effective way to meet the situation in Korea is to intensify and persevere in our present efforts to build up a self-governing and democratic Korea, neither subservient to nor menacing any power.
>
> . . . We intend to carry on an informational and educational campaign to sell to the Koreans our form of democracy. . . .
>
> Our commitments for the establishment of an independent Korea require that we stay in Korea long enough to see the job through and that we have adequate personnel and sufficient funds to do a good job. I am, therefore, requesting the agencies concerned to see that means are found to insure that General Hodge has the men and funds he needs to attain our objectives.[15]

The letter to Pauley caused the War Department to plan a program of increased military assistance to Korea, designed to implement the policies suggested by the president. On August 12 Truman wrote to Secretary of War Patterson to indicate his "particular interest" in the aid program. Truman assured Patterson that if the plan required additional funds, the secretary could count on his support. The president also informed Patterson that he had asked the State and Navy departments to assist in the accomplishment of this program. Truman repeated the belief expressed in his letter to Pauley: "I am convinced that we may be required to stay in Korea a considerable length of time in order to fulfill our pledge to aid in the establishment of a free and independent government." In his reply, Patterson assured the president that the War Department would do its utmost in working toward the attainment of American objectives in the Far East. By June, 1950, the United States had provided the Republic of Korea over $57 million in military equipment. Total economic assistance in the period between the end of World War II and the inception of the Korean War amounted to over $495 million.[16]

Early in 1947 it became apparent that the issue of Korean unification was completely stalemated by the failure of the United States and the Soviet Union to find a common ground for agreement. General Hodge was concerned enough about the attitude of the Russians to warn Washington that he "might be faced with a serious military situation at any time." The general had already warned Truman, in January and again in February, 1947, that a civil war between North and South Korea was in the offing if the two occupying powers could not find a solution. On the basis of Hodge's warnings, the Joint Chiefs of Staff decided to warn MacArthur, the Far East commander, that he faced "a possible critical military situation in Korea." [17] Late in May the United States made a final attempt to achieve a diplomatic accord through the Russo-American Joint Commission. These negotiations continued for several months, but they proved fruitless.

In May, 1947, Secretary of War Patterson, concerned over the severe cutbacks in personnel necessitated by budgetary limitations on military spending, recommended to Secretary of State Marshall that his department consider the advisability of withdrawing all American forces from Korea. Marshall and Truman were not ready to take such a step in May, but with the failure of diplomatic efforts in the joint commission meetings in September, the president ordered the joint chiefs to study and make recommendations on the withdrawal question. Their study was submitted on September 25, 1947. It was their opinion that, "from the standpoint of military security, the United States had little strategic interest in maintaining the present troops and bases in Korea." [18] The joint chiefs defended this conclusion by saying that the forty-five thousand men in Korea were a military liability: They could not resist an attack without heavy reinforcements; an American offensive operation in Asia would bypass the Korean peninsula; the Korean force was expensive to maintain, yet contributed little of lasting value to American security; and, given the existing military manpower shortages, the forces could be used more profitably elsewhere.[19] MacArthur agreed with this estimate. General Albert Wedemeyer, whom the president had sent to study the Far Eastern situation in the summer of 1947, reported substantially the same conclusions as the joint chiefs reached. However, he also recommended that the United States endeavor to strengthen the military forces of Korea prior to withdrawal, since they would surely fall to the far superior North Korean army otherwise.[20]

The failure of the joint commission to reach agreement on Korean unification and independence led Truman to conclude that it would be futile to continue direct negotiations with the Soviet Union. Therefore he directed the secretary of state to place the question of Korean independence before the General Assembly of the United Nations.[21] Marshall addressed the General Assembly on September 17, 1947. He acknowledged that the Russian and American representatives in the joint commission had been unable to agree on the means of implementing a process leading to the independence promised to Korea at Cairo in 1943. After summarizing the vain efforts to achieve agreement, Marshall proposed that the occupying forces hold elections in their respective zones of Korea. The elections should be supervised by a United Nations commission, which would also assist in the formation of the central government thus elected. Following this, Marshall suggested, the new government should arrange for the prompt withdrawal of the American and Soviet forces.[22]

Through the joint commission, the Russians offered a substitute proposal which called for the withdrawal of all foreign military forces from Korea early in 1948. The Koreans were to be left to their own devices in structuring a unified government. However, Truman was aware, from Wedemeyer's report and other intelligence information, that the North Korean army had been very well equipped and trained by the Soviet Union and that the constabulary forces of the South Koreans would be no match for them. Although it was really this fear that South Korea would be at the mercy of North Korea which motivated rejection of the Soviet proposal on October 18, the State Department informed the Russians that the United States could not enter into a bilateral agreement on troop withdrawal while the larger question of Korean independence was before the United Nations.[23] With the Soviet bloc objecting and abstaining, on November 14, 1947, the UN General Assembly voted forty-three to zero to hold legislative elections in all of Korea for a National Assembly which would then form a national government for Korea. The General Assembly resolution, which followed closely the recommendations made by the United States, provided that the elections should be held no later than March 31, 1948. Supervision of the elections was to be carried out by a nine-nation, United Nations temporary commission on Korea.[24] Shortly after the vote, Louise Kim, Korean Peoples Assembly Representative to the United Nations, wrote to the president expressing "the heartfelt thanks of the Korean people for your government's successful efforts on behalf of Korea at the United Nations." [25]

The UN temporary commission was refused access to North Korea by the Red army. It had to content itself with supervising elections held in the American zone in May, 1948. Syngman Rhee's party captured a majority of the seats. On June 25 the temporary commission on Korea certified to the United Nations that the election had been "a valid expression of the free will of the electorate." [26] On July 17 Korea adopted a constitution, and on July 20 Syngman Rhee became president. In a statement issued through the State Department on August 12, Truman recognized the Rhee government as the "Government of Korea" and named John J. Muccio as his special representative, with the personal rank of ambassador.[27] The State Department release implied that the new government was the government for *all* Korea, but neither the president nor the State Department could have seriously believed Rhee would govern above the 38th parallel. In fact, in a warm letter of congratulations to General Hodge on August 15, Truman wrote of the "constitutional government of southern Korea." The formal transfer of authority was completed in a ceremony on August 15 creating the Republic of Korea.[28] American military authority ended with this transfer of power.

In the spring of 1948, during the formative period of the new republic, the National Security Council made a study of the future military relationship of the United States and Korea for the president. The council informed Truman that several courses of action were open: abandonment of Korea; continuation of American political and military responsibility; extension of military training, equipment and assistance to Korea's security forces, as well as extensive economic aid to the burgeoning nation. The Security Council recommended the latter option to the president, which he approved.²⁹ Thus, when Korea became an independent nation in August, it was the avowed policy of the United States to militarily and economically assist the new republic, but to consider it outside America's defensive shield.

Red army forces were completely withdrawn from Korea by the end of December, 1948. The United States Army had withdrawn about twenty-nine thousand soldiers from Korea by that time. However, the State Department and President Rhee opposed any further rapid withdrawal. Their reasons were simply that the South Korean army was not ready to perform its primary functions of preserving internal security and preventing external (Communist) aggression. So it was that at the end of 1948, although all Soviet army personnel had left North Korea, sixteen thousand American troops were still stationed in South Korea.³⁰

On New Year's Day, 1949, the White House announced that the United States was now according full diplomatic recognition to the Republic of Korea. The statement was a legal technicality necessary to officially terminate the military occupation and relieve the army of responsibility for administering economic assistance programs for Korea.³¹ On March 22, 1949, the National Security Council reported to Truman on a review of the Korean military situation. Based on this study, Truman issued orders the next day, directing that all United States forces remaining in Korea be withdrawn. The president had already agreed to provide support for a sixty-five-thousand-man army in South Korea. When the withdrawal of American forces was completed (June 29), a five-hundred-man regimental combat team remained behind to supervise the training of the Korean army. The president had acted on the unanimous advice of the Joint Chiefs of Staff and the National Security Council in removing all forces from Korea. General MacArthur's opinion had also been solicited, and he had agreed that withdrawal was advisable.³²

The decision of the Truman administration to withdraw from Korea left that nation vulnerable to attack. In the cold light of power politics and the planning for global, not limited, war, Korea was of no strategic importance to the United States. Although sincere efforts were made to bolster the Republic of Korea (ROK) armed forces, Truman had difficulty in obtaining funds for this purpose from Congress in 1949–1950. The president also went along with his advisers in not supplying the ROK forces with offensive weapons, such as aircraft, tanks, and heavy artillery. President Rhee had often threatened to attack North Korea, so there was an obvious cause for reluctance to provide him with the means of doing so. The Mutual Defense Assistance Act, which Truman had signed on October 6, 1949, provided for $10.2 million in military aid for South Korea, but these aid items were just beginning to arrive when the fighting broke out.[33]

Secretary of State Acheson defined the new strategic military thinking of the Truman administration with regard to the Far East in a celebrated and controversial speech to the National Press Club in Washington on January 12, 1950. Acheson described the defensive perimeter of the United States in the Pacific by tracing an imaginary line from the Aleutian Islands through Japan and the Ryukyu Islands to the Philippines. Within the boundaries of this strategic perimeter, the United States had the resources, and assumed the responsibility, for reacting immediately against any aggressor. The line Acheson described had not been drawn by him, but by the Joint Chiefs of Staff, with the concurrence of the National Security Council and the president. In fact, in an interview in Tokyo nine months earlier, General MacArthur had described exactly the same line of defense.

The omission of Korea and Formosa, the latter by then the home of Nationalist China, from the perimeter defined by Acheson made the speech increasingly controversial, since the attack on South Korea occurred six months later. With respect to nations beyond the pale, Acheson said, "No person can guarantee these areas against military attack . . . should such an attack occur. . . . The initial reliance must be on the people attacked to resist it and then upon the . . . United Nations." [34] This was not new. This was a reiteration of an official policy of American military disengagement from the Asian mainland, Formosa, and Korea that was plainly evident. Acheson was saying that any nation attacked outside the American perimeter would have to defend itself. Should it prove unable to contain the aggressor, then the United Nations would come to that nation's aid. The United States would not automatically regard an act of aggression outside the perimeter as a cause for war, but would act in concert with the United Nations. Some critics have said that the Acheson speech "could have been interpreted by the Communists as a green light." [35] The criticism seems questionable, since by the same reasoning, the North Korean attack would never have taken place had the secretary of state not made this speech.

By 1950 the animosity between the two Koreas had increased to the point where military conflict seemed more and more a possibility. The North Koreans continually probed the 38th parallel with hit-and-run raids and sent bands of guerrillas into South Korea to foment internal disorder. The chief source of military intelligence on Korea for Truman was MacArthur's headquarters in Tokyo. The reports coming in in the spring of 1950 told of a rapid buildup of North Korean forces. The Central Intelligence Agency informed the commander in chief that the North Koreans were capable of a full-scale attack at any time they should choose.[36] A weekly intelligence cable from MacArthur's G-2 (intelligence section), dated March 10, 1950, contained a sentence stating that North Korea would invade South Korea in June of 1950. But attached to this report was a commentary stating that G-2 did not anticipate that such an attack would occur. "It is believed," read a March 25 cable from the same source, "that there will be no civil war in Korea this spring or summer." However, a MacArthur aide, Major General Courtney Whitney, has claimed "the record shows" that between June, 1945, and the June, 1950, attack the Far East Command had sent fifteen hundred warnings of impending attack on South Korea. And among them was the quite accurate prediction dated March 10.[37]

The intelligence data from Korea did indicate the possibility of armed conflict, but the president faced daily intelligence summaries from the CIA informing him of numerous other places around the world where the Soviet Union "possessed the capability" to attack. At the time of the invasion of South Korea, the abundant rumors of war were not at all confined to the Korean peninsula, and it would have been impossible for Truman to take immediate remedial steps as each of these warnings was received.[38] He would be especially disinclined to react to a warning from MacArthur's G-2, which had sounded the tocsin more than fifteen hundred times. In addition, since it was Truman's policy not to become unilaterally involved in conflict outside the Pacific defensive perimeter, it is difficult to imagine by what rationale he could have taken action on these reports warning that the "possibility" of attack existed.

President Truman was back in his home state of Missouri on June 9, 1950, to give the commencement address and receive an honorary degree at the University of Missouri. He spoke with pride of the path of international cooperation the nation had followed since 1945, rejecting the "dangerous futility of isolationism." He had praise for American support of the United Nations, the economic recovery of Europe, ratification of the NATO pact and "our military assistance to the common defense of free nations . . . part of our strong, positive program to achieve a just and lasting peace." After the speech, Truman went on to St. Louis to join his comrades of the Thirty-fifth Division in their annual reunion, highlighted by a parade on June 10 which Truman led on foot: "The President cut a jaunty figure as he marched proudly with his old World War I division, and especially with Battery D, 129th Field Artillery, of which he was captain." Two weeks later, Truman returned to Missouri, this time to spend a quiet weekend at home in Independence. But a telephone call from the secretary of state informed "Captain Harry" of a new call to arms.[39]

A cable from Ambassador Muccio in Seoul arrived at the State Department at 9:26 P.M., Saturday, June 24, 1950. Shortly after ten o'clock the message was decoded. Dean Rusk, assistant secretary for Far Eastern Affairs, called Secretary Acheson at his Maryland farm to inform him of Muccio's note. Acheson immediately called the president at his home in Independence to relay the message, which read, in part: "North Korean Forces invaded Republic of Korea territory at several points this morning. . . . It would appear . . . that it constitutes an all-out offensive against the Republic of Korea." Truman gave tentative approval to Acheson's suggestion that the matter be brought before the United Nations Security Council. He accepted Acheson's advice that he remain in Independence at least until morning when the situation would be clearer.[40]

During the night, reports continued coming in from the wire services, Ambassador Muccio, and Far Eastern Command headquarters in Tokyo, all confirming that the attack constituted an invasion, not just another border probe. Acheson called Truman again to tell him that the fighting in Korea was intensifying and that the State Department had drafted a resolution charging the North Koreans with breaching the peace by an act of aggression. Truman gave Acheson permission to request an emergency session of the UN Security Council. At 3:00 A.M. Trygve Lie, the secretary general, was asked to convoke a council meeting as quickly as possible.[41]

The Security Council assembled early in the afternoon of June 25 in response to the American request. By this time the UN commission in Korea had filed a report with the Secretariat, describing the conflict as "full-scale war" endangering international peace.[42] In the Security Council session the United States deputy representative, Ernest A. Gross, reviewed developments in Korea since 1945 and offered a draft resolution calling upon North Korea to end hostile actions and withdraw beyond the 38th parallel.[43] After some minor revisions the Security Council adopted the American draft resolution by a vote of nine to zero, Yugoslavia abstaining and the Soviet Union unrepresented.[44]

Truman received another call from Acheson as he was sitting down to Sunday dinner. It was the secretary's opinion that the North Koreans would ignore the Security Council resolution, in which case it would be necessary for the president to decide what the United States should do to assist the Republic of Korea. Truman told Acheson that he was leaving for Washington at once. In the meantime, he instructed the secretary to meet with the joint chiefs and the service secretaries and begin working out recommendations for a meeting to be held upon his return.[45]

The president's plane landed in Washington at 7:15 on the evening of June 25. He was met by Acheson and Defense Secretary Louis Johnson. Acheson was able to inform Truman that the Security Council had adopted the American resolution. During the ride in from the airport, the president gave the impression that he was determined to take firm action, but, as usual, he was not ready to specify any steps until hearing from all his advisers.[46]

Truman opened the Blair House meeting with a brief statement to the effect that he was maintaining an "open mind" as to possible actions. He wanted to hear fully from all his advisers, but planned to make no major decisions that night. Truman then asked Acheson to summarize the latest developments in Korea and present the recommendations that the State and Defense departments had prepared during the day. The secretary of state read the various reports received from Muccio and described the emergency session of the Security Council. He also sketched in the military situation which saw the North Koreans advancing along a broad front. In Acheson's words, "I gave a darkening report of great confusion." [47]

The secretary of state then presented the recommendations prepared for the president's consideration: (1) that American nationals, particularly dependents of the military and diplomatic missions to Korea, be evacuated; (2) that the U.S. Air Force be commanded to protect this evacuation by force, if necessary to keep the requisite ports and airfields open; (3) that General MacArthur be instructed to provide the Republic of Korea forces with arms and ammunition over and above current allocations; (4) that the Seventh Fleet be ordered into the Formosa Strait to prevent a Chinese Communist invasion of Formosa or vice versa; (5) that consideration of additional assistance for South Korea should be given, based on the Security Council resolution, or supplementary resolutions; (6) that military aid to Indochina be increased.[48]

Following his long-established routine in this type of meeting, the president then went around the table, asking each adviser in turn to state his opinion of these recommendations and soliciting any additional views they might have. The general consensus supported the recommendations made by Acheson, with varying degrees of enthusiasm for particular points. Truman's questions to the joint chiefs were quite extensive, leaving Defense Secretary Johnson with the impression that the commander in chief had a thorough knowledge of troop dispositions and the existing military situation. The military men told Truman that they did not believe the Soviet Union would use the Korean situation as a pretext for a general war. The air force and navy chiefs, Vandenberg and Sherman, told the president that their services would probably be able to provide enough assistance to the ROK army, if ordered, to enable them to stem the tide of the North Korean advance. The military men were not inclined to the use of ground forces in Korea because of the terrain and the uncertain conditions.[49]

As the first Blair House conference ended (about 11:00 P.M.), Truman began to make his decisions. He approved the use of military aircraft and ships for the evacuation of American nationals. He also authorized the use of naval and air units in combat if needed to protect the evacuation area (Inchon-Kimpo-Seoul) from falling into the hands of the North Korean forces. In no case were these operations to be conducted above the 38th parallel.[50] MacArthur was ordered to provide as much ammunition and military equipment as he deemed necessary to South Korea. The Seventh Fleet—the carrier *Valley Forge*, the *Rochester*, a heavy cruiser, eight destroyers, and some twelve lesser craft—was ordered to sail north to the Formosa Strait at once. Truman stipulated that no further orders to the fleet were to be transmitted until they arrived on station. Reflecting his belief that the invasion might be a Soviet ruse, Truman instructed Acheson to survey all areas of the world where the Russians might strike. Before midnight cables were being transmitted from the State Department to all diplomatic and military missions in the world, requesting an intelligence recheck of Soviet intentions. At about the same time, the Joint Chiefs of Staff were transmitting orders to MacArthur based on Truman's decisions.[51]

These first decisions by the commander in chief were tentative. They did not represent a positive commitment to the defense of South Korea. Truman had made minimal decisions because he wanted to wait until his military and diplomatic intelligence clarified the situation. However, there is every reason to believe that he was already resolved to take whatever action was required to defend South Korea. Truman wrote that one strong impression he had from the Blair House meeting was "the complete, almost unspoken acceptance on the part of everyone that whatever had to be done to meet this aggression had to be done. . . . This was the test of all the talk of the last five years of collective security." [52] The president and all of his major counselors were of one mind on the need for action to defend South Korea, with the degree of American involvement apparently to be determined chiefly by the ability of the Korean forces to resist the attack.

The White House issued a press release on Monday, June 26, 1950, in which Truman acknowledged that he had conferred with the leadership of the State and Defense departments Sunday evening. He avoided mentioning any decisions reached, except to state that the "type" of aid being furnished Korea under the Mutual Defense Assistance Program was being augmented and expedited. The president had praise for the Security Council resolution and words of warning to the aggressors: "Willful disregard of the obligation to keep the peace cannot be tolerated by nations that support the United Nations Charter." [53]

The president was subject to numerous pressures for action on Mon-

day. He began the day—as was his custom—by reading four major
newspapers (New York *Times*, New York *Herald Tribune*, Baltimore
Sun, and Washington *Post*) after breakfast. Two of the papers, the
Times and the *Sun*, called for firm and decisive action.[54] As the day
wore on, he received several appeals directly from Korea. A cable
from the Korean National Christian Council at Seoul was received at
the White House at 8:46 A.M. saying, "Large invading forces are pressing around us, begging your immediate help." The Korean National
Assembly appealed to the United States for immediate assistance. Truman also received a message from President Rhee bearing the same
urgent plea for assistance. At 3:50 P.M. Truman received the Korean
ambassador, John M. Chang, who delivered the messages from Rhee
and the National Assembly. Truman recalled Chang looking so de-
pressed that he tried to encourage him: "I told him to hold fast—that
help was on the way." [55]

Early on the evening of June 26 Dean Acheson called the president
to inform him that conditions in South Korea had seriously deteriorated during the day. The secretary suggested that another full-scale
conference was necessary so that Truman could hear these reports
directly and issue further instructions. The president told Acheson to
assemble his advisers at Blair House for a meeting at 9:00 P.M. The
group which assembled was essentially the same, although Francis
Matthews, secretary of the navy, was absent.

Truman first heard the military situation reports. He learned that
the South Korean government had abandoned Seoul in the face of a
rapidly advancing North Korean armored column. General Vandenberg
told the president that American fighter planes had been in combat
over the South Korean capital and that at least one North Korean aircraft had been destroyed. General Bradley then read Truman the latest
communiqué from MacArthur which indicated that a "complete collapse" was imminent.[56]

At the president's request, Acheson led off the discussion by making a number of recommendations for further American action. He
felt that a new resolution should be presented to the United Nations
asking the member states to furnish South Korea with all aid necessary
to repel the invasion and restore peace. Acheson also urged that the
Seventh Fleet be instructed to block any Chinese Communist attack on
Formosa and any Nationalist Chinese thrust at the mainland. The most

significant of his recommendations, however, was that the air force and navy should be allowed to provide full tactical support for South Korean forces, but that their military activities should not extend to areas above the 38th parallel.[57]

All the advisers present were asked to comment on Acheson's recommendations by Truman, who had already made it clear that he considered Korea, like Berlin, a test of American resolve that had to be met. Secretary of Defense Johnson had no recommendations of his own to offer. Generals Bradley and Collins of the army doubted that air and naval support could stem the momentum of the invasion. They also told the president that if American ground forces were needed, it would probably require at least a partial mobilization. Johnson objected to using ground troops in Korea, but Truman asked the joint chiefs to give immediate consideration to that possibility. Although the conferees discussed whether the Soviet Union might take the use of American air and navy as sufficient cause for intervention or expansion of the conflict into other areas, these possibilities were considered remote. None of the advisers present told the president that the United States should not use the air force and navy in the defense of South Korea. Truman approved the recommendations presented by Acheson. He ordered Secretary Johnson to contact General MacArthur and directly inform him of the decisions which had been made.[58] The conference broke up at 9:40 P.M. As Truman left the meeting room he remarked, "Everything I have done in the last five years has been to try to avoid making a decision such as I had to make tonight." [59]

At 10:00 P.M., shortly after leaving the meeting with his military advisers, Truman placed a call to Charles S. Murphy, special counsel to the president. He gave Murphy a list of congressional leaders he wished to attend a conference in his office at 11:30 the following morning, June 27.[60] During the session with his advisers, the president had apparently broached the subject of asking Congress for a joint resolution supporting his decisions, but had been dissuaded by Acheson on the grounds that it would precipitate attacks on him by hostile Republicans and generate lengthy discussions of the eventual effect and financial expenditures involved in this intervention. Truman then decided on this meeting with the legislative leadership to simply inform them of what had occurred and the decisions he had made.[61]

The meeting between the president and the congressional leaders was held in the Cabinet Room of the White House at 11:30 A.M., Tuesday, June 27. With Truman were the secretaries of state and defense and most of the other officials who had participated in the two conferences at Blair House. Acheson summarized all that had transpired in the past three days, stressing the desperate situation being faced by the South Korean forces and the administration's belief that a failure to respond to this invasion would inevitably lead to World War III. The president then spoke at some length, emphasizing that the United States was not acting unilaterally, but through the United Nations, which he believed would suffer the fate of the League of Nations if it failed to act in this instance. Truman told those present of his effort to get the Soviet Union to intercede with North Korea. He read the text of a statement he planned to release following the meeting which would make public the actions he had taken. Truman then asked for questions; a general discussion of the American role in the crisis followed.[62]

The senators and representatives posed several question as to military dispositions. They were assured by the joint chiefs that no American ground forces were being employed in Korea nor were there any plans for such a commitment. Senator Millard Tydings, chairman of the Armed Services Committee, informed Truman that his committee had that morning favorably reported out bills allowing the president to call up the National Guard and to extend the Selective Service Act of 1948. Truman personally assured the congressmen present that his actions were in full accord with the principles and policies of the United Nations. There is clear-cut agreement in the recollections of the participants that no one present disputed Truman's decisions. They were agreed that the administration's course was the proper response to the situation.[63] However, two of the patricipants, Secretary Johnson and Senator Alexander Smith, later recalled that Senator Smith and, perhaps, Senator Tom Connally as well, wanted to know why Truman had not consulted Congress before making the decision to intervene militarily. There is no evidence to indicate that the subject was discussed at this meeting, but it was at a subsequent meeting of Truman with these same conferees on June 30, three days later.[64]

Truman had entertained thoughts of obtaining a joint resolution from Congress, but he believed he was acting within the scope of his powers as commander in chief in ordering naval and air intervention without congressional sanction. Testifying a year later before Congress, Acheson supported this conclusion. The secretary of state was asked by Senator Harry Byrd how he could justify the president's action without the prior approval of Congress. Acheson replied "Those orders were issued by the President in exercise of his authority as President and Commander in Chief." [65]

As the meeting with the congressmen ended, the White House released to the press the president's statement on the American response to the Korean crisis. In it, he said that he had ordered air and sea units to provide cover and support for Korean troops. He had, Truman said, dispatched the Seventh Fleet to prevent a Chinese Communist attack on Formosa or a Chinese Nationalist attack on the mainland. He was sending more troops to the Philippines and more military assistance to that government. Also, he had ordered an increase in the military supplies being provided to the French in Indochina as well as ordering a military mission to the area.[66]

An editorial in the New York *Times*, commenting on Truman's statement described his decision as "momentous and courageous." In the same edition, correspondent James Reston wrote that Truman's decision had "produced a transformation in the spirit of the United States Government." Reston added that differences of opinion as to what reaction the United States should take "have apparently been swept away by the general conviction that the dangers of inaction were greater than the dangers of the bold action taken by the President." The New York *Herald Tribune*, in a front page editorial, declared: "The President has acted—and spoken—with a magnificent courage and terse decision. . . . It was time to draw a line." Scores of messages came to the White House endorsing Truman's action by a wide margin. One telegram was from Thomas E. Dewey, the Republican nominee in 1944 and 1948: "I wholeheartedly agree with and support the difficult decision you have made today." Columnist Arthur Krock noted that Truman had been determined "from the outset to adopt the forceful policy which was announced this morning." Joseph C. Harsch, writing in the *Christian Science Monitor*, said Truman's announcement was received in Washington with a sense of relief and a strong expression of unity and satisfaction.[67]

Truman's statement was read to the House on the afternoon of the twenty-seventh by Democratic Floor Leader John McCormack. As he concluded, the members rose as a body to cheer and applaud. Before the afternoon had ended, they had rushed to pass an extension of the Selective Service Act by a 315 to 4 vote. Truman was accorded unprecedented peacetime powers as commander in chief by this act, particularly in the provisions authorizing him to call up the National Guard and reserves for up to twenty-one months active duty. The only dissonant note struck in the House came from Vito Marcantonio, an American Labor party representative from New York. He charged that Truman "had usurped the powers of Congress by declaring war against North Korea." [68]

The Senate reaction to the reading of the president's statement was much more reserved, but it reflected a general bipartisan endorsement of the decision to intervene. Republicans such as William Knowland, Leverett Saltonstall, and Wayne Morse endorsed the president's statement as did Henry Cabot Lodge, Jr., who went further than his fellow Republicans in expressing the hope that Truman would use ground forces in Korea if the military felt they were needed. These senators were joined in their expressions of approval of the Korean decision by Democratic leaders like Herbert Lehman, Estes Kefauver, and Hubert Humphrey. Although no senator voiced open opposition to the announced decisions, Arthur Watkins and James Kem, both Republicans, challenged the president's decision not to obtain congressional approval. Kem, noting the passages in the statement ordering the Seventh Fleet to isolate Formosa and prevent attack, asked: "Does that mean he has arrogated to himself the authority of declaring war?" By way of rebuttal, Senator Scott Lucas told Kem that, "on 126 occasions in the past a President . . . acting in his capacity as Commander in Chief of the nation's armed forces, had deployed these forces . . . without asking a declaration of war of Congress." [69]

The most significant challenge to the president's authority to send American forces into foreign combat without the approval of Congress came from Senator Robert A. Taft, the Ohio Republican. Taft delivered a lengthy major speech on the floor of the Senate, Wednesday afternoon, June 28. The senator blamed the Korean crisis on the "outrageous, aggressive attitude" of the Soviet Union and the "bungling and inconsistent" policies pursued by Truman. Taft pointed out that Truman had not attempted to consult with Congress or request a resolution approving the action taken. Truman's actions, Taft charged, created a *de facto* condition of war between the United States and North Korea, without the constitutionally required approval of the Congress. It was the senator's opinion that these actions represented usurpation of power by the commander in chief. Taft believed that if the Senate did not protest, it would end forever the right of Congress to declare war. Taft saw Truman's decisions as representing a change of policy in the Far East, which he endorsed, but he expressed concern over whether the crisis in Korea was the right time or place for such a change. The senator acknowledged, however, that should a joint resolution be offered, asking the Congress to authorize the use of American military forces in Korea, he would vote in favor.[70]

The administration reacted quickly to Taft's challenge, even though the senator seemed to have little support for his position. Less than a week later, congressmen received copies of a lengthy memorandum, dated July 3, 1950, and titled, "On the authority of the President to repel the attack in Korea." The memorandum cited volumes of historical and legal precedents to justify the president's decision to use force in Korea. It offered as further justification the membership of the United States in the United Nations and the resolutions of the Security Council, June 25 and 27. The North Korean aggression had to be met, the memorandum argued, because it constituted a threat not only to international peace, but to the peace and security of the United States and the security of United States forces in the Pacific area. Concluding, the memorandum read: "These interests of the United States are interests which the President as Commander in Chief can protect by the employment of the Armed Forces of the United States without a declaration of war. It was they which the President's order of June 27 did protect. This order was within his authority as Commander in Chief." [71]

The military situation continued to worsen. Virtually unimpeded, a column of North Korean tanks entered Seoul on June 26 (Washington time). A spokesman for Rhee's government, which had to flee the city, said that the Korean President "is greatly disappointed with American aid; coming as late as it has it is very difficult to save anything. We have nothing to stop those tanks." On June 27 MacArthur's headquarters announced that American combat aircraft were engaged in bombing and strafing missions south of the 38th parallel in support of South Korean ground forces. United States forces were also engaged in limited action below the parallel. During the day, four Russian-built North Korean (YAK) fighters were shot down over Seoul by American aircraft.[72] One conclusion emerges from these combat reports: Truman ordered United States forces into combat in support of the South Korean armies prior to the passage of the Security Council resolution requesting member nations to intervene militarily. That resolution was not passed until late in the evening of the twenty-seventh.

Warren Austin, the United States representative at the United Nations, addressed the Security Council on Tuesday afternoon, June 27. Austin told the other delegates that North Korea's failure to accept their resolution of June 25 constituted an attack upon the United Nations itself. He informed the council that the United States stood ready to provide military aid to South Korea. Austin then offered a resolution asking member nations to provide South Korea with the forces necessary to repel the attack.[73] After long delays while the Indian and Egyptian delegates vainly attempted to receive voting instructions from their governments, at 10:45 P.M. the Security Council adopted the American-sponsored resolution seven to one, with two abstentions. The operative line of the document recommended "that the Members of the United Nations furnish such assistance to the Republic of Korea as may be necessary to repel the armed attack and to restore international peace and security in the area." [74]

That Truman sent American forces into combat before the sanctifying resolution was even proposed, thus presenting the Security Council with *a fait accompli*, is true, but of little consequence. The State Department had every assurance that the resolution would be approved that day. Additionally, a very broad interpretation of the June 25 resolution might be taken as justification for military intervention by UN members.[75]

The combat reports received in Washington on Wednesday gave little cause for optimism. The South Korean forces, driven from Seoul on Tuesday, had continued a "demoralized retreat" during the night. Early on June 28 (Washington time) the Korean forces were reportedly holding the enemy advance in check at the Han River, south of the capital. One report reaching Washington indicated that two of the seven understrength ROK divisions had "disintegrated." American B-29 bombers attacked Kimpo airfield (near Seoul) while jet fighters were seeing action against North Korean tanks and troops. The jets were not able to provide close support for ground troops because no direct ground-to-air communications had yet been established.[76]

The president met with the National Security Council on the afternoon of June 28. This was a regularly scheduled meeting of the council. Truman had not seen fit to call this body into special session since the Korean crisis had begun. The president began the meeting with a brief review of the bleak military picture in Korea. Vice-president Barkley, arriving late, informed Truman that the draft extension bill had just cleared the Senate by a unanimous vote. This meant that both houses of the Congress had shown almost total unanimity in conferring greater military authority on the president. Acheson cautioned that the present enthusiasm would wither away if Americans began to die and taxes rise because of Korea. "The President, mistaking my purpose," Acheson recalls, "insisted that we could not back out of the course upon which we had started." [77]

The remainder of the Security Council meeting dealt with the probable intentions of the Soviet Union and the desirability of making administration policy clear to MacArthur. Truman and many others were anticipating that the Soviet Union would take overt action somewhere in the world in order to capitalize on American preoccupation with Korea. Another consideration was direct military involvement by the Soviet Union in the fighting in Korea, particularly since the United States had entered the conflict. Army Secretary Pace told Truman that he had instructed military intelligence to be especially alert for signs of a Soviet move into Korea. Truman told Pace that he had already ordered an intensification of strategic intelligence efforts in the areas of northern Europe, Bulgaria and Yugoslavia. The president also ordered a thorough reappraisal of American policies in all areas contiguous with the USSR.[78]

During the National Security Council meeting of June 28, Air Force Secretary Thomas Finletter suggested to the president that General Vandenberg be sent to Tokyo to personally instruct MacArthur in the strategic thinking of the administration. Finletter was concerned that MacArthur might err in an initial response to new developments in Korea without such instructions. However, Truman vetoed this suggestion on the grounds that he needed the chiefs of staff with him in Washington during this crisis. The limited records available do not indicate whether or not the subject of employing American ground forces in Korea was discussed in this council session. It is known that General John Church had reported to MacArthur from the scene on Wednesday (Korean time), his belief that the 38th parallel could not be restored as the boundary line without the use of United States ground combat forces.[79]

General MacArthur flew to Korea from Tokyo at dawn, June 29 (Korean time). At some point in the flight he dictated an order to Lieutenant General George E. Stratemeyer to be sent by radiogram to Major General Earl E. Partridge, who, in Stratemeyer's absence, was commanding the Far East air force. The order read: "Take out North Korean Airfield immediately. No publicity. MacArthur approves." The Far East commander took this action without consultation or approval from Washington. General Whitney, who was on the flight to Korea, explained that MacArthur felt that allowing North Korea a sanctuary above the 38th parallel "would not be giving to the South Korean defenders the 'effective military assistance' that the U.N. had directed him to give. He concluded . . . that implicit in his directive was the discretion normal to field command." MacArthur was, of course, never actually under the "direction" of the United Nations. The directive from his superiors in Washington had specifically drawn the 38th parallel as the outer limits of United States military activity. There is no record of any countermanding order or message of censure from Washington. Instead, less than twenty-four hours later, the president sent MacArthur authorization to do precisely what he had already done.[80]

The reports arriving in Washington from Korea on Thursday, June 29, continued to describe the ROK position as desperate. The North Koreans were massing along the Han River for another push southward. The South Korean army was sustaining very heavy casualties, and its ability to continue resistance was diminishing hourly. Shortly before noon, Secretary Johnson called Truman to suggest that he hold another meeting with the National Security Council. The president agreed, and the meeting was scheduled for 5:00 that evening.[81]

One hour before his meeting with the Security Council, Truman held his regular weekly press conference, the first since the crisis in Korea erupted. In response to a reporter's question, Truman said that the United States was not at war. Asked to elaborate, he said that South

Korea had been "unlawfully attacked by a bunch of bandits." A reporter then asked if it would be accurate to refer to American assistance as a "police action" under the aegis of the United Nations. "That is exactly what it amounts to," was the president's reply. The unfortunate phrase became part of the language and a source of embarrassment to Truman. The president wanted action in Korea to be undertaken through the United Nations. In a personal letter written in July, he revealed this concern: "Every effort is being made to line up the United Nations in a practical way on our side. I hope we can get it worked out so that all the allies on our side will be in the fight." [82]

In the Security Council meeting following his press conference, Truman listened as Secretary Johnson presented the text of a proposed directive to MacArthur which had been drafted by the Joint Chiefs of Staff. Johnson said that the major difficulties encountered by the United States forces in carrying out the assigned mission of aiding Korea were many: A lack of proper ground-air liaison existed between American fighters and the ROK army; support missions being flown from Japan could spend only minutes over Korea because of fuel expenditure on the long flights; transportation facilities available in Korea made supplying American munitions difficult; the prohibition of aerial and naval operations above the 38th parallel provided the enemy with a sanctuary and secure base of supply. The directive proposed to offset these disadvantages by allowing MacArthur to strike above the 38th parallel (the conferees being apparently unaware that MacArthur had already given such an order), by allowing the use of army service units of the Signal Corps and transport companies to provide air-ground communications and transport of munitions, and by allowing the use of army combat forces to be stationed in the Pusan-Chinhae area to protect the port and guard an airfield to be used by American fighter aircraft.[83]

In the general discussion that followed Johnson's presentation, the proposed directive underwent substantial revision. Both Secretary Pace and Truman were reluctant to allow a blanket endorsement for military action in North Korea. Truman also deleted some lines from the directive that implied that the United States was planning for war with the Soviet Union. After some modifications the president approved the directive for MacArthur, the major decisions being that military operations against North Korea were permitted and that the first ground combat units were committed, although not for actual combat purposes, since the Pusan area was some two hundred miles south of the existing battle lines.[84]

Later in the evening of June 29 Acheson called upon Truman to deliver to him the text of an offer just received from President Chiang Kai-shek. The generalissimo offered to provide thirty-three thousand combat troops to South Korea. The offer was apparently contingent upon American willingness to provide the transportation necessary from Formosa.[85] In his eagerness to involve other UN member nations in the Korean fighting, Truman wanted to accept the offer immediately. Acheson opposed this, arguing that the Chinese were probably not properly equipped and that they performed a much more valuable service by protecting Formosa, which was vulnerable to attack from the Chinese mainland. Although Truman was still disposed to accepting the offer, he agreed to postpone a decision until a conference the following day with Acheson, Johnson, and the joint chiefs.[86]

While these deliberations were going on in Washington, MacArthur was completing a personal reconnaissance of the Korean battlefields. The general later recalled that the battle-front scenes he witnessed convinced him that the South Koreans had already depleted their defensive potential. American naval and air support was not sufficient to reverse the tide: "Only the immediate commitment of ground troops could possibly do so. The answer I had come to seek was there. I would throw my occupation soldiers into this breach." [87] On the flight back to Tokyo, MacArthur drafted his report to the Pentagon. It called for a commitment to Korea far greater than Truman or his advisers had anticipated five days earlier.

About three o'clock on Friday morning, June 30, the Pentagon received a cable from MacArthur containing his report. The general said that the ROK forces were disorganized and ill equipped to repel the North Korean invaders. Unless some new factor was introduced, there was nothing to prevent the conquest of the entire peninsula. MacArthur felt that the only way to stop the North Korean advance and retake the lost ground was by employing United States ground combat forces. The cable concluded with a dire warning: "Unless provision is made for the full utilization of the Army-Navy-Air team . . . our mission will at best be needlessly costly in life, money and prestige. At worst, it might be doomed." [88]

Truman received a call from Army Secretary Pace shortly before five o'clock. Pace explained the substance of MacArthur's messages from Tokyo, stressing that the general was emphatic in his insistence that a combat troop authorization was of the utmost urgency. The army secretary asked Truman for instructions: "I told Pace to inform General MacArthur immediately that the use of one regimental combat team was approved." Within moments, the command decision Truman had reached alone in his bedroom at Blair House had been relayed to MacArthur. A few hours later the first units of the combat regiment began arriving by airlift at Pusan.[89]

A colonel from the Joint Staff came to Blair House from the Pentagon at seven o'clock to brief the president fully on all of the telegraphic conversations and the existing military situation in Korea. As soon as the briefing was completed, Truman called Secretary Johnson and said that he wanted a full-scale conference with his military and diplomatic advisers (the original Blair House conferees) in his office in 2½ hours. The president said his advisers should be prepared to discuss and make recommendations on MacArthur's request for two combat divisions and on the Nationalist Chinese troop offer.

The June 30 conference began with Truman asking his advisers if it would be worthwhile to accept the thirty-three thousand troops offered by Chiang Kai-shek. Acheson was against the idea for reasons expressed to Truman the previous evening. Additionally, he felt their use might encourage the Red Chinese to intervene in Korea. The joint chiefs were agreed that the best of Chiang's troops were not properly equipped or trained for modern combat operations. They believed that the available transport could be better used to transfer American forces to Korea. "I accepted," Truman wrote later, "the position taken by practically everyone else at this meeting; namely, that the Chinese offer ought to be politely declined." [90]

The discussion of committing other divisions into combat was brief. There is no indication that any adviser present dissented from the view that MacArthur should be allowed to use available United States infantry forces to stop the North Korean advance. Truman ordered that the limitations imposed upon American troop use in the directive of the previous evening be rescinded and that MacArthur be given full discretionary authority to use the ground forces of his command in Korea. The order did not limit MacArthur to the two divisions which he had requested. At Admiral Sherman's suggestion, Truman also approved a second order to the Far East Command, establishing a naval blockade of the entire coastline of North Korea. The meeting was over in thirty minutes. There seems to have been little consideration given to the eventual cost in lives and treasure that could and did ensue from this decision. The employment of land armies on foreign soil is usually regarded as an irrevocable commitment. This distinction is not accorded to aerial and naval combat, probably because of their remote and impersonal character.[91]

The president met with the congressional leadership at eleven o'clock in order to inform them of the decisions he had just reached. Some thirty officials of the administration were joined in the Cabinet Room of the White House by fifteen senators and representatives. Truman began the meeting by summarizing the actions taken by both the United States and the United Nations during the preceding five days. The president then acquainted the gathering with the latest battle reports from Korea, which described an increasingly desperate general retreat by the South Korean forces. Truman then told the congressional leaders of his recent decision to send in combat units. There was a stunned silence, followed by several comments indicating general approval.[92]

A few members of Congress present registered varying degrees of disapproval with the way Truman had decided, but none challenged the decision itself. Senator Connally, not by way of censure, but "for the record," asked Truman if this were a unilateral action by the United States, or in support of the UN resolutions. The president assured him that this step was taken in concert with the United Nations.[93] Senator Kenneth Wherry questioned the legal authority of the commander in chief to make such a decision without the consent of Congress. Truman replied that this was an emergency situation requiring immediate action; that it was his duty to act and he had. Senator Alexander Smith suggested that Truman could still seek a congressional resolution approving his decision and the president agreed to consider such a step. Wherry began again to question Truman's right to act, but he was cut off by Representative Dewey Short, the ranking Republican on the Armed Services Committee. Short told Truman that he was certain he spoke for "practically everyone in Congress" in thanking the president for the quality of his leadership in the present crisis. On that note, the meeting adjourned.[94]

Shortly after the meeting with the congressional leadership, the White House released a presidential statement to the press explaining that they had been given a complete review of military activities in Korea. The statement also noted that consonant with the UN Security Council resolution, Truman had ordered the air force to attack designated military targets in North Korea, ordered the navy to blockade the entire Korean coast, and authorized General MacArthur "to use certain supporting ground units." The press release was deliberately left vague for reasons of security. However, the congressional leaders were told very little more than that in the meeting with regard to the number of troops that were to be committed or how they would be employed.[95]

The decisions made on Friday morning, June 30, were conclusive; Truman had committed the United States to defense of South Korea. He found no difficulty in explaining why: "We could not stand idly by and allow the Communist imperialists to assume that they were free to go into Korea or elsewhere. This challenge had to be met—and it was met." [96] But the president, in meeting this challenge, went to great lengths to point out that the United States was merely acting as a member of the United Nations, diligently upholding the principle of collective security. In truth, considerations of power politics and the American doctrine of containment weighed heavily in the decision to intervene. As Robert Osgood phrased it, "Our eagerness to represent American intervention as an altruistic act of pure collective security tended to obscure the underlying basis of *Realpolitik* without which intervention, regardless of UN sanction, would have been unjustified." [97]

There is no doubt that Truman's decision to intervene in Korea was initially accorded strong public acceptance. As measured by public opinion pollsters, Truman's popularity was at one of its lowest points just prior to the Korean crisis. The Gallup poll taken a few days before the fighting began showed 37 percent of the public approving of his leadership. The record indicates that the president was under no significant pressure from either domestic or foreign sources either to intervene or stay out of the Korean conflict. Also it is known that Truman deliberately excluded any consideration of domestic political repercussions from the conferences held during the week in which these decisions were made. It is possible that, as an old political hand, he knew intuitively that his decision would receive strong public support.

In any event, such was the case. A Roper poll taken in August, 1950, claimed that a total of 73 percent of the people agreed that Truman was right in sending the troops into Korea.[98]

This military intervention in Korea, which Truman later called his "toughest" decision, was made without calling on the National Security Council, which his unification reforms had established as the primary advisory body on major military and foreign policy decisions. The council did not have contingency plans available, because the Korean peninsula had not been included in long-range strategic planning. The deliberative process of the council, in which policy recommendations evolve gradually from a series of position papers drafted by several agencies which must be coordinated at different administrative levels, was too time consuming to be utilized in a crisis requiring immediate decisions. However, even while Truman bypassed his Security Council for the sake of expediency, almost all of the members of that body were present at the five informal meetings from which these major policy decisions emerged. Truman preferred to work through the conventional staff and command structure created by his administration, but he was flexible and confident enough to find *ad hoc* solutions in an emergency condition.[99]

Truman's decision to forego asking Congress for authorization to intervene in Korea has far more profound implications than his decision to ignore the formal machinery of the National Security Council. He bypassed Congress on the advice of Secretary Acheson: "I . . . recommended that the President should not ask for a resolution of approval, but rest on his constitutional authority as Commander in Chief of the armed forces." As with the decision not to involve the National Security Council, Truman was partially motivated by pressing considerations of time. Certainly historical precedent supports the commander in chief's prerogative of committing troops without prior approval of Congress. However, it is difficult to comprehend why Truman did not ask Congress to sanction his decisions after they were made. In the first weeks of the war, with the nation responding with generous ardor, aflush with crusading zeal at yet another opportunity to safeguard democracy, the consent of Congress was an absolute certainty.[100] Since Truman chose to act alone, he also stood alone as the martial spirit faded from the nation when confronted by the bitter reality of defeat in the bleak hills of Korea.

11 / The Policeman I

This is the Greece of the Far East. If we are tough enough now, there won't be any next step.[1]

—HARRY S. TRUMAN

Once the decision was made to intervene in Korea, Truman established a procedural system wherein he kept a close supervisory control over the conduct of the war. Each morning at about ten o'clock, General Bradley or an officer from the Joint Staff would call on the president and provide him with a full briefing on the battle reports received from Korea in the preceding twenty-four hours. As commander in chief, Truman insisted that all directives concerning the Korean War, except those involving the most routine of matters, had to be presented to him for approval prior to their being transmitted to the Far East Command.[2]

The day-to-day strategic direction of the war was handled by the Joint Chiefs of Staff. Military problems were referred to the joint chiefs from the Far East Command, the United Nations Command, the National Security Council, the three service secretaries and the State Department. These problems were then channeled to the Joint Staff of the Joint Chiefs of Staff for deliberation and the drafting of a paper. The joint chiefs would then consider the paper's proposals. If their decision necessitated a directive to the commander in chief, Far East (CINCFE), it was transmitted to the president through the secretary of defense and the National Security Council. If Truman assented, the order was then forwarded to the theater commander by the joint chiefs. While very few commands to the military bore Truman's name, they were all cleared through him. For the remainder of his presidency, Truman never slackened this close control. He considered it part of his function as commander in chief to make all final decisions and approve all strategic plans dealing with the fighting in Korea. Truman's military chiefs and civilian administrators in the Pentagon clearly assumed a subordinate role under this style of leadership. As Wilber Hoare wrote in his essay on Truman as commander in chief, "The actions of the Secretary of Defense and of the JCS all fell into one of two categories—advice to the commander in chief or implementation of his directives." [3] The system worked because the civilian advisers and the military chiefs worked well together, free from most of the interservice bickering that had fragmented efforts at unified command in the past.

From the very beginning of the war, Truman gave increased prestige and importance to the deliberations and recommendations of the National Security Council. The president ordered the council to meet weekly, and he regularly sat in on these sessions, a practice he had deliberately avoided in the past. On July 6, the first time the Security Council met following the decision to send in land armies, Truman gave instructions to all present that he did not want unilateral proposals regarding Korea sent to him directly. He said that recommendations requiring presidential action must be transmitted to him through the machinery of the National Security Council.[4] Except in extraordinary circumstances, policy was formulated and decisions made through this highly institutionalized civil-military staff structure.

General MacArthur, who was seventy years old in 1950, shouldered a heavy burden. He was supreme commander for the Allied powers in Japan (SCAP), the single executive authority for the administration of the Japanese nation. He was commander in chief, Far East, the overall authority for all American military forces in the Far East. The general was also military governor of the Ryukyu Islands and was in technical control of all United States ground forces operating in the Far Eastern theater. And, as of July 8, he was also commander in chief, United Nations Command (CINCUNC), exercising command responsibilities over the military forces of all nations operating in and around Korea.[5] MacArthur had accepted this additional command although the sum of his existing responsibilities would have easily broken a far younger, less gifted man.

The placing of all forces in Korea under a United Nations banner did not, in fact, substantially change anything. While Truman had to practice some restraint in order to maintain United Nations support of the Korean operations, the links in the chain of command remained the same. MacArthur still reported to the army chief of staff (J. Lawton Collins) and through him to the joint chiefs, secretary of defense, National Security Council, and finally, to the commander in chief, who was not obliged to clear anything with the United Nations. MacArthur himself later testified: "My connection with the United Nations was largely nominal. . . . Everything I did came from our own Chiefs of Staff. . . . I had no direct connection with the United Nations whatsoever." [6] Had the administration been obliged to act through the Security Council, there would have been problems. On August 1 the Soviet Union ended a seven-month boycott of the sessions. Shortly thereafter the Soviet representative became president of the council.

By early July, 1950, American ground troops were actively engaged in combat against the North Korean People's Army (NKPA). MacArthur became quickly aware that his first estimate of two divisions would be insufficient to repulse the aggressors. The general sent several requests to Washington for various infantry, airborne and marine units, as well as three medium tank battalions and seven hundred more combat aircraft. On July 7 MacArthur told the joint chiefs that turning back the North Koreans would require 4½ full-strength infantry divisions and numerous other support forces. He reported that he found the enemy to be "both skillful and resourceful." Intelligence estimates at the time held that the North Korean invading force numbered about ninety thousand. MacArthur had ten thousand Americans and twenty-five thousand ROK forces with which to meet the enemy.[7]

Reports coming in from the Far East Command during the second week of July continued to emphasize the need for more troops and the gross underestimation of the training and equipment of the North Korean People's Army. On the ninth, MacArthur informed the joint chiefs that his tactical situation continued to worsen. He asked that four more divisions, with all components, be sent to him, over and above those already requisitioned. "The situation," MacArthur concluded, "has developed into a major operation." On the sixteenth, General Collins, army chief of staff, sent his own estimate of the tactical position of the United Nations Command to Truman. Collins praised MacArthur's leadership and the effectiveness with which the general had committed and employed his forces. However, Collins added, the North Koreans were "well-equipped, well-led, and battle-trained and . . . have at times out-numbered our troops by as much as twenty to one." [8]

Although MacArthur was certain that he had to have more troops at once, he was optimistic in a personal communication to Truman on July 19. He told the president that with the full deployment of the Eighth Army having by then been accomplished, the possibility of a North Korean victory had ended. MacArthur said his hold upon southern Korea was now a "secure base" and that he anticipated being able to establish a final stabilization line. The general said that the North Korean People's Army had enjoyed the advantages of surprise, overwhelming force, speed, and superior weapons. But the extraordinary speed with which the Eighth Army had deployed robbed the enemy of these advantages: "His supply line is insecure. He has had his great chance but failed to exploit it. We are now in Korea in force, and . . . we are there to stay." [9]

MacArthur recalled being amazed when his initial request for more troops was denied by Washington. He was told that his request was disapproved because no increase in troop strength had been authorized, shipping was in short supply and there was a need to maintain the American military posture in other areas of the world. MacArthur dismissed this as faulty reasoning which placed the Far East on the bottom of the priority list. The general felt it should have been obvious, "even to the non-military mind" that Soviet military deployment in eastern Europe was defensive, not offensive. Truman later wrote that area commanders always lack a global perspective and believe that their command should receive top priority. The president said this was understandable to him because during World War I he had considered his artillery battery to be the center of the entire war effort and had continually fought for more consideration for his unit.[10]

The administration had not completely disapproved MacArthur's troop recommendations, as he implied. Decision was postponed on any major commitment of American forces in Korea over and above the units performing occupational duties in the Far East. Truman was reluctant to engage a large body of troops without positive confirmation that the Soviet Union would not take action elsewhere in the world. To this end, he had asked the State and Defense departments to consider the probable course of Soviet conduct and report to him at a cabinet meeting on July 14, 1950. The report concluded that the Soviet Union possessed the military capability, either alone or in concert with satellite nations, of beginning a general war or applying pressure at numerous locations along common borders. Acheson told the president that Defense and State could not agree on which area the Soviets might select to apply military pressure. However, he told Truman that the two agencies were in complete agreement that such a danger existed. Truman was also informed that should such military action occur, the United States did not possess sufficient military power to make an adequate response.[11]

The report of the secretaries of state and defense recommended that Truman take several steps that represent the first efforts to implement NSC–68, the major policy-planning paper drafted just prior to the outbreak of the Korean conflict. The president was urged to request an increase in the authorized manpower levels of the armed forces from Congress, as well as substantial appropriations for an increased production of military goods and the power to allocate supplies of certain critical raw materials. Truman approved these proposals and five days later (July 19), sent a special message to Congress requesting everything the report had called for.[12]

The president's message of July 19 traced the course of recent events in Korea and elsewhere in the world, insisting that circumstances dictated that the United States increase its total military strength, not just to meet the needs in Korea, but to prepare the common defense of all free nations to resist further anticipated aggression. The requested increments fell into three categories: (1) more men, supplies, and equipment were required to meet the situation in Korea; (2) over and above the needs for defending Korea, the force levels of the armed services as well as the supporting matériel must be substantially increased; (3) American military support of other nations must be augmented by increased appropriations. The president told Congress he had instructed the secretary of defense to exceed budgeted levels for military personnel in the army, navy and air force. The Selective Service System had been ordered to increase the draft in order to fill the allocated spaces. Truman's message also revealed that he had directed the secretary of defense to activate as many National Guard units and army, navy and air force reserve components as might be required. The day after his message was sent to Congress, Truman received a note from John Foster Dulles of the State Department. Dulles told the president that talks he had with the Republican leadership on the message indicated he would receive strong bipartisan support.[13]

Truman found the Congress most cooperative in providing the manpower levels and additional appropriations which he requested in this and other messages during the next few months. Before requesting additional force levels from Congress, he had already authorized the army to increase its manpower by 110,000 "spaces" above the total strength of 592,000 at the beginning of July. On the day Truman's message went up to Congress (July 19), a bill was introduced which would remove all statutory limitations on personnel ceilings for the services for the next four years. The bill was approved on August 8, 1950. In the next few months a bewildering series of measures flowed swiftly through the Congress moving the country, as Acheson put it, "in a somewhat disorderly way into a more formidable military posture." The rapidity of this partial mobilization was amazing. For example, within eleven months the size of the army had almost tripled. The assumptions which guided Truman and his planners in this urgent rearmament effort were taken largely from NSC–68.[14]

To the small American force first committed to battle in early July, the additional troops and equipment came too late. They were committed to fighting a superior force with outdated equipment. In a letter to Eleanor Roosevelt, Truman denied that the forces were ill equipped for combat, an accusation made in a story in the New York *Herald Tribune* on August 8, 1950. The president told Mrs. Roosevelt that he had checked with "no less an authority than General Bradley himself," and the general had assured him that the story was untrue. Apparently the story had been leaked to the press by someone high in the administration, for Truman wrote: "Nevertheless, I fervently wish that some of my top men would learn the old, old lesson about the golden quality of silence." [15] But even the official army history of the Korean War does not support Truman and Bradley's contention that these forces were properly equipped. One of the major problems noted in the account of early fighting, for example, was the lack of any ordnance capable of stopping the powerful Russian-built T–34 tank with which the North Koreans were armed. Almost all equipment was of World War II vintage; much of it was obsolete and worn and not combat serviceable. "Equally bad," was the term used by the official army historian to describe the physical condition of military vehicles and combat weaponry employed in the first months of the fighting in Korea.[16]

The ground combat forces initially committed in Korea fought gallantly and suffered great losses. Essentially, they were involved in a delaying action, trading space for time. MacArthur felt they did admirably, causing the enemy to delay and redeploy in a conventional line of battle, rather than pressing through with their unstoppable tank columns. This miscalculation of American strength by the North Koreans gave MacArthur time to place enough force in Korea to establish a secure foothold on the southeastern tip of the peninsula. By early August the Korean and American defenders were crowded into the "Pusan Perimeter," an area roughly the size of the state of Connecticut. The perimeter was maintained by Lieutenant General Walton H. Walker, commander of the Eighth Army, to whom MacArthur had delegated field command over all ground forces in Korea.[17] The important thing about the perimeter was that it fixed the enemy in a relatively static position on the end of a very long, vulnerable line of supply.

MacArthur had always intended, once he was able to halt the North Korean advance, to strike deep behind the enemy, cutting supply and communication lines and blocking the escape routes. This would place the main body in an untenable position, between the "hammer" and the "anvil" of military jargon. Early in July, MacArthur had informed Washington that this was his intention: "Once he (NKPA) is fixed, it will be my purpose fully to exploit our air and sea control, and by amphibious maneuver, strike him behind his mass of ground force." [18] Given MacArthur's extraordinary success in World War II with amphibious sweeps striking at his opponent's rear, it was natural for him to devise such a tactical maneuver for relieving the pressure on the Pusan Perimeter.

It was MacArthur's genius as a tactician to choose the one site the enemy would consider least likely as an invasion target and the one locale that would bring the quickest military rewards if successful. The general's problem was that he alone, among the military hierarchy, believed that such an assault could succeed. For MacArthur selected the port city of Inchon (Inch'on) on the western coast of Korea. The second largest port in South Korea, Inchon is located on the Yellow Sea, some twenty-five miles west of the capital city of Seoul, which is a point of convergence for the highways and rail lines of Korea. However desirable a target the Inchon-Seoul area was, the physical geography created seemingly insurmountable obstacles to a massive amphibious assault. As one of MacArthur's planning staff for Inchon remarked:

"We drew up a list of every conceivable and natural handicap and Inchon had them all." [19]

MacArthur was firmly convinced that Inchon must be the attack site. On July 23 he wired the Pentagon for clearance of the operation, telling his superiors that the alternative would be an expensive, protracted breakthrough from the Pusan Perimeter. The general waited three weeks for a response. When it came, it was a wire informing him that army Chief of Staff Collins and Chief of Naval Operations Sherman were flying to Tokyo to discuss the proposed operation with him. MacArthur believed Collins and Sherman were sent to dissuade him, not to discuss his plans. Behind Washington's opposition to the Inchon invasion, according to MacArthur, were General Bradley and President Truman; the former believing that amphibious operations were obsolete, the latter opposing any use of the marines except as a police force.[20]

MacArthur and his staff met with Collins and Sherman on August 23, to discuss the Inchon invasion. A naval briefing team began the meeting by explaining that many hazards were present at Inchon. Most notably, one of the greatest tides in the world, that on the anticipated invasion date (September 15) would fall about thirty feet at full ebb, leaving mud flats extending from the shore as much as two miles. This meant that landing craft would have about two hours in the morning and two and a half hours in the evening to land troops, neutralize defenses, secure a beachhead and prepare for counterattack. The rest of the time the landing craft would be stuck helplessly in mud awaiting the next full tide. The marine invaders would face sixteen-foot seawalls in an attack on a highly built up area offering extensive cover to the defensive forces.[21]

MacArthur took the floor and in a very eloquent forty-five-minute discourse, made believers of almost all of the skeptics present. He argued that the value of striking at Seoul was simply that it was the key to the extended enemy supply line. He recognized all of the navy's objections as real but not insuperable obstacles. To those who doubted, he cited the example of James Wolfe at Quebec in 1759, who won a pivotal battle of the French and Indian War by attacking the Marquis de Montcalm at the one point where the French deemed an attack to be impossible. In closing, MacArthur said that he would be at Inchon, and if the defenses were too strong, he would order withdrawal: "The only loss then will be my professional reputation. But Inchon will not fail. Inchon will succeed. And it will save 100,000 lives." [22]

Following their meeting with MacArthur, Sherman and Collins returned to Washington to discuss Inchon with the other joint chiefs. The plans were subsequently brought to Truman with the joint chiefs' recommendation that they be approved. The president agreed, later writing: "It was a daring strategic conception. I had the greatest confidence that it would succeed." Truman's enthusiasm after the fact is quite strong, but the joint chiefs' directive he approved for transmission to MacArthur carried qualifications. He was to be allowed to attack Inchon if the defenses there proved ineffective. But he was urged to consider some other site south of Inchon along the western coast of the Korean peninsula. [23]

Since the invasion of Inchon had not been ruled out, MacArthur concentrated on it with single-minded purpose. It is a tribute to his military brilliance that the Inchon landing went off on September 15 exactly as planned. The Tenth Corps, especially created for this attack, captured Inchon against unexpectedly light resistance. The American force pushed inland against stiffer opposition, with one arm heading south to seize Suwon and the other moving relentlessly toward Seoul, which was recaptured on the twenty-eighth. On September 16 General Walker had begun to push out of the Pusan Perimeter. His Eighth Army gained slowly at first, but the North Korean People's Army, cut off from supplies and reinforcements and aware of the impending envelopment, broke into disorderly retreat on September 23. Three days later, elements of the Tenth Corps and Eighth Army linked up. Allied troops continued to roll back the North Korean army with little difficulty once the rout began. At the end of September organized resistance had ceased south of the 38th parallel. [24]

The joint chiefs had doubted the wisdom of Inchon from the very beginning, but willingly acknowledged MacArthur's triumph: "You have exploited to the utmost all capabilities and opportunities. Your transition from defensive to offensive operations was magnificently planned, timed and executed." Truman sent a message praising the "brilliant maneuver" that had culminated in the liberation of Seoul. [25]

In the midst of the Inchon-Seoul campaign the Defense Department acquired a new secretary, for Truman found it expedient to replace

Louis Johnson. As secretary of defense, Johnson had come under critical fire for the lack of preparedness of the American military that had been made evident by the early fighting in Korea. Although this condition was caused mainly by the budget cuts imposed by Truman and the Congress on the military establishment, the secretary was the natural target of criticism. Additionally, it was widely known that Johnson was unable to get along with Dean Acheson and the State Department. Johnson testified in 1951 that he had no idea why he had been made to resign, but it would seem that his feud with Acheson and an unfavorable press made him an expendable liability to Truman. Johnson's testimony makes it clear that his resignation was a result of pressure from the White House. He said he did not know why he was "ousted" and regretted *having* to resign three days before the Inchon landing, which he felt would end much of the criticism, since he had favored the plan from the outset. When the White House failed to deny an Associated Press story that he was to be removed and Acheson was to remain in the cabinet, he called Truman and later resigned as a result of that telephone conversation.[26]

In his letter of resignation, dated September 12, Johnson recalled telling Truman when accepting the post that in performing his tasks as secretary he would probably make more enemies than friends and now admitted, "somewhat ruefully," that he had been right. He closed by recommending that Truman appoint as his successor a man whose stature would promote unity, General George C. Marshall. Truman accepted Johnson's resignation in a letter dated the same day. He spoke of the "terribly regrettable circumstances" that had arisen, forcing him to "concur" in Johnson's decision to resign, effective September 19. The president also accepted the recommendation that Marshall be appointed as the new secretary of defense. Johnson departed without rancor and full of praise for Truman and Marshall.[27] For seventy-year-old General Marshall to be appointed, Truman would have to change the law, since the National Security Act of 1947 in Section 202(a) wisely prohibited service by a military officer as secretary of defense.

Truman was prepared to act on Marshall's appointment. The day after Johnson's letter of resignation, he sent the necessary draft legislation to the chairmen of the House and Senate Armed Services Committees. In a covering letter, Truman explained that he believed strongly in the "general principle" that civilians should direct the Department of Defense. "However," Truman wrote, "in view of the present critical circumstances and of General Marshall's unusual qualifications, I believe that the national interest will be served best by making an exception in this case." The Congress was willing. On September 18, only five days after submitting his draft legislation, Truman was able to sign the bill into law. Senate confirmation quickly followed, and Marshall took the oath of office on September 20, 1950.[28]

The defeat of the aggressors in South Korea in the last week of September restored the status quo antebellum. It must have seemed to many that MacArthur's bold strike at Inchon had dramatically achieved the objective for which the United States had fought. At the outset Acheson had said that American intervention was "solely for the purpose of restoring the Republic of Korea to its status prior to the invasion from the north." But the expulsion of the North Korean attackers led to a decision to change objectives from maintaining the independence of South Korea to the conquest and political unification of all Korea. Truman's decision to cross the 38th parallel was a tragic miscalculation.[29]

The first suggestion that the United Nations forces should carry the fight into North Korea came from MacArthur. On July 13 he told Generals Collins and Vandenberg that the destruction of the enemy forces might necessitate the occupation of all North Korea. On July 31, 1950, the Joint Chiefs of Staff completed a study of crossing the parallel, which was submitted to the State and Defense departments for comment. The plan recommended that MacArthur be allowed to cross the boundary line in order to defeat the North Korean People's Army and occupy the entire country. The proposal carried three contingent assumptions: (1) that the Americans would provide the men and matériel sufficient to the task without depleting forces in other strategic areas around the world; (2) that no threat of Soviet or Chinese intervention in Korea or elsewhere then existed; (3) that Truman, Congress, and the United States accepted the unification and independence of all of Korea as a new war objective.[30]

The National Security Council proposals, incorporating some modifications suggested by the Joint Chiefs of Staff, were approved by Truman on September 11, 1950. The president also allowed the joint chiefs to send MacArthur a tentative advisory in respect to operations above the 38th parallel. The message to MacArthur, dated September

15, informed him that final decisions on future operations could not be made until several factors were added to the equation regarding Soviet and Chinese intentions, the risk of general war involved, and the viewpoint of friendly members of the United Nations. However, MacArthur was told that it was Washington's belief that legal justification for crossing the parallel into North Korea already existed on the basis of the UN resolution of June 27. The directive instructed MacArthur to make plans for the invasion and occupation of North Korea, but to execute the order only with the express consent of President Truman. The general was also cautioned not to undertake ground action into North Korea if Soviet or Chinese Communist units were found to occupy the area, although he could continue to attack with his air and naval units. One last warning was a portent of the future: MacArthur was informed that if a major Chinese Communist force penetrated below the 38th parallel, he was to resist this incursion as long as it was militarily feasible to do so, but that the United States would not—as a matter of policy—allow itself to be drawn into a general war with China.[31]

Six days after MacArthur was instructed to prepare for an advance into North Korea, a reporter asked Truman if he had decided what American troops would do when they reached the 38th parallel: "No, I have not. That is a matter for the United Nations to decide." Asked in a press conference on September 28, seven days later, if MacArthur had been granted specific authority to cross the boundary, the president replied that he could not answer the question publicly yet. The questioner persisted, asking Truman if he considered that MacArthur had implied authority to cross the 38th parallel. Truman replied: "General MacArthur is under direct orders of the President and the Chief of Staff, and he will follow those orders." Truman had inadvertently tripped on the thread of fiction which held that the United Nations, not the United States, was determining the course of action in Korea. A reporter reminded him that a week earlier he had said that crossing the 38th parallel was a decision to be made by the United Nations, but he was now saying that the United Nations commander would take orders directly from him on whether or not to cross the parallel. Truman tried to salvage the sinking myth by saying that while it was he who would give orders to MacArthur, the United Nations would have to first decide the matter and then request that he command MacArthur to act.[32]

On the day prior to this press conference of September 28, Truman had approved a directive which the joint chiefs transmitted to MacArthur. Based on the National Security Council policy statement the president had endorsed on the eleventh, it began: "Your military objective is the destruction of the North Korean armed forces. In attaining this objective, you are authorized to conduct military operations north of the thirty-eighth parallel in Korea." The directive also specifically commanded that the general was not to allow his ground, sea, or air elements to cross the borders of North Korea into Manchuria or the USSR. MacArthur was further instructed to use only Korean ground forces in those provinces bordering China and the Soviet Union. Decisions as to the "character of occupation of North Korea" would be made later as circumstances warranted.[33]

Why Truman and his advisers decided to cross the 38th parallel, having already achieved their limited objective of containment, seems to have been based on considerations largely divorced from the original purpose. The explanation favored by Acheson was that it was a tactical decision. Not to pursue the retreating North Korean force and destroy it would have violated a fundamental principle of warfare. The North Korean army, if not pursued and conquered, would be able to regroup in its sanctuary and launch another offensive. At the same time, barring an unknown factor such as Chinese intervention, the political unification of Korea would constitute a desirable by-product of this purely military operation.[34]

That an imperative military need to cross into North Korea motivated Truman's decision is unlikely, at best. The very fact that the secretary of state took the initiative in urging this step would argue against such an assumption. The unexpectedly swift conquest of the invading army after months of clinging tenaciously to a toe-hold on the peninsula had created a new atmosphere of confidence. Additionally, the opportunity to accomplish the long-frustrated promise of a unified, independent Korea must have been an irresistible temptation, seemingly easy to achieve. The threat of Chinese intervention was not taken too seriously. One other factor may have been weighed in the balance by the president: His administration's Far Eastern policies had been severely criticized since the fighting began and the midterm congressional elections were only weeks away. There is no justification for saying that Truman ordered the invasion of North Korea in response to domestic political pressures, but the fact is that the pressure existed. The subconscious mind is a trackless labyrinth and it would be presumptuous to attempt to measure its influence on conscious decisions. On the other hand, it would be naïve to assume that Truman was superior to personal and political considerations that influence the best of men.

Having received authority to invade North Korea in the September 27 directive from Washington, MacArthur submitted his plans for this attack to the Joint Chiefs of Staff. He proposed to send the Eighth Army up the western coastal corridor through Kaesong and Sariwon to Pyongyang, the capital of North Korea. By an amphibious operation, the Tenth Corps was to attack Wonsan, a port city on the eastern coast, roughly parallel to Pyongyang. Following a juncture along the Wonsan-Pyongyang road by his separate commands, MacArthur proposed to advance northward toward the Yalu River. Since his directive had instructed him not to use non-Korean forces close to the Russian and Chinese borders, the general's plan called for the use of South Korean forces only, north of a line (Chungjo-Yongwon-Hungnam) fifty miles beyond the Pyongyang-Wonsan line and approximately sixty miles below the mouth of the Yalu. MacArthur ended by saying he had no indication of entry into Korea by major Russian or Chinese Communist armies. Both Secretary of Defense Marshall and Secretary of State Acheson recommended MacArthur's operational plans to Truman, who gave his consent.[35]

The General Assembly of the United Nations adopted a resolution on October 7, 1950, which had the effect of sanctioning the invasion of North Korea by the United Nations Command. The resolution recommended that "all appropriate steps be taken to ensure conditions of stability throughout Korea . . . including the holding of elections . . . for the establishment of a unified, independent and democratic government in the sovereign State of Korea." The thinking behind this act seemed to be more than just an effort to place the United Nations behind a decision already made by the American commander in chief. The United Nations was also changing objectives in the light of MacArthur's success, from simple preservation of the independence of South Korea, to the unification of all Korea as called for in the resolution of November 14, 1947.[36]

Truman received a message from President Rhee of South Korea following the liberation of Seoul that expressed deep gratitude: "The

Korean people will always cherish the memory of your bold leadership in defense of liberty." On October 11, ten days after this message, the president met with representatives of the Korean government. They thanked him for liberating their country and expressed the hope that now all of Korea could be united under the rule of President Rhee. Truman avoided committing himself on the question of unification, saying only that the United States would have to be guided by the forthcoming survey report of the United Nations commission.[37] The following day the UN interim committee resolved that South Korean civil authority extended only to the 38th parallel, and all civil control north of the border was delegated to General MacArthur. The United States endorsed the interim committee resolution on October 13. The resolution was declared "unacceptable" by the South Korean government on the following day. A week later President Rhee announced that it was his intention to rule over all of Korea.[38] The intervention of the Chinese forces would spoil these plans.

At nine o'clock on the morning of October 9, 1950 (Korean time), the American Eighth Army began its initial advance across the 38th parallel. It had been preceded by several divisions of the ROK army a few days earlier. The Korean units made excellent progress, particularly along the eastern seaboard. They captured Wonsan on October 10, two weeks before landings could be made there by units of the U.S. Tenth Corps. In the west, however, the Eighth Army met very strong resistance in its drive toward the North Korean capital city of Pyongyang. By October 14, the Eighth Army had moved approximately one third of the distance along the axis of advance toward its immediate objective, penetrating the major prepared defensive positions that the enemy had established between the 38th parallel and Pyongyang. The North Korean forces were now in confusion; an integral front line of resistance had ceased to exist. However, a few Chinese Communist soldiers had been captured by this time, an ominous portent of the full-scale intervention which China had been threatening since American troops first massed along the parallel.[39] At this point, on October 15, a unique meeting was held between the commander in chief of the United Nations Command and his commander in chief.

The White House released a presidential statement to the press on October 10, 1950, in which Truman announced that he would meet with MacArthur over the weekend in the Pacific to discuss the last phase of the United Nations operations in Korea and other matters relating to the Far East Command. Truman explained in his *Memoirs* that he had several reasons for wanting to talk with MacArthur: "The first and the simplest reason . . . was that we had never had any personal contacts at all, and I thought that he ought to know his Commander in Chief and that I ought to know the senior field commander in the Far East." Writing years later, Truman said that he also made the trip because MacArthur was out of touch with America, having been away for fourteen uninterrupted years. This long separation caused MacArthur to consider things from a limited perspective which gave priority to Far Eastern affairs. Truman hoped to help the general adjust his thinking to a broader picture. The president was also concerned about intelligence reports and repeated threats from Peking that Chinese forces would intervene in Korea. As for the timing of his trip to the mid-Pacific (they met on Wake Island), Truman had to speak on October 17 in San Francisco and a week later address the UN General Assembly in New York; he wanted to bring back a first-hand report from the United Nations commander.[40]

Secretary of State Acheson was invited by the president to join him in this conference with MacArthur. Acheson asked to be excused since he found the whole idea repugnant. He told Truman that the general already had many of the attributes of a foreign ruler and was just as difficult to control. Acheson thought it unwise for the president to go to MacArthur. To the secretary this was tantamount to acknowledging the general's image as a sovereign. "I wanted no part of it," Acheson later wrote, "and saw no good coming from it. . . . Talk should precede, not follow, the issuance of orders." In terms of protocol, the normal procedure would be for the commander in chief to summon a field commander to Washington. However, Truman was willing to go to MacArthur rather than pull him away from his command at this critical juncture.[41]

The timing of Truman's visit was probably most influenced by his concern over Chinese intentions and an incident on October 9 in which two F–80 fighter aircraft attacked a Soviet air station. The base was located sixty-two miles north of the Korean border and eighteen miles to the southwest of the Russian port of Vladivostok. When the Soviet Union protested this "gross violation" of its territory, an air force spokesman in Tokyo denied any knowledge of the charges, and the State Department said it was a matter to be taken up with the United Nations, since the planes operated under its auspices. But the day following the attack, Truman announced he was going to meet with MacArthur.[42]

Although the incident was not widely noted at the time, it may have had a dramatic effect on the president. From the outset of the fighting he had been vitally concerned with keeping Korea a limited conflict, to avoid giving China or the Soviet Union a reason to intercede and widen the war. Nations had gone to war in the past for less provocation than that generated by the errant F–80s. Four days after the Wake Island meeting, Ambassador Warren Austin presented a report to the Security Council from MacArthur. The report attributed the attack to navigational miscalculation by the pilots and failure to identify the target prior to their attack. Austin stated that disciplinary action was being instituted against the two pilots and that the commander of their air group had been relieved.[43]

Truman came to Wake Island bearing gifts; a five-pound box of candied plums for Mrs. MacArthur and a fourth Oak Leaf Cluster to add to the general's Distinguished Service Medal. For his part, MacArthur said he had been warned about Truman's "quick and violent temper and prejudices," but that he found the president to be courteous and humorous: "He has an engaging personality, a quick and witty tongue, and I liked him from the start." Truman recalled that MacArthur—they were meeting for the first and last time—was friendly and that he "found him a most stimulating and interesting person." [44] The two men met privately for approximately forty-five minutes and then met with other members of their staffs for a general conference lasting about ninety minutes.

What transpired in the private meeting is open to conjecture. MacArthur declined to testify as to the substance of their conversation during the hearings on his dismissal in 1951, which was proper, since it represented a privileged communication. General Whitney, MacArthur's aide and biographer, felt constrained to reveal part of what the general told him about the conversation. Whitney claims a passing reference was made to Formosa and that the bulk of the conversation dealt with "the fiscal and economic problems of the Philippines." In his *Memoirs*, Truman recalled that only a brief reference was made to

Formosa, but made no mention of the Philippines. Instead, he wrote that MacArthur assured him victory in Korea was a certainty and that Chinese Communist intervention was quite unlikely.[45]

The general conference at Wake Island started immediately after the private session between Truman and MacArthur.[46] The meeting began with the general telling the president that formal resistance in all of Korea should end by Thanksgiving. If this proved to be the case, he planned to withdraw the Eighth Army to Japan by Christmas. Mac-Arthur expressed the hope that the United Nations would be able to conduct elections in North Korea soon after the first of the year, following which he proposed to pull out all occupation forces. Later in the meeting, Bradley asked MacArthur if he would be able to spare a division for redeployment to Europe in January. MacArthur said he could have the Second Division by then. When asked by Army Secretary Pace if there was any more that needed to be done in terms of cooperation with the Far East Command, MacArthur replied: "No commander in the history of war has ever had more complete and adequate support from all agencies in Washington than I have." [47]

Toward the close of this meeting, Truman asked MacArthur to estimate the chances of Soviet or Chinese intervention in Korea. "Very little," the general replied. "Had they intervened in the first or second months it would have been decisive. We are no longer fearful of their intervention." MacArthur went on to explain that the Soviet Union had no appreciable ground forces nearby and that the Chinese, who had about 125,000 troops along the Yalu River, could only commit about 60,000 across the river. Because they lacked a proper air force for support, MacArthur believed that "if the Chinese tried to get down to Pyongyang there would be the greatest slaughter." As to the possible combination of Russian air support of Chinese ground operations, the general believed that liaison would be too difficult to be effective.[48] Shortly after this meeting ended, MacArthur flew back to Japan and Truman departed for San Francisco.

In a statement issued following the Wake Island conference, Truman described the meeting as "highly satisfactory," and indicated that a "very complete unanimity of view" had prevailed. The president said that he had primarily discussed with MacArthur the military aspects of the Korean situation and the further steps which would be required to bring peace and security to the area. Speaking at the War Memorial

Opera House in San Francisco two days later, Truman said that there was no need for speculation about why he went to Wake Island: "I went because I wanted to see and talk to General MacArthur. . . . There is no substitute for personal conversation with the commander in the field who knows the problems there from first-hand experience." [49]

Five days after the Wake Island conference, the Eighth Army enveloped and captured the North Korean capital city of Pyongyang. Resistance to the United Nations' advance became increasingly sporadic, often confined to guerrilla-type actions of limited effect. Truman cabled MacArthur his congratulations for the remarkable progress made since their meeting at Wake Island. The general's confidence that the fighting was over shows clearly in a message to the joint chiefs on October 21. He informed his superiors that he hoped to start the movement of the Eighth Army back to Japan before Thanksgiving and intended to complete the transfer before Christmas.[50]

The ROK forces driving northward from Pyongyang were moving too slowly to satisfy General MacArthur. On October 24, without prior consultation with Washington, he advised his commanders that he was lifting all restrictions on the use of non-Korean forces close to the Chinese border. He instructed the field commanders to ignore the restraining line he had previously imposed upon them and to use any and all forces at their command necessary to complete the capture of North Korea. This order countermanded the joint chiefs' directive of September 27, which had restricted operations in the northern provinces to Korean troops exclusively. The joint chiefs informed MacArthur on the same day that they were sure he had good reasons for taking this action, but wished to be informed as to what these reasons were.[51] Replying on October 25, MacArthur said that his orders were a matter of "military necessity" because the strength and leadership of the ROK forces were insufficient for the accomplishment of his objective. He indicated that Secretary Marshall's message to him of September 30 provided him with the "necessary latitude" to modify his instructions to suit the combat situation. MacArthur also said that the whole subject had already been covered in his meeting with Truman on Wake Island. Although the joint chiefs apparently were still convinced that MacArthur had violated his instructions, they did not move to countermand his orders. Nor is there any indication that Truman was consulted. The matter was simply dropped, the Defense Department being unwilling to overrule a field commander arguing military necessity, particularly a general of MacArthur's prestige.[52]

During the Blair House meetings in which the decision was made to involve the United States in Korea, consideration was given to the possibility of Communist China entering the war. There was general agreement then that while a risk did exist, such intervention was not likely to occur. It will be recalled that the directive to MacArthur regarding his operations above the 38th parallel, which Truman had approved in September, carried a restrictive proviso in the event of major intervention by Soviet or Chinese Communist forces. Acheson testified later that it was the belief of the president's advisers that crossing the 38th parallel probably would not cause China to intervene.[53] This belief must have been based on the assumption that the Chinese were only bluffing, for they had indicated otherwise on several occasions.

General Nieh Yen-jung, acting chief of the Communist general staff, had discussed the American crossing of the 38th parallel with the Indian ambassador at Peking, Sardar K. M. Panikkar, on September 25. He informed the ambassador that China would not permit the United States to advance to the Yalu River. In public speeches on September 31 and October 1, China's foreign minister, Chou En-lai, said that his country would resist foreign aggression against its North Korean neighbors. On October 3 Chou summoned Panikkar and informed him that if American troops advanced across the parallel, China would enter the war. It was Panikkar's understanding that if only South Korean forces entered North Korea, this would not precipitate Chinese intervention.[54]

The president and his advisers believed that Chou En-lai's warnings were designed to blackmail the United Nations. However, Truman concluded that the possibility of Chinese intervention was too great to be ignored. He ordered the joint chiefs to send a directive to MacArthur to be followed in the event that Chinese Communist forces were committed in North Korea. The instructions to the Far East commander, dated October 9, read, in part:

> In light of the possible intervention of Chinese Communist forces in North Korea the following amplification of our directive . . . is forwarded for your guidance:
>
> Hereafter in the event of the open or covert employment anywhere in Korea of major Chinese Communist units, without prior announce-

ment, you should continue the action as long as, in your judgment, action by forces now under your control offers a reasonable chance of success. In any case you will obtain authorization from Washington prior to taking any military action against objectives in Chinese territory.[55]

Truman considered the October 9 directive to be a restrictive, cautionary gesture. In fact it allowed MacArthur greater latitude. The September 27 directive had prohibited advancement into North Korea if Chinese actions constituted a major threat of intervention. The corollary of October 9 allowed MacArthur to continue his advance northward even if the Chinese did attack, so long as the general felt he could win. This willingness to risk a confrontation with a fresh new opponent was a product of the optimism generated by the triumph at Inchon and a failure of military and political intelligence. Inchon had made the long-sought goal of Korean unification seem within easy grasp. MacArthur's military intelligence had informed him that Chinese armies were being moved to the banks of the Yalu. But it was assumed that with the North Korean army in disarray and the presumed ability of American air power to prevent any sizable movement southward by the Chinese, the logic of the military situation argued against an invasion.[56]

In the closing days of October, the evidence that Chinese troops were involved in North Korea had begun to accumulate. Truman had received a memorandum on the twentieth from the CIA that the Chinese would be moving into North Korea to establish a protective perimeter around several power plants on the Yalu which serviced Manchuria. ROK units close to the Yalu began to engage in battle with Chinese units and on October 26 captured the first prisoners from these units. The prisoners informed their captors that their units had crossed the Yalu on October 16. This was, Truman later wrote, "only one day after General MacArthur had assured me on Wake Island that if any Chinese were to enter Korea they would face certain disaster but that he did not expect them to try anything that foolish." [57] By October 30 there were reports that elements of the Chinese Thirty-ninth, Fortieth, and Forty-second armies were in North Korea. The Far East Command informed Washington that there was no confirmation of these reports and that the Chinese engaged were probably volunteers. Truman ordered the joint chiefs to secure a complete and up-to-date assessment of the Chinese incursion from MacArthur.

On November 4 General MacArthur told the Joint Chiefs of Staff that available combat intelligence was insufficient for the purpose of adequately estimating the degree of Chinese involvement. He felt it was most likely that China would provide some volunteers and military aid surreptitiously to the North Koreans. Regarding a full-scale military intervention by the Chinese Communist government, MacArthur said that it was a distinct possibility, but that there were several logical reasons why they would not try. He closed by cautioning against drawing premature conclusions pending accumulation and appraisal of military data. On November 6 MacArthur issued a special communiqué which began with the declaration that the North Korean army had been decisively beaten and the Korean war had been brought to a practical end. But the United Nations Command now faced a "fresh army of Communist Chinese." The statement closed by asserting that it was now the mission of the UN Command to destroy the force newly deployed against it in North Korea.[58]

MacArthur had cautioned Washington on November 4 against making hasty judgments regarding Chinese intervention. But on the following day he sent extraordinary orders to his air chief, General George E. Stratemeyer, telling him to concentrate his forces on the destruction of the Korean end of all bridges crossing the Yalu. Stratemeyer's first objective was to take out the bridges connecting Sinuiju, North Korea and Antung, China. Three hours before the intended strike, a copy of Stratemeyer's orders were received by the Pentagon. Under Secretary of Defense Lovett immediately met with Acheson and Dean Rusk, assistant secretary of state. Lovett expressed a fear that MacArthur's order might cause the bombing of the Manchurian city. He also believed that destroying the bridges would not materially affect the flow of Chinese troops into North Korea. Rusk reminded Acheson of the American commitment to consult with Great Britain before moving against Manchurian targets. The three were in agreement that the proposed attack should be postponed pending consultation with the president. Acheson called Secretary of Defense Marshall, who agreed to order the joint chiefs to countermand MacArthur's orders to Stratemeyer, pending new instructions from Truman.[59]

Shortly after talking with Marshall on November 6, Acheson was able to reach the president by telephone in Kansas City, where he had gone to cast his ballot in the off-year elections. After being brought up to date by ths secretary of state, Truman said that he was willing to authorize any action necessary for the safety of the troops. However, MacArthur's last message (on the fourth), had given no indication of movement across the Yalu that would justify such an action. Truman approved the temporary cancellation of the bombing mission until Mac-Arthur explained why the attack was necessary.[60] Accordingly, less than two hours before the massive flight of bombers was to leave Japan, the countermanding order was radioed to Far East headquarters by the Joint Chiefs of Staff. MacArthur was informed that the implications of his proposed air strike were being considered on a governmental level. He was told of the need to consult with the British prior to taking action which might involve Manchuria. Until such time as orders were issued to the contrary, MacArthur was instructed to adhere to a previous joint chiefs' directive which prohibited him from bombing targets within five miles of the Manchurian border. The Far East Commander was also ordered to provide Washington with a new estimate of the military situation and an explanation for his order to destroy the Yalu bridges.[61]

MacArthur quickly drafted a dramatic response to the joint chiefs' request for justification. His message said that Chinese troops and military supplies were "pouring" across the target bridges. It was his belief that this movement not only endangered his troops, but also threatened to accomplish the total destruction of the armies under his command. MacArthur said that only destruction of the bridges could prevent reinforcement of the enemy. He also advocated full utilization of his air power to accomplish the destruction of all installations in northern Korea which could contribute to the support of the Chinese forces. The tone of MacArthur's report was unusually adamant, revealing the fervor of his conviction that his superiors were in error. He said that what he had ordered was within the scope of his directives and did not constitute a belligerent act against Chinese territory. The general said he could not overemphasize the "disastrous effect" of the combat restrictions they were imposing upon him. MacArthur made a most unusual appeal over the heads of the joint chiefs, directly to the commander in chief: "I trust that the matter be immediately brought to the attention of the President as I believe your instructions may well result in a calamity of major proportion." [62]

Upon receipt of this message in Washington, General Bradley called the president and read him the text. Truman was very concerned about the danger of precipitating a far wider war. "But," he wrote later, "since General MacArthur was on the scene and felt so strongly that this was of unusual urgency, I told Bradley to give him the 'go-ahead.' " In their message transmitting the President's decision to MacArthur, the joint chiefs acknowledged that bombing the bridges would contribute to the security of his forces. However, this action might bring full intervention by China or the Soviet Union and his force would be in greater danger and the war vastly extended to a degree hazardous to American self-interest. MacArthur was allowed to proceed with his bombardment, but the directive expressly enjoined against attacks on dams or hydroelectric plants along the Yalu. The concept of limited warfare is evident throughout the message. Most notably, MacArthur was advised to be absolutely certain not to violate Manchurian soil or airspace, "because it is vital in the national interests of the U.S. to localize the fighting in Korea." [63]

A military intelligence estimate by MacArthur arrived in Washington on November 7. In it the Far East commander reaffirmed his belief that the Chinese attack did not constitute a full-scale intervention. The troops that had crossed the Yalu could be reinforced, however, to the point where they could check the completion of his advance northward and, possibly, force him into a retrograde movement. MacArthur said he intended to advance against these new units in order to estimate their potential strength.[64] Truman already had in hand a Central Intelligence report (dated November 6) which estimated that about two hundred thousand Chinese troops were poised in a striking position in Manchuria. The CIA estimate agreed with MacArthur that intervention by these troops would halt his advance and probably force a retreat. The drafters of the report were convinced that China was aware that such involvement could bring about a general war. The CIA also told Truman that the Soviet Union was not inclined to join directly in the Korean fighting but hoped to keep the United States deeply involved there, thus allowing them freer rein in Europe.[65]

In a second message on November 7 General MacArthur told of the ever-increasing number of Russian-built MIG-15 jet fighter aircraft that were attacking his air units operating near the Yalu. The MIGs were using very effective hit-and-run tactics, striking quickly and then breaking contact and retreating across the border into Manchurian airspace. Since MacArthur had been ordered not to penetrate the border, pursuing aircraft had to halt at the Yalu River, the area beyond constituting a sanctuary. The general described this as an abnormal condition having a debilitating effect on combat efficiency and the morale of air and ground troops. He requested new instructions from Washington. What MacArthur wanted was the right of "hot pursuit," which he subsequently defined as permission "to pursue an attacking enemy plane to the death, whether it was over the border line or not." [66]

The principle involved in "hot pursuit" was clearly established in international law and by historical precedents involving the rules of warfare. The Joint Chiefs of Staff, Defense Department, State Department, and Truman were all willing to allow this latitude to pursuing aircraft. Secretary Acheson believed it proper to inform the other nations with forces involved in Korea that such an order was to be issued. Accordingly, on November 13, he dispatched a message to the American embassies in the nations concerned asking the ambassador to inform the government to which he was accredited that United Nations aircraft might soon be granted permission to pursue attacking aircraft up to a limit of three minutes' flying time into Manchuria. Acheson concluded his message by saying that since only limited application of the pursuit doctrine was involved and because the order was based on "military necessity and elementary principles of self-defense," the concurrence of the respective countries was not being sought. [67]

Concurrence of the allies was not requested in Acheson's "hot pursuit" notification, but they responded—unanimously and negatively— to the whole idea. The ambassadors reported that these nations regarded hostile action over Manchuria as undesirable and dangerous. In the face of such general opposition, the matter was dropped. The president's views on the aerial pursuit question are not altogether clear. Acheson does not recall Truman being consulted at all. [68] In his *Memoirs* Truman did not offer any personal judgment on the question; he merely recorded MacArthur's message asking for a new directive to meet the situation. However, he follows MacArthur's message with commentary that reveals how he felt he had to conduct this unique type of limited, coalition warfare:

> I valued the expression of MacArthur's opinions, and so did the Joint Chiefs. There was never any question about my high regard for MacArthur's military judgment. But as President I had to listen to more than military judgments, and my decisions had to be made on the basis

of not just one theater of operations but of a much more comprehensive picture of our nation's place in the world.

. . . . neither he [MacArthur] nor I would have been justified if we had gone beyond the mission that the United Nations General Assembly had given us.

There was no doubt in my mind that we should not allow the action in Korea to extend into a general war. All-out military action against China had to be avoided, if for no other reason than because it was a gigantic booby trap.[69]

The deep misunderstanding that developed between the commander in chief and his field commander was not lessened by the limitations imposed on the conduct of operations above the 38th parallel. The restrictive policy Truman adopted was designed to avoid any activity that would alienate the allies or serve to justify the enemy's expansion of the conflict into a general war. Nor were these self-imposed limitations designed solely to prevent the onset of World War III. They were also part of an implicit bargain with the Communists. Although Truman did not allow MacArthur to violate the Manchurian sanctuary, the enemy also allowed the United States privileged sanctuary. Enemy air power was very rarely employed against American ground units, supply depots, railroads, or bridges. Shipping was not endangered by enemy actions. Port facilities could off-load military supplies at night, fully illuminated and inviolate. While it is difficult to speculate on the enemy's motivations, save to suggest that they, too, may not have desired a general war, it should be remembered that both sides imposed quite restrictive limitations upon their own conduct.[70] The comparison to nature, wherein wild animals of the same species fight over territorial imperatives, but by some instinctual urging stop short of destroying each other, seems inescapable.

Amidst the uncertainties of Chinese Communist intentions in the first week of November, Truman instructed the joint chiefs to provide him with their recommendations respecting intervention. He was given a three-point memorandum on November 8. The joint chiefs recommended first, that all available political and diplomatic means should be employed to assure China that the UN forces in North Korea did not constitute a threat to their security. Secondly, since the military objectives and degree of involvement by the Chinese Communists were still unknown, orders should remain unchanged, pending later review. Lastly, all planning and preparations by the United States should

210 The Awesome Power

henceforth be predicated on the assumption that the possibility of global conflict had been increased.[71]

The National Security Council met on November 9 to discuss the joint chiefs' recommendations and review the changing conditions of the war. Truman was not present. Speaking for the joint chiefs, Bradley said that the Chinese had three possible intentions: establishing a buffer zone to protect the hydroelectric facilities along the Yalu; forcing the United States to fight a war of attrition that would weaken the nation decisively in the event of a global conflict with the Soviet Union; driving the UN command completely off the Korean peninsula. If the latter was their objective, Bradley stated, it would require a degree of Soviet assistance that might bring about world war. MacArthur should be able to hold off an attack along his present line, but the proscription against attacking Manchurian bases left this questionable. Bradley did not agree with MacArthur that destroying the Yalu bridges could halt the Chinese. The Yalu would soon freeze over and be passable without bridges. Secretary Marshall told the council members that MacArthur's eastern flank was dangerously thin and dispersed over a very wide area. The meeting ended in general accord with the principles expressed in the Joint Chiefs of Staff memorandum of the eighth.[72] The meeting demonstrated that Truman's civil and military advisers agreed on the potential capacity of Chinese forces to destroy what had been accomplished. But they could not solve the great riddle of Chinese intentions, so they agreed that MacArthur's strategic disposition should remain unchanged while the administration sought answers through indirect diplomacy.

What Truman's advisers did not know was that while they deliberated the Chinese were in the process of completing a massive infiltration into North Korea. MacArthur, after his earlier concern that the Chinese constituted a genuine threat to his forces, was convinced, from November 9 until the last days of the month, that the air force could prevent any major Chinese reinforcement across the Yalu and that his ground forces would soon dispatch the remaining opposition in North Korea. His reports in this period reflect calm assurance and heartening optimism. Meanwhile, the Chinese Communists were moving the last units of a force of 300,000 into the mountains of North Korea. Moving only at night, in a very effective "march and bivouac" discipline, the Chinese accomplished one of the great secret mass troop movements in military history. American military intelligence, aerial observers, and aerial photographs all failed entirely to detect this infiltration which had begun some time in October.[73]

As part of the diplomatic initiatives recommended to Truman by the Joint Chiefs of Staff, a resolution was introduced in the UN Security Council on November 10. It asked the Chinese to desist from continued intervention in Korea and affirmed that it was UN policy, "to hold the Chinese frontier with Korea inviolate and fully to protect legitimate Chinese and Korean interests in the frontier zone." Speaking in support of the resolution in a public statement on November 16, his remarks clearly directed at China, Truman said that the United States fully endorsed and was acting within the scope of limits imposed by United Nations policy in Korea. He said that American policy "never at any time" envisioned carrying the war into Chinese territory. The Security Council resolution was vetoed by the Soviet Union on November 30, 1950.[74]

On November 11 units of General Walker's Eighth Army, advancing northward, encountered stiff resistance just above the Chongchon (Ch' ongch' on) River. Walker reported to MacArthur that the opposition came from "fresh, well-organized, and well-trained units, some of which were Chinese Communist forces." Six days later, determined to test the full extent of Chinese involvement and, if possible, complete the conquest of North Korea, MacArthur informed the Pentagon that he was launching a general offensive on November 24, designed to bring his whole line of advance up to the Yalu. Before the offensive got off, forward elements of the Tenth Corps on the eastern flank reached the Yalu on November 21. But on the northwestern flank, the Eighth Army, advancing in widely separated columns, was finding it increasingly difficult to move forward.[75]

MacArthur flew to Eighth Army headquarters on the Congchon to launch the "final" offensive himself. He announced that the assault should bring an end to the war. He also told his corps commanders that he hoped American troops could be pulled out of Korea by Christmas. On the flight to Korea, the general had ordered his plane to fly along the Yalu so that he might observe the area for himself. Upon his return to Tokyo, MacArthur issued a statement saying, "an air reconnaissance behind the enemy's line and along the entire length of the Yalu River border showed little sign of hostile military activity." On the day of this statement Far East headquarters had been provided with a copy of a CIA report which estimated that the minimal response from the Chinese Communists that could be expected was an increase in their military operations. They would, the CIA claimed, seek to immobilize the UN forces, wage a prolonged war of attrition, and attempt to preserve the semblance of a Communist North Korean state. The Chinese also had sufficient strength, if employed, to force the UN armies into withdrawal and a defensive posture.[76]

The first two days of the offensive went well against light opposition. But on the twenty-sixth of November 200,000 Chinese Communist troops struck in the wide gap between the Eighth Army and the Tenth Corps. In a matter of hours they had swept through the ROK Second Corps and all but eliminated the right flank of Eighth Army. Walker's army began a retreat that continued until the Chinese temporarily broke contact, a distance of some forty miles. In the eastern sector, Tenth Corps advance units—First Marine Division and Seventeenth Infantry Regiment—were surrounded and cut off by several Chinese divisions.[77]

It was the president's usual routine to meet with the White House staff before his business day began. On November 28, in a quiet, solemn voice, he told the staff that he had received a telephone call from General Bradley at 8:15 that morning. He had told Truman of a "terrible message" just received from the Far East. "MacArthur said there were two hundred and sixty thousand Chinese troops against him out there," Truman told his staff. "He says he's stymied. He says he has to go over to the defensive. . . . The Chinese have come in with both feet." MacArthur acknowledged that the Chinese attack had shattered the hopes he had entertained that his offensive would bring a prompt end to the fighting: "We face," he said, "an entirely new war." [78]

12/ The Policeman II

General MacArthur was ready to risk general war. I was not.[1]
—HARRY S. TRUMAN

The Chinese intervention in Korea snatched from Truman both the victory that seemed within his grasp and the opportunity to cap his second term on a note of triumph. More important, it raised the specter of a far wider war, something he wanted desperately to prevent. He spent the remaining two years of his presidency in a successful effort to keep the Korean conflict limited and an unsuccessful effort to achieve a negotiated settlement to end the war.

Truman convened a special session of the National Security Council on November 28, 1950, to examine policy in light of the dramatic reversal of military fortunes in Korea. All of the president's military advisers—the secretaries of defense, army, navy, air force and the Joint Chiefs of Staff—were in full agreement that the war had to remain limited. The United States should not allow itself to be drawn into a general war with China. Not only could the Communists draw on an enormous manpower reserve, but no additional reinforcements would be available for Korea until March of 1951. Additionally, an all-out war against China would necessitate halting the buildup of the military defenses of western Europe (which was a primary objective set by NSC–68, the global policy statement drafted by this same council). The president's advisers offered no recommendations, being content, for the time being, to wait for the battlefield situation to clarify.[2]

MacArthur was in a difficult position. The prohibitions against bombing Manchuria and the Yalu dams and hydroelectric stations remained, as did the denial of hot pursuit. His force was badly outnumbered and facing a fresh enemy and he was informed that he should

213

not expect even limited reinforcements until the following March and few replacements before January.[3] On November 29, a message arrived from General MacArthur asking the administration to accept the offer of thirty-three thousand Chinese Nationalist troops made by Chiang Kai-shek at the outset of the war. After a long talk with the State and Defense departments, Truman ordered the joint chiefs to tell MacArthur that the subject was under study. But the message made it clear that for numerous diplomatic reasons, the proposal was not favorably received.[4]

MacArthur's general offensive of November 24, which he subsequently referred to as a "reconnaissance in force," had at least revealed Chinese intentions. Critics have said the operation was a miscalculation leading to "one of the most ignominious defeats in American history." [5] MacArthur denied this, saying that his advance was designed to determine enemy capability and that his reversal was a strategic withdrawal, accomplished in "magnificent order and shape." [6] The truth lies somewhere between these extremes, but it is worthwhile to note that—at the time—Truman's faith in MacArthur's generalship had not wavered. Queried about the developing crisis, Truman said that those who were criticizing MacArthur did not understand military affairs. He did not expect his generals to win every day. "I'm not upset, like most people, about these reverses MacArthur is taking." [7]

The Chinese continued to press their advantage in the last days of November. They had driven a large wedge between the Eighth Army and Tenth Corps. The Chinese Communist forces apparently planned to envelop the inland flanks of both commands, drive them into defensive pockets on the coasts, and destroy them. Meanwhile, the major thrust of the Chinese attack would be southward through the central breach down the entire peninsula. In a message received by the Joint Chiefs of Staff on November 30, MacArthur explained that if enemy pressure continued to develop at its current rate, he would contract the Tenth Corps into a defensive sector between the deep-water ports of Hungnam and Wonsan on the eastern seaboard. The joint chiefs expressed concern over the exposed positions of Tenth Corps. They suggested that MacArthur attempt a sufficient coordination of Eighth Army with Tenth Corps to prevent their being outflanked or allowing any large Chinese Communist force to advance between them. If it became necessary, Tenth Corps should be evacuated.[8]

On the morning these messages were being exchanged, the president held a press conference. He began by reading a statement to the reporters regarding Chinese intervention, which he described as a "new act of aggression in Korea" by which China was being "forced or deceived into serving the ends of Russian colonial policy in Asia." [9] Although the battlefield situation was then uncertain, Truman said that the United Nations did not intend to abandon its mission. He described the attack as part of a global pattern that endangered all free nations, and he emphasized the necessity for rapidly expanding military defenses and establishing an integrated NATO force in Europe. The president said that he would immediately submit a request to Congress for supplemental appropriations, which would include additional funds for the Atomic Energy Commission, as well as the army, navy, and air force. The purpose of these budgetary requests would be to expand the armed forces and increase the effectiveness of the entire military-defense system.[10]

Following his statement, Truman opened the press conference to questions. He defended MacArthur by explaining that he, as commander in chief, was kept fully informed by the general of "every detail" in tactical planning. As the questioners persisted, Truman responded by telling them that MacArthur was doing a good job and had not exceeded his command authority. To further questioning, the president revealed that he was still not going to use Nationalist Chinese troops in Korea and, although he refused to say whether MacArthur would be allowed to bomb beyond the Yalu, he did acknowledge that if the UN authorized such a step, it would be taken. Elaborating, he said that he was prepared to take whatever steps were necessary to meet the new military situation. A reporter asked if this included use of the atomic bomb. Truman replied, "That includes every weapon we have." [11] Continuing, in response to several more queries, the president went on to say that although the atomic bomb was a "terrible weapon" he did not want to employ, its use in the Korean War was, and always had been, under active consideration. Asked if atomic weapons would be used against military or civilian objectives, he said, "It's a matter that the military people will have to decide. I'm not a military authority that passes on those things." [12]

Truman's atomic policy statement makes little sense from any angle. In the first place, he had told a reporter in July that he was *not* considering use of the atomic bomb in Korea.[13] Also, he was the only human being in the world who had ever decided on the use of atomic devices and the type of target they were to be used against. After World War II he had wisely insisted that all atomic weapons policy decisions rest exclusively with the commander in chief. Surely he had no intention of allowing any "military authority" to decide whether to destroy military or civilian targets. Apparently someone had second thoughts about the implications in Truman's statement, for a clarification was issued by the White House shortly after the press conference ended, emphasizing that the president exercised exclusive control over all nuclear weaponry. Some American allies in Korea, most notably Great Britain, were quite alarmed by Truman's remarks to the press and required additional assurance that the bomb would not be used.[14]

The message to Congress requesting supplemental appropriations was sent up on December 1, 1950. In it the president asked that an additional $1.05 billion be provided the Atomic Energy Commission to increase its capacity to produce fissionable materials and fabricate nuclear weapons. He asked that $16.8 billion more be added to the Department of Defense budget for fiscal 1951. Truman said that this latter increment was necessary to sustain America's military participation in the UN action in Korea and to increase the readiness of the military to respond to provocation in other areas of the world. He justified the need for additional funds and forces with much the same logic and language employed in the statement he read to his press conference the previous day. To Truman the Chinese attack was but one facet of a global strategy directed by the Soviet Union. In the process of implementing this policy, the Russians were knowingly running the risk of bringing on a third world war.[15]

Truman's assumption regarding Soviet intentions was neither provable then, nor is it subject to documented refutation now, but it became the operating premise which guided the determination of American military policy for the remainder of his administration. In retrospect, while China's intervention may have neatly meshed with existing Soviet policy, national self-interest was the most likely primal determinant. The Chinese border was threatened by a large armed force representing a hostile political ideology. China intervened, at least in part, to preserve a neighboring Communist nation's existence. However, it would be inaccurate to conclude that the president overreacted to the

Chinese incursion by falsely assuming that it was part of a Soviet master plot. The Central Intelligence Agency had provided him with a great deal of data substantiating just such a conclusion. This intelligence appreciation was concurred in by Secretaries Marshall and Acheson.[16] It could be that the American build-up and countervailing movements frustrated Soviet intentions.

In a lengthy report to the Joint Chiefs of Staff on December 3, MacArthur described the Eighth Army's situation as "increasingly critical" and said that he was moving the Tenth Corps into a beachhead as rapidly as possible. A continuous defensive line across the peninsula was militarily unsound because of the size of the enemy forces. MacArthur claimed the effectiveness of his air power was diminished by the terrain and "enormously" hampered by the prohibition against attacking across the international boundary. Because the enemy was concentrating force along deep interior lines, amphibious maneuvers and naval gunfire support were rendered ineffective. Thus MacArthur's air and naval superiority was of little use. He said that unless he received ground reinforcements "of the greatest magnitude," he would have to continue a costly withdrawal tactic or form beachhead bastions. He insisted that political decisions had to be made and strategic plans implemented adequate to the new situation he faced, or "attrition leading to final destruction can reasonably be contemplated." [17]

MacArthur's message, which Army Secretary Lovett characterized as a "posterity paper," prompted a meeting between officials of the Defense and State departments and a subsequent meeting with Truman. In the Pentagon session the military advisers expressed the belief that MacArthur's forces would face a crisis within three days. They believed that the Tenth Corps had to be evacuated and that Walker's Eighth Army might eventually be forced to evacuate as well, unless a cease-fire could be arranged. Acheson opposed asking for a cease-fire. Evacuation of all UN forces from the Korean peninsula—they were all agreed—should be undertaken only as a last resort. MacArthur's decision not to attempt to form a continuous defensive line would not be countermanded. The reason for this, as explained by the army chief of staff, was that it was the established policy of the joint chiefs not to override a theater commander.[18] Apparently the joint chiefs reasoned that MacArthur, conducting the war in Korea from Japan, four hundred miles away, had a better perspective than they did in Washington,

seven thousand miles from the battlefield. There may have been another reason. General Matthew Ridgway, as the meeting ended, asked
General Vandenberg, the air force chief, why the Joint Chiefs of Staff
did not simply tell MacArthur what to do. Vandenberg responded,
"What good would that do? He wouldn't obey orders. What *can* we
do?" [19]

The president was apprised of the conclusions reached in this session shortly afterward by Marshall and Acheson. He immediately ordered the joint chiefs to dispatch a message to MacArthur which read:
"We consider that the preservation of your forces is now the primary
consideration. Consolidation of forces into beachheads is concurred
in." [20] During this meeting with Truman, the secretary of state urged
him to declare a state of national emergency. Acheson reasoned that
this would alert the public to the serious situation the government faced
as well as provide the president with the extraordinary powers he
would now need to control wages, prices, and production. Truman
accepted the suggestion and preparations to take this step were initiated. Also, on the suggestion of Marshall and Acheson, the president
directed General Collins to depart immediately for Tokyo and Korea
to assess the combat situation and discuss operational planning with
General MacArthur. [21]

Collins returned on December 8 to report his findings to the president in a meeting held in the Cabinet Room of the White House. Also
present were British Prime Minister Atlee, the British ambassador, Sir
Oliver Franks, General Bradley, and Secretaries Marshall and Acheson. The army chief of staff explained to this gathering that it was no
longer possible to hold the Seoul-Inchon area. He reported that General Walker felt he could hold again in the Pusan region, especially if
he were reinforced by the Tenth Corps which, by now (MacArthur
agreed) would have to be evacuated from the Hungnam-Wonsan
bridgehead on the eastern coastline. [22]

In the early days of December, Truman was subjected to severe
pressures as numerous interest groups tried to influence his thinking
on the Korean crisis. Much of this activity was generated by press reports, which in turn were based on information emanating from Mac-
Arthur's headquarters, to the effect that the general could win the war
were it not for the unparalleled restrictions placed upon him by Truman. [23] In a letter dated December 6 the national commanders of the

four largest veterans' organizations in America petitioned the president to "give General MacArthur full authority to employ such means as may be necessary." These former warriors told Truman he must end the restrictions and delays and lift the "imposed limitations" because American soldiers "must not be sacrificed to delusions of appeasement." [24] In a joint letter on December 5, eight congressman urged Truman to resist the pressures put on him to "buy peace in the Orient" by appeasing the Chinese Communists. They also wanted to know why he had not used the Nationalist Chinese troops, who could make an important military contribution, and would also serve to refute the charge that Korea represented an attack by white men on Orientals.[25]

Senator Joseph McCarthy wired the president on December 2, saying that American mothers demanded to know why he was allowing Acheson and the rest of the "crimson clique in the State Department" to "run amuck" with the lives of American soldiers. It would be necessary to impeach Truman unless he ended "this treasonable farce," removed Acheson, and brought the Formosan forces into the fight.[26] John Chang, the Korean ambassador, met with the president on December 6, imploring him to continue the military action in Korea in spite of the reversals. Truman assured the ambassador that he would do all within his power to save Korea.[27] A day earlier the chairman of the Korean National Assembly had informed Truman that a successful conclusion to the existing crisis called for an increase in American military assistance to build up the ROK forces.[28] The strain is evident in a diary note Truman wrote on December 9: "I have worked for peace for five years and six months and it looks like World War III is near. I hope not—but we must meet whatever comes—and we will." [29]

Truman called a meeting of the National Security Council on December 11 to discuss with them a cease-fire resolution soon to be proposed in the General Assembly. He told his advisers that he and Prime Minister Atlee had agreed not to seek a cease-fire in Korea unilaterally, but that they were undecided as to what position to assume with regard to the forthcoming resolution. Additionally, he informed them that he had an understanding with Atlee that the UN command would not surrender; it would leave Korea only if driven off the peninsula by force of arms. The joint chiefs and secretary of defense opposed a cease-fire for the present, particularly one without preconditions. Truman said he had no intention of accepting any armistice without first arriving at terms. Secretary Marshall asked if MacArthur should be ordered to withdraw to the 38th parallel in anticipation of its becoming the cease-fire line. Truman told him to let MacArthur's orders stand (holding to his existing positions), until the Tenth Corps was safely evacuated from the east coast and a satisfactory cease-fire arrangement had been concluded. Marshall pointed out that Joint Chiefs of Staff planning called for a gradual retirement southward and asked if the president objected to this. Truman explained that he was opposed only to a hurried withdrawal based on political expediency; the rate of withdrawal should be determined by military considerations alone.[30]

The Tenth Corps's successful evacuation from Hungnam, which Truman described as "the best Christmas present" he could have, began on December 13.[31] The following day the UN General Assembly adopted a resolution creating a three-member group to determine the basis for a satisfactory cease-fire. The United States voted for the resolution. The member states participating in the unified command subsequently indicated general agreement on the 38th parallel as an acceptable cease-fire line. This decision represented a return to the original objective in Korea and a tacit repudiation of the October 7 resolution which sought unification of Korea under one government. However, on the seventeenth a Communist Chinese envoy rejected the UN proposal, calling it a trap and stated that the conditions for peace were an end to American aggression and complete withdrawal from Korea.[32]

Truman spent a substantial part of the second week of December working on plans for declaring a state of national emergency. A brief survey of the available presidential powers had been made at the beginning of the Korean fighting. Although the president had available to him a vast range of powers to control the domestic economy and achieve industrial mobilization, most of these legislative grants of authority were contingent upon a declaration of national emergency.[33] The decision to declare such a condition was discussed by Truman in numerous sessions with White House aides and speechwriters, at a cabinet meeting on December 8, in two meetings with the National Security Council and in a stormy session with the congressional leadership on Wednesday, December 13. In the latter conference, Republican Senators Taft and Wherry insisted that Truman had not shown just cause for the proposed proclamation. However, the majority present accepted the president's explanation.[34] On the evening of the fourteenth, Truman reviewed an address he planned to deliver the following day with his speechwriters. He told them they would have to delete a line that read: "Our troops are well able to take care of themselves." Truman explained that he could not give any such assurance, for he had just heard from Tokyo that the Eighth Army's right flank was extremely vulnerable. He hoped that the Tenth Corps, having been evacuated from the east coast, could fill in the gaps and secure the line.[35]

In his message to the nation, Truman said that the Chinese intervention had pushed the world to the brink of general war, with the very future of civilization dependent upon American action. He set "four tasks for national security" in his speech: continued support for the principles of the United Nations; continued cooperation to strengthen collective security; a buildup of the army, navy, and air force and the requisite weaponry; and an expansion of the entire economy, with safeguards against inflationary wage-price spirals. During the course of the speech, Truman indicated he was raising the military manpower level from the existing 2½, to 3½ million personnel. He also raised selective service quotas and ordered two additional National Guard divisions to active duty.[36] The formal proclamation establishing a state of national emergency was issued by the White House the following morning. By this action, provisions of some seventy separate legislative acts became operative, significantly increasing the executive authority of the president.[37] In addition, Truman asked for, and received, legislation extending and amending Title II of the War Powers Act of 1941, which was generally concerned with governmental contracting powers.[38]

General Walker's Eighth Army had established a continuous defensive line across the Korean peninsula just north of the 38th parallel. This line was fortified by elements of the evacuated Tenth Corps, now amalgamated into the Eighth Army. But this line was thinly spread and could not hold against any serious Chinese pressure. The enemy had broken off pursuit, but intelligence reports indicated they were preparing for an all-out resumption of the offensive on New Year's Day.

The Eighth Army lost its commander in a fatal traffic accident on December 23. MacArthur immediately requested that General Matthew B. Ridgway, then deputy chief of staff for Operations and Administration, be appointed as Walker's replacement. Truman gave his approval and Ridgway was briefed by MacArthur on the twenty-sixth and warned not to underestimate the ability of his enemy.[39] By the next day Ridgway found himself in full tactical command of an endangered army, far removed from the serene corridors of power in the Pentagon.

With the knowledge that no immediate reinforcements were available for the United Nations Command and a resumption of the massive Chinese Communist assault in the offing, Truman's military advisers were increasingly insistent that ways be considered for withdrawing "with honor" from Korea. However, Acheson and the State Department felt the troops should not leave Korea unless they were driven out. This divergence of views caused Truman to summon Generals Bradley and Marshall and Secretary Acheson to Blair House on December 26. The generals made it clear that they believed a major war was near and that Korea was definitely not the place to fight it. Acheson argued that the stakes involved in Korea were so high that the UN should fight on until Chinese strength and resolution had been fully tested. Then, Acheson said, if required by "dire military necessity," Korea should be evacuated. The secretary of state suggested to Truman that MacArthur's directives be revised to allow him to inflict maximum attrition against the enemy up to the point where his own force was in danger of destruction. MacArthur should be warned against risking the loss of his command, since upon these forces the ultimate safety of Japan depended. Marshall and Bradley accepted this, and Truman instructed them to prepare a new directive.

The Joint Chiefs of Staff transmitted the approved directive to MacArthur on December 29. Acheson has provided a concise summary:

1. If with present UN strength, we could resist at some point in Korea without our incurring serious losses, and if the apparent military and political prestige of Chinese Communists could be deflated, it would be of great importance to our national interests.

2. "In the face of increased threat of general war" the Joint Chiefs of Staff would not commit additional U.S. forces in Korea. Major war should not be fought in Korea.

3. "Therefore . . . your directive now is to defend in successive positions, subject to safety of your troops as your primary consideration, inflicting as much damage to hostile forces in Korea as is possible."

4. Decision was to be made ahead of time by the Joint Chiefs on

the last reasonable opportunity for orderly evacuation, General Mac-Arthur's views were requested on the conditions which should determine evacuation.[40]

The directive reflects a change of policy of considerable magnitude. The objective of Korean unification was not mentioned. The objectives of repelling aggression and restoring peace and security were to be abandoned if unobtainable with the existing force. MacArthur was to take extreme care that his force was not placed in jeopardy, since— the directive emphasized—his primary objective was preservation of the security of Japan, not Korea.[41] The directive asked much: without any increase in forces, or lessening of the restrictions upon operations, a war of attrition was to be waged against a superior force without endangering the troops. MacArthur would insist that none of this was possible. Ridgway would accomplish it all.

MacArthur's reaction to the December 29 directive was that it indicated the administration had lost the will to win in Korea: "President Truman's resolute determination to free and unite that threatened land had now deteriorated almost into defeatism." MacArthur responded on December 30 to the joint chiefs' directive, saying that the continued restrictions on his air and naval operations deprived him of the available military capacity. The additional potential represented in utilizing Chinese Nationalist troops was also being ignored. The greater part of MacArthur's message dealt with the advantages which would ensue from declaring war on Communist China. The general tone of this communication was one of thorough dissatisfaction with the new directive and an urgent repetition of his request that all tactical and political limitations be removed.[42] The resumption of the Chinese offensive made an end to this policy dispute essential.

As predicted, the Chinese did resume the offensive on New Year's Day, forcing the United Nations Command to abandon the South Korean capital of Seoul as they gave ground southward. Meanwhile, Washington considered a reply to MacArthur's message of December 30. On the ninth of January, Truman approved a Joint Chiefs of Staff message which informed the Far East commander that the retaliatory steps he advocated had been given thorough consideration. The administration fully appreciated the difficulties he now faced because of Chinese intervention. However, reconsideration of existing conditions led to the acceptance of certain new operating assumptions. Among these now accepted by the joint chiefs (and Truman) was the feeling that conditions outside of Korea did not justify a strengthening of United States military forces there. Additionally, the proposals for a naval blockade and use of Chinese Nationalist troops were viewed with disfavor for diplomatic reasons. As for the bombing of objectives in China, this would be undertaken only in response to a Chinese attack on UN forces *outside* Korea. The Joint Chiefs of Staff's message concluded by repeating the instructions sent to MacArthur on December 29: "To defend in successive positions, inflicting maximum damage to hostile forces in Korea," with evacuation to be undertaken if essential to the preservation of his command in order to carry out the primary mission, defense of Japan.[43]

Like MacArthur, President Rhee of South Korea had a plan for turning the tide of the war which he pressed upon Truman during the early days of January. Rhee proposed that the United States underwrite a dramatic increase in the size of the Republic of Korea army. When queried about this by the joint chiefs, MacArthur replied on January 6 that given the performance levels of ROK army units and friendly guerrillas, the military equipment involved could be put to better use if given to the newly formed National Police Reserve of Japan.[44] Rhee persisted, however. In a personal letter to Truman, dated January 10, he told him that "even now you can save the situation," by fully arming and equipping a half-million Korean youths. The South Korean president also asked Truman to grant MacArthur the authority to use the atomic bomb. Truman ignored Rhee's message until February 10, when he sent a noncommittal response written for him by the State Department.[45]

Truman and the Pentagon brass found General MacArthur not as easy to ignore. He was irritated by the joint chiefs' message of January 9, for it left all decisions contingent upon tactical actions initiated by the enemy. MacArthur requested a clarification of his orders, since it was self-evident to him that his command was not of sufficient strength to carry out the twin tasks of holding in Korea and simultaneously protecting Japan from assault. He could hold a beachhead line temporarily, but at great cost. His troops, MacArthur said, were embittered and worn out, with their morale at such an ebb that their battle efficiency would be severely impaired "unless the political basis upon which they are asked to trade life for time is clearly delineated, fully understood, and so impelling that the hazards of battle are accepted cheerfully." If no such basis existed, MacArthur said his command should be removed from Korea as rapidly as possible.

> The issue involves a decision of highest national and international importance. . . . Therefore, my query amounts to this: is it the present objective of United States political policy to minimize losses by evacuation as soon as it can be accomplished, or to maintain a military position in Korea—indefinitely, for a limited time?
>
> Under the extraordinary limitations and conditions imposed upon the command in Korea, as I have pointed out, its military position is untenable, but it can hold, if overriding political considerations so dictate, for any length of time up to its complete destruction. Your clarification requested.[46]

General MacArthur's message shifted responsibility for any disaster involving Korea or Japan back to Washington, unless the "extraordinary limitations" were lifted. Reaction to the message was strong. Admiral Sherman believed that it brought about a serious impairment of the normal command relationship between MacArthur and the Joint Chiefs of Staff. Secretary Acheson has written of the January 10 cable: "Nothing further was needed to convince me that the General was incurably recalcitrant and basically disloyal to the purposes of his Commander in Chief." Aware of the gravity of MacArthur's message, Marshall brought it to the president soon after receiving it. Truman recalled being "deeply disturbed" by MacArthur's words: "The Far East commander was, in effect, reporting that the course of action decided upon by the National Security Council and by the Joint Chiefs of Staff and approved by me was not feasible." [47] He reacted to MacArthur's message by putting the joint chiefs to work studying recourses and ordering a special meeting of the National Security Council to convene on January 12.

The joint chiefs drafted another directive for MacArthur, but in consultation with the State Department a dispute arose over the inclusion of foreign policy matters in a military directive. The disagreement was laid before Truman in the Security Council meeting of the twelfth. He resolved it by agreeing to write a personal letter to MacArthur regarding the political policy matters the State Department wished to emphasize, and he approved the purely military directive which was dispatched immediately. This new directive began with the joint chiefs informing MacArthur that, based primarily on information he had provided, they recognized that it would not be feasible to hold in Korea under extant conditions for any protracted period. However, national interests, the worldwide prestige of the United States, and the future of the UN and NATO organizations rested upon his ability to inflict "maximum practicable punishment" on the aggressors. He was to evacuate only when compelled to do so by military considerations.[48] The sense of the message was that MacArthur's orders remained unchanged.

The personal message Truman agreed to send MacArthur on national policy is dated January 13. Because of its importance, it merits substantial quotation:

> I wish in this telegram to let you have my views as to our basic national and international purposes in continuing the resistance to aggression in Korea. . . . This present telegram is not to be taken in any sense as a directive. Its purpose is to give you something of what is in our minds regarding the political factors.
>
> 1. A successful resistance in Korea would serve the following important purposes:
>
> (a) To demonstrate that aggression will not be accepted by us or by the United Nations. . . .
>
> (b) To deflate the dangerously exaggerated political and military prestige of Communist China. . . .
>
> (c) To afford more time for and to give direct assistance to the organization of non-Communist resistance in Asia. . . .
>
> (d) To carry out our commitments of honor to the South Koreans. . . .
>
> (e) To make possible a far more satisfactory peace settlement for Japan and to contribute greatly to the post-treaty security position of Japan in relation to the continent.
>
> (f) To lend resolution to many countries not only in Asia but also in Europe and the Middle East . . . to let them know that they need not now rush to come to terms with Communism on whatever terms they can get, meaning complete submission.
>
> (g) To inspire those who may be called upon to fight against great odds if subjected to a sudden onslaught by the Soviet Union or by Communist China.
>
> (h) To lend point and urgency to the rapid build-up of the defenses of the western world.
>
> (i) To bring the United Nations through its first great effort on collective security and to produce a free-world coalition of incalculable value to the national security of the United States.
>
> (j) To alert the people behind the Iron Curtain that their masters are bent upon wars of aggression and that this crime will be resisted by the free world.

2. Our course of action at this time should be such as to consolidate the great majority of the United Nations. . . . Further, pending the build-up of our national strength, we must act with great prudence in so far as extending the area of hostilities is concerned. Steps which might in themselves be fully justified and which might lend some assistance to the campaign in Korea would not be beneficial if they thereby involved Japan or Western Europe in large-scale hostilities.

3. We recognize, of course, that continued resistance might not be militarily possible with the limited forces which you are being called upon to meet larger Chinese armies. Further, in the present world situation, your forces must be preserved as an effective instrument for the defense of Japan and elsewhere. However, some of the important purposes mentioned above might be supported, if you should think it practicable, and advisable, by continued resistance from off-shore islands of Korea . . . if it becomes impracticable to hold an important portion of Korea itself. In the worst case, it would be important that, if we must withdraw from Korea, it be clear to the world that that course is forced upon us by military necessity and that we shall not accept the result politically or militarily until the aggression has been rectified.

4. In reaching a final decision about Korea, I shall have to give constant thought to the main threat from the Soviet Union and to the need for a rapid expansion of our armed forces to meet this great danger. . . .

6. The entire nation is grateful for your splendid leadership in the difficult struggle in Korea and for the superb performance of your forces under the most difficult circumstances.[49]

By any measure, Truman's message was an extraordinary document. Not only was it a uniquely candid communication between the commander in chief and a theater commander, but also a concise, thorough delineation of the goals of national military and diplomatic policy. In paragraph (2) of the telegram, Truman provided a definition of his concept of limited warfare by acknowledging that there were militarily advisable steps which were not being taken because of the danger of precipitating a wider war. MacArthur's reaction on receipt of the message was to inform his staff that the question of evacuation was settled; there would be none.[50]

MacArthur's message of January 10 had galvanized the Washington hierarchy into feverish activity. The special session of the National Security Council, the joint chiefs' directive, and Truman's telegram have already been noted. Two other developments can also be attributed to MacArthur's message: first, a study proposing numerous courses of action received tentative approval by the Joint Chiefs of

Staff and was submitted by Marshall to the National Security Council for initial consideration on the twelfth. Second, in the Security Council session, Truman approved a recommendation that two members of the joint chiefs—Collins and Vandenberg—be sent immediately to Japan and Korea for a fresh evaluation of the military situation.[51]

The study tentatively accepted by the Joint Chiefs of Staff was prepared by its own Joint Staff. It contained sixteen courses of action which might be undertaken in the Far East in the event the United Nations force had to evacuate Korea, and a full-scale war with China developed. The proposals were military, economic, and diplomatic in nature and included the four retaliatory measures against China which MacArthur had recommended on several occasions.[52] On January 12 the National Security Council deferred discussion of the joint chiefs' study until their next scheduled session five days later. By that time their appreciation of the military situation had improved to the point where active consideration of the documents was halted. Thus, while several of the proposed actions were later instituted, in whole or part, the full study was never implemented as a national policy directive.[53]

MacArthur had been briefed on the joint chiefs' study in a meeting with Generals Collins and Vandenberg, who had just arrived from Washington on January 15 (Tokyo time). They also discussed the joint chiefs' directive and the president's telegram to MacArthur. Soon afterward, Collins and Vandenberg left for an extensive tour of the Korean battlefields. Collins already knew, from private communication with Ridgway, that the Eighth Army leader was far more confident than MacArthur that his forces could not be driven from the peninsula.[54] In his talks with Ridgway and numerous other commanders in Korea, the army chief of staff's belief that they could hold and fight effectively was confirmed. In a message radioed to Bradley on the seventeenth and a subsequent meeting with Truman following his return to Washington, Collins said that the Eighth Army was in "good shape" and that the morale of the troops was "very satisfactory" under the circumstances. The Chinese were having severe logistical difficulties and had made no serious effort to advance beyond the Han River (just south of Seoul). Collins later recalled that Truman and his advisers seemed reassured by the reports that he and Vandenberg brought back from Korea: "Though it was realized that rough times were still ahead of us, no longer was there much talk of evacuation. General Ridgway alone was responsible for this dramatic change." [55]

By the third week of January it was evident that the Communist offensive had halted at a point just above the 37th parallel. The enemy could not sustain the offensive because of overextended lines of communication and supply. Their logistical problems were made more difficult by persistent aerial interdiction. The bulk of the enemy force was withdrawn northward from the line of contact. Sensing this, Ridgway sent out reinforced probes which encountered only thin screening forces. Accordingly, he began to move cautiously to the offensive with reconnaissances-in-force in various sectors along the battle line. Meeting with success, on January 25 Ridgway ordered the western flank of his Eighth Army, the First and Ninth corps, on a general sweep forward. January ended with these forces encountering their first really stiff resistance from a Communist delaying action near the outskirts of Seoul.[56]

Stalled on the western flank, on February 5 Ridgway ordered the American Tenth and ROK Third corps to advance in hopes of reducing the deep salient in the central sector of his front line. This advance met strong opposition and a concentrated counterattack that was launched on February 11. The center sagged; but reinforced by all available reserves, it held, and the advance recommenced ten days later, eliminating the salient. On the western front, to avoid being flanked, the enemy withdrew all forces below Seoul on February 9, enabling UN forces to recapture Inchon and Kimpo airfield the next day. The combined Chinese and North Korean forces mounted a stubborn defense in the capital city of South Korea and held it until mid-March. Ridgway, who was more concerned with destroying the enemy and maintaining the integrity of his line than with the acquisition of places, did not press an attack against Seoul. By the end of February, 1951, the UN forces occupied a line just south of Seoul, running from Inchon in the west to Kangnung in the east, having advanced roughly half the distance between the 37th and 38th parallels.[57]

Truman had by now given up any thought of reconquering North Korea, since that would entail a ground war against the almost limitless manpower reserves of China. But MacArthur was still actively devising such a campaign. In long-range plans developed in February,

MacArthur intended to first regain the Seoul line as a base of operations. He would then destroy the enemy's rear by massive air strikes along the top of North Korea. If still not permitted to bomb enemy reinforcements in Manchuria, as he anticipated, MacArthur intended to lay vast fields of radioactive wastes across all major enemy supply lines in North Korea. Then, using American and Nationalist Chinese reinforcements, he would launch simultaneous airborne and amphibious strikes against both the east and west coasts of North Korea. "It would be something like Inchon," he said, "but on a much larger scale." [58]

On March 7 General Ridgway began a new offensive push, its objective being the destruction of enemy forces and the attainment of a new front-line located just south of the 38th parallel. As this movement advanced, it resulted in the bracketing of Seoul, leaving the enemy defenders in an untenable position. Without opposition, the Eighth Army recaptured the city on the morning of March 15. Korean President Rhee wrote to Truman expressing gratitude for the return of Seoul. In the same letter Rhee urged the president not to listen to the "pro-Communist" appeasers who were urging him to stop at the 38th parallel and seek a cease-fire. He repeated his request that the United States immediately provide arms and equipment for over a quarter-million Korean youths who would be of material assistance in driving the Chinese Communists back into Manchuria to stay.[59] By the final week in March, Ridgway's forces were at the 38th parallel, and he proposed to advance and stabilize his position at a line slightly above the parallel. The Eighth Army commander was instructed to hold below the line, pending an attempt by the administration to negotiate a settlement.

Truman's advisers in the State and Defense departments had been meeting continuously, since Ridgway's success in January indicated to them the need to prepare new policy recommendations for the president. From the viewpoint of the State Department in early February, five possible courses of action existed: abandoning Korea; unifying the entire peninsula by force; extending the war into China; enduring an indefinite stalemate at the current positions; and trying for a negotiated settlement. The planners were at loggerheads; the State Department was reluctant to offer political objectives until the Eighth Army's military capabilities were clearly established and the Joint Chiefs of Staff insisted political goals had to be set before military recommendations could be made. At the same time it appeared that the majority of the

UN member nations, including those engaged in Korea, were against any general advance across the parallel.

Secretary Marshall received a draft memorandum from Acheson on February 23 which the latter proposed forwarding as a joint statement to the president. The memorandum cautioned against any general allied advance beyond the 38th parallel, but recognized that MacArthur should feel free to continue air and naval operations along with any necessary, limited ground action north of that line. Marshall referred Acheson's note to the joint chiefs and the three service secretaries.[60] The latter groups responded in agreement with Acheson's memorandum that the UN resolution allowing advances north of the 38th parallel was "permissive not mandatory." They further agreed that the UN forces should not make a general advance beyond the parallel except for tactical reasons to acquire favorable defensive terrain. Army Secretary Pace and Air Secretary Finletter also agreed that this policy should be made a matter of public record. On this last, Acting Secretary of the Navy Daniel A. Kimball demurred, believing it would "hamper effective military action." [61]

The Joint Chiefs of Staff reported to Marshall their direct disagreement with the service secretaries and Acheson's draft memorandum for the president. They argued that since there had been no change in the stated political objectives of the United Nations or the United States, no political reason existed for halting military operations beyond the parallel. MacArthur needed freedom of maneuver to keep the enemy off balance and ensure the safety of his own forces. The joint chiefs urged that until such time as a new political objective was formulated, MacArthur's directive remain unchanged. Backed by these opinions, Marshall told Acheson he would not sign the memorandum to Truman. The defense secretary joined the joint chiefs in emphasizing the necessity for a definitive statement on political objectives in Korea. Truman did not see the memorandum in question, since State and Defense were so far apart on its terms.[62] However, there existed a tacit understanding that the nation must return to its original political objective of preserving South Korea. Except for General MacArthur and President Rhee, no one seriously proposed the reconquest of North Korea.

It was the success of General Ridgway's forces in March that forced the Truman administration to a policy decision. By mid-March the

State and Defense departments, as well as the National Security Council, were in substantial agreement that the time was opportune to seek a cease-fire, looking toward a negotiated peace settlement. It was felt that the president, acting as executor for the United Nations, should initiate such an approach by a public appeal to the Communists, a position with which Truman agreed.

The draft of a statement was prepared for the president by the State Department and agreed to by all the principals on March 19. On the following day a message to MacArthur requested his recommendations:

> State planning a Presidential announcement shortly that with clearing of bulk of South Korea of aggressors, United Nations now prepared to discuss conditions of settlement in Korea. United Nations feeling exists that further diplomatic efforts toward settlement should be made before any advance with major forces north of the thirty-eighth parallel. . . .
>
> Recognizing that the parallel has no military significance, State has asked Joint Chiefs of Staff what authority you should have to permit sufficient freedom of action for next few weeks to provide security for United Nations forces and maintain contact with the enemy. Your recommendations desired.[63]

MacArthur responded on March 21, telling the joint chiefs that his existing directive was adequate and requesting that no additional restrictions be imposed upon his command. Also, MacArthur granted final approval to Ridgway's proposed offensive which would carry UN forces slightly above the 38th parallel. This was entirely proper for MacArthur to do, for without new instructions from Washington, crossing the line into North Korea was simply a tactical decision.[64] However, Truman did not consider MacArthur's next action to be proper at all.

On March 24 (Tokyo time), MacArthur issued a communiqué which he described as "routine" and which Secretary Acheson described as "defiance of the Chiefs of Staff, sabotage of an operation of which he had been informed, and insubordination of the grossest sort to his Commander in Chief." [65] In this controversial document, MacArthur dwelt at length on the military weaknesses demonstrated in the fighting by the Chinese and on the success of his forces in spite of the inhibitions placed on their activities. The enemy should be aware, MacArthur said, that if the United Nations were to drop its tolerant efforts at keeping the war limited and allow operations against China, that nation risked total military collapse. Although the fundamental questions at issue in Korea were political and subject only to diplomatic solutions, MacArthur announced his willingness to negotiate with the enemy commander with a view to finding military means for achieving the political objectives of the United Nations in Korea.

The president called a meeting the following morning (March 24, Washington time) to discuss MacArthur's communiqué. In attendance were Acheson and Rusk from State and Lovett and all the chiefs of staff. At the time, the process of clearing the proposed presidential statement with the thirteen nations having forces in Korea was just being completed. Nevertheless, Truman ordered the cancellation of his message, which would have proposed a cease-fire, to be followed by mutual withdrawal, leaving to the United Nations the final solution of the Korean question. Truman later wrote that what was more important than the cancellation of his message and the furor among the allies was that "once again General MacArthur had openly defied the policy of his Commander in Chief, the President of the United States." [66] After ascertaining that everyone present agreed that his order of December 6, 1950, regarding the clearance of all public statements was at issue, Truman personally dictated an order to MacArthur:

> The President has directed that your attention be called to his order as transmitted 6 December, 1950, In view of the information given you 20 March, 1951 any further statements by you must be coordinated as prescribed in the order of 6 December.
> The President has also directed that in the event Communist military leaders request an armistice in the field, you immediately report that fact to the JCS for instructions.[67]

Truman stated—after the fact—that he had decided to relieve General MacArthur of command upon receipt of the March 24 communiqué, which he regarded as extreme insubordination. However, another indiscreet statement by MacArthur two weeks later occurred before Truman acted. The final incident which confirmed the president in his resolve concerned an exchange of letters between MacArthur and Representative Joseph W. Martin, Jr., leader of the Republican minority in the House. Early in March, Martin wrote to the general soliciting his views on Far Eastern policy and strategy. In a reply dated March 20, MacArthur said he favored the conventional military approach of "meeting force with maximum counter-force." He also said Martin's suggestion that the Nationalists on Formosa be allowed to open a second front in Asia was consistent with logic and tradition. The letter concluded with the now-famous line, "There is no substitute for victory." [68]

Without first obtaining MacArthur's approval, Congressman Martin read the letter from the floor of the House on April 5. A series of meetings began between Truman and various officials of the State and Defense departments the following day. The culminating session came on Monday morning, April 9, with Marshall, Acheson, Harriman, and Bradley present, the latter reporting that the joint chiefs were unanimous in recommending the immediate relief of General MacArthur from command. All present concurred, including Truman, who revealed for the first time that he had arrived at this decision following MacArthur's statement of March 24. The president directed Bradley to prepare the order which was transmitted April 11 (Washington time): "I deeply regret that it becomes my duty as President and Commander in Chief of the United States military forces to replace you as Supreme Commander, Allied Powers; Commander in Chief, United Nations Command; Commander in Chief, Far East; and Commanding General, U.S. Army, Far East." [69]

The president appointed Lieutenant General Matthew Ridgway to MacArthur's commands. Lieutenant General James A. Van Fleet was ordered from the United States to take command of the Eighth Army. Ridgway recalls that upon taking over his new post he was determined not to exercise the tight tactical control which MacArthur had exercised but to allow Van Fleet the latitude necessary to field command. When he took over, Ridgway said, "clear policy decisions" had been communicated to him by Truman and the joint chiefs, "the most immediate of which was to avoid any action that might result in an extension of hostilities and thus lead to a worldwide conflagration." [70]

By mid-April, as the change of commanders took place, UN forces had generally secured the "Kansas" line, a front about six to eight miles above the 38th parallel. On April 22 twenty-one Chinese and nine North Korean divisions began a massive counteroffensive along the entire front, but with major stress against the western flank, aiming at a recapture of Seoul. The Eighth Army was compelled to give ground, but did so in good order, moving to successive delaying positions in preestablished defensive fortifications. Van Fleet was thus able to contain the attack a few miles above Seoul. The fighting ended five days later with the enemy's withdrawal northward. The Communist forces resumed their offensive on May 16, this time against the eastern flank, where they gained some thirty miles before being halted. The human-wave assault tactics of these two offensives cost the enemy an estimated 200,000 casualties, or roughly one third of the total Communist strength in Korea. Once the Communist offensive had been blunted, Van Fleet's forces had little trouble driving them back until, by mid-June, they reoccupied their previous line. Since no enthusiasm existed for advancing to the Yalu, either in Washington or the allied capitals, Van Fleet ordered his corps commanders to fortify the line in depth. This was accomplished by construction of log-and-sandbag bunkers connected by deep, narrow trenches across the entire line of the peninsula, quite reminiscent of World War I entrenchments. The fluid phase of the Korean War had ended. From June, 1951, until the final settlement in 1953, military activity consisted mainly of constant patrolling and small, localized clashes.[71]

The character of the Korean War was altered by a pivotal meeting of the National Security Council on May 16, 1951. It was the conclusion of this body—subsequently approved by Truman—that a distinction must henceforth be made between military and political objectives in Korea. The political aim would remain the same, establishment of a unified, democratic, independent Korean state. However, the military objective was now repulse of the invaders and an end to the fighting through an armistice agreement. Following such a cease-fire, American purpose would be the securing of autonomy for the Republic of Korea south of a line not substantially below the 38th parallel, mutual withdrawal of non-Korean forces, and a buildup of ROK forces to a point where they would constitute an effective deterrent to renewed aggression. Truman wrote that this policy "represented no change," when, in fact, it was a return to the original objective of American involvement.[72]

Trygve Lie, UN secretary-general, announced on June 1 that a cease-fire established in the proximity of the 38th parallel would accomplish the objectives of the United Nations in Korea. Speaking on the seventh, Acheson took the same position. Two days earlier, George F. Kennan, on leave from the department but acting as Acheson's agent, had an "unofficial" conversation with Jacob Malik, chief Soviet delegate to the United Nations. Kennan learned that the Soviet Union desired a peaceful and rapid solution in Korea. On June 23, speaking on a UN radio program in New York, Malik said that his nation believed that it was time for the belligerents in Korea to discuss peace. The Peking *People's Daily*, a semiofficial organ of the Chinese government, endorsed Malik's statement two days later.[73] Grasping at this, on June 29 Truman ordered Ridgway to transmit an armistice feeler to the enemy commander.[74]

A favorable response to this message was received from the Communist commander on the first day of July. He suggested that the meeting place be the town of Kaesong, a site between the lines, quite near the 38th parallel. The first plenary session of the truce talks was held on July 10, 1951, with hostilities to continue until an armistice was agreed upon. It would take another 158 such sessions, stretched out over more than two years of bitter disputation before the fighting was at last stopped.

Throughout it all, until the end of his term of office, Truman maintained an active supervision of the limited military operations and of the frustrating efforts to obtain a satisfactory cease-fire. Now, along with the daily battlefield reports he also received a daily account of the truce proceedings. As he recalled, "No major steps were taken without specific approval of the President, even to the wording of announcements made by the Far East commander or the chief negotiator at crucial points." [75] The fact is that there was little need for Truman to exercise his powers as commander in chief following the removal of MacArthur and the decision to halt and seek a settlement near the 38th parallel. While he continued to act as an overseer and exercise final authority, the decreased level of combat and smooth functioning of his subordinates sharply diminished his active participation in the conduct of the war. As the war scaled down, some personnel changes were made. Truman lost his trusted secretary of defense, General Marshall, who retired for personal reasons in September, 1951, but was quite pleased with Marshall's successor, Robert A. Lovett. In May, 1952, Eisenhower resigned as supreme allied commander in Europe in order to seek the Republican presidential nomination. Truman ordered General Ridgway to assume the NATO command, which is some indication of the declining importance placed on the limited military activity in Korea. General Mark W. Clark served as Ridgway's successor.[76]

The policy adopted for military operations in Korea in mid-1951 was held relatively constant by Truman until the end of his term. His adherence to this policy was reinforced by a recommendation of the National Security Council in December, 1951, that any broadening of the Korean effort was undesirable. The president did not shortchange the troops serving in Korea, for he insisted that the overriding priority on all military production was to be accorded to combat consumption requirements. However, Truman did keep the troop levels in Korea substantially unchanged for the remainder of his presidency.[77] This assured a battlefield stalemate and may have contributed to the protracted truce negotiations.

In June, 1952, a public opinion poll revealed that 43 percent of those surveyed believed that the United States should have been bolder in Korea, "even at the risk of starting World War III." Asked what policy should be adopted in Korea, a majority (53 percent) felt that the United States should "stop fooling around and do whatever is necessary to knock the Communists out of Korea once and for all." [78] But the president was convinced that his course was the only proper one. In a meeting with the Joint Chiefs of Staff and the secretary of defense on September 15, 1952, Truman did authorize a very limited increase in military pressure in hope of forcing a more conciliatory attitude out of the Communist truce negotiators. But he told his advisers that he could envision no genuine prospect for any armistice other than by persisting with the established course of action.[79]

The campaign to select Truman's successor was heating up by this time, as were the Republican condemnations of his strategy in the Korean War. Although an armistice at the time would have been of inestimable value to his party and a desirable climax to his presidency, Truman refused to allow personal or political considerations to influence his position on a negotiated settlement. His determination was revealed in a meeting in the White House with his principal advisers on September 24, 1952. He said that he did not want an armistice just for the sake of having one, if it meant leaving the Chinese in a situation where they could renew the fighting. A transcript of this session records Truman as saying that he "had been conducting his administration for seven years in an effort to avoid World War III. . . . Nevertheless, he would not weaken on the principles that we are striving to maintain." [80]

The Communists, finding American peace terms unacceptable, broke off negotiations in October, 1952. On the twenty-fourth of the month, the Republican nominee, General Eisenhower, made a major campaign address at Detroit in which he bitterly denounced the Korean policies of his former commander in chief. He said that Korea and the twenty thousand Americans who had died there were "a measure—a damning measure—of the quality of leadership we have been given." Eisenhower said that the Korean War was a direct result of Acheson's "perimeter" speech. If elected, he would not be diverted by political considerations (the implication being that Truman had), but would go personally to Korea to determine how best to bring about an honorable settlement.[81]

Truman had written to Eisenhower on August 13, inviting him to attend cabinet meetings and receive full briefings from the White House staff. He also told the Republican candidate that he had arranged for the CIA to provide him and his Democratic opponent, Adlai Stevenson, with weekly intelligence summaries on the world situation. Replying the next day, Eisenhower declined the invitation so as to remain free to "analyze publicly" the present administration. While welcoming the weekly CIA reports, Eisenhower cautioned that he would not consider them a restriction on his freedom to discuss foreign policy. The response made Truman furious. In a personal note he told Eisenhower that he was very sorry that the latter had allowed "a bunch of screwballs" to come between them. His closing sentence reads: "From a man who has always been your friend and who always intended to be!" [82]

The presidential campaign of 1952 must have been doubly disappointing to Truman. Not only because the result could be interpreted as a repudiation of his Korean policies, but also because Eisenhower, whom he greatly admired and counted as a friend, chose unfairly (in Truman's view) to attack administration policy. In the years between World War II and the 1952 campaign, the president had given every indication of his great faith in the general. In 1946 he had appointed Eisenhower to the permanent rank of general of the army for life. Truman subsequently made Eisenhower chief of staff of the army, later chairman of the joint chiefs and, finally, NATO supreme commander. Their correspondence throughout these years is replete with mutual assurances of respect and loyalty. Eisenhower, for example, wrote early in 1948 of the great sense of honor and privilege he felt for the opportunity to serve under Truman and his gratitude for the president's understanding, encouragement, and friendship. Resigning from the chairmanship of the joint chiefs in 1949, the general assured Truman that it had been "a great honor and privilege to do what I could . . . under your direction as Commander-in-Chief." When Eisenhower resigned as army chief of staff in January, 1948, Truman told him: "You have my heartiest good wishes in whatever you may decide to do—and my friendship and admiration always." [83]

Despite his personal pique at Eisenhower, Truman sent him a message of congratulations immediately after the election and offered the use of the presidential aircraft should he still desire to go to Korea. This was the first of a series of messages exchanged between the two men in the next few days, in all of which Truman emphasized his strong desire to keep the president-elect abreast of the international scene as well as to bring about as effortless a change of administrations as possible.[84] Truman's sincerity in this was displayed in a letter he addressed to all of the principal officers of his administration in December, asking their full cooperation in facilitating an orderly transition. He required that each of them report to him on the steps taken to bring this about. In compliance with this request, Secretary Lovett reported that the Defense Department had provided General Eisenhower with transportation, accommodations, and military intelligence on his trip to Korea, accompanied throughout by Omar Bradley, the chairman of the Joint Chiefs of Staff. Eisenhower, as well as the men he designated as appointees to the various posts in the departments, was being fully briefed and constantly acquainted with the military and administrative information necessary for the conduct of office.[85]

Truman's efforts resulted in a governmental changeover brought about with minimal friction or disruption. However, he had little faith in his successor's ability to govern. MacArthur has recorded that while he and the president were talking privately at Wake Island, the conversation got around to politics. Truman remarked that while he liked the general personally, "Eisenhower doesn't know the first thing about politics. Why, if he should become President, his Administration would make Grant's look like a model of perfection." Truman recalled an observation by Sam Rayburn, powerful House Democrat, who, when asked to comment on the possibility of Eisenhower running for the presidency said: "No, won't do. Good man, but wrong business." [86] Contemplating the possibility of an Eisenhower victory in the summer of 1952, Truman reportedly commented: "He'll sit here and he'll say, 'Do this! Do that!' *And nothing will happen.* Poor Ike—it won't be a bit like the Army. He'll find it very frustrating." [87]

Certainly Truman found his own last months in office very frustrating. He relinquished leadership on January 20, 1953, and left Washington for his home in Independence, his every effort to find a solution to the Korean conflict having ended in abject failure. Too politically weak at home to make peace and too inherently wise to embark on military adventures that might result in general war, he left office with the great issue of his second term unresolved. But Eisenhower faced no such dilemma and was able to end the fighting (July 27, 1953), by accepting a settlement for which Truman would have been damned, a peace without victory.[88]

13/The Defender of the Faith

He was insubordinate and I fired him, just like Lincoln fired McClellan. Sure I knew there would be a lot of stink about it, but I didn't give a damn. It was the right thing to do and I did it.[1]
—HARRY S. TRUMAN

At the end of World War II, President Truman had boundless respect for his European and Pacific theater commanders, Generals Eisenhower and MacArthur. But his regard for both men was diminished by their separate challenges to his decisions as commander in chief during the Korean War. Although Eisenhower's bid for the presidency in 1952 was based on his credentials as a professional soldier, it was as a nominally civilian candidate that he disputed Truman's military policies in the political arena. The American system can tolerate this type of dissent. But the challenge with which MacArthur confronted his commander in chief endangered the very basis of the civil-military relationship, if not the democratic system itself.

The man destined to clash with Truman over Korean strategy was unlike the president in almost every respect. Where Truman had failed to even qualify for the United States Military Academy, MacArthur had graduated from West Point with a superlative record. The blunt, earthy Truman was so avowedly middle class, middle American that he seemed at times to be a caricature of the virtues and foibles ascribed to the type. His frequent trips back to his small hometown in Missouri seemed to be a necessary restorative. The suave, articulate MacArthur, on the other hand, was the regal, proud heir of his father (Arthur), a Medal of Honor winner, who retired in 1909 with the rank of lieutenant-general. Douglas MacArthur had not even visited the United States for over a dozen years prior to his relief in 1951. Aside from their both being born in the 1880s and both being sincere, dedicated Americans, there are few common denominators in the lives of the president and the general.

241

The potential for conflict had always been there. Truman was a firm believer in the principle of civil supremacy. MacArthur later testified to his acceptance of the fundamental concept of military subordination to civilian authority.[2] But there was a lofty, imperious attitude about the general, probably fostered by his years as American proconsul for Japan, that belied these assurances. Perhaps the best indicator of the attitude that led MacArthur into contention with Truman can be found in a framed quotation from Livy which was prominently displayed on the wall of his office in the Dai-Ichi Building, his headquarters in Tokyo. The lines caution that those who seek to advise a military commander should join him on the battlefield and share the danger. It concludes, "We shall pay no attention to any councils but such as shall be framed within our camp." [3] MacArthur did not ignore the "councils" framed by the joint chiefs and the commander in chief. But there is ample evidence that he fought mightily against any of their orders which ran counter to his own thinking. Also, he was not above giving an interpretation to his directives which had the effect of accommodating administration policy to his strategic concepts.

The first indication that MacArthur did not feel absolutely bound by the injunctions in his directives can be found in his order to the Far East air force on June 29, 1950 (Korean time), prior to the president's decision to become completely involved in Korea. MacArthur had ordered that airfields in North Korea be destroyed. His operating directive, dated June 26, gave the Far East commander the authority to attack by air all military targets *south* of the 38th parallel. The general made no effort to obtain clearance for an attack upon a nation with which the United States was not even "unofficially" at war. Courtney Whitney, MacArthur's aide and apostle, explained that the general had made a discretionary decision within the "normal latitude" granted to field commanders. Only an extraordinarily broad reading of the directive would allow such an interpretation. In any event, on the following day (June 29 in Washington) Truman approved an order giving MacArthur the authority he had already assumed—to attack beyond the 38th parallel.[4]

MacArthur paid a brief visit to Formosa on July 31, 1950. While the general did not say so specifically, Truman received the clear impression from newspaper accounts and statements by Chiang Kai-shek and his aides, that MacArthur rejected the president's decision to neutralize the Nationalist Chinese refuge. Truman was concerned enough about the comments in the press to send Averell Harriman to Tokyo to give MacArthur an account of the administration's views on foreign policy, particularly about the Far East. Harriman later reported to the president that MacArthur denied making any political comments in his conversations with Chiang and that while he disagreed on Formosan policy he would "as a soldier, obey any orders that he received from the President." [5]

Truman later recalled that he erred in assuming "General MacArthur would accept the Formosa policy laid down by his commander in chief." Two weeks after Harriman's return, on August 26, Truman was given a copy of a message from MacArthur to Clyde A. Lewis, commander of the Veterans of Foreign Wars. The message, sent at Lewis' request, was to be read to the national encampment in Chicago on August 28. MacArthur told the VFW that he believed it to be in the public interest that he clear up the "misconceptions currently being voiced concerning the relationship of Formosa to our strategic potential in the Pacific." He then went into detail on the great strategic importance that the island of Formosa represented, describing it as the keystone of the protective shield defending the Pacific area and the Americas. After establishing that Formosa was pivotal to maintenance of the defensive perimeter in the Pacific, MacArthur said that if this line were lost, war would inevitably result. The neutralization of Formosa, on the grounds that it lacked strategic importance and that any other course might alienate continental Asia—which was Truman's policy as communicated to MacArthur by Harriman—was fallacious reasoning by those who understood neither "broad strategic concepts" nor the Oriental mind. To MacArthur, existing policy was defeatism and appeasement. He closed with high praise for the president's decision to intervene in Korea.[6]

MacArthur later wrote that his VFW message was apolitical and in full support of Truman's policy respecting Formosa. He said he did not know how his message could have been construed to imply the reverse of the intended meaning, nor how the president could be so "easily deceived," presumably, by his military or political advisers. Truman, on the other hand, believed that the tone of the entire message was an expression of criticism of the policy MacArthur had told Harriman he would support, and that this was the way the general intended it to read. The president felt that the VFW message was a direct contradiction of his statements to Congress as well as his announcement of June 27 which neutralized Formosa. It was also, he felt, contrary to a letter Ambassador Austin had just written to the UN secretary-general on his instructions.[7]

Shortly after reading a copy of the VFW message on August 26, Truman attended a previously scheduled meeting with the secretaries of state, defense, and treasury, the joint chiefs, and Harriman. Acheson recalls that the president entered the room obviously disturbed, his lips "white and compressed." He read them MacArthur's message and then asked each in turn if he had any prior knowledge of the document. All responded negatively. Truman then instructed Secretary of Defense Johnson to inform MacArthur that he (the president) was ordering him to immediately withdraw his statement to the VFW.[8] Truman was aware that the message, having been released by MacArthur's staff to the press in Tokyo, had already appeared in several newspapers and at least one national magazine when he ordered it withdrawn. But by ordering its recall he could demonstrate that the general's views did not represent national policy, on which, Truman said, there could be only one voice—his. The order read: "The President of the United States directs that you withdraw your message for . . . Veterans of Foreign Wars because various features with respect to Formosa are in conflict with the policy of the United States." [9]

Personal memoirs are particularly suspect on such points but Truman has recorded that it was at this juncture he first gave serious thought to relieving MacArthur. He considered taking only the field command in Korea away from him and giving it to Omar Bradley. But he claims to have rejected the idea since it would appear he was demoting MacArthur, whom he had no desire to injure personally. Instead, he decided on a far milder course, a note to his Far East commander explaining the necessity for his order to withdraw the VFW message.[10]

Truman wrote to MacArthur on August 29, enclosing a letter he had written to Ambassador Austin, and calling the general's attention to a letter from Austin to UN Secretary-General Lie, a copy of which had been forwarded to Far East headquarters on the date it was written, August 25. The president's note was brief, explaining that he was certain that once MacArthur had read these letters he would understand why the withdrawal order was given. The letter Truman sent to Austin, dated the twenty-seventh, the day after he became aware of MacArthur's message to the VFW, was released to the press by the White House. An obvious effort to counter the effect of the VFW message, it restated the points made in Austin's letter to the secretary-general, emphasizing that the ambassador's letter accurately reflected the fundamental position of the government respecting neutralization of Formosa and a desire to limit conflict in the Far East.[11] The controversy died down soon afterward, smothered by the news of MacArthur's smashing triumph in the Inchon invasion and the subsequent elimination of the aggressors from South Korea.

Truman and MacArthur had their only face-to-face meeting on Wake Island, October 15, 1950, a month after Inchon. Two years later Truman said, regarding Wake Island: "I made a 14,400 mile trip to get a lot of misinformation." [12] He described the misinformation from MacArthur as the assurance that China would not intervene, that the war was over, and that it would be possible to release a regular army division from Far East service for occupation duties in Germany.[13] There is ample evidence that MacArthur did make these estimates and that they were gross miscalculations of what subsequently transpired; but the general was guilty only of overconfidence. The same intelligence information upon which he based his unfortunate estimates was also known to the president, the chairman of the Joint Chiefs of Staff, and the others present at this meeting. No one saw fit at the time, nor, in fact until events proved otherwise, to challenge MacArthur's assertions.

In his post–Wake Island statements, the president went to great pains to emphasize that there were no disagreements on policy between himself and MacArthur. In a statement issued the day of the meeting, Truman spoke of "the very complete unanimity of view which prevailed." Two days later, speaking at San Francisco, the president admitted that one of his reasons for going to Wake Island was that he felt a need to make it clear, by talking with MacArthur, "that there is complete unity in the aims and conduct of our foreign policy." To a press conference the following day, Truman explained, "There is no disagreement between General MacArthur and myself." [14] MacArthur did not see it this way. When asked at his dismissal hearing if Truman's statement regarding their complete accord, particularly regarding Formosa, was a misinterpretation, MacArthur agreed that it was. The day after his return to Tokyo, MacArthur testified, "I issued a statement . . . that there had been absolutely no change on my part on any views I held as to the strategic value of Formosa." [15] This is most revealing of MacArthur's inability to completely subordinate himself to the president's authority. It seemed never to occur to him that a soldier on active duty should not issue press releases counter to statements made by his commander in chief.

Two incidents which occurred shortly after the Wake Island meeting demonstrate MacArthur's irresponsible disregard for the limitations imposed by modern warfare. On October 24 he told his commanders to use American units in their drive to the Yalu, in unquestionable violation of a directive received a month earlier, stipulating that only Korean forces were to be used in the northern provinces. Less than two weeks later (November 5), MacArthur ordered the air force to destroy the Korean end of all bridges crossing the Yalu River. Again, his order was not consistent with his instructions regarding aerial operations near the Manchurian border. In both instances the Far East commander did not request a change of orders. In both instances the general later explained away his preemptory actions on the basis of military necessity and a broad, unique interpretation of his directives that was never envisioned by their authors.[16] MacArthur won both cases. In the first the joint chiefs deferred to his judgment, although aware he had violated orders. In the second he successfully appealed over the heads of his military superiors to the commander in chief. In winning these two skirmishes against Washington, MacArthur converted the strong likelihood of massive Chinese intervention into a certainty, and then lost the last battle of his brilliant career.

The overwhelming Chinese onslaught in late November brought about a dramatic military reversal and marked the beginning of the second and final phase of the conflict between the president and the general. Truman, while believing that the general northward assault begun on the twenty-fourth was ill-advised, did not blame MacArthur for failing to defeat a vastly superior army. What the president found inexcusable was MacArthur's resorting to public attacks on the administration, alleging that extraordinary limitations made his defeat inevitable.

From the time China intervened until his relief, MacArthur persisted in taking his case to the people, arguing that the military limitations imposed upon him were all that stood in the way of a decisive victory. On November 28 MacArthur denied that he had made the "home by Christmas" statement when launching the general offensive on the twenty-fourth.[17] Two days later, responding to a radiogram from Arthur Krock, MacArthur said that every strategic and tactical movement made by his forces was in accord with UN resolutions and his directives from Washington. He had taken no major steps without full prior approval. MacArthur told Krock that no authoritative source had ever suggested he halt his advance at any point before the Yalu River boundary. (The joint chiefs had made such a suggestion.) China's intervention, MacArthur continued, was long premeditated. "It is historically inaccurate to attribute any degree of responsibility for the onslaught of the Chinese Communist armies to the strategic course of the campaign itself." [18]

On the first day of December, MacArthur granted an interview in which he was asked how his military operations were affected by the imposed limitations, particularly regarding the Manchurian sanctuary. The general described these limitations as "an enormous handicap, without precedent in military history." [19] In a telegram to the United Press on the same date, MacArthur expressed similar sentiments. He said that he was faced with a new war against vastly superior numbers, a situation brought about by his having to accept military odds, "without precedent in history—the odds of permitting offensive action without defensive retaliation." [20] Comments in a similar vein from MacArthur were contained in a general press release to the Tokyo press corps on December 2.[21]

In all these statements to the press, MacArthur consistently stressed four points. First, he denied that his movements toward the Yalu had in any way triggered China's intervention. Second, his "end the war" (or "home by Christmas" or "reconaissance in force") offensive launched on November 24 had forced the enemy to commit forces prematurely and had totally disrupted the enemy's strategic plans, which called for the conquest of all Korea by a continuous sweeping movement southward. Third, MacArthur took exception to reports that his forces were in full retreat, explaining that his troops were executing a predetermined retrograde movement in magnificent order. Fourth, he was unable to defeat the Chinese because of the unreasonable strictures imposed upon the conduct of his operations.[22]

Truman grew quickly out of patience with the press barrage coming from his Far East commander. He was concerned, too, over the confusion regarding American policy that MacArthur's statements were generating in other nations. The president sent the following memorandum to all government agencies on December 6:

> In the light of the present critical international situation, and until further written notice from me, I wish that each one of you would take immediate steps to reduce the number of public speeches pertaining to foreign or military policy made by officials of the departments and agencies of the executive branch. This applies to officials in the field as well as in Washington.
>
> No speech, press release, or other public statement concerning foreign policy should be released until it has received clearance from the Department of State.
>
> No speech, press release, or other public statement concerning military policy should be released until it has received clearance from the Department of Defense.
>
> In addition to the copies submitted to the Departments of State or Defense for clearance, advance copies of speeches and press releases concerning foreign policy or military policy should be submitted to the White House for information.
>
> The purpose of this memorandum is not to curtail the flow of information to the American people, but rather to insure that the information made public is accurate and fully in accord with the policies of the United States Government.[23]

In a memorandum to the secretaries of state and defense the same day, Truman instructed them to order all overseas officials, "including military commanders," to be extremely cautious in their public utterances and to obtain clearance for all but the most routine statements. Additionally, they were to be instructed, in Truman's words, "to refrain from direct communication on military or foreign policy with newspapers, magazines, or other publicity media in the United States." [24] Although these messages were not addressed directly to MacArthur, there can be no doubt that he was the target. General Bradley later testified that prior to MacArthur's press statements such an order had never been necessary, "because it is tradition and custom and common practice of military men, when speaking on policy matters, to submit them, submit their views, for approval." [25]

For the second time Truman considered dismissing MacArthur, but rejected the idea. He said he did not because it would appear that MacArthur was being fired for the failure of the November offensive. Truman said that he had no desire to hit the general while he was down. He did not even wish to reprimand him directly.[26] This, then, is the apparent reason for the "scatter-gun" technique of issuing orders that every government employee must clear military and foreign policy statements.

The target of Truman's orders must have been hit by the salvo, for MacArthur was silent on policy questions throughout December and January. He continued to struggle with the joint chiefs, but through the proper, nonpublic channels. Then, a "leak" developed in MacArthur's headquarters on February 6, 1951. The Associated Press reported that MacArthur had recommended the use of Chinese Nationalist forces against the Chinese mainland and in Korea. The unidentified source also indicated that the general had, on three occasions, sought permission to bomb the privileged sanctuary in Manchuria. MacArthur was reportedly stressing that there could be no turning back in the struggle against Communism, not just in Korea, but throughout the Orient.[27] A week later, under his own name, MacArthur issued a public statement which attacked strategic proposals then under active consideration by the joint chiefs, the National Security Council and the president. He said that he was still fighting a war of maneuver, and dismissed "the concept being advanced by some" that a switch be made to positional warfare by the establishment of a defensive line across the Korean peninsula. This, MacArthur said, was strategically unsound and would result in the piecemeal destruction of UN forces. He again lashed out at the unprecedented military advantage which sanctuary gave to the Chinese, who were "engaging with impunity in undeclared war against us." [28]

General MacArthur must have come to a decision in February that he could no longer remain publicly silent on policy. Whether he sought only personal exculpation from the defeat in Korea, or still hoped to garner victory by forcing Truman and the Defense Department to yield to mass popular support for his ideas is not certain. He begins to emerge as a Billy Mitchell-type figure, striving to change the strategic thinking of a static bureaucracy. There was one significant difference: MacArthur wished to revert to an older concept of warfare, one that recognized no political limitations.

The depths of MacArthur's bitterness and frustration can be gathered from a conversation he had in February with General Mark Clark, then chief of army field forces. MacArthur dwelt on the errors in policy of "great magnitude and danger" being made in Washington. His views and recommendations, he told Clark, had largely been ignored at critical times. In this regard, he was most critical of the joint chiefs. MacArthur found it incomprehensible that the administration continued to allow sanctuary, providing the enemy with a secure base of supply and air operations. Clark, who would eventually replace Ridgway in the Far East command post, agreed with MacArthur on the sanctuary question then and later.[29]

The Far East commander was back on his most persistent theme, the "abnormal conditions" affecting his command, in another public statement issued March 7, 1951. MacArthur closed this release by insisting that important politico-military decisions, far beyond his authority, had yet to be made. These decisions, he said, would have to provide "on the international level an answer to the obscurities which now becloud the unsolved problems raised by Red China's undeclared war in Korea."[30] Later, when asked by Senator Lyndon Johnson if the closing lines of this release complied meticulously with the president's directive, Secretary of Defense Marshall testified that he did not think it did. The secretary of state had an even stronger reaction to a statement by MacArthur to Hugh Baille, president of United Press, on March 15. The general criticized the decision to halt at the 38th parallel, since this did not achieve the mission of Korean unification. Acheson believed that MacArthur's March 15 statement was a new move, from private harassment of the administration, to open defiance of Truman's order regarding unauthorized comment on national policy.[31]

The conflict between Truman and MacArthur was rapidly intensifying. On March 20, as previously described, the joint chiefs informed MacArthur that the State Department was in the process of drafting a statement in which Truman would seek a negotiated settlement. In a release from Tokyo four days later, MacArthur stated his willingness to negotiate a military settlement with the enemy commander. His statement also contained a thinly veiled threat that if a settlement were not reached, the United Nations might well extend military operations to the coastal areas and interior bases of China, which would bring about its military collapse.[32]

An administration spokesman quickly informed the press that Mac-

Arthur's statement involved political issues beyond his responsibility as a field commander.[33] However, convinced that any possibility for negotiations had been temporarily forestalled, Truman abandoned the effort. In the president's view, MacArthur's statement flouted UN policy. The general, Truman said, was in open defiance of the commander in chief, challenging the very basis of the civil authority of the president over the military established in the Constitution. "By this act," Truman wrote, "MacArthur left me no choice—I could no longer tolerate his insubordination." Despite this emphatic statement (in his *Memoirs*), Truman waited over two more weeks before relieving the Far East commander. His only immediate act was to order the joint chiefs to tell MacArthur that he (the president) was directing his attention to the December 6 order and stipulating that any further statements be cleared through channels.[34]

Millions of copies of MacArthur's March 24 statement had been printed and air-dropped over enemy territory on his authority. He explained later that this was part of "psychological warfare." He said that his statement was a cold military appraisal designed to end the bloodshed and bring peace. It had, he said, no relationship to the joint chiefs' message of the twentieth regarding the drafting of a peace feeler for issue by the president. Nor, according to MacArthur, was his message designed to embarrass Truman "or anyone else working to bring about peace." [35] Less than six months later, addressing the American Legion, MacArthur said that his statement had prevented a disgraceful plot to appease China by surrendering Formosa and turning Nationalist China's United Nations seat over to Peking in return for peace in Korea. MacArthur told the Legionnaires that he had "unquestionably wrecked" this plot.[36]

House Minority Leader Joseph W. Martin precipitated MacArthur's dismissal by disclosing the letter received from him on the floor of the House, April 5, 1951. Martin had written to MacArthur on March 8 requesting his views on the Far East. The now-famed response was not unique, but dwelt on the same basic themes: release from the imposed limitations, utilization of Chinese Nationalist armies, and recognition that while Europe received all of the attention, he was fighting the Battle of Armageddon in Asia. MacArthur considered the exchange of letters with Martin innocuous, just another courtesy to a Congressman, phrased in very general terms.[37] Viewed as a piece of private correspondence, it was just that. When Martin chose (without Mac-Arthur's consent) to make the letter public, it became a controversial document.

Writing in his *Memoirs*, Truman dealt at length with the letter to Representative Martin. He dissected the two principal paragraphs, noting MacArthur's inconsistency on the employment of Formosan troops, disagreeing with the general's "Asia-first" philosophy, and holding that the idea of "meeting force with maximum counterforce" was not part of the American tradition. He ended his examination of MacArthur's letter with the following comments: "MacArthur's letter to Congressman Martin showed that the general was not only in disagreement with the policy of the government but was challenging this policy in open insubordination to his Commander in Chief." [38]

It was not the Martin letter that determined the issue. Truman wrote that after March 24 he could no longer tolerate this insubordination.[39] He had already decided to fire MacArthur; only the means and timing were undetermined. The Martin letter was merely a catalyst to the process.

Shortly after Martin read MacArthur's letter to the House of Representatives, Secretary of State Acheson received a call from the White House instructing him to meet with the president and Secretary of Defense Marshall the next morning. Acheson had no doubt about the subject of this meeting. General Bradley also received a call that afternoon, although he was not able to recall who it was from, advising him that the president was very concerned about MacArthur's statements. Bradley held a brief meeting with the chiefs of staff immediately afterward, warning them that they should consider what recommendations they would make respecting the military implications of a possible relief of General MacArthur.[40]

Truman met with Acheson, Marshall, Bradley, and Harriman in his office, Friday morning, April 6. He asked for their views on what should be done about MacArthur's open defiance. Knowing that his views would influence the advice he received, Truman did not contribute to the discussion. Harriman offered the opinion that MacArthur should have been dismissed two years earlier. The three other advisers present were more conservative. Marshall wanted time to reflect. He also told Truman that firing MacArthur might cause problems in getting the military appropriations bill through Congress. Bradley believed that on the basis of his statements, the president would be justified in relieving MacArthur, but indicated a desire to consult with the other members of the joint chiefs before making a final recommendation. Acheson agreed on the question of dismissal, but was concerned about the political, military, and diplomatic repercussions. He cautioned against making a hasty decision, since basic questions were involved, particularly the prerogatives and duties of the president as commander in chief in his relationship to one of his most important military subordinates. He warned the president that if the decision were made to relieve MacArthur, he would face the greatest political battle of his administration. Truman made no decisions. He asked those present to meet among themselves and then meet again with him the following morning.[41]

The meeting together of the four advisers Friday afternoon and their subsequent meeting with the president on Saturday, April 7, were inconclusive. In the Friday meeting General Marshall asked the others for their opinions on the possibility of ordering MacArthur to Washington for consultation and arriving at a final determination after that. Acheson, Bradley, and Harriman were all opposed. Truman's session with the same four advisers on Saturday morning was brief. Marshall told the president that he had read all the communications received from MacArthur since 1949 and now agreed with Harriman that he should have been fired two years earlier. Truman directed Bradley to obtain the opinions of the chiefs of staff from a "purely military" point of view. He accepted a suggestion that all present dwell privately on the question over the weekend and instructed them to be prepared to make their final recommendations to him on Monday.[42]

General Bradley met with the chiefs of staff at the Pentagon on Sunday afternoon, April 8, in order to obtain their views. They all concurred; MacArthur should be dismissed. There was discussion among them as to the feasibility of relieving MacArthur of the Korean command but allowing him to remain in his post as supreme commander of the Allied powers for Japan, but this was ruled out as impractical. As later reported by General Bradley, the joint chiefs had three basic reasons for concurring in the removal. First, the general's official communications and public statements indicated a lack of sympathy with the limited war policy in Korea; second, MacArthur had violated the president's directive relative to clearing public statements; third, "The

Joint Chiefs of Staff, have felt and feel now that the military must be controlled by civilian authority in this country," and MacArthur's actions were jeopardizing this control.[43]

Meeting with the president at nine o'clock Monday morning, Bradley informed him of the unanimous concurrence of the joint chiefs. Marshall, Acheson, and Harriman, each in his turn, indicated agreement that General MacArthur should be immediately relieved of all his commands. It was only then that Truman told them that he had come to that decision after MacArthur's statement of March 24. The president directed that orders be prepared relieving MacArthur and appointing General Ridgway as his successor. These orders and a draft public statement were brought to the president at three o'clock, Tuesday, April 10, and he approved them.[44]

An unfortunate series of events disrupted the process by which MacArthur was to be informed of his relief. It was originally planned that the secretary of the army, Frank Pace, who was then in Korea, would personally inform the general in Tokyo. The orders were to be wired in State Department code to Ambassador Muccio in Pusan for delivery to Pace, who, it was assumed, was with Muccio. However, Pace was visiting the front with Ridgway at the time. In addition, a power unit failed at Pusan, delaying receipt of the message from the State Department. At this point, General Bradley came to Blair House to tell Truman that the news had apparently leaked and was to be published by a Chicago paper in the morning, long before Pace could reach MacArthur. Truman, perhaps to avoid giving his antagonist an opportunity to resign before he was fired, ordered that MacArthur be informed immediately and directly over the army's own communications network.[45]

At one o'clock in the morning, April 11, reporters were summoned to the White House and given a series of hurriedly reproduced copies of the dismissal order, a statement by the president, and several "background" documents.[46] In his statement, Truman said it had become necessary to remove the general because he could not give wholehearted support to the policies of the United States and the United Nations. Acknowledging that "full and vigorous debate" is a vital element in democracy, the president went on to say: "It is fundamental, however, that military commanders must be governed by the policies and directives issued to them in the manner provided by our laws and constitution." [47] Truman also addressed the nation by radio on the evening of April 11. The bulk of the speech explained basic policies in Korea. Only two paragraphs mentioned the dismissal of MacArthur, and they were largely a rephrasing of the statement he had issued earlier that morning. [48]

General MacArthur was informed of his dismissal by his wife, who learned of it from an aide listening to a news broadcast. The relief process was abrupt and lacked the courtesy many felt he should have been accorded. His relief came, MacArthur said, "just when victory was within my grasp." Shortly after the news was received, General Whitney told the Tokyo press corps melodramatically: "I have just left the General. He received the word magnificently. . . . His soldierly qualities were never more pronounced. I think this has been his finest hour." MacArthur's own estimate of his personal worth was never higher than when he described in his memoirs the world's reaction to the news of his dismissal: "Moscow and Peiping rejoiced. The bells were rung and a holiday atmosphere prevailed. The left-wingers everywhere exulted. But in the Far East, there was bewilderment and shock." [49]

Much of the initial response to MacArthur's dismissal in the United States took the form of vehement attacks on Truman. He was burned in effigy in numerous cities. Dock workers in New York walked out in a protest strike. The Los Angeles city council adjourned to sorrowfully contemplate the "political assassination" of MacArthur. The legislatures of Illinois, Michigan, Florida, and California all passed resolutions condemning Truman's action. [50] One national magazine commented, "Seldom has a more unpopular man fired a more popular one." [51] Many in the Senate were incredulous. Senator William Jenner announced solemnly that "a secret inner coterie" directed by Soviet agents was running the government of the United States. Senator Richard M. Nixon saw the dismissal as rank appeasement of communism. He suggested that the Senate censure the president and insisted that he reinstate MacArthur to command. Senator Joseph McCarthy said the president must have made his decision while drunk on benedictine and bourbon. McCarthy added, "The son of a bitch ought to be impeached." [52]

Writing at the time of the dismissal, journalist Arthur Krock said that it is a basic American principle that the authority of the president as commander in chief must not be undermined by military officers: "This basic principle General MacArthur disregarded with increasing openness, but it certainly does not seem to be disapproved by millions of Americans." [53] Telegrams poured into Congress at a ratio of ten to one against Truman's decision. If internal White House reports can be accepted on this subject, Truman faired better in messages addressed directly to him. By the end of the fifth week following MacArthur's relief, Truman had received 46,389 letters and telegrams described as "Pro MacArthur" and 37,708 that were "Pro President." [54] Apparently many of Truman's correspondents became quite abusive in their denunciations of his decision. Memoranda from the White House mail room listed a total of 1,745 letters and cards "critical of the President" as having been referred to the Secret Service.[55]

Untold millions of Americans may have opposed Truman's recall of MacArthur, but an overwhelming majority of the working press supported his decision. An extensive survey of 332 newspaper and periodical correspondents in Washington, Korea, Tokyo, and at the United Nations was made a few weeks after the dismissal. Eighty-five percent of the reporters questioned believed Truman to be right in removing the general; only thirteen percent felt he was wrong. Most also agreed that the decision was "delayed too long and delivered too bluntly." The main reasons given by those correspondents who agreed that the recall was warranted were almost identical to the reasons stated by the Joint Chiefs of Staff. The reporters saw MacArthur as obviously out of sympathy with national policy. More importantly, they emphasized the necessity for civilian control: "We must preserve the Constitutional right of the Commander-in-Chief to remove an insubordinate general." [56]

The emotional fever was running high as MacArthur arrived in San Francisco from the Far East. The defeated commander, stripped of all powers and accused of flagrant insubordination, was driven about the streets, not in a tumbrel, but in a Cadillac limousine of the type used for a conquering hero or a visiting monarch. In the minds of many, he was both. MacArthur described his welcome home as "tumultuous." With unabashed conceit he wrote: "It seemed to me that every man, woman, and child in San Francisco turned out to cheer us." Having been invited to address a joint session of the Congress on April 19, he flew on to Washington where, the general recalled, "it looked as though the whole District of Columbia greeted our arrival." [57]

MacArthur's speech to the Congress was a forensic masterpiece. He began by depicting himself as just another American "in the fading twilight of life," desiring only to serve his country. In the body of the speech he emphasized the importance of the Far East and his role there, glossed over the reasons for his recall, reiterated his belief that there was no substitute for total victory, and dismissed the president's policies as appeasement. He closed with the touching, now-famous lines about old soldiers not dying, but just fading away, promising to do likewise.[58]

The "fading away" process was protracted and voluble. It began with MacArthur's being borne from the Congress down Pennsylvania Avenue to the Washington Monument in another ceremonial automobile. As he rode between ranks of cheering admirers, formations of Air Force jet fighters and bombers provided an aerial escort. In ceremonies at the monument grounds, MacArthur was awarded a silver tea service by his followers along with a seventeen-gun salute.[59] Truman, sitting in the White House a short distance from this scene, had anticipated it all. In a letter to a friend on the day he signed the dismissal order, he had written: "It will undoubtedly create a great furor but under the circumstances I could do nothing else and still be President of the United States." [60]

Through these ceremonies and numerous addresses, General MacArthur had ample opportunity to present his case to the public. The climax came in the Senate investigation of the reasons for MacArthur's dismissal, which began on May 3, 1951. Thirteen witnesses were heard in a forty-two-day period in which a total of 2,450,000 words were recorded on 3,691 pages of printed testimony. MacArthur, the lead-off witness, testified for three days. The general assured his questioners that he did not in any way question the president's decision to fire him or his right to do so. But he repeatedly dismissed as completely invalid the reason Truman gave for dismissing him—a lack of sympathy with established policies—by claiming that while he sometimes disagreed with the wisdom and judgment of the orders and directives he received, he carried them out to the best of his ability.[61]

There appeared to be an area of agreement between MacArthur

and Truman over the command latitude that must be accorded by the commander in chief to a theater commander. MacArthur testified that once war began, a theater commander had to direct—politically, economically, and militarily—the whole area encharged to him: "You have got to trust at that stage of the game when politics fails, and the military takes over, you must trust the military." Later in his testimony, he said, "There should be no non-professional interference in the handling of troops in a campaign. You have professionals to do that job and they should be permitted to do it." [62] Truman once related in an interview his belief that one of MacArthur's tactical decisions seemed wrong, but that he did not countermand it because the general was commander in the field. He explained: "You pick your man, you've got to back him up. That's the only way a military organization can work." [63] Truman's belief in allowing commanders tactical latitude was more than an abstract principle to him. He never publicly criticized his commander's conduct of field operations, nor dictated troop dispositions to him, except in the broad, strategic sense. For example, in July, 1950, he told reporters: "I am not in charge of the military in Korea . . . a report is made every day by General MacArthur, and he is the one to evaluate the situation. I rely on his evaluation." [64] To this extent, the general and the president were in agreement on the civil-military relationship.

A major area of disagreement between Truman and MacArthur which was highlighted in the latter's testimony was, of course, the political restrictions which the president's limited war policy placed on the conduct of military operations. "I do unquestionably state," MacArthur said, "that when men become locked in battle, that there should be no artifice under the name of politics, which should handicap your own men." [65] In voicing public opposition to these limitations, MacArthur believed he was performing a service, because the American public had the right to know the truth, and Truman had no right to "gag" him. In his memoirs, MacArthur quoted British Field Marshall Lord Alanbrooke, who had defended MacArthur's actions by saying that any general who is unable to obtain the political advice and guidance he seeks has a responsibility to act on his own.[66] The fullest expression of MacArthur's revolutionary interpretation of his responsibility to civilian authority can be found in an address he made to the legislature of Massachusetts three months after his dismissal: "I find in existence a new and heretofore unknown and dangerous concept that the members of the Armed Forces owe their primary allegiance and loyalty to those who temporarily exercise the authority of the executive branch of the government, rather than to the country and its Constitution they are sworn to defend. No proposition could cast greater doubt on the integrity of the Armed Forces." [67]

The Truman administration did not sit passively by during this period, but counterattacked; the basic argument being that the really "new and dangerous concept" was embodied in MacArthur's public challenge to the policies of his commander in chief. A major response to the charges MacArthur was publicizing at the time was delivered by General Bradley one week after the dismissal. Speaking at Chicago, Bradley refuted MacArthur point by point. Whereas MacArthur said there was no Korean policy, Bradley listed its primary objectives, making it plain that appeasement—another MacArthur charge—was not part of that policy. Without naming him specifically, Bradley described MacArthur's solutions for Korea as not being militarily feasible. Bradley emphasized that the Korean conflict had to be understood as part of a worldwide American commitment to contain communism and prevent the onset of a third world war.[68] To counter rumors to the contrary, on April 19, 1951, the Pentagon issued a statement saying that "the action taken by the President in relieving Gen. MacArthur was based upon the unanimous recommendations of the President's principal civilian and military advisers, including the Joint Chiefs of Staff." [69]

Truman remained publicly aloof from the controversy engendered by MacArthur's dismissal throughout April, issuing no statements in rebuttal and responding noncommitally to pointed questions in his press conferences. Privately, he was not as disinterested. For example, in a note to Averell Harriman on April 24, Truman wrote: "He [Eisenhower] seems to be on top of the situation and he also seems to understand the international situation better than another 5-star General I can name." In a press conference held the day MacArthur began his testimony in the hearings on his dismissal, Truman joined the battle to defend his own policies for the first time. The president said that it was MacArthur's persuasion at Wake Island that convinced him the

Chinese Communists would not intervene in North Korea. Truman also told the assembled reporters that he was confident he would be vindicated once testimony in the hearings was completed.[70]

In a nationally broadcast address on May 7, the president struck back repeatedly at the various charges leveled by MacArthur in his just completed testimony. Acknowledging that he had refused to extend the Far East conflict, he explained that such action offered no real promise of ending the war, but posed the very real threat of expanding and protracting the hostilities. As to the suggestion by MacArthur that the United States "go it alone," if the Allies were unwilling to attack China, Truman said this would destroy the United Nations, NATO, and the entire collective security system. Throughout, he returned to the overall guiding principle of his policy decisions, the prevention of a third world war. MacArthur was never mentioned by name, but he was unquestionably the main topic, a point not lost to the press in their accounts the next day.[71]

In the lengthy, often tedious pages of the hearings in Congress can be found the vindication which Truman had predicted. No objective reading of these pages can lead to any other conclusion but that the president was amply justified in removing MacArthur from command. Virtually all of the testimony which followed MacArthur's rebutted his basic contentions. This evidence, cited at length throughout the present and preceding chapters, does not require restatement here. The case for MacArthur's dismissal was cogently summarized by General Marshall:

> The responsibilities and the courses of action assigned to a theater commander necessarily apply to his own immediate area of responsibility. It is completely understandable and, in fact, at times commendable that a theater commander should become so wholly wrapped up in his own aims and responsibilities that some of the directives received by him from higher authority are not those that he would have written for himself. There is nothing new about this sort of thing in our military history. *What is new, and what has brought about the necessity for General MacArthur's removal, is the wholly unprecedented situation of a local theater commander publicly expressing his displeasure at and his disagreement with the foreign and military policy of the United States.*
> It became apparent that General MacArthur had grown so far out of sympathy with the established policies of the United States that there was grave doubt as to whether he could any longer be permitted to exercise the authority in making decisions that normal command

functions would assign to a theater commander. In this situation, there was no other recourse but to relieve him.[62]

Douglas MacArthur had described the onset of the Korean conflict as "Mars' last gift to an old warrior."[73] Fate seemed to have handed him the capstone for an already legendary career; up to the moment of Chinese intervention, the final chapter was ending in fairy-tale fashion. Fortune, however, shown a hero, wrote a tragedy. It was not the defeat, or even the conceit that could not acknowledge failure, which finally tarnished the heroic figure. It was his paranoidal assault on civilian authority, which struck at the very base of the system to which he had devoted over fifty years of his life.

Wilber Hoare has described MacArthur as a "politico-military anachronism," whose "sense of frustration and rage at being denied an unequivocal victory were not those of a man who understood the reasons for denial and opposed them, but of one who did not understand at all."[74] But in view of MacArthur's acknowledged brilliance, it is difficult to believe that he had no comprehension of the concept of limited warfare. Rather, it seems, he fully grasped the concept intellectually, but rejected it as a principle for the conduct of military operations. Then, failing to win acceptance for his views through the established channels, he took his case to the public in clear and open opposition to the commander in chief.

A Civil War buff like Truman could not overlook the historical parallel between Lincoln's difficulties with General George McClellan and his own with MacArthur. He recognized a basic difference, in that he was trying to keep a checkrein on MacArthur, whereas Lincoln was trying desperately to get McClellan to attack. But Truman implies that McClellan (like MacArthur) was fired for politically opposing his commander in chief, when in truth he was dismissed for his failures as a general. The real parallel may well be, as one writer noted, that like McClellan, MacArthur was "confusing his popularity as a symbol of patriotism in a nation at war with his duty as a general on active service."[75] Had MacArthur first retired and then opposed Truman's policies in the political arena (as Eisenhower did), he would have been beyond reproach. But by attacking from within, he forced his own dismissal.

The basis for the disagreement between Truman and MacArthur rested upon fundamental strategic policy determinations. Truman had decided that extending military operations beyond Korea itself, in order to obtain a victory in Korea, involved too great a risk of general war. Also, the president decided that victory—in the sense of Korean unification—was neither worth the increased effort that would be required, nor essential to American security. MacArthur, of course, considered the Far Eastern struggle to be the pivotal, climactic contest between the forces of capitalism and communism. Truman came to accept a military stalemate which preserved South Korean sovereignty as achievement enough; MacArthur could accept no alternative to complete victory. Since Truman neither could nor would relinquish his authority as commander in chief to conduct the war, MacArthur had to go.

The restrictions placed upon MacArthur by the limited war policy—a few were later lifted—did represent a significant check by the president on the conduct of military operations. Raymond G. O'Connor correctly maintains that these controls represented an enlargement of the president's role as commander in chief. He is correct in holding that the conflict with MacArthur was an understandable consequence of Truman's exercising this role. But O'Connor stands on shakier historical ground when he asserts that Truman's "detailed control of battlefield operations" was without any precedent. "Even Lincoln," O'Connor says, "did not match Truman's interference with military tactics." [76] So long as MacArthur (and his successors) operated within the strategic guidelines imposed by the president and the Joint Chiefs of Staff, tactical decisions were neither dictated nor countermanded. Truman did not believe that the field deployment and utilization of forces was a proper function of a commander in chief. Lincoln, particularly when McClellan was in command in the East, was actively engaged in tactical direction of armies in the field.

Truman commented often, after the event, on MacArthur's dismissal and its meaning. He believed that MacArthur did not deliberately set out to challenge his authority as commander in chief, but that his actions did endanger the principle of civilian control which Truman considered fundamental to the existence of a free society. As he wrote to the president of the University of Virginia: "I regret very much that the action had to be taken but the civilian control of the military was at stake and I simply had to do something about it." Or, in a similar vein, to the mayor of Paterson, New Jersey: "In time,

people will realize and understand that military commanders must be
governed by the policies and directives issued to them in the manner
provided by our laws and Constitution." [77]

A college student once asked the former president the rationale behind MacArthur's firing. Truman said he fired him for disobeying
orders. He added that "maybe" he should have court-martialed him
as well.[78] When an interviewer asked him if he considered relieving
MacArthur the most courageous act of his presidency, Truman told
him that it had not involved courage. The general was insubordinate
and was fired. That was all.[79] But at the time of the dismissal, Truman
was not as cavalier as he was in his later comments. A week after the
recall, he told Representative Carl Albert that MacArthur's distinguished record of military service made his decision very difficult. Two
days later the president wrote to another correspondent about the difficulty he had in determining to dismiss "one of our greatest military
commanders." From Truman's letters in the weeks after the recall
order there emerges a constant emphasis: He had acted only after
being forced to by MacArthur in consideration of his constitutional
responsibilities as commander in chief: "In justice to my own responsibility . . . I found myself compelled to take this distressing action." [80]

A new philosophy must enter into the training of military leaders.
It must be made clear that the objective in limited warfare is not neces-
sarily victory in the classic sense, but a *modus vivendi*, a reasonable
peace which precludes general war. MacArthur would have considered
this a shameful compromise with "evil." But Truman knew that in a
nuclear age there could be no victors.

In a letter to Dwight Eisenhower, then NATO supreme commander,
Truman expressed himself on MacArthur's recall with characteristic
bluntness: "Dear Ike," he wrote on April 12, "I was sorry to have to
reach a parting of the way with the big man in Asia but he asked for
it and I had to give it to him." [81] And so he did.

14/ The Commander in Chief

I will leave it to future historians to judge how well I have done.[1]

—HARRY S. TRUMAN

The American presidency has evolved with the times. The less hectic tempo of the first half of the twentieth century allowed the presidents time for personal direction of the government, time to examine all sides of an issue, time for an endless procession of *pro forma* ceremonials, and time to relish the perquisites of the office. The Roosevelt administration may be viewed as a transitional phase. World War II greatly accelerated the continuous process of social, political, and technological change with which a president must contend. The pace and complex interrelationships of postwar issues have been such that the executive authority has expanded along with the difficulties of administering the office effectively.

Harry Truman was the first incumbent in the "new" presidency. The preceding chapters represent only a selective recounting of events relating to exercise of the military function during his terms in office. But there is enough here to suggest the enormity of the task which Truman faced. Considering this, Clinton Rossiter wrote: "It was no mean achievement simply to have gone through the motions of being President in these eight years." [2] Truman believed that no one person could truly fill the office because the responsibilities had become too many and too great. But he also believed that there was a quality about the presidency that could make one equal to the task: "It *is* a tremendous job. . . . A really huge job. One to make a person stop and think. . . . Any man faced with this job, no matter what he's like, no matter how much or how little he's capable of to begin with—any man will be lifted up by the dignity and responsibility of this job to a place where he can meet it." [3]

264

Truman was a man of strong convictions. Despite a lack of formal education, his own extensive reading in history and government provided him with as clear a comprehension of presidential function as any of his predecessors. However, lacking the charismatic quality of presidents like Lincoln and Franklin Roosevelt, or the political abilities of leaders like Lyndon Johnson, his performance of these functions was often unequal to the task at hand. At his best, he consciously emulated strong "liberals" like Jefferson, Jackson, Lincoln, Wilson, and the two Roosevelts. He was constantly wary of congressional encroachment on executive functions, believing entirely in the separation-of-powers principle, even to the point of refusing a subpoena from a House committee on those grounds after his presidency.

"The President," Truman wrote, "must use whatever power the Constitution does not expressly deny him." [4] Despite all the powers given to the office by the Constitution and legislative enactments, Truman felt that the prime power of the chief executive was exhortation: "The principal power that the President has is to bring people in and try to persuade them to do what they ought to do without persuasion. . . . That's what the powers of the President amount to." [5] Commenting on the same subject in a 1947 meeting, he said that most of his time as president was taken up soothing hurt feelings and "saluting the backsides of a large number of people." [6] On another occasion, without being anatomically specific, Truman told an interviewer: "I sit here at the President's desk talking to people and kissing them on both cheeks trying to get them to do what they ought to do without getting kissed." [7]

The Constitution, in particularizing the powers of the president, invests him with only one substantive title, that of commander in chief. The title and the military function it designates are inseparable from the office. Like many another president, however, Truman liked to think of his military command responsibility as one of the separate and distinct "jobs" or "hats" incumbent within the executive office. [8] As commander in chief, he conceived of his function as being executor of all military policy. He defined the issues and objectives but did not personally determine these policies. Rather, the staff process, channeled through the National Security Council, presented him with military policy recommendations which he accepted, rejected, or revised. [9]

Truman did not attempt to direct the military, but he did exercise complete supervisory control. He usually enjoyed a harmonious relationship with the joint chiefs and the defense secretary, but never allowed them to intrude upon his presidential prerogatives. Maintaining this control meant devoting much time and study to each military proposal and directive. By requiring that all but the most routine of military matters receive his personal approval prior to issuance of orders, he precluded the possibility of a strong, independent military arising to intimidate the civilian leadership. He trusted his military advisers (notably Bradley and Marshall) because they gave him no cause to mistrust them. He was also willing to allow theater commanders freedom of tactical action, so long as they remained within established policy guidelines. Time and again he emphasized that he did not believe the commander in chief should become involved in tactics: "I am not a desk strategist and don't intend to be one," Truman told reporters in 1950. "I leave that to the military men." [10] Or, again in 1951: "That is a military matter, and the President of the United States has never interfered with military maneuvers in the field, and he doesn't expect to interfere in it now." [11]

Truman's direction of the military, unlike that of his predecessor, was not based on personal leadership, or any particular insight or intuition. In fact, one of the characteristics of his incumbency was an institutionalization of the presidential command functions. The structural components have not always operated as designed, but the military command system of today (somewhat modified), is that instituted by Truman.[12] In an age of intercontinental missiles and thermonuclear weaponry, it can be validly argued that this structure is too cumbersome. Truman himself bypassed the staff mechanism when the occasion demanded.

In the crisis over Berlin, Truman acted without waiting for policy recommendations to evolve. It was his decision alone to stay in Berlin and supply the city by airlift. In the early days of the Korean War, Truman unhesitatingly ordered a regimental combat team into action solely on his own authority as commander in chief, thus creating a condition of war without a declaration of war. In the entire week-long process of decision committing the United States to the armed defense of South Korea, the president did not once convene the National Security Council. Also, Truman decided to fire MacArthur and then went through the motions of obtaining the recommendations of his military advisers.

In retrospect, one of Truman's most serious errors as commander in chief was allowing the success of the Inchon invasion to influence a departure from the original objective in Korea. The United States had gone to war to repel the North Korean invaders. The Inchon assault had restored the status quo. Truman then allowed an essentially defensive action to become offensive by permitting MacArthur to cross the 38th parallel. Through military means the administration hoped to gain a political objective—Korean unification.

The Chinese Communist intervention in November forced Truman to choose between committing far more resources and modifying his war aims. He did not immediately act, but waited until UN forces had regained the 38th parallel before accepting status quo antebellum as an appropriate basis for negotiation. It was in the hearings on MacArthur's recall that this new policy was publicly acknowledged. Acheson testified that the "political objective" of the United States since 1945, and of the United Nations since 1947, was the establishment of a free, unified, democratic Korean state. The "military mission" was to repel the North Korean aggressors and establish peace and security in the area. "Unhappily," Acheson said, "the intervention of the Chinese Communists threw our forces back and made it militarily difficult, if not impossible, to achieve the political objective." [13]

Truman's decision to invade and conquer North Korea was a revision of the containment doctrine. In previous applications of this policy—Greece, Turkey, and Berlin—the American military response had been carefully gauged so as to counter Communist actions and restore things as they had been. Once this was achieved, diplomatic means were found to end the confrontation.[14] But by insisting on the unification of all Korea, Truman had embarked upon a military adventure intent upon the destruction of a Communist satellite nation. The Communist version of containment then required a response which restored equilibrium and culminated in a negotiated settlement that returned the peninsula to its prewar condition.

American strategic policy under Truman was generally based not on action, but reaction, to stimuli. In each case, the stimulus has been provided by "Communist aggression." This defensive posture, requisite in a democratic system, takes away any advantages that accrue to an aggressor, such as picking the time and place for disputation.

The limited-action/limited-response military decisions made by Truman were *ad hoc* adaptations to a succession of tense confrontations in a sadly polarized world. His decision in each instance was designed to avoid the atomic maelstrom of another total war. In Truman's words, "The one purpose that dominated me in everything I thought and did was to prevent a third world war." [15] As the sole human being ever to press the nuclear trigger, Truman must have been more aware than anyone that atomic technology made total war the ultimate irrationality. "The atomic bomb," John Spanier aptly observed, "made the world safe only for limited wars." [16] Viewed in that context, the fear of nuclear holocaust has returned a measure of rationality to military confrontations, reason dictating strict limitations on both means and ends.[17] It is to Harry Truman's credit that he established a Cold War precedent based on this proposition.

There was certainly no diminution in the powers of the commander in chief during Truman's tenure of office. In his exercise of the military functions of the presidency, Truman did, in fact, enlarge upon the traditional role. This is particularly true in consideration of his disregard for the military authority of the Congress. Truman decided to aid Turkey and Greece, defy the blockade of Berlin, and intervene in a foreign civil war, all without the prior approval of Congress. Also, after the Korean War began, Truman sent four Army divisions into Europe to bolster NATO defenses in the mistaken belief that the attack in Asia was simply a feint by the Soviet Union. The president did so despite strong opposition from the Senate. This action represents a positive expansion of the commander in chief powers, since it established a peacetime precedent for ordering American troops into other lands to honor the terms of an international alliance.[18]

Through his efforts as commander in chief, Truman made the military establishment over, generally, for the better. His desegregation of the military services, although it may have been politically motivated and was not vigorously pursued, was important in itself and had an immeasurable influence upon the domestic civil rights movement in the 1950s and 1960s. His unification of the armed forces did not achieve all that he had envisioned. It did modernize the command system and make the military establishment somewhat more responsive to civilian direction. But, for the most part, the massive Pentagon monolith absorbed the imposed reforms of unification and continued without marked change, except that it obtained greater political strength from unity. By the passage of the Atomic Energy Act of 1946 and his resistance to subsequent military encroachment on atomic weapons policy, Truman preserved for future commanders in chief the ultimate decision on utilization of the ultimate weapon.

In the long view of history, Harry Truman will doubtlessly be most remembered for his first major decision as commander in chief, his decision to drop the atomic bombs on Japan. That is to say that his memory will be marred by this act, particularly if the revisionist historians succeed in proving that his motivations were entirely political. Even if his reasons were entirely military, which is most unlikely, he was not wise enough to see that a test demonstration in an unpopulated area would have been a far more humane means of obtaining the same objective.

Aside from the atomic-bombing decision, Harry Truman was the kind of leader whom, in Clinton Rossiter's words, "history will delight to remember." [19] The very foibles and contradictions for which he was scorned will set him apart from the mass of his predecessors and successors who have been too often absorbed with posturing for posterity. He was certainly not the most intelligent, articulate, or inspiring president this nation has ever had, and he was aware of that. Knowing it, he worked all the harder. One of his favorite, oft-repeated anecdotes about the way he would like to be remembered, concerned a gravestone in Arizona which bore the inscription: "Here lies Jack Williams, he done his damnedest." [20] For Harry Truman's presidency no more fitting epitaph could be devised. Four days after taking the oath of office as president he had said, "I ask only to be a good and faithful servant of my Lord and my people." [21] And so it was; for whatever his shortcomings, the nation has never known a more dedicated or faithful servant.

Notes

CHAPTER 1

1. *Truman Speaks* (New York: Columbia University Press, 1960), 6.
2. Clinton Rossiter (ed.), *The Federalists Papers* (New York: New American Library, 1961), 418, also No. 74, p. 447. See also Ernest R. May, "The President Shall Be Commander in Chief," in May (ed.), *The Ultimate Decision: The President as Commander in Chief* (New York: Braziller, 1960), 4.
3. At the beginning of the twentieth century, Secretary of War Elihu Root accomplished a major reorganization of the War Department. Root was influenced in these reforms by the "New Hamiltonianism," which was an adaptation of business organizational techniques to governmental operations advocated by the Progressives. The Root reforms were predicated on the assumption that "clear lines of accountability provide effective political control." See Paul Y. Hammond, *Organizing for Defense: The American Military Establishment in the Twentieth Century* (Princeton, N.J.: Princeton University Press, 1961), 23.
4. Quoted in Edward S. Corwin, *The President: Office and Powers, 1787–1957* (New York: New York University Press, 1957), 228. See also Clarence A. Berdahl, *War Powers of the Executive in the United States* (Urbana: University of Illinois Press, 1920), 117.
5. Clinton Rossiter, *The Supreme Court and the Commander in Chief* (Ithaca, N.Y.: Cornell University Press, 1951), 2.
6. U.S. Senate, Committees on Foreign Relations and Armed Services, *Powers of the President to Send the Armed Forces Outside the United States*, 82nd Cong., 1st Sess., 1–2. See also *House Reports*, 82nd Cong., 1st Sess., No. 127, pp. 50–52; Rossiter (ed.), *Federalist Papers*, No. 23, p. 154; Rossiter, *Supreme Court and the Commander in Chief*, 8.
7. Dorothy B. James, *The Contemporary Presidency* (New York: Pegasus, 1969), 159, 165. See also *House Miscellaneous Documents*, 84th Cong., 2nd Sess., No. 443, pp. 16–17.
8. James, *Contemporary Presidency*, 165.
9. Charles S. Murphy to Richard B. Russell, February 19, 1951, in Papers of Charles S. Murphy, White House Files, Presidential Powers folder, Harry S. Truman Library, Independence, Mo., hereinafter cited as Murphy Papers. See also *House Miscellaneous Documents*, 84th Cong., 2nd Sess., No. 443, pp. 2, 8. In an article on the war powers, a national magazine wrote: "U.S. Presidents have ordered troops into position or action without a formal congressional declaration a total of 149 times." *Time*, XCVI (June 1, 1970), 37. A list of the occasions on which U.S. troops were engaged on foreign territory appears in *House Report*, 82nd Cong., 1st Sess., No. 127, pp. 55–62. A similar, more detailed list may be found in U.S. Senate, Committee on Foreign Relations, *War Powers Legislation: Hearings before the Committee on Foreign Relations on S. 731, S.J. Res. 18 and S.J. Res. 59*, 92nd Cong., 1st Sess., 359–79, hereinafter cited as *War Powers Hearings*.
10. Rossiter, *Supreme Court and the Commander in Chief*, 66; Henry H. Fowl-

er, *War Powers of the President* (Washington: Industrial College of the Armed Forces, 1948), 12–14; *House Report*, 82nd Cong., 1st Sess., No. 127, p. 19.

11. Arthur H. Vandenberg, Jr. (ed.), *The Private Papers of Senator Vandenberg* (Boston: Houghton Mifflin, 1952), 342, Senator Vandenberg, a Republican from Michigan, was chairman of the Senate Foreign Relations Committee in the 80th Congress.

12. Unsigned Report, "Constitutional Power of the President and of Congress to Determine Roles and Missions for the Armed Forces," Record Group (RG) 340, Office of Administrative Assistant, Secretary of the Air Force, Special Interest File 4A, National Archives.

13. Charles Murphy to John McCormack, February 19, 1951, White House Files, Presidential Powers Folder; Murphy Papers; Berdahl, *War Powers of the Executive*, 121; Fowler, *War Powers of the President*, 18; Rossiter, *Supreme Court and the Commander in Chief*, 75–77; *Background Information on the Use of United States Forces in Foreign Countries*, 50–54; Edward H. Foley, Jr., "Some Aspects of the Constitutional Powers of the President," *American Bar Association Journal*, XXVII (August, 1941), 486.

14. Otis A. Singletary, *The Mexican War* (Chicago: University of Chicago Press, 1960), 150–51; U.S. Army, Office of the Chief of Military History, *American Military History* (Washington: U. S. Government Printing Office, 1969), 166.

15. Leonard D. White, "Polk," in May (ed.), *Ultimate Decision, 58.*

16. *Ibid.*, 60. Since general military terminology must be employed throughout, it is necessary to define what is meant by some of these terms. *Tactics* refers to the choice of battle formations and the actual direction of forces when actively engaged with an enemy. *Strategy* originally meant the planning of operations by a nation's commanding generals, utilizing the personnel and matériel made available by the civilian leadership. With the growing technological complexity of modern warfare in the twentieth century, for the U.S. at least, this has come to mean that the civilian leaders in the executive branch determine general strategy and exercise control over all major operational decisions in the theaters of command. In either case, strategy is designed to implement *policy*, the latter being defined as the purpose for which a war is fought. Policy is formulated by civilian leaders, usually the president, who determine the priorities of men and supplies to be allocated to the military. These definitions are taken, in large part, from T. Harry Williams, *Americans at War* (Rev. ed.; New York: Collier Books, 1962), 13–14, 49–50; White, "Polk," 73.

17. White, "Polk," 74–75.

18. Text of Lincoln's "Spot Resolution," introduced in the House of Representatives, December 22, 1847, is in Roy P. Basler (ed.), *The Collected Works of Abraham Lincoln* (New Brunswick, N.J.: Rutgers University Press, 1953), I, 420–22; Lincoln to William H. Herndon, February 1, 1848, *ibid.*, 446–48.

19. The newspaper account of Lincoln's speech at Wilmington on June 10, 1848, is taken from the *Delaware State Journal*, June 13, 1848, as reprinted in Basler (ed.), *Collected Works of Lincoln*, I, 475–76.

20. Speaking in January, 1848, Lincoln said he hoped Polk could prove that Mexico attacked American territory, since he (Lincoln) was concerned

about the "doubtful propriety" of some of his votes on the war. Speech, January 12, 1848, *ibid.*, 431–32.
21. Lincoln to Herndon, February 15, 1848, *ibid.*, 451–52.
22. Williams, *Americans at War*, 55; Robert A. Dahl, *Pluralist Democracy in the United States: Conflict and Consent* (Chicago: Rand, McNally, 1967), 96. The term, *dictator*, is used here only to indicate the extent of Lincoln's powers and the absence of any efficacious method of dividing the decisive powers with Congress. Lincoln's actions were justified by the emergency condition. While he often acted without statutory authority, the Congress willingly, ex post facto, provided him with the legislative sanctions. Lincoln was a democratic ruler, granted a dictatorial range of powers as an expedient. Had he been a dictator in truth, he would not have submitted to a popular election in 1864.
23. *House Reports*, 82nd Cong., 1st Sess., No. 127, p. 18.
24. Corwin, *The President*, 229. Similar lists, varying only in detail, can be found in *American Military History*, 189–90; Edward S. Corwin and Louis W. Koenig, *The Presidency Today* (New York: New York University Press, 1956), 32; T. Harry Williams, *Lincoln and His Generals* (New York: Knopf, 1952), 7.
25. Lincoln, Message to Congress in Special Session, July 4, 1861, Basler (ed.), *Collected Works of Lincoln*, IV, 421–41; Corwin and Koenig, *Presidency Today*, 32–33; *House Report*, 82nd Sess., No. 127, p. 18.
26. Clinton Rossiter, *The American Presidency* (New York: New American Library, 1956), 18.
27. William A. Dunning, *Truth in History and Other Essays* (New York: Columbia University Press, 1937), 165–66.
28. Lincoln, Message to Congress in Special Session, July 4, 1861, Basler (ed.), *Collected Works of Lincoln*, IV, 430; Fowler, *War Powers of the President*, 17.
29. Lincoln to James C. Conkling, August 26, 1863, Basler (ed.), *Collected Works of Lincoln*, VI, 408.
30. Lincoln to Albert G. Hodges, April 4, 1864, *ibid.*, VII, 281.
31. Walter Millis, *Arms and Men: A Study of American Military History* (New York: New American Library, 1956), 245.
32. John E. Wiltz, *From Isolation to War, 1931–1941* (New York: Crowell, 1968), 81.
33. Corwin and Koenig, *Presidency Today*, 35. See also Dahl, *Pluralist Democracy*, 96; Selig Adler, *The Uncertain Giant, 1921–1941: American Foreign Policy Between the Wars* (Toronto: Collier-Macmillan, 1965), 249–51.
34. Corwin, *The President*, 237.
35. James, *Contemporary Presidency*, 146; Corwin and Koenig, *Presidency Today*, 34–35; Millis, *Arms and Men*, 249–51; Wiltz, *From Isolation to War*, 85–87. Senator Wheeler is quoted in an undated report, "Power of the President to Send Troops Abroad" (Appendix D), in White House Files, Murphy Papers.
36. William R. Emerson, "Roosevelt," in May (ed.), *Ultimate Decision*, 136–37.
37. New York *Times*, April 13, 1945; Maurice Matloff, "Roosevelt as War Leader," in Abraham S. Eisenstadt (ed.), *American History: Recent Interpretations* (New York: Crowell, 1969), II, 425–26; Emerson, "Roosevelt," 176.

CHAPTER 2

1. Harry S. Truman, *Mr. Citizen* (New York: Popular Library, 1961), 111.
2. Luther Huston, New York *Times*, April 15, 1945; Harry S. Truman, *Year of Decisions*, Vol. I of *Memoirs* (Garden City, N.Y.: Doubleday, 1955), 112–25 *passim*.
3. Quoted in Alfred Steinberg, *The Man from Missouri: The Life and Times of Harry S. Truman* (New York: G. P. Putnam, 1962), 51.
4. Jonathan Daniels, *Man of Independence* (Philadelphia: J. B. Lippincott, 1950), 75–84. See also Truman, *Memoirs*, I, 126–27; Irving Brant, "Harry S. Truman—I," *New Republic*, CXII (April 30, 1945), 578; John Hersey, "Profiles—Mr. President," Pt. 2, "Ten O'Clock Meeting," *New Yorker*, XXVII (April 14, 1951), 38.
5. Harry S. Truman, *Years of Trial and Hope*, Vol. II of *Memoirs* (Garden City, N.Y.: Doubleday, 1956), 46.
6. Daniels, *Man of Independence*, 89–90; Truman, *Memoirs*, I, 125–28; Steinberg, *Man from Missouri*, 42.
7. New York *Times*, April 13, 1945; Truman, *Memoirs*, I, 128–31; Daniels, *Man of Independence*, 92. See also Cabell Phillips, *The Truman Presidency: The History of a Triumphant Succession* (New York: Macmillan, 1966), 13.
8. *Public Papers of the Presidents of the United States, Harry S. Truman: Containing the Public Messages, Speeches, and Statements of the President, 1945* (Washington: U.S. Government Printing Office, 1961–66), p. 14, hereinafter cited as *Public Papers . . . Truman* [year].
9. Truman, *Memoirs*, I, 138–39.
10. Phillips, *Truman Presidency*, 14; Truman, *Memoirs*, I, 133–36; Daniels, *Man of Independence*, 113–14.
11. In Missouri, county judges are actually administrators, performing a function similar to that of county boards of supervisors in other states. Truman, *Memoirs*, I, 139, 140; Phillips, *Truman Presidency*, 17; New York *Times*, April 15, 1945.
12. Truman, *Memoirs*, I, 141. See also New York *Times*, April 15, 1945; Steinberg, *Man from Missouri*, 113–14.
13. "I was a New Dealer from the start," Truman wrote. "In fact, I had been a New Dealer back in Jackson County. . . . I believed in the program from the time it was first proposed." *Memoirs*, I, 141, 149. See also Phillips, *Truman Presidency*, 24; Steinberg, *Man from Missouri*, 120.
14. Brant, "Harry S. Truman—I," 577; Phillips, *Truman Presidency*, 18–19, 24–25; Daniels, *Man of Independence*, 165–66. Nowhere is it more evident that Truman's image was not permanently tarnished by his alliance with the Kansas City machine than in a *Times* editorial following his assumption of the presidency: "There is no need to blink at the one-time association with Pendergast," the editorial reads. The writer describes Truman as a "practical politician" who, along with Al Smith, was educated in "the hard, tough schools of the ward machines . . . whose experience in the practical ways of accomplishing sound public purposes . . . [make] them particularly useful to their country in a time of crisis." New York *Times*, April 14, 1945.
15. Phillips, *Truman Presidency*, 18, 20.
16. *Time*, XLI (March 8, 1943), 15. See also Brant, "Harry S. Truman—I," 577–78.

17. Truman, *Memoirs*, I, 147–48. Truman did receive assignment to the Military Affairs Committee in his second term. Arthur M. Schlesinger, Jr., *The Coming of the New Deal*, Vol. II of *The Age of Roosevelt* (Boston: Houghton Mifflin, 1960), 554.
18. Truman, *Memoirs*, I, 159–61; Brant, "Harry S. Truman—I," 579.
19. Truman, *Memoirs*, I, 164–65; Steinberg, *Man from Missouri*, 180–81. See also Phillips, *Truman Presidency*, 33–34; Daniels, *Man of Independence*, 215–16. Commenting in a 1950 interview, Truman said: "I came back and set up the Truman Committee. If I hadn't taken that drive, I'd still be just Senator Truman instead of being in all this fix." John Hersey, "Profiles—Mr. President," Pt. 1, "Quite a Head of Steam," *New Yorker*, XXII (April 7, 1951), 45.
20. Truman, *Memoirs*, I, 165–66. See also Phillips, *Truman Presidency*, 34.
21. Steinberg, *Man from Missouri*, 182; Truman, *Memoirs*, I, 166. See also, New York *Times*, April 15, 1945.
22. Truman, *Memoirs*, I, 189; Steinberg, *Man from Missouri*, 184. A few months prior to U.S. entry into World War II and shortly after entry, resolutions were offered in Congress to create a "joint committee on the conduct of national defense." Both efforts were blocked by the Democrats, who argued that military policy matters must reside with the president. A. Russell Buchanan, *The United States and World War II* (New York: Harper and Row, 1964), II, 314–15.
23. Quoted in Steinberg, *Man from Missouri*, 184.
24. Truman, *Memoirs*, I, 168, 188–89. See also Irving Brant, "Harry S. Truman—II," *New Republic*, CXII (May 7, 1945), 635; William Hillman (ed.), *Mr. President: The First Publication from the Personal Diaries, Private Letters, Papers and Revealing Interviews of Harry S. Truman, Thirty-Second President of the United States of America* (New York: Farrar, Straus and Young, 1952), 94.
25. Truman, *Memoirs*, I, 167; Buchanan, *United States and World War II*, Vol. II, 315; Brant, "Harry S. Truman—II," 635–36; Phillips, *Truman Presidency*, 35–37. See also New York *Times*, April 15, 1945; Cecil V. Crabb, Jr., *American Foreign Policy in the Nuclear Age: Principles, Problems and Prospects* (Evanston, Ill.: Row, Peterson, 1960), 117–18.
26. Truman, *Memoirs*, I, 186; Hersey, "Profiles," Pt. 1, p. 45; Hillman (ed.), *Mr. President*, 94.
27. Richard N. Current, *Secretary Stimson: A Study in Statecraft* (New Brunswick, N.J.: Rutgers University Press, 1954), 204–205.
28. Transcription of interview with Truman, "March of Time" radio broadcast, November 26, 1942, Truman Papers, RG-1, Senatorial Files, "National Defense Committee-General," Truman Library, hereinafter cited as Truman Papers.
29. Truman to Joseph P. Smithers, April 4, 1942, in Special Senate Committee to Investigate the National Defense Program-General, Senatorial Files, Truman Papers.
30. Wilfred E. Binkley, *President and Congress* (3rd rev. ed.; New York: Random House, 1962), 328. See also Daniels, *Man of Independence*, 221; *Time*, XLI (March 8, 1943), 13. Quoted in Brant, "Harry S. Truman-II," 638.

31. Truman to Marian J. Bowles, March 13, 1943, in Special Senate Committee to Investigate the National Defense Program-General, Senatorial Files, Truman Papers.
32. *Truman Speaks*, 38.
33. Brant, "Harry S. Truman-I," 577; New York *Times*, April 14, 15, 1945. See also, Binkley, *President and Congress*, 328.
34. Forrestal to Truman, January 6, 1943, transcript, Patterson testimony before Truman Committee (undated), Nelson to Truman, January 9, 1943, all in Special Senate Committee to Investigate the National Defense Program-General, Senatorial Files, Truman Papers.
35. New York *Times*, April 15, 1945; *New Republic* (April 23, 1945), 540. For a detailed listing of the major accomplishments of the Truman Committee, see Brant, "Harry S. Truman-II," 636.
36. *Time*, XLI (March 8, 1943), 13.
37. For a view somewhat contrary to that expressed here, see Wilbur W. Hoare, Jr., "Truman," in May (ed.), *Ultimate Decision*, 181–82.
38. Truman to Henry Wallace, August 3, 1944, in Truman, *Memoirs*, I, 185–86; Resolution (undated), Special Senate Committee to Investigate the National Defense Program–1944, Senatorial Files, Truman Papers.
39. New York *Times*, April 14, 1945; Truman, *Memoirs*, I, 53, 56, 195. A recent monograph maintains unconvincingly that "though short in duration, Truman's vice presidency was an important and constructive apprenticeship." See Arthur F. McClure and Donna Costigan, "The Truman Vice Presidency: Constructive Apprenticeship or Brief Interlude?" *Missouri Historical Review*, LXV (April, 1971), 341.
40. Truman, *Memoirs*, I, 5.

CHAPTER 3

1. Harry S. Truman to Martha Truman, April 16, 1945, in Truman, *Memoirs*, I, 43–44.
2. New York *Times*, April 13, 1945.
3. When Truman took office the cabinet consisted of Edward R. Stettinius, Jr., secretary of state; Henry Morgenthau, Jr., secretary of the treasury; Henry L. Stimson, secretary of war; Francis Biddle, attorney-general; James Forrestal, secretary of the navy; Frank C. Walker, postmaster general; Claude R. Wickard, secretary of agriculture; Harold L. Ickes, secretary of the interior; Henry L. Wallace, secretary of commerce; and Francis Perkins, Secretary of Labor.
4. Item No. 1, *Public Papers . . . Truman, 1945*, 1; New York *Times*, April 13, 1945.
5. Louis W. Koenig (ed.), *The Truman Administration: Its Principles and Practices* (New York: New York University Press, 1956), 30.
6. *Truman Speaks*, 66; Truman, *Memoirs*, I, 50–51; Winston S. Churchill to Truman, April 13, 1945, in Winston Churchill, *Triumph and Tragedy*, Vol. VI of *The Second World War* (Boston: Houghton Mifflin, 1953), 479–80.
7. New York *Times*, April 14, 1945.
8. Truman, *Memoirs*, I, 14. The military intelligence reports were compiled by a central intelligence staff headed by Major General Hoyt S. Vandenberg. See Arthur Krock, New York *Times*, July 16, 1946.

9. State Department, Memorandum to the President, April 13, 1945, in Truman, *Memoirs*, I, 14–17.
10. Truman, *Memoirs*, I, 17; New York *Times*, April 13, 14, 1945. See also Vincent J. Esposito (ed.), *West Point Atlas of American Wars* (New York: Frederick A. Praeger, 1959), II, Sec. 2, Map Plate No. 70. The military leaders at the time were: General George C. Marshall, chief of staff, army; Admiral Ernest J. King, chief of naval operations; Secretary of War Stimson; Secretary of the Navy Forrestal; Lieutenant General Barney M. Giles, Army Air Force; General A. A. Vandergrift, Marine Corps commandant; Admiral William D. Leahy, chief of staff to the commander in chief. Stephen E. Ambrose, *Eisenhower and Berlin, 1945: The Decision to Halt at the Elbe* (New York: W. W. Norton, 1967), 73–79. See also Cornelius Ryan, *The Last Battle* (New York: Simon and Schuster, 1966), 209–13.
11. Buchanan, *United States and World War II*, Vol. II, 575–78. For detailed maps and a textual explanation of these bombings, see Esposito (ed.), *West Point Atlas*, II, Sec. 2, Map Plate No. 166.
12. Truman, *Memoirs*, I, 17; Buchanan, *United States and World War II*, Vol. II, 578.
13. Truman, *Memoirs*, I, 18. One scholar of the Cold War period, D. F. Fleming, sees the retention of Leahy as military adviser to Truman as a factor in the coming of the Cold War. Fleming says that Leahy, because of these daily briefings, was in a unique position to influence the president and that the admiral had "a long time aversion to the Russians." Fleming perceives a Leahy-influenced anti-Soviet bias emerging in Truman some ten days after taking office. See *The Cold War and Its Origins, 1917–1960* (Garden City, N.Y.: Doubleday, 1961), I, 266. Cabell Phillips, in his study of Truman, disagrees with Fleming. He claims that Leahy, along with Stimson and Marshall, advocated "getting along with the Russians at all costs." *Truman Presidency*, 71.
14. Truman, *Memoirs*, I, 19. See also New York *Times*, April 14, 1945. Eden to Churchill, April 16, 1945, in Churchill, *Triumph and Tragedy*, 474–75.
15. Item No. 2, *Public Papers . . . Truman, 1945*, 1–6. Text is also in New York *Times*, April 17, 1945. See also Truman, *Memoirs*, I, 42.
16. Truman, *Memoirs*, I, 328–29; New York *Times*, April 15, 1945.
17. Hoare, "Truman," 182; *Truman Speaks*, 6; Truman, *Memoirs*, I, 88.
18. Quoted in Richard G. Hewlett and Oscar E. Anderson, Jr., *The New World, 1939–1946*, Vol. I of *A History of the United States Atomic Energy Commission* (University Park: Pennsylvania State University Press, 1962), 347.
19. Hoare, "Truman," 182–83; Truman *Memoirs*, I, 210.
20. Buchanan, *United States and World War II*, Vol. II, 456–58; Esposito (ed.), *West Point Atlas*, II, Sec. 2, Map Plate No. 71.
21. Truman, *Memoirs*, I, 211–12; Buchanan, *United States and World War II*, Vol. II, 453–54. For a discussion of the underlying political and diplomatic factors involved, see Ambrose, *Eisenhower and Berlin*, 27–29, 60–62.
22. Churchill to Truman, April 18, 1945, in Truman, *Memoirs*, I, 61–62, 211, 213.
23. Ambrose, *Eisenhower and Berlin*, 83–84.
24. Churchill to Truman, April 30, 1945, in Churchill, *Triumph and Tragedy*, 506. See also Truman, *Memoirs*, I, 216.

25. Truman, *Memoirs*, I, 216.
26. Truman to Churchill, May 1, 1945, in Truman, *Memoirs*, I, 216–17. See also Churchill, *Triumph and Tragedy*, 506; Ambrose, *Eisenhower and Berlin*, 85.
27. Truman, *Memoirs*, I, 214.
28. Churchill to Truman, April 18, 1945, in Truman *Memoirs*, I, 62. See also Churchill, *Triumph and Tragedy*, 508–10.
29. Himmler falsely claimed that Hitler had suffered serious brain damage and that he was in effective command and able to make a legitimate surrender offer. Truman, *Memoirs*, I, 88–91. Truman to Stalin, April 25, 1945, *ibid.*, 94.
30. Item No. 12, *Public Papers... Truman, 1945*, 25–26.
31. Item No. 21, *ibid.*, 32. See also Item No. 20, *ibid.*, 31; Truman, *Memoirs*, I, 201.
32. Hitler apparently took his own life on April 30. Prior to this, on April 28, he had denied any authority to Himmler or Hermann Goering, his Luftwaffe chief. Both had attempted to take command in the last weeks of the fighting. As head of the government and the military Hitler named Admiral Doenitz, who assumed command on May 1, 1945. Forrest C. Pogue, *The Supreme Command* (Washington: U.S. Government Printing Office, 1954), 474. See also Buchanan, *United States in World War II*, Vol. II, 461–63.
33. Truman to Eisenhower, May 8, 1945, Eisenhower to Truman, May 10, 1945, in Eisenhower Papers, Personal Files 108, "Truman, Harry S. (1)," Dwight D. Eisenhower Library, Abilene, Kan., hereinafter cited as Eisenhower Papers. Text of message to Eisenhower also appears as Item No. 29, *Public Papers... Truman, 1945*, 51–52.
34. Truman, *Mr. Citizen*, 181, 185–86. Other examples abound: "I have said it many a time ... I think General Marshall is the outstanding man of that war period." Item No. 4, *Public Papers ... Truman, 1949*, 9. For a similar tribute, see Truman, *Memoirs*, I, 235.
35. Churchill to Truman, May 6, 1945, quoted in Churchill, *Triumph and Tragedy*, 501; Truman to Churchill, May 9, 1945, in Truman, *Memoirs*, I, 298.
36. Truman, *Memoirs*, I, 79, 262, 298–99.
37. Truman to Churchill, June 13, 1945, quoted in Truman, *Memoirs*, I, 303; Churchill, *Triumph and Tragedy*, 604–605. Because of a Soviet-requested delay, the actual removals did not begin until July 1, 1945.
38. *Truman Speaks*, 22–23. Truman had earlier noted this same determination when he wrote: "My intention was always to carry out to the letter all agreements entered into by Roosevelt with our allies." *Memoirs*, I, 305–306. Since the question of whether Truman was simply carrying out the Yalta Agreement or not deals with matters almost entirely diplomatic and political, it will not be examined at length here. See Gar Alperovitz, *Atomic Diplomacy: Hiroshima and Potsdam, the Use of the Atomic Bomb and the American Confrontation with Soviet Power* (New York: Simon and Schuster, 1965), 41–90 *passim*.
39. Document No. 10, Agreements of the Yalta Conference, February, 1945, in William Appleman Williams, *The Shaping of American Diplomacy: Readings and Documents in American Foreign Relations, 1750–1955* (Chicago: Rand McNally, 1956), 930–35. See also Draft Statement, W.

Averell Harriman to Senate Armed Services and Foreign Relations Committee, August (?), 1951, in Papers of Theodore Tannenwald, "MacArthur—Copies of Memorandums re Hearings," Truman Library, hereinafter cited as Tannenwald Papers. Harriman's statement is reprinted in U.S., Congress, Senate, Committees on Armed Services and Foreign Relations, *Military Situation in the Far East: Hearings to Conduct an Inquiry into the Military Situation in the Far East and the Facts Surrounding the Relief of General of the Army Douglas MacArthur from His Assignments in That Area*, 5 Parts, 82nd Cong., 1st Sess., Pt. 5, Appendix NN, 3328–42, hereinafter cited as *Far East Hearings*. For full description and text of the Yalta Agreements, see U.S., Department of State, *Foreign Relations of the United States, Diplomatic Papers: The Conferences at Malta and Yalta, 1945* (Washington: U.S. Government Printing Office, 1955). As with other security matters, Truman did not learn of the secret portions of the Yalta Pact until he became president. See Memorandum (unsigned) to Theodore Tannenwald, June 12, 1951, in Tannenwald Papers.

40. Truman, *Memoirs*, I, 314–15, 322–23, 411; Phillips, *Truman Presidency*, 96–97; Walter Millis (ed.), *The Forrestal Diaries* (New York: Viking Press, 1951), 78–79. Stalin had first agreed to declare war on Japan—following the defeat of Germany—in October, 1943, at the Moscow Conference of Foreign Ministers. At the Teheran Conference the following month, the Soviet premier personally reaffirmed this commitment to Roosevelt and Churchill. At Yalta, in February, 1945, Stalin agreed to a general date of "two or three months" after Germany's surrender for Russian entry into the Pacific fighting. In May, in talks at Moscow with Harriman and Harry Hopkins, Stalin said he would be ready to strike by August 8, with the actual date of entry dependent upon Chinese acceptance of the terms of the Yalta Agreement on the Far East. Hopkins to Truman, May 28, 1945, quoted in Truman, *Memoirs*, I, 264. See also Hewlett and Anderson, *The New World*, 351–52.

41. Memorandum, JCS to Roosevelt, January 23, 1945, quoted in Draft Statement, Harriman to Senate Armed Services and Foreign Relations Committees, August (?), 1951, MacArthur Hearings, Tannenwald Papers. This document is reprinted in *Far East Hearings*, Pt. 5, Appendix NN, 3332.

42. William L. Neumann, *After Victory: Churchill, Roosevelt, Stalin and the Making of the Peace* (New York: Harper and Row, 1967), 165. The chief reason was, of course, that the Red army could hold or destroy Japanese forces in Manchuria, thus facilitating the planned American invasion of the Japanese home islands. Truman, *Memoirs*, I, 265, 314–15, 403. The Joint Chiefs of Staff were unanimous in earnestly desiring Soviet entry, as General Marshall later testified in the *Far East Hearings*, Pt. 1, pp. 562-63. See also Dean Acheson testimony, in the *Far East Hearings*, Pt. 3, p. 1989. General Douglas MacArthur, commanding general, Pacific Theater, was also in complete agreement. See Memorandum, George A. Lincoln to Marshall, March 8, 1945, quoted in Barton J. Bernstein and Allen J. Matusow (eds.), *The Truman Administration: A Documentary History* (New York: Harper and Row, 1966), 316–17.

43. Churchill, *Triumph and Tragedy*, 639; Phillips, *Truman Presidency*, 97; Truman, *Memoirs*, I, 77–79, 84–85; Draft Statement, Harriman to Senate Armed Services and Foreign Relations Committees, August (?), 1951,

MacArthur Hearings, Tannenwald Papers; Kennan to Harriman, April 24, 1945, quoted in George F. Kennan, *Memoirs, 1925–1950* (Boston: Little, Brown, 1967), 238.

44. Truman, *Memoirs*, I, 382. The Sino-Soviet Agreement was signed at Moscow on August 14. But the Soviet Union had declared war and invaded Manchuria on August 8, six days earlier. The Russian timetable was probably changed by the atomic destruction of Hiroshima on the sixth. For a detailed account of the Potsdam deliberations, see Herbert Feis, *Between War and Peace: The Potsdam Conference* (Princeton, N.J.: Princeton University Press, 1960).

45. Truman, *Memoirs*, I, 396. See also Hewlett and Anderson, *The New World*, 387.

46. Churchill, *Triumph and Tragedy*, 641–42. See also Lord Moran's diary entry for July 18, 1945, in which he quotes from Churchill's dictated notes on his meeting with Truman, printed in Charles Wilson (Lord Moran), *Churchill, Taken from the Diaries of Lord Moran: The Struggle for Survival* (Boston: Houghton Mifflin, 1966), 293–94.

47. Item No. 28, *Public Papers . . . Truman, 1945*, 50.

48. Truman, *Memoirs*, I, 396–97; Hewlett and Anderson, *The New World*, 397. See also James F. Byrnes, *Speaking Frankly* (New York: Harper and Brothers, 1947), 205; Buchanan, *United States and World War II*, Vol. II, 589.

49. Truman, *Memoirs*, I, 416–17; Millis (ed.), *Forrestal Diaries*, 66; Hewlett and Anderson, *The New World*, 352, 363; Feis, *Between War and Peace*, 115; Louis Morton, "The Decision to Use the Atomic Bomb," in Kent R. Greenfield (ed.), *Command Decisions* (Washington: Office of the Chief of Military History, 1960), 507. The SWNCC was a group composed of the assistant secretaries of the State, War and Navy departments. It was established in 1944 to assist these three agencies in integrating their policy recommendations to the administration. It had separate subcommittees for Germany and Japan. See Current, *Secretary Stimson*, 223–24.

50. Truman, *Memoirs*, I, 417.

51. Current, *Secretary Stimson*, 232. See also Byrnes, *Speaking Frankly*, 206; Lansing Lamont, *Day of Trinity* (New York: Atheneum, 1965), 145; Urs Schwarz, *American Strategy: The Growth of Politico-Military Thinking in the United States* (Garden City, N.Y.: Doubleday, 1967), 57; Henry L. Stimson and McGeorge Bundy, *On Active Service in Peace and War* (New York: Harper and Brothers, 1947), 620–24. President Truman gave "general approval" to Stimson's memorandum. For text of the July 2 memo, see Stimson, "The Decision to Use the Atom Bomb," St. Louis *Post-Dispatch*, January 28, 1947.

52. Hewlett and Anderson, *The New World*, 384–85, 389; Byrnes, *Speaking Frankly*, 206.

53. The report is quoted in Morton, "Decision to Use the Atomic Bomb," 504–505.

54. Neumann, *After Victory*, 176; Hewlett and Anderson, *The New World*, 385. All the text of the declaration eventually said was that the conquerors would restore the government to Japanese control as soon as, "There has been established in accordance with the freely-expressed will of the Japanese people, a peacefully-inclined and responsible government."

55. Hewlett and Anderson, *The New World*, 392–93; Truman, *Memoirs*, I,

429; Herbert Feis, *Japan Subdued: The Atomic Bomb and the End of the War in the Pacific* (Princeton, N.J.: Princeton University Press, 1961), 78–79.
56. *Truman Speaks*, 74.
57. Truman, *Memoirs*, I, 387, 390–92; Lamont, *Day of Trinity*, 263; Hewlett and Anderson, *The New World*, 395. For a full official account of the Potsdam Conference see U.S. Department of State, *Foreign Relations of the United States, Diplomatic Papers: The Conference of Berlin (Postdam), 1945* (Washington: U.S. Government Printing Office, 1960).
58. Steinberg, *Man from Missouri*, 259. See also, Phillips, *Truman Presidency*, 59; Fleming, *The Cold War*, I, 304.
59. Feis, *Japan Subdued*, 97. See also Current, *Secretary Stimson*, 232–33; Hewlett and Anderson, *The New World*, 395–96.
60. For details of the settlement see Item No. 91, *Public Papers . . . Truman, 1945*, 179–95 *passim*. Quoted in Steinberg, *Man from Missouri*, 259; Esposito (ed.), *West Point Atlas*, II, Sec. 2, Map Plates Nos. 161, 165.
61. In all, American aircraft delivered incendiary attacks against 66 Japanese cities, destroying about 169 square miles of these urban areas, killing 260,000 and leaving 9,200,000 homeless. See *West Point Atlas*, II, Sec. 2, Map Plate No. 166. For other accounts of the effectiveness of these fire raids, see Buchanan, *United States and World War II*, Vol. II, 579–80; Fleming, *The Cold War*, I, 297–98; Carl Spaatz (commanding general, Army Strategic Air Forces) to Henry H. Arnold (commanding general, Army Air Forces), August 6, 1945, RG18, Army Air Force (AAF), 312.1—Operations Letters—1945, National Archives.
62. Truman, *Memoirs*, I, 222.
63. Memorandum, Brehon Somervell to George C. Marshall, RG18, AAF, Judge Advocate General (JAG) 400.336-Lend Lease, National Archives; Truman to Clement Atlee, August 15, 1945, *ibid*. See also Buchanan, *United States in World War II*, Vol. II, 504–505.
64. Presidential Directive, July 6, 1945, quoted in memorandum, Thomas Goodman (Acting Air Judge Advocate) to General Hood, August 29, 1945, RG18, AAF, JAG, 400.336-Lend Lease, National Archives. A change in lend-lease policy, which he approved, was recommended to Truman in August. See memorandum (unsigned), Foreign Economic Administration to Truman, August 13, 1945, *ibid*. A full statement of Truman's interim policy respecting lend-lease can be found in a directive, secretary of war, "Presidential Policy on Military Lend-Lease," August 15, 1945, *ibid*. See also Truman, *Memoirs*, I, 227–28, 231. In a directive dated August 21, 1945, Truman canceled all lend-lease operations. For text, see Item No. 107, *Public Papers . . . Truman, 1945*, 232.
65. Truman, *Memoirs*, I, 232, 234. Emphasis supplied.
66. Quoted in *Far East Hearings*, Pt. 5, Appendix NN, 3332. See also draft statement, Harriman to Senate Armed Services and Foreign Relations Committees, August (?), 1951, MacArthur Hearings, Tannenwald Papers.
67. Schwarz, *American Strategy*, 56; Hewlett and Anderson, *The New World*, 348–49. Reports from intelligence experts supported the army's view that bombings and blockades would not likely force surrender prior to an invasion. Morton, "The Decision to Use the Atomic Bomb," 504.
68. Paul Freeman, Jr., to George C. Marshall, February 13, 1945, in Bernstein and Matusow (eds.), *The Truman Administration*, 315–16; Mac-

Arthur to Marshall, April 20, 1945, quoted in Morton, "The Decision to Use the Atomic Bomb," 501; Marshall testimony, *Far East Hearings*, Pt. 1, pp. 563–64.

69. Hewlett and Anderson, *The New World*, 350–51; Truman, *Memoirs*, I, 236.
70. Marshall testimony, *Far East Hearings*, Pt. 1, p. 563; Esposito (ed.), *West Point Atlas*, II, Sec. 2, Map Plate No. 167; Hewlett and Anderson, *The New World*, 351; Frazier Hunt, *The Untold Story of Douglas MacArthur* (New York: Devin-Adair, 1954), 392–94.
71. Truman, *Memoirs*, I, 416. Although no one disagreed with the plans, several offered related views. For example, Stimson hoped to find some approach to the Japanese that would bring about surrender short of actual invasion. He was doubtlessly thinking of the upcoming Potsdam Declaration and the availability of the atomic bomb. Admiral Leahy denounced the unconditional surrender formula adopted at Casablanca as making the invasion necessary. Admiral King told Truman that entry of the Soviet Union was still desirable, but was no longer considered indispensable to victory. Hewlett and Anderson, *The New World*, 363–64. For a detailed description of Marshall's recommendations to Truman regarding the joint chiefs' strategic proposals, see U.S. Department of State, *Foreign Relations of the United States, Potsdam Papers: 1945*, I, 904–909.
72. Morton, "The Decision to Use the Atomic Bomb," 501–502; Schwarz, *American Strategy*, 56–57.
73. Truman, *Memoirs*, I, 415. In a subsequent meeting on July 24, Churchill and Truman received the final report of the Combined Chiefs of Staff. They approved of this document, whose recommendations showed little change from the original joint chiefs' memorandum to Roosevelt of January 22, 1945. For text of the latter, see *ibid.*, 381–82. For text of the combined chiefs' memorandum of July 24, see *Far East Hearings*, Pt. 5, Appendix NN, 3338–39. As Louis Morton commented, "The question of the bomb was divorced entirely from military plans and the final report of the conference accepted as the main effort the invasion of the Japanese home islands." See "The Decision to Use the Atomic Bomb," 512.

CHAPTER 4

1. Quoted in Cabell Phillips, "Truman at 75," *New York Times Magazine* (May 3, 1959), 107.
2. Stimson and Bundy, *On Active Service*, 615–16; Stimson, "Decision to Use the Atom Bomb," St. Louis *Post-Dispatch*, January 28, 1947. In a biography of FDR, James MacGregor Burns claims (without documentation) that in December, 1944, Roosevelt favored a *non*-military demonstration as a warning to the Japanese. *Roosevelt: Soldier of Freedom* (New York: Harcourt, Brace and Jovanovich, 1970), 550. Most writers have taken the view that had Roosevelt lived, he would have used the bomb directly against Japan. See, for example, Buchanan, *United States and World War II*, Vol. II, 582; Morton, "Decision to Use the Atomic Bomb," 496; Matloff, "Roosevelt as War Leader," 434.
3. Elting E. Morison, *Turmoil and Tradition: A Study of the Life and Times of Henry L. Stimson* (Boston: Houghton Mifflin, 1960), 616. For Truman's version, which varies somewhat in details, see *Memoirs*, I, 10–11. See also Hillman (ed.), *Mr. President*, 247–48. This was not the only instance of Truman respecting military security. In May, 1942, Julius H.

Amberg, special assistant to Stimson, asked the then Senator Truman to quash an investigation by his committee counsel, Hugh Fulton, into an experimental project on target-seeking bombs. Again, Truman agreed without complaint or question. See Amberg to Truman (and reply), May 7, 16, 1942, Senatorial Files, "National Defense Committee-General," in Truman Papers.

4. Stimson, "Decision to Use the Atom Bomb," St. Louis *Post-Dispatch*, January 28, 1947; Stimson to Truman, April 24, 1945, in Truman, *Memoirs*, I, 85.

5. Stimson and Bundy, *On Active Service*, 634–36; Hewlett and Anderson, *The New World*, 343; Arthur H. Compton, *Atomic Quest: A Personal Narrative* (New York: Oxford University Press, 1956), 237–38. See also Morton, "Decision to Use the Atomic Bomb," 496; Truman, *Memoirs*, I, 87. Strangely enough, almost a month after this briefing Budget Director Smith, in a conversation with Truman, mentioned the "Manhattan Project." Truman asked him what it was. Apparently no one had mentioned the project's overall code name to him. Diary Entry, May 21, 1945, Papers of Harold D. Smith, copy in Truman Library of original in Franklin D. Roosevelt Library, hereinafter cited as Smith Diary.

6. Hewlett and Anderson, *The New World*, 343; Phillips, *Truman Presidency*, 54. General Groves had made substantially the same report to Roosevelt just prior to the Yalta Conference. Bourke Hickenlooper to Groves (and reply), June 25, 1951, printed in *Far East Hearings*, Pt. 4, pp. 3119–20, 3132.

7. Truman, *Memoirs*, I, 419. The membership of the committee was as follows: Stimson, chairman; George L. Harrison, adviser to Stimson and president, New York Life Insurance Co., cochairman; James F. Byrnes, personal representative of the president; Ralph A. Bard, undersecretary of the navy; William L. Clayton, assistant secretary of state; Vannevar Bush, director, Office of Scientific Research and Development and president, Carnegie Institute; Karl L. Compton, chief, Office of Field Services in OSRD and president, Massachusetts Institute of Technology; James B. Conant, chairman, National Defense Research Committee and president, Harvard University. Among those advising the interim committee were Generals Marshall and Groves and distinguished nuclear scientists, such as Enrico Fermi, Arthur Compton, and J. Robert Oppenheimer.

8. Lamont, *Day of Trinity*, 103–104; Morison, *Turmoil and Tradition*, 624–25.

9. Truman, *Memoirs*, I, 419. See also Morton, "Decision to Use the Atomic Bomb," 497; Stimson and Bundy, *On Active Service*, 617.

10. Byrnes, *Speaking Frankly*, 261–62. Urs Schwarz believes that no serious consideration was given to *not* using the bomb. *American Strategy*, 65. Interim committee member Ralph Bard does not recall discussion of the subject, nor does physicist J. Robert Oppenheimer. Arthur Compton, on the other hand, recalls that "fullest consideration" was given to alternatives, but that it was his impression that the committee viewed it as a "foregone conclusion that the bomb would be used." Morison, *Turmoil and Tradition*, 625–27.

11. Byrnes, *Speaking Frankly*, 261–62; Schwarz, *American Strategy*, 66. See also Morison, *Turmoil and Tradition*, 626; Compton, *Atomic Quest*, 238–39.

12. Truman, *Memoirs*, I, 419.

13. Morton, "Decision to Use the Atomic Bomb," 502; Hewlett and Anderson,

The New World, 117, 364; Morison, *Turmoil and Tradition*, 630–31.
14. Feis, *Japan Subdued*, 40–42; Franck Committee Report, in Bernstein and Matusow, (eds.), *The Truman Administration*, 10–13; Current, *Secretary Stimson*, 230–31.
15. Scientific Advisory Committee Report, in Bernstein and Matusow, (eds.), *The Truman Administration*, 15. See also Compton, *Atomic Quest*, 240.
16. Bard Memorandum, June 27, 1945, in Bernstein and Matusow (eds.), *The Truman Administration*, 15–16.
17. Petition, Leo Szilard, *et. al.* to the President of the United States, July 17, 1945, in Bernstein and Matusow (eds.), *The Truman Administration*, 16–17. See also Fleming, *The Cold War*, I, 300–301. Szilard had perhaps a greater feeling of responsibility for the bomb than most other scientists. He had helped convince Albert Einstein to write the fateful letter to FDR that brought about the creation of the Manhattan Project. Feis, *Japan Subdued*, 40*n*.
18. Hewlett and Anderson, *The New World*, 399–400; Bernstein and Matusow (eds.), *The Truman Administration*, 18–20.
19. Bernstein and Matusow (eds.), *The Truman Administration*, 16–17. See also Lamont, *Day of Trinity*, 146; Hewlett and Anderson, *The New World*, 399–400. The Szilard petition could have been forwarded to Truman, for he received White House mail pouches which were flown in daily to him at Potsdam. Truman, *Memoirs*, I, 330–31. Herbert Feis, *Japan Subdued* (p. 63), feels it was "improbable" that the Szilard petition was forwarded to Truman. Steinberg claims, without offering any documentation, that Truman was aware of the Chicago poll. *Man from Missouri*, 259.
20. Harrison to Stimson, July 16, 17, 1945, and Groves to Stimson, July 18, 1945, *Foreign Relations of the United States: Potsdam Papers*, II, 1360–68. See also David Rees, *The Age of Containment: The Cold War, 1945–1965* (New York: St. Martin's Press, 1967), 13.
21. Hewlett and Anderson, *The New World*, 360; Lamont, *Day of Trinity*, 108–109.
22. Oppenheimer testimony, quoted in Bernstein and Matusow (eds.), *The Truman Administration*, 20–21; Truman, *Memoirs*, I, 415; Lamont, *Day of Trinity*, 228.
23. Churchill, *Triumph and Tragedy*, 639; Lamont, *Day of Trinity*, 136–37, 146.
24. Churchill, *Triumph and Tragedy*, 637–38, 640–41. See also Truman, *Mr. Citizen*, 201; Hewlett and Anderson, *The New World*, 386.
25. Truman, *Memoirs*, I, 416.
26. Churchill, *Triumph and Tragedy*, 670. Secretary of State Byrnes, who was also present, corroborates both Truman and Churchill's accounts of the brief encounter with Stalin. *Speaking Frankly*, 263. All three men were clearly surprised by Stalin's mild reaction to Truman's information about the atomic bomb. In their accounts Truman and Byrnes did not note the possibility that Stalin already knew much more than Truman told him. Churchill stated emphatically that Stalin's response was proof that the Soviet Union had not penetrated the project's security prior to this meeting. See *Triumph and Tragedy*, 669–70. For a detailed description of espionage at Alamogordo see Lamont, *Day of Trinity*.
27. Those present at the July 17 meeting were Stimson, Byrnes, Leahy, Marshall, Arnold, and King. Stimson and Bundy, *On Active Service*, 618.

There is no clear agreement on Japanese determination to fight on. One who has taken exception to Stimson's interpretation of these reports is Alexander H. Leighton, who was codirector, Foreign Morale Analysis Division, Bureau of Overseas Intelligence. Leighton holds that Japan would have surrendered without the atomic bomb *or* Russian intervention and prior to the planned invasion of the home islands. See Leighton, "Was Atomic-Bombing of Japan Necessary?," Richmond *Times-Dispatch*, April 20, 1947. Leighton was a member of a survey team that inspected Japan at the end of the war. What he says is quite similar to the conclusion reported by the United States Strategic Bombing Survey Report, reprinted in Bernstein and Matusow (eds.), *The Truman Administration*, 45. D. F. Fleming believes that Soviet intervention alone would have been sufficient to force Japanese surrender. *The Cold War*, I, 305.

28. Stimson and Bundy, *On Active Service*, 619.
29. "Marshall . . . was deeply disturbed at the idea of a surprise atomic attack on Japan." Lamont, *Day of Trinity*, 264. Louis Morton says that, "No one at this time, or later in the conference, raised the question of whether the Japanese should be informed of the existence of the bomb." Morton, "Decision to Use the Atomic Bomb," 511. Interviewed in 1960, Eisenhower said that when informed by Stimson of the bomb he said he hoped that America would not be the first to use such a weapon, especially against an almost defeated nation. Feis, *Japan Subdued*, 178*n*. Quoted in Hillman (ed.), *Mr. President*, 248.
30. Hewlett and Anderson, *The New World*, 389–90.
31. Quoted in Raymond G. O'Connor, "Harry S. Truman: New Dimensions of Power," in Edgar E. Robinson, *et al.*, *Powers of the President in Foreign Affairs, 1945–1965* (San Francisco: Commonwealth Club of California, 1966), 29; Churchill, *Triumph and Tragedy*, 638–39. "When I talked to Churchill he unhesitatingly told me that he favored the use of the atomic bomb if it might aid to end the war." Truman, *Memoirs*, I, 419.
32. Truman, *Memoirs*, I, 420. See also Hillman (ed.), *Mr. President*, 248; Lamont, *Day of Trinity*, 264–65; Current, *Secretary Stimson*, 233. Current errs in placing Truman in Washington during this period.
33. Truman, *Memoirs*, I, p. ix. In a similar vein Truman said: "The Presidential chair is the loneliest place a man can be." See "Harry S. Truman—The Government Story," Group W television network broadcast, July 19, 1969.
34. Hillman (ed.), *Mr. President*, 248. The date of Truman's decision was probably July 23. A cable from Stimson to George Harrison of the interim committee, dated the twenty-third, indicated that the bombing decision had now "been confirmed by highest authority." Quoted in Bernstein and Matusow (eds.), *The Truman Administration*, 25.
35. Truman, *Memoirs*, I, 420. Full text of orders appears in Bernstein and Matusow (eds.), *The Truman Administration*, 25–26. See also Feis, *Japan Subdued*, 91. A copy of the orders was sent to General MacArthur, and this was probably his first knowledge of the new weapon. MacArthur said he first learned of the bomb "just prior" to its use on Hiroshima. See Douglas MacArthur, *Reminiscences: General of the Army Douglas MacArthur* (New York: McGraw-Hill, 1964), 262. See also Charles A. Willoughby and John Chamberlain, *MacArthur, 1941–1951* (New York: McGraw-Hill, 1954), 286.
36. Truman, *Memoirs*, I, 421. See also Schwarz, *American Strategy*, 58–59.

37. Hillman (ed.), *Mr. President*, 248–49; Truman, *Memoirs*, I, 421. Secretary Stimson felt that Suzuki had rejected the ultimatum: "In the face of this rejection we could only proceed to demonstrate that the ultimatum had meant exactly what it said . . . destruction of Japanese forces and devastation of the homeland." Stimson and Bundy, *On Active Service*, 625. Morton errs in saying that following the Suzuki statement, "Truman held off orders on the use of the bomb for a few days." See "Decision to Use the Atomic Bomb," 513. As indicated textually, no orders had to be given after the order to General Spaatz, and none were given as far as can be determined from available sources.
38. General Spaatz to General Arnold, August 6, 1945, RG18, AAF, 312.1— Operations Letters—1945, III, National Archives. The time noted is for Japan. It was 7:15 P.M., August 5, in Washington.
39. Lamont, *Day of Trinity*, 265. In a research study in progress at Hiroshima's Institute of Nuclear Medicine and Biology, sociologist Minoru Yuzaki offers "highly tentative projections" placing the city's death toll at 200,000. *Time*, XCVI (August 10, 1970), 31; Truman, *Memoirs*, I, 421.
40. Item No. 93, *Public Papers . . . Truman, 1945*, 197–200. Full text is reprinted as Doc. No. 1315, in Richard L. Watson, Jr. (ed.), *The United States in the Contemporary World, 1945–1962*, (New York: Free Press, 1965), IX, 42–45.
41. Buchanan, *United States and World War II*, Vol. II, 585; Truman, *Memoirs*, I, 426.
42. Truman, *Memoirs*, I, 426; Feis, *Japan Subdued*, 116n; Schwarz, *American Strategy*, 59.
43. Lamont, *Day of Trinity*, 304–305. The idea originated with Admiral William R. Purnell of the Military Policy Committee.
44. Truman, *Memoirs*, I, 420, 423. Groves's deputy on Tinian, General Thomas F. Farrell, was in direct field command of the bombings. He believed that it was Groves's wish that a second atom bomb should follow the first as rapidly as possible. With this in mind, Farrell "decided to rush and risk the attack on the 9th rather than wait out the forecasted worse weather." Feis, *Japan Subdued*, 116n.
45. *Truman Speaks*, 73.
46. See, for example, Gar Alperovitz, *Atomic Diplomacy*. See also Feis, *Japan Subdued*; Hanson W. Baldwin, *Great Mistakes of the War* (New York: Collins-Knowlton-Wing, 1950), 88–107. The distinguished diplomatic historian Richard W. Leopold said in a 1970 interview: "I do not think there is any doubt that if those who made the decision knew what we know now, the bomb would not have been dropped." See "The United States in World Affairs, 1941–1968," in John A. Garraty (ed.), *Interpreting American History: Conversations with Historians* (New York: Macmillan, 1970), II, 230. Norman Cousins and Thomas K. Finletter have written: "The first error was the atomic bombing of Hiroshima." See "A Beginning for Sanity," *Saturday Review of Literature*, XXXIX (June 15, 1946), 6.
47. Fleming, *The Cold War*, I, 297; Feis, *Japan Subdued*, 178n; Alperovitz, *Atomic Diplomacy*, 236–39. Admiral Leahy wrote that the atomic bomb, "was of no material assistance in our war against Japan. The Japanese were already defeated and ready to surrender." Leahy, *I Was There* (New York: McGraw-Hill, 1950), 441.
48. For examples of the revisionist approach, see Alperovitz, *Atomic Diplo-*

macy; Fleming, *The Cold War*; William Appleman Williams, *Tragedy of American Diplomacy* (New York: World, 1962); William Appleman Williams (ed.), *Shaping of American Diplomacy*, 946. The first important statement of this thesis appeared in the article by Cousins and Finletter, "A Beginning for Sanity." See also P. M. S. Blackett, *Fear, War and the Bomb* (New York: McGraw-Hill, 1948). For an attack on the revisionists, particularly W. A. Williams, see Robert J. Maddox, *The New Left and the Origins of the Cold War* (Princeton, N.J.: Princeton University Press, 1973).

49. Truman, *Mr. Citizen*, 202; Item No. 97, *Public Papers . . . Truman, 1945*, 212.

50. In recommending the fire bombings of Japan and the use of the atomic bomb, Stimson was, according to Bundy: "implicitly confessing that there could be no significant limits to the horrows of modern war." Stimson and Bundy, *On Active Service*, 632–33; Feis, *Japan Subdued*, 179. The insidious factor in atomic weapons is, of course, the radioactive fallout. As Leahy said: "It [the bomb] is a poisonous thing that kills people by its deadly radioactive reaction, more than by the explosive force it develops." *I Was There*, 441. It has not been possible to determine how much information on radioactivity had been made available to Truman prior to the use of this weapon.

51. For example, a poll taken in October, 1945, showed only 4 percent indicating the bomb should not have been used; 14 percent favored a test on an unpopulated area first; 54 percent accepted the two-bomb tactic used; and 23 percent felt Truman should have used "quickly used many more of them before Japan had a chance to surrender." Elmo Roper, *You and Your Leaders: Their Actions and Your Reactions, 1939–1956* (New York: William Morrow, 1957), 124.

52. James MacGregor Burns, *Presidential Government: The Crucible of Leadership* (Boston: Houghton Mifflin, 1966), 215–16; Truman, *Memoirs*, I, 419. Truman repeatedly avowed that it was his decision alone, often in almost exactly the same language. See, for examples, Truman, *Mr. Citizen*, 202; Hillman (ed.), *Mr. President*, 248–49; Phillips, "Truman at 75"; *Truman Speaks*, 73; New York *Times*, May 3, 1959.

53. For an incisive examination of politico-military thinking in the decision-making process, see Schwarz, *American Strategy*, 59–60. Schwarz's attack on such thinking is substantially the same as that used by Bundy in defense of Stimson. Stimson and Bundy, *On Active Service*, 629–30.

54. Burns, *Presidential Government*, 216.

55. Quoted in Hillman (ed.), *Mr. President*, 248. Emphasis supplied. See also Burns, *Presidential Government*, 215–16.

56. Quoted in Lamont, *Day of Trinity*, 303.

57. Entry, October 5, 1945, Smith Diary.

58. David E. Lilienthal, *The Atomic Energy Years, 1945–1950* (New York: Harper and Row, 1964), II, 391. Again, when talking of the bomb in private (in 1949), Truman mentioned a book by a British author which contended that the bomb was just another weapon of war. Truman said that this was "a very serious mistake," and added: "This isn't just another weapon, not just another bomb." Journal Entry, February 14, 1949, *ibid.*, 474. When Admiral William S. Parsons wrote an article for the *Saturday Evening Post* to the effect that the atomic bomb was just another weapon,

Truman, acting through his special counsel, Clark Clifford, ordered that the article *not* be published because he considered it contrary to the national interests. Memoranda, Lilienthal to Clifford, December 14, 1948; Clifford to the president, December 29, 1948; Clifford to Forrestal, December 31, 1948, all in Papers of Clark M. Clifford, Atomic Energy file, Truman Library, hereinafter cited as Clifford Papers. When asked in a November, 1950, press conference if the bomb was being considered for use in Korea, Truman said, "There has always been active consideration of its use. I don't want to see it used. It is a terrible weapon, and it should not be used on innocent men, women, and children who have nothing whatever to do with this military aggression. That happens when it is used." Item No. 295, *Public Papers . . . Truman, 1950,* 727.

59. Stimson and Bundy, *On Active Service,* 626–27; Truman, *Memoirs,* I, 427–28; Byrnes, *Speaking Frankly,* 209; Hillman (ed.), *Mr. President,* 125; Hewlett and Anderson, *The New World,* 405.

60. Byrnes, *Speaking Frankly,* 209–10; Arnold A. Rogow, *Victim of Duty: A Study of James Forrestal* (London: Rupert Hart-Davis, 1966), 145–46. See also Truman, *Memoirs,* I, 428–29. Full text of the Byrnes note is printed in Herbert Feis, *Contest over Japan* (New York: W. W. Norton, 1967), 162–63. Harriman to Truman, August 9, 11, 1945, in Truman, *Memoirs,* I, 425–32; Item No. 94, *Public Papers . . . Truman, 1945,* 200.

61. Item No. 100, Press Conference, August 14, 1945, *Public Papers . . . Truman, 1945,* 216. For text of Japanese surrender message, see *ibid.,* 217–18.

62. Truman to JCS, August 13, 1945; Marshall to MacArthur, August 13, 14, 1945, JCS to MacArthur, September 6, 1945, all quoted in Truman, *Memoirs,* I, 438–39, 451–53, 457.

63. Presidential Proclamation No. 2714, December 31, 1946, *Federal Register,* XII (January 1, 1947). In a speech to Congress on September 6, 1945, Truman had explained the need for continuing the war powers granted to the president. Basically, he said they would facilitate demobilization and reconversion. Item No. 128, *Public Papers . . . Truman, 1945,* 276–77. By the December 31 proclamation, Truman terminated fifty-three statutes granting his office various war powers. However, the declared "state of military emergency" was not terminated, so he retained numerous extraordinary powers. Colonel Robert Wood to all army commands. December 31, 1946, RG165, War Department, Plans and Operations, 387.4— (011, Case 62), National Archives.

64. Walter Lippman, "Roosevelt Has Gone," New York *Herald-Tribune,* April 14, 1945.

65. Wilber Hoare, in his essay on Truman as commander in chief, would disagree, particularly with regard to the decision to use the bomb. See "Truman," 182.

66. Memorandum, Truman to Forrestal, September 7, 1945, Hillman (ed.), *Mr. President,* 49.

CHAPTER 5

1. Quoted in Lilienthal, *Atomic Energy Years,* 391.
2. Item No. 116, *Public Papers . . . Truman, 1945,* 243–45.
3. Truman to secretary of the navy (Forrestal), *et al.,* October 23, 1945, A17-24 (1), Historical Records Division, Chief of Naval Operations, Navy Yard, Washington, D.C., hereinafter cited as CNO, Navy Yard. Alben

Barkley, chairman of the joint committee, finding many reluctant to testify despite the president's memorandum, asked the White House for a more forceful statement. Over Judge Rosenman's objections, Truman issued such a statement. See Barkley to Matthew J. Connelly, November 2, Truman to joint chiefs, November 7, Rosenman to Truman, November 9, 1945, in Rosenman Papers, Subject File, 1945, Pearl Harbor Investigation, Truman Library; hereinafter cited as Rosenman Papers; Summary, Presidential Actions in re Pearl Harbor Hearings, White House Files, Presidential Powers folder, in Murphy Papers.

4. Truman to secretary of war (Stimson), *et al.*, August 15, 1945, memorandum, Truman to secretary of war, *et al.*, August 30, 1945, in RG107, Office of the Secretary of War (OSW), 471.6—Atomic Bomb, 031.1, National Archives; Truman, *Memoirs*, I, 524.

5. Stimson and Bundy, *On Active Service*, 635–36; Truman, *Memoirs*, I, 523.

6. Item No. 93, Item No. 97 in *Public Papers . . . Truman, 1945*, 199–200, 212–13.

7. For full text of Stimson's memorandum to the president, September 11, 1945, see Stimson and Bundy, *On Active Service*, 642–46.

8. Hewlett and Anderson, *The New World*, 419; Truman, *Memoirs*, I, 524–25. See also Item No. 164, President's News Conference at Tiptonville, Tenn., October 8, 1945, *Public Papers . . . Truman, 1945*, 381–82. Stimson resigned for reasons of health and age. The last cabinet meeting he attended was held on his seventy-eighth birthday. See Item No. 139, *Public Papers . . . Truman, 1945*, 329; Stimson and Bundy, *On Active Service*, 656–57. Truman appointed Robert P. Patterson, the undersecretary of war, to replace Stimson.

9. Dean Acheson, *Present at the Creation: My Years in the State Department* (New York: W. W. Norton, 1969), 123. Acheson, as acting secretary of state, represented Byrnes at this meeting.

10. Truman, *Memoirs*, I, 526–29. See also Rogow, *Victim of Duty*, 154–55; Acheson, *Present at the Creation*, 124; C. Joseph Bernardo and Eugene H. Bacon, *American Military Policy: Its Development since 1775* (Harrisburg, Penn.: Stackpole, 1961), 462; Arthur Krock, *Memoirs: Sixty Years on the Firing Line* (New York: Funk and Wagnalls, 1968), 248–49.

11. Item No. 156, *Public Papers . . . Truman, 1945*, 362–66. See also Acheson, *Present at the Creation*, 124–25; Truman, *Memoirs*, I, 530–33.

12. Text of statement is in Truman, *Memoirs*, I, 542–44.

13. Stimson and Bundy, *On Active Service*, 645; Truman, *Memoirs*, I, 544; Acheson, *Present at the Creation*, 125.

14. Acheson, *Present at the Creation*, 152–54. See also Walter LaFeber, *America, Russia, and the Cold War, 1945–1966* (New York: John Wiley, 1967), 34; Bernard M. Baruch, *The Public Years*, Vol. II of *My Own Story* (New York: Holt, Rinehart and Winston, 1960), 360–63. For Acheson's version of his dispute with Baruch, see *Present at the Creation*, 154–56. For Truman's account, see his *Memoirs*, II, 7–10. See also Byrnes, *Speaking Frankly*, 270.

15. New York *Times*, June 15, 1946. For the full text of the U.S. proposal, see U.S. Senate, Committee on Foreign Relations, *A Decade of Foreign Policy: Basic Documents, 1941–1949*, 81st Cong., 2nd Sess., 1079–1087.

16. Acheson, *Present at the Creation*, 155–56; Bernardo and Bacon, *American Military Policy*, 465; LaFeber, *America, Russia, and the Cold War*, 35;

Editor's Note, Koenig (ed.), *Truman Administration*, 336; Lloyd C. Gardner, *Architects of Illusions: Men and Ideas in American Foreign Policy, 1941–1949* (Chicago: Quadrangle Books, 1970), 194–96; Truman to Baruch, July 10, 1946, quoted in Baruch, *Public Years*, 374.

17. Illustrative of this is a newspaper headline in March, 1947: "U.S. Stand on Atom in the U.N. Unchanged," New York *Times*, March 7, 1947. See also New York *Herald-Tribune*, March 28, 1947. The United Nations Commission on Atomic Energy adjourned *sine die* in May, 1948, resumed hearings in February of 1949 and gave up again in July.
18. Item No. 239, *Public Papers ... Truman, 1948*, 789.
19. At this writing, a quarter-century later, significant progress has not been made, although Strategic Arms Limitation Talks (SALT) are being held.
20. Wallace to Truman, July 23, 1946 (and reply), August 8, 1946, in Subject File, Unification (Pt. 3), Clifford Papers.
21. Truman, *Memoirs*, I, 559.
22. Patterson and Forrestal to Truman, September 18, 1946, RG107, OSA, RPP/White House, National Archives; Baruch to Truman, September 24, 1946, Atomic Energy folder, in Clifford Papers. Truman to Martha Truman, September 20, 1946, quoted in Truman, *Memoirs*, I, 560. The original draft of Truman's public statement of September 20, firing Wallace is in Subject File, "Wallace, Henry," Clifford Papers.
23. Item No. 156, *Public Papers ... Truman, 1945*, 364.
24. See Editor's Note, Koenig (ed.), *Truman Administration*, 126.
25. Patterson to Sam Rayburn, October 3, 1945, RG107, OSW, 471.6—Atomic Bomb, National Archives. A copy of the draft is not in the files, but it is outlined in the body of the letter. An earlier letter to Truman's counsel, Judge Rosenman, from the War Department reads: "An Interim Committee has completed the recommendations for (atomic bomb) legislation which are now in Mr. Byrnes' hands together with War Department comments." Colonel H. M. Pasco to Rosenman, September 1, 1945, Subject File, 1945, in Rosenman Papers. A memorandum to the president from the secretary of war notes that the undersecretary of war "worked with the House Military Affairs Committee" on the May-Johnson bill. Patterson to Truman, December 27, 1945, RG107, OSW, 471.6—Atomic Bomb, National Archives.
26. Hewlett and Anderson, *The New World*, 438; Item No. 172, *Public Papers ... Truman, 1945*, 403.
27. Truman, *Memoirs*, II, 2.
28. Hewlett and Anderson, *The New World*, 436–39. See also Entries, October 5, 30, 1945, in Smith Diary; Truman, *Memoirs*, II, 3.
29. Truman to Patterson and Forrestal, November 28, 1945, RG107, OSW, 471.6—Atomic Bomb, National Archives.
30. Truman, *Memoirs*, II, 2–3; Rogow, *Victim of Duty*, 148. In addition to Forrestal, Patterson, and Groves, Admiral Leahy, Truman's chief military adviser, also objected to the lack of military authority proposed in the McMahon bill. Diary entry, February 13, 1946, Millis (ed.), *Forrestal Diaries*, 133.
31. Patterson to Truman, December 27, 1945, RG107, OSW, 471.6—Atomic Bomb, National Archives.
32. Truman to Patterson and Forrestal, January 23, 1946, in Truman, *Memoirs*, II, 3–4. See also Hewlett and Anderson, *The New World*, 489. (Truman

dates the prior memo "November 30," whereas the secretary of war's copy was dated November 28.) The importance of the last paragraph of this January 23 memorandum can be seen in that on the day it was written, Forrestal was testifying to the Senate Special Committee on Atomic Energy in opposition to the Truman proposal for a five-member AEC serving "at the pleasure of the President." Rogow, *Victim of Duty*, 150.
33. Truman, *Memoirs*, II, 4–5. See also Hewlett and Anderson, *The New World*, 490–91.
34. Diary entry, March 14, 1946, in Vandenberg, *Private Papers*, 256–57; Rogow, *Victim of Duty*, 152.
35. Truman, *Memoirs*, II, 7.
36. Item No. 61, *Public Papers. . . Truman, 1946*, 157.
37. Public Law 585, 79th Cong., 2nd Sess. See also Brief of S.1717, Subject File, Atomic Energy folder, in Clifford Papers.
38. James, *Contemporary Presidency*, 89.
39. Warner R. Schilling, "The Politics of National Defense: Fiscal 1950," in Schilling, Paul Y. Hammond and Glenn H. Snyder (eds.), *Strategy, Politics, and Defense Budgets* (New York and London: Columbia University Press, 1962), 173.
40. Journal entry, December 11, 1946, Lilienthal, *Atomic Energy Years*, 118.
41. Clarification of those functions relative to security and exercise of other atomic project powers was discussed in messages from Secretary of War Patterson to the president: Patterson to Truman, February 27, 1946, RG407, The Adjutant General-(WDCSA), 471.6—Atomic, National Archives; Patterson to the president, September 23, 1946, Subject File, Atomic Energy folder, in Clifford Papers.
42. Item No. 106, Item No. 193, *Public Papers . . . Truman, 1945*, 224, 495. Truman's statement generated a good deal of speculation in the press. On December 7, Patterson asked the president for permission to issue a joint public statement with Forrestal to the effect that tests were to be conducted. Patterson to Truman, December 7, 1945, RG107, OSW, 471.6—Atomic Bomb (031.1), National Archives.
43. The JCS request to the president is quoted in a memorandum informing Truman of progress made subsequent to his approval of the tests. See Kenneth G. Royall and Forrestal to the president, January 7, 1946, RG107, OSW, 471.6, National Archives.
44. William W. Carpenter to W. Stuart Symington, August 2, 1946, RG340, Secretary of the Air Force, Office of Administrative Assistant, General Files, Special Interest File 4A, National Archives; New York *Times*, May 18, 1948. See also Journal Entry, May 17, 1948, Lilienthal, *Atomic Energy Years*, 340–41; New York *Herald-Tribune*, May 18, 1948; Truman to Forrestal, May 17, 1948, RG407, AG201.22, National Archives.
45. Acheson, *Present at the Creation*, 125, 155; New York *Times*, September 21, 1945.
46. Journal Entry, February 14, 1949, Lilienthal, *Atomic Energy Years*, 473–74; Truman, *Memoirs*, II, 306–307. See also Lamont, *Day of Trinity*, 280. Truman used the occasion of publicly announcing the Soviet bomb test to call again for a "truly effective enforceable international control of atomic energy." Item No. 216, *Public Papers . . . Truman, 1949*, 485.
47. Warner R. Schilling, "The H-Bomb Decision: How to Decide Without Actually Choosing," *Political Science Quarterly*, LXXVI (March, 1961),

29. This article is an excellent, detailed analysis of the decision-making process. For other effects of the Soviet atomic test on American politico-military thinking, see Millis, *Arms and Men,* 291; Robert Endicott Osgood, *Limited War: The Challenge to American Strategy* (Chicago: University of Chicago Press, 1957), 157–59. See also Paul Y. Hammond, "NSC-68: Prologue to Rearmament," in Schilling, Hammond, and Snyder, *Strategy, Politics, and Defense Budgets,* 285–86.

48. Lilienthal, *Atomic Energy Years,* 624.

49. Monroe (La.) *Morning World,* March 17, 1969; Lilienthal, *Atomic Energy Years,* 624, 627–32; Schwarz, *American Strategy,* 76; Richard G. Hewlett and Francis Duncan, *Atomic Shield, 1947–1952,* Vol. II of *A History of the United States Atomic Energy Commission* (University Park: Pennsylvania State University Press, 1969), 406–408.

50. Lilienthal, *Atomic Energy Years,* 632–33. See also Schilling, "H-Bomb Decision," 36ff; Hewlett and Duncan, *Atomic Shield,* 408.

51. Item No. 26, *Public Papers . . . Truman, 1950,* 138.

CHAPTER 6

1. Item No. 174, *Public Papers . . . Truman, 1945,* 409.

2. U.S. War Department, "General Principles of National Military Policy to Govern Preparation of Post-War Plans: Extracts from Directives by General George C. Marshall, Chief of Staff," Circular No. 347 (August 25, 1944); O'Connor, "Harry S. Truman: New Dimensions of Power," 32. For an interesting historical background on UMT, see Millis, *Arms and Men,* 274–76.

3. Truman, *Memoirs,* I, 153, 510; Item No. 36, *Public Papers . . . Truman, 1947,* 147; Russell F. Weigley, *Towards an American Army: Military Thought from Washington to Marshall* (New York and London: Columbia University Press, 1962), 247.

4. Item No. 44, *Public Papers . . . Truman, 1945,* 78. See also Washington *Post,* June 2, 1945. One major difference between Truman and the services was over the timing of the training period. The president, in an unused plan developed in June, 1945, hoped to split the year of active service into several periods over a four-year span, to be followed by three years of inactive reserve service. The army and navy, on the other hand, wanted the trainee for one unbroken year of active service. Draft, "Plan for Universal Military Training under Postwar Conditions," June 23, 1945, Subject File, Universal Military Training, in Rosenman Papers. In the same file, see also *The War and Navy Department Views on Universal Military Training* (undated, 38-page pamphlet; cover bears handwritten notation: "publd. about 10 May 1945").

5. Washington *Post,* June 11, 1945. No signs of public apathy can be found in the Gallup polls taken on the question in May and July. They recorded about 70 percent in favor of UMT. See *ibid.,* May 8, July 18, 1945. New York *Times,* June 16, 1945; New York *Herald-Tribune,* June 16, 1945; Baltimore *Sun,* June 16, 1945. The New York *Times* reported (October 28, 1945) that General Marshall, "has made a virtual crusade for UMT."

6. Baltimore *Sun,* June 16, 1945. Eisenhower's statement was contained in a letter to Clifton Woodrum, chairman of the committee. Text of the letter appears in the New York *Times,* June 16, 1945. A summary of the principal arguments against UMT can be found in a memorandum, George M.

Elsey to James K. Vardaman, August 18, 1945, Subject File, Universal Military Training, in Rosenman Papers.

7. *House Reports,* 79th Cong., 1st Sess., No. 857. See also Lauris Norstad to Commanding General, Continental Air Forces, August 8, 1945, RG18, Army Air Force (AAF), AF353-UMT, 1945, National Archives.

8. See, for example, Joseph Loftus, "Military Training Issue Quiescent but Not Dead," New York *Times,* July 22, 1945; [Anonymous], "Conscription or Enlistment?," *The Nation,* CLXI (July 14, 1945), 32–34. Item No. 106, *Public Papers . . . Truman, 1945,* 227. See also Washington *Post,* August 17, 1945.

9. Truman, *Memoirs,* I, 510.

10. Item No. 128, *Public Papers . . . Truman, 1945,* 127–28. In a letter to the secretary of war, Truman restated the passage cited here and told the secretary he wanted the War Department to, "make the necessary studies, prepare material, assist in drafting, present testimony to Congress, and in general, follow the progress of the legislation in Congress." The secretary was further instructed to send progress reports to the White House on the first and fifteenth of each month. Truman to Patterson, October 4, 1945, RG407, OSW, AG011 (October 4, 1945), National Archives; Rosenman to Truman, October 9, 1945, Subject File, Universal Military Training, in Rosenman Papers.

11. Item No. 174, *Public Papers . . . Truman, 1945,* 407.

12. *Ibid.,* 407–408.

13. *Ibid.,* 408–409. Truman said in his *Memoirs* (I, 510) that he sent the UMT message up to Congress on the twenty-second. In fact, he delivered the speech personally to a joint session of Congress beginning at 12:31 P.M., October 23. See *Public Papers . . . Truman, 1945,* 413; New York *Times,* October 28, 1945. Truman's plan had the backing of the secretary of war and the army chief of staff. Patterson to Truman, October 18, 1945, Subject File, Universal Military Training, in Rosenman Papers.

14. Item No. 18, *Public Papers . . . Truman, 1946,* 52; Bernardo and Bacon, *American Military Policy,* 448; New York *Times,* October 28, 1945.

15. Entry, January 4, 1946, in Smith Diary.Forrestal's diary entry for July 30, 1945, corroborates this recollection by Smith. Forrestal says Truman had talked "a good deal" about citizen-soldiers and of destroying the "political cliques that run the Army and Navy." In the same conversation Forrestal recalls Truman describing West Point and Annapolis as "finishing schools." Millis (ed.), *Forrestal Diaries,* 88–89.

16. Patterson to Andrew J. May, February 28, 1946, RG407, AG353 (December 10, 1945), National Archives; Item No. 53, Item No. 76, *Public Papers . . . Truman, 1946,* 145, 187–88.

17. Bernardo and Bacon, *American Military Policy,* 448–49.

18. The letters enclosed were Jefferson to Thaddeus Kosciusko, February 26, 1810; Jefferson to James Madison, June 18, 1813. In his note to Patterson, Truman inadvertently referred to the program as Universal *Military* Training. He had come to avoid the term, *military,* ordinarily preferring to speak of it as his "Universal Training" program. Truman to Patterson, October 9, 1946, RG107, OSW, RPP/White House, National Archives.

19. Arthur A. Ekirch, Jr., *The Civilian and the Military: A History of the American Antimilitarist Tradition* (New York: Oxford University Press, 1956), 281; Patterson to the president, November 5, 1945, RG407, AG353,

National Archives; Truman to Patterson, November 13, 1945, Subject File, Universal Military Training, in Rosenman Papers.

20. Item No. 268, *Public Papers . . . Truman, 1946*, 509; New York *Times*, December 21, 1946. See also Washington *Post*, December 23, 1946; Truman, *Memoirs*, II, 534. New York *Herald-Tribune*, December 21, 1946.

21. Lewis B. Hershey to Truman, December 5, 1946; Patterson to Truman, February 4, 1947; Marshall to Truman, February 6, 1947. all in Subject File, National Military Establishment: Selective Service, Clifford Papers. See also New York *Times*, March 4, 1947; Washington *Post*, March 15, 1947. Text of Truman's special message to Congress is in *Public Papers . . . Truman, 1947*, 163–64.

22. Ekirch, *Civilian and the Military*, 281–82. Summary of the Commission Report is in New York *Times*, June 2, 1947. See also Bernardo and Bacon, *American Military Policy*, 449–50; Truman, *Memoirs*, II, 54–55.

23. Bernardo and Bacon, *American Military Policy*, 450. Truman publicly urged UMT passage regularly. For example, in his second State of the Union message, January 6, 1947, *Public Papers . . . Truman, 1947*, 11–12. In June, speaking at Princeton's Bicentennial, the president made the need for universal training the subject of an address which was not too warmly received, according to Alfred Friendly in the Washington *Post*, June 18, 1947. Ten days later, Truman told reporters that UMT was essential for national security. New York *Times*, June 27, 1947. The same theme was repeated by the president in statements made in August and October. See New York *Times*, August 29, 1947; Washington *Post*, October 25, 1947. Forrestal to secretary of the air force, *et al.*, December 18, 1947, RG340, Office of the Secretary of the Air Force (SAF) AF381, National Archives.

24. Item No. 5, *Public Papers . . . Truman, 1948*, 26; Forrestal to Walter Andrews, April 2, 1948, RG330, Office of the Secretary of Defense (OSD), CD9-1-4, National Archives.

25. Millis (ed.), *Forrestal Diaries*, 393–94, 397–98. See also Paul Y. Hammond, "Super Carriers and B-36 Bombers: Appropriations, Strategy and Politics," in Harold Stein (ed.), *American Civil-Military Decisions: A Book of Case Studies* (Tuscaloosa: University of Alabama Press, 1963), 473–76. For text of Truman's special message to the Congress, see Item No. 52, *Public Papers . . . Truman, 1948*, 182–86. Truman emphasized the urgency of his requests in New York City the same day (March 17) in an address before the Society of the Friendly Sons of St. Patrick. Truman, *Memoirs*, II, 242–43. Text of this address appears in New York *Herald-Tribune*, March 18, 1948.

26. Forrestal to Walter Andrews, April 2, 1948, RG330, OSD, CD9-1-4, National Archives; Bernardo and Bacon, *American Military Policy*, 450. Truman signed the Selective Service Act into law on June 24, 1948, less than a day after passage. New York *Times*, June 25, 1948.

27. For example, in October of 1948, Omar Bradley, then army chief of staff was still strongly urging that the services should try to obtain enabling legislation on UMT in the next congressional session. Bradley to Royall, October 4, 1948, RG330, OSD, CD9-2-4, National Archives. Secretary of Defense Forrestal, while believing in the UMT idea, had given up hope of getting it through Congress by the summer of 1948. See entries, April 24, 30, 1948, Millis (ed.), *Forrestal Diaries*, 425–28.

28. Item No. 225, *Public Papers . . . Truman, 1950,* 601–602. See also Item No. 272, *ibid.,* 687–89.
29. Marshall to Johnson, January 17, 1951, RG340, AF353, UMT, National Archives; Bernardo and Bacon, *American Military Policy,* 451; Robert Payne, *The Marshall Story: A Biography of General George C. Marshall* (New York: Prentice-Hall, 1951), 314–16.
30. "Recommendations of the Secretary of Defense of Materials for Inclusion in the State of the Union Message," draft attached to a letter of transmittal, John G. Adams to Charles Coolidge, November 26, 1951, RG330, OSD, 031.1, National Archives.
31. E. W. Kenworthy, "Taps for Jim Crow in the Services," *New York Times Magazine* (June 11, 1950), 12. Kenworthy served as executive secretary on the President's Committee on Equality of Treatment and Opportunity in the Armed Forces. See also Richard M. Dalfiume, *Desegregation of the U.S. Armed Forces: Fighting on Two Fronts, 1939–1953* (Columbia, Mo.: University of Missouri Press, 1969), 38–39. For a detailed, but generally uncritical, study of the Negro soldier in World War II, see Ulysses Lee, *The Employment of Negro Troops,* in Stetson Conn (ed.), *United States Army in World War II* (Washington: U.S. Government Printing Office, 1966).
32. Kenworthy, "Taps for Jim Crow in the Services," 12. See also Jean Byers, "A Study of the Negro in Military Service" (263-page mimeographed, restricted document, "reproduced for departmental use," January, 1950), 1. Copy in RG340, S/AF, Special Interest File, 1948–49, National Archives.
33. Ira Baker to Joseph T. McNarney, June 2, 1945, RG118, AAF, 312.1-Operations ltrs.-1945 (v.3), National Archives.
34. Byers, "A Study of the Negro in Military Service," 262–63. Copy in RG340, S/AF, Special Interest File, 1948–49, National Archives.
35. William C. Berman, *The Politics of Civil Rights in the Truman Administration* (Columbus, Ohio: Ohio State University Press, 1970), 8–39 *passim.*
36. Dalfiume, *Desegregation of the U.S. Armed Forces,* 142–44; Berman, *Politics of Civil Rights,* 53–54.
37. Truman, *Memoirs,* II, 180. See also Item No. 9, *Public Papers . . . Truman, 1947,* 98–99.
38. *"To Secure These Rights": A Report of the President's Committee on Civil Rights* (Washington: U.S. Government Printing Office, 1947), 151–73; John P. Roche, *The Quest for the Dream: The Development of Civil Rights and Human Relations in Modern America* (Chicago: Quadrangle Books, 1968), 238. See also Dalfiume, *Desegregation of the U.S. Armed Forces,* 155–56; Truman, *Memoirs,* II, 181. For Truman's message praising the report, see Item No. 215, *Public Papers . . . Truman, 1947,* 479–80.
39. Item No. 20, *Public Papers . . . Truman, 1948,* 121–26.
40. *New York Times,* May 28, 1948. Forrestal, who believed completely in the idea, had begun work upon receipt of the president's orders. See, for example, his interim progress report in a memorandum, Forrestal to Truman, February 29, 1948, RG330, OSD, CD25-1-11, National Archives.
41. *New York Post,* June 6, 1948.
42. Executive Order 9981, July 26, 1948 (13 *F.R.,* 4314). Text of both orders is in Joint Army and Air Force Bulletin No. 32 (August 2, 1948). See also Berman, *Politics of Civil Rights,* 116–18; Richard J. Stillman, *Integration*

of the Negro in the U.S. Armed Forces (New York: Praeger, 1968), 41–42. The original idea for the committee was Clark Clifford's: "I would suggest . . . a defense establishment board . . . charged with the development of a uniform racial policy in the Services consistent with the President's two goals of equal opportunity and non-discrimination." See original draft of the order and also Clifford to Truman, May 11, 1948, both in Subject File, Segregation in the Armed Forces, Clifford Papers. Clifford repeated this proposal in a memorandum to Forrestal, May 13, 1948, Subject File, Unification: Secretary of Defense, in Clifford Papers.

43. New York *Times*, April 27, 1948; Baltimore *Sun*, April 27, 1948. See also Berman, *Politics of Civil Rights*, 100; Dalfiume, *Desegregation of the U.S. Armed Forces*, 165–66; Stillman, *Integration of the Negro in the U.S. Armed Forces*, 40; Barton J. Bernstein, "The Ambiguous Legacy: The Truman Administration and Civil Rights," in Bernstein (ed.), *Politics and Policies of the Truman Administration* (Chicago: Quadrangle Books, 1970), 286–87.

44. Royall to Forrestal, September 22, 1948, RG330, OSD, CD30-1-2, National Archives.

45. Eugene M. Zuckert to Symington, January 12, 1949, RG340, S/AF, Special Interest File, 35-Staff, National Archives. The original draft of Symington's order to all commanding officers is in RG 340, S/AF, Special Interest File (35), Negro Affairs—1949, National Archives.

46. R. E. Nugent to Symington, *et al.*, January 3, 1949, RG340, S/AF, Special Interest File, 35-Staff, National Archives; Transcript, "Meeting of the President and the Four Service Secretaries with the President's Committee on Equality of Treatment and Opportunity in the Armed Services, 12:15 P.M., 12 January, 1949, Cabinet Room, White House," RG 330, OSD, D54-1-16, National Archives. See also, Symington to Forrestal, January 6, 1949, RG330, OSD, CD30-1-2, National Archives.

47. Johnson to secretaries of army, navy, air force and chairman, Personnel Policy Board, April 6, 1949, RG330, OSD, SD291.2—Negroes, National Archives. For the secretary of defense's explanation of the need for his servicewide directive of April 6, see letter, Louis Johnson to Lyndon B. Johnson, July 8, 1949, RG330, OSD, D54-1-6, National Archives. Secretary of the Army Royall resigned effective April 27. See Truman to Royall, April 21, 1949, OF, 1285-B, Department of the Army (1949), in Truman Papers.

48. For an excerpted version of the report, see Item No. 121, Freedom to Serve, Report of the President's Committee on Equality of Treatment and Opportunity in the Armed Services, Leslie H. Fishel, Jr. and Benjamin Quarles (eds.), *The Black American: A Brief Documentary History* (Glenview, Ill.: Scott, Foresman, 1970), 312–14. See also Dalfiume, *Desegregation of the U.S. Armed Forces*, 198–200; Kenworthy, "Taps for Jim Crow in the Services," 24. There is evidence that Truman had to intervene directly with Gordon Gray, the new secretary of the army, to have the racial quotas dropped. See Gray to Truman, March 1, 11, 1950, OF, 1285B, Department of the Army, in Truman Papers; Truman to Gray, March 27, 1950, RG335, Office of the Secretary of the Army (OSA), 291.2, National Archives.

49. For example, in July, 1951, General Marshall, then secretary of defense, was able to tell two senators who inquired that racially segregated units had been almost totally eliminated in the Far Eastern Command (Korea

and Japan) and that progress was being made in other areas, "to carry forward the principle of integration in a planned and orderly manner." Marshall to Herbert H. Lehman and Hubert H. Humphrey, July 20, 1951, RG330, OSD, SD291.2, National Archives. General Matthew B. Ridgway recommended and was very active in bringing about the integration of the units in his Far Eastern Command. See Walter G. Hermes, *Truce Tent and Fighting Front*, in Stetson Conn (ed.), *United States Army in the Korean War* (Washington: U.S. Government Printing Office, 1966), 104–105.

CHAPTER 7

1. Item No. 86, *Public Papers . . . Truman, 1946*, 207.
2. Entry, July 30, 1945, Millis (ed.), *Forrestal Diaries*, 88–89.
3. Truman, *Memoirs*, II, 46–47; Truman, "Our Armed Forces Must Be Unified," *Collier's*, CXIV (August 26, 1944), 63.
4. Truman, "Our Armed Forces Must Be Unified," 16, 63–64. See also Hoare, "Truman," 184–85. Truman's own summation of this article appears in his *Memoirs*, II, 47–48. Questioned about the article in a press conference (August 30, 1945), Truman admitted his statements about a lack of cooperation between commands at Pearl Harbor were incorrect, but he stated that he still believed, as he always had, in unity of command. Item No. 118, *Public Papers . . . Truman, 1945*, 246–48.
5. Truman, *Memoirs*, II, 46–47. See also Elmer E. Cornwell, Jr., "The Truman Presidency," in Richard S. Kirkendall (ed.), *The Truman Period as a Research Field* (Columbia, Mo.: University of Missouri Press, 1967), 221–22.
6. While there was some thought given to unification prior to World War II, the results of such activity were inconsequential. The Morrow Board (1925) and the Baker Board (1934), while principally concerned with national aviation policies, did comment on the feasibility of integration of the armed services. The former concluded that unification would create too complex and unwieldy a structure. The latter made some passing allusions to a need for greater coordination between the armed services. Excerpts from both the Morrow and Baker board reports can be found in Walter Millis (ed.), *American Military Thought* (New York: Bobbs-Merrill, 1966), 387–417 *passim*.
7. Rogow, *Victim of Duty*, 187–88. See also U.S. Senate, Committee on Armed Services, *National Defense Establishment: Unification of the Armed Services, Hearings on S. 758*, 80th Cong., 1st Sess., Pt. 1, pp. 7–8, hereinafter cited as *Hearings, National Defense Establishment*. The War Department plan is usually called the McNarney Plan, after Lieutenant General Joseph T. McNarney, deputy chief of staff, who presented it. Representatives from the House Naval Affairs and Military Affairs committees made up the membership of the select committee, chaired by Clifton Woodrum.
8. *Hearings, National Defense Establishment*, Pt. 1, p. 5; Rogow, *Victim of Duty*, 188–89. Forrestal committed suicide by defenestration shortly after resigning as secretary of defense.
9. Entries, June 13, 19, 1945, Millis (ed.), *Forrestal Diaries*, 62–63; Rogow, *Victim of Duty*, 191.
10. "Excerpts from the Eberstadt Report," in Henry M. Jackson (ed.), *The National Security Council: Jackson Subcommittee Papers on Policy-Making*

at the Presidential Level (New York: Praeger, 1965), 291–94. See also Bernardo and Bacon, *American Military Policy*, 455; *Hearings, National Defense Establishment*, Pt. 1, pp. 6, 8–9.

11. St. Louis *Post-Dispatch*, October 22, 1945. For a summary of Forrestal's testimony in favor of the Eberstadt Plan and against the army's proposals, see Rogow, *Victim of Duty*, 193–94. For the principal proposals of the War Department, see *Hearings, National Defense Establishment*, Pt. 1, pp. 6, 9. A transcript of General Collins' statement to the committee is in Subject File, Unification, Clifford Papers.

12. Bernardo and Bacon, *American Military Policy*, 456; Marshall Testimony, October 18, 1945 (transcript), Subject File, Unification, in Clifford Papers. General Eisenhower was in full agreement with Marshall on all points. He warned the committee that failure to unify would invite another Pearl Harbor. New York *Times*, November 17, 1945. A transcript of Patterson's testimony is in Subject File, Unification of the Armed Services, Rosenman Papers.

13. H. W. Bowman to Hoyt S. Vandenberg, October 2, 1945, RG18, AAF, 312.1—Operations—1945, National Archives. See also F. F. Everest to Nathan F. Twining, October 5, 1945, *ibid.*; Hanson W. Baldwin, "The Military Move In," *Harper's Magazine*, CXCV (December, 1947), 488.

14. Statement by General of the Army H. H. Arnold (transcript), Subject File-1945, Unification of the Armed Services, in Rosenman Papers.

15. Chicago *Tribune*, October 26, 1945; "Unification of the Armed Services: Analytical Digest of Testimony Before the Senate Military Affairs Committee, 17 October to 17 December, 1945" (n.a., n.d., mimeographed), 105. Copy in RG330, OSD, Office of the Director of Administration, National Archives; Baltimore *Evening Sun*, October 25, 1945.

16. Forrestal to Truman, November 8, 1945, RG107, OSA, Single Department-National Defense, National Archives. See also Forrestal to Patterson, November 9, 1945, *ibid.*

17. Entry, October 30, 1945, in Smith Diary; Item No. 193, *Public Papers . . . Truman, 1945*, 496.

18. Truman, *Memoirs*, II, 49.

19. "I assume you wish to adopt the Army view," Rosenman wrote to the president. Rosenman to Truman, November 13, 1945, Subject File, Unification of the Armed Services, in Rosenman Papers. See also entry, December 13, 1945, wherein the budget director received the same impression, in Smith Diary.

20. Leahy to Rosenman, December 17, 1945, Subject File, Unification of the Armed Services, in Rosenman Papers.

21. H. H. Arnold to Rosenman, December 18, 1945, Howard C. Peterson to Rosenman, December 18, 1945, Rosenman to Harold Smith, December 17, 1945, Rosenman to Forrestal (and reply) December 17, 18, 1945, Forrestal to Rosenman, December 18, 1945, *ibid.*

22. Full text is in *Public Papers . . . Truman, 1945*, 546–60. See also Cornwell, "The Truman Presidency," 222–23. For a description of the differences and areas of agreement between Truman's proposal and the Navy (Forrestal) Plan, see Millis (ed.), *Forrestal Diaries*, 119–20. For a summary of the Truman Plan, see *Hearings, National Defense Establishment*, Pt. 1, pp. 9–10.

23. Entries, December 18, 19, 1945, Millis (ed.), *Forrestal Diaries*, 118–19;

New York *Mirror*, December 20, 1945; Item No. 221, *Public Papers . . . Truman, 1945*, 565.

24. Eisenhower to Patterson, January 28, 1946, Personal File/Dwight D. Eisenhower (PF/DDE), Patterson folder, in Eisenhower Papers.

25. Eberstadt, "Memorandum of Discussions Between Judge Patterson, Mr. Forrestal, and Myself," March 14, 1946, RG107, OSA (Patterson), Single Department-Misc., National Archives.

26. Entry, March 18, 1945, Millis (ed.), *Forrestal Diaries*, 148–49.

27. *Hearings, National Defense Establishment*, Pt. 1, pp. 6–10. The subcommittee consisted of Elbert D. Thomas (chairman, Utah); Warren Austin (Vt.), and Lister Hill (Ala.); Truman, *Memoirs*, II, 50.

28. Item No. 78, *Public Papers . . . Truman, 1946*, 194–95. In another press conference held on the seventeenth, Truman repeated his charge that the admirals were still actively lobbying and speaking against unification. Item No. 84, *ibid.*, 204.

29. Rogow, *Victim of Duty*, 197–98; Millis (ed.), *Forrestal Diaries*, 151–52; Eisenhower to Patterson, April 27, 1946, PF/DDE, Patterson folder, in Eisenhower Papers.

30. Truman, *Memoirs*, II, 50. See also Rogow, *Victim of Duty*, 201; Entry, May 13, 1946, Millis (ed.), *Forrestal Diaries*, 160–62.

31. Patterson and Forrestal to Truman, May 31, 1946, Subject File, Unification, Correspondence-General, in Clifford Papers.

32. Truman, Memoirs, II, 50; Entry, May 22, 1946, in Smith Diary. On May 15 Forrestal received a joint letter from Senator David Walsh, chairman of the Senate Naval Affairs Committee and Representative Carl Vinson, chairman of the House Naval Affairs Committee, stating their belief that any unification measure could get through Congress if it proposed a single department of the armed forces. Walsh's committee opened hearings on S.2044 on April 30 and closed them July 11, 1946. The bill was not reported out of committee. *Hearings, National Defense Establishment*, Pt. 1, pp. 6–7.

33. Truman to Patterson and Forrestal, June 15, 1946, RG330, OSD, Hoover Commision Report, Unification of the Armed Forces, National Archives.

34. Truman to Andrew J. May, June 15, 1946, Correspondence-General, in Clifford Papers. The president sent identical letters to Senators Thomas and Walsh and Representative Vinson. Text of the letter is printed as Item No. 137, *Public Papers . . . Truman, 1946*, 303–305. Senator Thomas amended S.2044 to conform with the recommendations in Truman's letter. See U.S. Senate, *S.2044*, Committee Print (as amended), 79th Cong., 2nd Sess.

35. Patterson to Truman, June 17, 1946, RG407, OSW, AG381, National Archives; Forrestal to Truman, June 24, William E. Carpenter to Stuart Symington, August 2, 1946, RG340, AF, Special Interest File 4A, *ibid.*; Symington was specifically charged by the secretary of war with responsibility for all unification matters. See Patterson to Symington, April 11, 1946, RG18, AF381, Unification, *ibid.*

36. Forrestal to Clifford, September 7, 1946, in Subject File, Unification: Correspondence-General, Clifford Papers; Editor's Note, Millis (ed.), *Forrestal Diaries*, 203.

37. In addition to Truman, present were Patterson, Leahy, Forrestal, Eisenhower, Nimitz, and Clifford. Entry, September 10, 1946, Millis (ed.), *Forrestal Diaries*, 203–205.

300 *Notes to pages 104 to 106*

38. Forrestal and Patterson to Truman, January 16, 1947, in Subject File, Unification (Pt. 2), Clifford Papers; Truman to Patterson and Forrestal, January 16, 1947, RG330, OSD, Hoover Commission Report, Unification of the Armed Forces, National Archives. Both letters are printed in full in *House Documents*, 80th Cong., 1st Sess., No. 56 p. 2. *New York Times*, January 17, 1947; New York *Herald-Tribune*, January 17, 1947. No attempt has been made to describe the struggles between the War and Navy departments between the September meeting and this agreement, since it would be largely repetitious. The participants took the same stands detailed earlier and agreed only when they had to. The New York *Times* article recounts much of the substance of these meetings, as does Admiral Forrest Sherman in his testimony on the bill. See *Hearings, National Defense Establishment*, Pt. 1, pp. 159–67.
39. Truman to Joseph W. Martin, January 17, 1947, in House Documents, 80th Cong., 1st Sess., No. 56, p. 102. See also Item No. 12, *Public Papers . . . Truman, 1947*, 101–102.
40. Chan Gurney to Patterson, February 21, 1947, Subject File, Correspondence-Unification Bill, in Clifford Papers. See also Patterson to Clifford, February 21, 1947, *ibid.* (The Armed Services Committee was established by a congressional reorganization at the end of 1946. It replaced the Military Affairs and Naval Affairs committees.)
41. Clifford to Secretaries of War and Navy, February 24, 1947, *ibid.*
42. Patterson to Truman, Forrestal to Truman, February 25, 1947, *ibid.* The President's letter of transmittal and the text of the draft bill are published in *House Documents*, 80th Cong., 1st Sess., No. 149, Pt. 1, pp. 11–12. *Hearings, National Defense Establishment*, Pt. 1, p. 22; Rogow, *Victim of Duty*, 204–205. See also Washington *Post*, March 19, 1947.
43. Stimson to Gurney, April 21, 1947, in *Hearings, National Defense Establishment*, Pt. 2, pp. 457–60; Pt. 3, pp. 709–10. Among the few who took issue with the bill were Marine Commandant Vandergrift, who wanted statutory protection for the traditional functions of the Marine Corps, and Admiral King, who opposed establishing the office of secretary of defense. See *ibid.*, Pt. 2, p. 412, Pt. 3, p. 561; New York *Times*, May 8, 1947.
44. Public Law 253, 80th Cong., 1st Sess.; William H. Baumer, "National Security Organization," *Military Engineer*, XL (March, 1948), 5. For a description of the changes made in the act by the House, see Clifford to Truman, July 22, 1947, Subject File, Correspondence-Unification Bill, in Clifford Papers. Text of Executive Order 9877 is in RG330, SAF, Special Interest File 4A, National Archives.
45. "Staff Report of the Subcommittee on National Policy Machinery," December 12, 1960, in Jackson (ed.), *National Security Council*, 30. See also Cornwell, "The Truman Presidency," 224–25; Hoare, "Truman," 188–89; Ernest R. May, "The Development of Political Military Consultation in the United States," *Political Science Quarterly*, LXX (June, 1955), See also John Fischer, "Mr. Truman's Politburo," *Harper's Magazine*, CCII (June, 1951), 30. Marshall Testimony, *Far East Hearings*, Pt. 1, p. 584; Raymond P. Brandt, St. Louis *Post-Dispatch*, February 29, 1948.
46. Entry, September 17, 1947, Millis (ed.), *Forrestal Diaries*, 316, 320; Cornwell, "The Truman Presidency,'" 225. See also testimony by Sidney Souers, executive secretary, NSC, to Senate Subcommittee on National Policy Machinery, May 10, 1960, excerpted in Jackson (ed.), *National Security*

Council, 100, 108–109. For a fuller description of how Truman wanted the NSC to operate, see a draft memorandum, Truman to Souers (undated), Subject File, National Military Establishment—Security Council, in Clifford Papers.

47. Truman to Secretaries of State, War, and Navy, January 22, 1946, Subject File, National Intelligence Authority, in Clifford Papers. Text of the directive is printed in *Hearings, National Defense Establishment*, Pt. 3, p. 495. See also Truman, *Memoirs*, I, 98–99, 226; II, 55–58. Truman was originally opposed to changing the Central Intelligence Group into a full-fledged agency but was apparently persuaded to do so by Clark Clifford and members of the CIG, who found it ineffective in operation. Memorandum for file, George M. Elsey, July 17, 1946, Subject File, National Intelligence Authority, in Clifford Papers.

48. Baumer, "National Security Organization," 5; Bernardo and Bacon, *American Military Policy*, 459; Hillman (ed.), *Mr. President*, 14; John Hersey, "Profiles—Mr. President," Pt. 3, "Forty-Eight Hours," *New Yorker* (April 21, 1951), 36. For a critical view of the disadvantages of the CIA to a president, see James, *Contemporary Presidency*, 150–51.

49. Charles Fairman, "The President as Commander-in-Chief," *Journal of Politics*, XI (February, 1949), 150. See also Cornwell, "The Truman Presidency," 224.

50. Public Law 253, 80th Cong., 1st Sess., (61 *Stat.*, 495); Report, "Six Months of Unification," RG330, OSD, D67-1-32, National Archives.

51. *Far East Hearings*, Pt. 1, pp. 150–51, Pt. 2, pp. 904, 1256, 1475, 1606, 1622. See also, May (ed.), *Ultimate Decision*, xii–xv; Fairman, "The President as Commander-in-Chief," 151–52; *Truman Speaks*, 23.

52. Forrestal to Truman, July 28, 1947, Official File (OF), 1285, in Truman Papers; Item No. 182, *Public Papers . . . Truman, 1947*, 420. A month earlier, Hanson Baldwin had correctly picked each one of these appointments, including Forrestal's, in the New York *Times*, July 20, 1947. See also Washington *Post*, July 19, 1947; Millis (ed.), *Forrestal Diaries*, 295–96, 298–99.

53. O'Connor, "Harry S. Truman: New Dimensions of Power," 47–48.

54. Chicago *Tribune*, January 29, 1947.

55. Millis, *Arms and Men*, 280.

56. *The Hoover Commission Report on Organization of the Executive Branch of the Government* (New York: McGraw-Hill, 1949), 187, 190–91, hereinafter cited as *Hoover Commission Report*. Hanson Baldwin felt that the Joint Staff under the JCS was a "potentially dangerous" body, resembling the Greater German General Staff idea. "The Military Move In," 487–88.

57. O'Connor, "Harry S. Truman: New Dimensions of Power," 47–48; Baldwin, "The Military Move In," 484; Hammond, "NSC-68," 273–75, 277–79.

58. Editor's Note, Millis (ed.), *Forrestal Diaries*, 153.

59. Forrestal to Secretaries of Army, Navy, Air Force, and Joint Chiefs of Staff, January 20, 1948, RG330, OSD, D70-1-5, National Archives; Forrestal to Secretaries of Army, Navy, Air Force, February 3, 1948, RG340, S/AF, Reorganization of NME, Special File 4A, DG52-A53-307, *ibid.*

60. Forrestal to Truman, February 27, 1948, RG330, OSD, D70-1-5, National Archives.

61. NME Press Release No. 38–48, OSD, "Secretary Forrestal Announces Re-

sults of Key West Conference," March 26, 1948, Subject File, National Military Establishment—Misc., in Clifford Papers. Present at Key West were Admirals Leahy and Denfield, Generals Bradley and Spaatz, their aides, and Secretary Forrestal. Forrestal to Truman, March 27, 1948, RG330, OSD, D70-1-5, National Archives.

62. Clifford to Truman, April 13, 1948, OF, 1285, in Truman Papers. Clifford sent a memorandum to Forrestal, informing him that Truman wanted the phrase, "by direction of the President" added. Forrestal replied that such a phrase would have appeared in the original draft statement, "but for the fact that we wished to refrain from using the President's name in the document prior to the time you and he had an opportunity to go over it." See Clifford to Forrestal, April 15, 1948, Subject File, National Military Establishment—Misc., in Clifford Papers; Forrestal to Clifford, April 16, Truman to Forrestal, April 21, 1948, RG330, OSD, D70-1-5, National Archives; Forrestal to Symington, April 21, 1948, RG340, S/AF, Special Interest File 4A, Reorganization of NME, National Archives. See text of statement of service functions, *ibid.* See also *Joint Army and Air Force Bulletin*, No. 13, May 13, 1948.

63. Eberstadt to Forrestal, May 31, 1948, RG340, S/AF, Special File 4B, Hoover Commission—Reorganization of NME, National Archives; Forrestal to Secretary of the Air Force, et al., June 2, 1948, *ibid.* The Commission on Organization of the Executive Branch of the Government, directed by Herbert Hoover, was established by Congress at Truman's request, in December of 1945. Forrestal's old friend and associate, Ferdinand Eberstadt, was chairman of the Committee on the National Security Organization of the Hoover Commission. Truman, *Memoirs*, I, 486, II, 52–53; Forrestal to Secretaries of Army, Navy, Air Force, August 4, 1948, RG330, OSD, D70-1-5, National Archives.

64. Sullivan to Forrestal, September 1, 1948, RG330, OSD, D70-1-5, National Archives.

65. Symington to Forrestal, September 14, 1948, RG340, S/AF, Special File 4B, Hoover Commission—Reorganization of the NME, National Archives.

66. The Security Council advisory is quoted in a memorandum, Forrestal to Truman, September 16, 1948, RG330, OSD, CD22-1-5, National Archives; Rogow, *Victim of Duty*, 270.

67. Marx Leva to Clifford, December 3, 1948, Subject File, National Military Establishment: Security Council, in Clifford Papers. The draft memorandum, dated January 24, 1949, is in Subject File, Unification: Amendment of National Security Act, 1949, Clifford Papers. The draft of February 10, 1949, can be found in PF/DDE, Truman folder (2), Eisenhower Papers.

68. Item No. 50, *Public Papers . . . Truman, 1949*, 163–66. See also Forrestal, *et al.*, to Truman, February 10, 1949, RG340, S/AF, AF381, National Archives. A Defense Department staff paper comparing the Truman and Eberstadt recommendations is Tab C to a memorandum, Marx Leva to Forrestal, April 7, 1949, RG330, OSD, D70-1-5, National Archives. For the recommendations made by the Hoover Commission, see "Recommendations of Hoover Commission on National Security Organization," Subject File, National Military Establishment, Security Resources Board, in Clifford Papers. See also the excerpted version of Eberstadt's report in *Hoover Commission Report*, 192–97.

69. Item No. 177, *Public Papers . . . Truman, 1949*, 417.

70. Public Law 216, 81st Cong., 1st Sess. (63 *Stat. 578*).
71. Forrestal to Truman, March 2, 1949, OF, 1285, in Truman Papers; Item No. 46, *Public Papers . . . Truman, 1949*, 160. Forrestal was apparently suffering from severe mental strain. In late 1948 and early 1949 he became increasingly indecisive and forgetful. He began to act quite erratic and paranoidal, convinced he was constantly being followed and that his telephone was tapped. Columnists, with Drew Pearson taking the lead, had been attacking him and suggesting that Truman wanted him out of the cabinet. See, for example, Pearson's column in the Washington *Post*, June 10, 1948. Rogow claims that the Secret Service reported to Truman "late in 1948 or early in 1949," that Forrestal was suffering from "a total psychotic breakdown . . . characterized by suicidal features." See *Victim of Duty*, 271–73, 277–80, 306. See also Millis (ed.), *Forrestal Diaries*, 518–19, 544–47, 550–53; Krock, *Memoirs*, 252–57.
72. Truman, *Memoirs*, II, 53.
73. Truman, *Mr. Citizen*, 145–46.
74. *Time*, XCVI (August 10, 1970), 8.

CHAPTER 8

1. Item No. 128, *Public Papers . . . Truman, 1945*, 287.
2. Truman, *Memoirs*, I, 506; R. Alton Lee, "The Army 'Mutiny' of 1946," *Journal of American History*, LIII (December, 1966), 556–57.
3. Item No. 107, *Public Papers . . . Truman, 1945*, 233; *American Military History*, 530; Truman, *Memoirs*, I, 506.
4. Item No. 128, *Public Papers . . . Truman, 1945*, 288.
5. *Ibid.*, 277–78, 288–89. In a letter on August 23, 1945, to Senator Elbert Thomas, chairman of the Military Affairs Committee, Truman said that the necessary force levels could not be attained by enlistments and induction alone and that some World War II veterans would have to be retained in the service. Quoted in Lee, "The Army 'Mutiny' of 1946," 557. The portion of Truman's message to Congress dealing with selective service and retention of veterans, as well as the letter to Senator Thomas, were drafted by General Marshall, then army chief of staff. See Marshall to Truman, August 23, 1945, Subject File, Message to Congress, in Rosenman Papers.
6. Item No. 128, *Public Papers . . . Truman, 1945*, 288.
7. See, for example, "For the Common Defense: Biennial Report of the Chief of Staff, July 1, 1943 to June 30, 1945," quoted in Millis (ed.), *American Military Thought*, 436–37.
8. Item No. 138, *Public Papers . . . Truman, 1945*, 327–28; Truman, *Memoirs*, I, 507–508.
9. Lee, "The Army 'Mutiny' of 1946," 558–63; *American Military History*, 530.
10. Item No. 8, *Public Papers . . . Truman, 1946*, 15.
11. Truman, *Memoirs*, I, 509. There is ample evidence that both the president and the military agreed as to the dire effects of the program. For example, Eisenhower wrote to Truman about the "demoralization" of the "entire Army" that was brought about by the "drastic demobilization program." Eisenhower to Truman, January 30, 1946, RG407, OSW, AG370.01, National Archives.

12. Eisenhower to Matthew J. Connelly, July 27, 1946, PF/DDE, Truman Folder (1), in Eisenhower Papers; Osgood, *Limited War*, 154. See also O'Connor, "Harry S. Truman: New Dimensions of Power," 30–31; David S. McLellan and John W. Reuss, "Foreign and Military Policies," in Richard S. Kirkendall (ed.), *The Truman Period as a Research Field* (Columbia: University of Missouri Press, 1967), 76–77. It is well to note here, that while the armed services were reduced to levels well below those desired by Truman and the military, this still left the country with the largest peacetime military establishment in its history. By 1947 one third of the total national budget was being appropriated to the military. Ekirch, *Civilian and the Military*, 273.

14. Quoted in an entry, June 5, 1945, in Smith Diary. In a similar vein Truman wrote: "I knew . . . that Army and Navy professionals seldom had any idea of the value of money. They did not seem to care what the cost was." *Memoirs*, I, 88.

15. *American Military History*, 530–31. The 80th Congress, which convened in January, 1947, with both houses dominated by the Republicans, forced much greater economies on the military than Truman ever had.

16. Forrestal to Truman, November 2, 1945, Historical Records Division, Chief of Naval Operations (CNO), (SC) A4-1 (11), Navy Yard; Entries, September 13, 1945, February 18, 1946, in Smith Diary. Forrestal to Truman, August 21, Truman to Forrestal, October 9, 1946, Historical Records Division, CNO, (SC) L1-1, Navy Yard; Truman, *Memoirs*, II, 34.

17. Item No. 148, *Public Papers . . . Truman, 1947*, 344–45. An "air group" as defined by General Vandenberg was structured similarly to an Army division. There were groups of fighter aircraft (75 per group), and of light, medium, and long-range bombers, with fifty, thirty-six, and thirty planes per group respectively. Vandenberg testimony, *Far East Hearings*, Pt. 2, p. 1427.

18. Bernardo and Bacon, *American Military Policy*, 473; Rogow, *Victim of Duty*, 254. The Congressional Aviation Policy Board (known as the Brewster-Hinshaw Board), submitted its report to Congress on March 1, 1948. Item No. 5, *Public Papers . . . Truman, 1948*, 27–28.

19. Millis, *Arms and Men*, 277; Symington to James E. Webb, December 16, 1947, Subject File, National Military Establishment: Air Force, in Clifford Papers; Hammond, "Super Carriers and B-36 Bombers," 471; Millis, *Arms and Men*, 276–77.

20. Symington to Forrestal, Symington to Clifford, Symington to Webb, December 16, 1947, Subject File, National Military Establishment: Air Force, in Clifford Papers.

21. Forrestal's requests to the Armed Services Committee were based on figures worked out with Truman earlier and confirmed in a letter, Truman to Forrestal, March 26, 1948, OF, 1285, in Truman Papers. Forrestal to Chan Gurney, April 2, 1948, RG340, S/AF, Reorganization of the National Military Establishment, Special File 4A, Roles and Missions—Correspondence, National Archives. In a Pentagon press release (OSD No. 44–48), Forrestal made his letter to Gurney public. Copy in Subject File, National Military Establishment: Air Force, Clifford Papers. Forrestal to the Joint Chiefs of Staff, March 27, 1948, RG340, S/AF, Reorganization of the National Military Establishment, Special File 4A, Roles and Missions—Correspondence, National Archives.

22. Rogow, *Victim of Duty*, 258–59.
23. Schilling, "Politics of National Defense," 43–44; Millis, *Arms and Men*, 287.
24. New York *Times*, April 22, 1948.
25. "Statement by the President to the Secretary of Defense, the Secretaries of the Three Departments, and the Three Chiefs of Staff," May 13, 1948, in Papers of James E. Webb, President folder, Truman Library, hereinafter cited as Webb Papers. See also, Schilling, "Politics of National Defense," 154–55; Millis (ed.), *Forrestal Diaries*, 435–39.
26. Truman to Forrestal, May 13, 1948, Subject File, National Military Establishment—Misc., in Clifford Papers.
27. Millis (ed.), *Forrestal Diaries*, 435.
28. Truman to Air Force Chief of Staff, *et al.*, May 13, 1948, OF, 1285, in Truman Papers.
29. Schilling, "Politics of National Defense," 44–46. See also Rogow, *Victim of Duty*, 265.
30. New York *Times*, May 22, 1948. See also Item No. 106, *Public Papers . . . Truman, 1948*, 272; Millis, *Arms and Men*, 287. In a letter dated June 3, 1948, Truman set the maximum troop strengths for all services and stipulated the active aircraft inventory for the Navy and Air Force at 6000 and 9240, respectively. See Truman to Forrestal, June 3, 1948, RG330, OSD, CD9-2-4, National Archives.
31. Discussing the budget for fiscal year 1950 in a press conference, Truman said of the Air Force: "You never can satisfy them. I have to put my foot down and tell them what they can have. If you didn't do that they would take all the money in the budget." Item No. 7, *Public Papers . . . Truman, 1949*, 34.
32. Hammond, "Super Carriers and B-36 Bombers," 470–71.
33. Louis Johnson to Sullivan, April 23, Sullivan to Johnson, April 24, 1949, RG330, OSD, D16-2-44, National Archives.
34. Sullivan to Johnson, Sullivan to Truman, Truman to Sullivan, April 26, 1949, OF, 1285C, in Truman Papers. See also Hammond, "Super Carriers and B-36 Bombers," 495; Truman, *Memoirs*, II, 53.
35. Bernardo and Bacon, *American Military Policy*, 473. See also Feis, *Between War and Peace*, 291, 337.
36. A summation of the charges made by Van Zandt and Symington's 79-page rebuttal statement are both attached to a memorandum, Glenn W. Martin to Clifford, July 22, 1949, Subject File, National Military Establishment—B-36 Investigation, in Clifford Papers. The source of Van Zandt's generally unsubstantiated charges was an anonymous civilian employee in the Navy Department.
37. Among the naval officers who attacked the prevailing policies during the controversy were Captain John G. Crommelin and Admirals William Halsey, Ernest King, Gerald Bogan, Arthur Radford, Thomas Kincaid, William Blandy, Ralph Ofstie, Chester Nimitz, Raymond Spruance, and General Vernon Magee of the Marine Corps. Bernardo and Bacon, *American Military Policy*, 473–76; Hammond, "NSC-68," 280–82.
38. Matthews to Truman, October 27, 1949, Subject File, National Military Establishment—Navy, in Clifford Papers. In a memorandum to Johnson's aide, an assistant general counsel in the Pentagon discussed the power of the president to remove the chief of naval operations from office. He offered numerous legal precedents justifying such an action and added that

it was "self-evident" that the president, in his constitutional role as commander in chief, had the unquestioned right to change the duty assignment of any subordinate officer as he pleased. Nathaniel Goodrich to Marx Leva, October 26, 1949, Subject File, National Military Establishment—Navy, in Clifford Papers.

39. Hammond, "NSC-68," 281. Robert Osgood feels that Truman placed an "overwhelming reliance on nuclear retaliation as the military means of containing Communism," because of a preoccupation with the threat of a third world war and a fascination with the "vast and strange power of the atomic bomb." *Limited War*, 151.

40. Byrnes, *Speaking Frankly*, 301; Alexander DeConde, *A History of American Foreign Policy* (New York: Charles Scribner's, 1963), 667. Truman had been willing to go much further at Potsdam. He had urged the internationalization of the Rhine, Danube, and Dardanelles, because, he claimed, all the wars of the preceding two centuries had originated in Central Europe. Neumann, *After Victory*, 173–74.

41. Acheson, *Present at the Creation*, 195; DeConde, *History of American Foreign Policy*, 667; Phillips, *Truman Presidency*, 170.

42. Acheson, *Present at the Creation*, 195; Phillips, *Truman Presidency*, 171.

43. Acheson, *Present at the Creation*, 196.

44. LaFeber, *America, Russia, and the Cold War*, 44. See also Byrnes, *Speaking Frankly*, 299–300; *Major Problems of United States Foreign Policy, 1951–1952* (Washington: Brookings Institution, 1951), 365–66.

45. Acheson, *Present at the Creation*, 217; Truman, Memoirs, II, 99–100. See also Fleming, *The Cold War*, I, 438–39; Sidney Warren, *The President as World Leader* (Philadelphia: Lippincott, 1964), 310–11.

46. Acheson, *Present at the Creation*, 218–19; Fleming, *The Cold War*, I, 439–40. In a subsequent meeting with the congressional leadership (including Senator Taft), on March 10, Acheson felt the atmosphere was somewhat cooler. Although Vandenberg was favorably disposed, no legislator was willing to commit himself to the message proposals. Acheson, *Present at the Creation*, 222. Truman, discussing the same session, described it differently: "There was no opposition to what had to be done." *Memoirs*, II, 105. See also Vandenberg, *Private Papers*, 343–44.

47. Truman, *Memoirs*, II, 100; Acheson, *Present at the Creation*, 219.

48. Truman, *Memoirs*, II, 102. See also McLellan and Reuss, "Foreign and Military Policies," 57.

49. Item No. 56, *Public Papers . . . Truman, 1947*, 178–79. It was the vagueness and universality of the doctrine which brought belated objections from George F. Kennan, director of the Policy Planning Board of the State Department. See his *Memoirs*, 319–22.

50. New York *Times*, March 12, 1947; Baltimore *Sun*, March 13, 1947; Philadelphia *Inquirer*, March 13, 1947; New York *Herald-Tribune*, March 18, 1947; Chicago *Tribune*, March 13, 1947; Washington *Post*, March 13, 1947; *Izvestia*, March 13, 1947, quoted in Williams (ed.), *Shaping of American Diplomacy*, 1003–1005.

51. Philadelphia *Bulletin*, March 29, 1947.

52. As enacted, the bill is Public Law 75, 80th Cong., 1st Sess., (61 *Stat.* 103). See also Truman, *Memoirs*, II, 108; LaFeber, *America, Russia, and the Cold War*, 45–46; DeConde, *History of American Foreign Policy*, 670.

53. Item No. 100, *Public Papers . . . Truman, 1947*, 254–55; Executive Order

9857, March 22, 1947 (3 *C.F.R.*, 1943–48 Comp., 646); Marshall to Patterson, April 30, 1947, RG165, USA, 092-Plans and Operations, Case No. 96, National Archives.
54. Truman, *Memoirs*, II, 108; Marshall to Truman, June 27, Truman to Royall, August 30, 1947, RG407, AG091.3, National Archives.
55. *Major Problems of United States Foreign Policy*, 264–65; Truman, *Memoirs*, II, 109. Some observers have noted a curious lack of uniformity in U.S. policy towards Greece and China. In the same period of time that the United States was providing the wherewithal to suppress Communist insurgents in Greece, the American government provided some military and technical aid to the Nationalist Chinese, but encouraged them to form a coalition government with the Communists. See Osgood, *Limited War*, 162.
56. Phillips, "Truman at 75," 107; *Truman Speaks*, 70.
57. Hammond, "Super Carriers and B-36 Bombers," 472–73. See also Phillips, *Truman Presidency*, 194. Robert Osgood says that Greek-Turkish aid reflected a view in the White House and among the foreign and military advisers to the president that the Middle East and the Mediterranean regions formed a strategic unity, no part of which could be allowed to fall to Russian imperialism if the U.S. were to preserve the geopolitical basis of its security. Yet, Osgood notes, it was not in these terms that the decision was presented to Congress and the general public. See *Limited War*, 146–47; *Major Problems of United States Foreign Policy*, 28.

CHAPTER 9

1. Truman, *Mr. Citizen*, 204.
2. Quoted from George F. Kennan ("Mr. X"), "Sources of Soviet Conduct," *Foreign Affairs*, XXV (July, 1947), 567.
3. Truman, *Memoirs*, II, 290.
4. *Ibid.*, 120.
5. W. Phillips Davison, *The Berlin Blockade: A Study in Cold War Politics* (Princeton, N. J.: Princeton University Press, 1958), 3–6.
6. Eisenhower to Truman, October 26, 1945, PF/DDE, Truman folder (1), in Eisenhower Papers. See also Truman to Eisenhower, November 2, 1945, *ibid.*
7. Davison, *Berlin Blockade*, 8–9; Truman, *Memoirs*, II, 120.
8. Davison, *Berlin Blockade*, 4; Steinberg, *Man from Missouri*, 258. Steinberg claims that Truman blamed Eisenhower for the lack of a written agreement but offers no proof.
9. Arthur Krock, *In the Nation: 1932–1966* (New York: McGraw-Hill, 1966), 175.
10. Cable is quoted in Millis (ed.), *Forrestal Diaries*, 387.
11. Millis, *Arms and Men*, 255. During the Berlin crisis, members of Forrestal's staff prepared a report for him on the power of the president to declare a state of national emergency. The report said the commander in chief could declare a state of limited or unlimited national emergency upon his own discretion and that the consent of Congress, while desirable, was not necessary. Memorandum (unsigned) to Forrestal, March 29, 1948, RG330, OSD, President, 1947–1949, National Archives.
12. Item No. 52, *Public Papers ... Truman, 1948*, 183–85.

13. Davison, *Berlin Blockade*, 73; Millis (ed.), *Forrestal Diaries*, 408; Truman, *Memoirs*, II, 122.
14. Millis (ed.), *Forrestal Diaries*, 407; Truman, *Memoirs*, II, 122.
15. Truman, *Memoirs*, II, 122.
16. LaFeber, *America, Russia, and the Cold War*, 70; Rees, *Age of Containment*, 28. See also "Berlin Airlift," a report in RG330, OSD, D70-1-5, National Archives. It seems evident that the "technical difficulties" the Soviet Union used to explain the full blockade of the twenty-fourth were, in reality, the currency reforms. The exchange of old for new currency was to begin on the twenty-fifth. Davison, *Berlin Blockade*, 105–106, also 33–34.
17. Truman, *Memoirs*, II, 123. See also Millis, *Arms and Men*, 288; Millis (ed.), *Forrestal Diaries*, 451–52; Davison, *Berlin Blockade*, 75, 106–107, 131; John Lukacs, *A History of the Cold War* (Rev. ed.; Garden City, N.Y.: Doubleday, 1962), 70.
18. "Berlin Airlift," RG330, OSD, D70-1-5, National Archives; Truman, *Memoirs*, II, 125.
19. Davison, *Berlin Blockade*, 105, 112, 150–51; Millis (ed.), *Forrestal Diaries*, 452–54; New York *Times*, July 5, 1948. In addition to Forrestal, among those present at the June 27 meeting were Undersecretary Lovett, Secretaries Royall and Sullivan of the army and navy respectively, and Generals Bradley and Norstad.
20. Millis (ed.), *Forrestal Diaries*, 454; O'Connor, "Harry S. Truman: New Dimensions of Power," 42–43.
21. Millis (ed.), *Forrestal Diaries*, 454–55. See also Davison, *Berlin Blockade*, 110–11.
22. Truman, *Memoirs*, II, 123–24.
23. In an editorial note, Walter Millis cites many of the same factors mentioned here. He sees the June 27 Pentagon session as an *ad hoc* response which bypassed "the formal machinery of the Security Act to take large (if rather vague) politico-strategic decisions." *Forrestal Diaries*, 454.
24. "Berlin Airlift," RG330, OSD, D70-1-5, National Archives; Davison, *Berlin Blockade*, 195; Rees, *Age of Containment*, 28.
25. Millis (ed.), *Forrestal Diaries*, 457; Davison, *Berlin Blockade*, 129–30; *Arms and Men*, 289.
26. Rogow, *Victim of Duty*, 183–84; Millis (ed.), *Forrestal Diaries*, 458.
27. Millis (ed.), *Forrestal Diaries*, 458.
28. *Ibid.*, 460–61. Forrestal records Truman repeating these political considerations with General Marshall present on September 16. See *ibid.*, 490.
29. Davison, *Berlin Blockade*, 156; Millis (ed.), *Forrestal Diaries*, 487; Schilling, "Politics of National Defense," 173–74.
30. Millis, *Arms and Men*, 288–90.
31. Millis (ed.), *Forrestal Diaries*, 459.
32. Hillman (ed.), *Mr. President*, 140.
33. Truman, *Memoirs*, II, 124–25; Millis (ed.), *Forrestal Diaries*, 459; Davison, *Berlin Blockade*, 126. Robert Murphy, a State Department representative who accompanied General Clay from Germany, was quoted in *Time* magazine (June 1, 1970) as having said he regretted that he had not resigned at the time of the blockade as a protest. Murphy felt that the U.S. should have challenged the Soviet blockade with more vigor.
34. Truman, *Memoirs*, II, 125–26.
35. *Ibid.*, 128.

36. Hillman (ed.), *Mr. President*, 141.
37. Davison, *Berlin Blockade*, 250; Truman, *Memoirs*, II, 129; Symington to Forrestal, November 24, 1948, RG340, S/AF, Vittles, folder (1), National Archives.
38. Truman, *Memoirs*, II, 130–31; Symington to Forrestal, November 20, 1948, RG340, S/AF, 031.1, National Archives.
39. D. F. Fleming, "America's Responsibility," in Brian Tierney, Donald Kagan, and L. Pearce Williams (eds.), *The Cold War—Who Is to Blame?* (New York: Random House, 1967), 14–15; Glenn D. Paige, *The Korean Decision, June 24–30, 1950* (New York: The Free Press, 1968), 54–55.
40. O'Connor, "Harry S. Truman: New Dimemsions of Power," 43.
41. John W. Spanier, *American Foreign Policy Since World War II* (2nd rev. ed.; New York: Praeger, 1965) 49–50. See also U.S. Senate, Committee on Governmental Operations, Subcommittee on National Security and International Operations, *The Atlantic Alliance—Basic Issues: A Study*, Committee Print, 89th Cong., 2nd Sess.
42. Item No. 52, *Public Papers . . . Truman, 1948*, 184.
43. Truman, *Memoirs*, II, 243.
44. *Ibid.*, 244; Acheson testimony in U.S. Senate, Committee on Government Operations, Subcommittee on National Security and International Operations, *Hearings, The Atlantic Alliance*, 89th Cong., 2nd Sess. (April 27–August 15, 1966), Pt. 1, p. 9, hereinafter cited as *Atlantic Alliance Hearings*.
45. Text of Vandenberg Resolution is in Bernstein and Matusow (eds.), *Truman Administration*, 274–75. See also Henry M. Jackson (ed.), *The Atlantic Alliance: Jackson Subcommittee Hearings and Findings* (New York: Praeger, 1967), 8.
46. The signatory nations were Belgium, Canada, Denmark, France, Great Britain, Iceland, Italy, Luxembourg, the Netherlands, Norway, Portugal, and the United States. Truman provides a detailed account of the negotiations that led to the NATO treaty in his *Memoirs*, II, 244–50.
47. Item No. 75, *Public Papers . . . Truman, 1949*, 206–207.
48. O'Connor, "Harry S. Truman: New Dimensions of Power," 58. Senatorial efforts to check the commander in chief with respect to the NATO agreement are described in *Powers of the President to Send the Armed Forces Outside the United States*. The problem is also discussed in Krock, *In the Nation*, 161–63. See also Robert Taft, "A Conservative Opposes the Treaty," in Lawrence S. Kaplan (ed.), *NATO and the Policy of Containment* (Lexington, Mass.: Heath, 1968), 8.
49. Text of the North Atlantic Treaty is officially published in *U.S. Statutes at Large* (63 *Stat.* 2241). It is reprinted in Jackson (ed.), *The Atlantic Alliance*, 281–83.
50. Schwarz, *American Strategy*, 135; Leopold, "United States in World Affairs," 233. See also *Major Problems of United States Foreign Policy*, 156–57; McLellan and Reuss, "Foreign and Military Policies," 61, 66–68; Richard W. Leopold, *The Growth of American Foreign Policy* (New York: Knopf, 1962) 658.
51. *American Military History*, 543; McLellan and Reuss, "Foreign and Military Policies," 62; Hammond, "NSC-68," p. 283.
52. Item No. 163, *Public Papers . . . Truman, 1949*, 398–99.
53. Vandenberg, quoted in Acheson, *Present at the Creation*, 309ff. Here

Acheson provides a thorough, if slightly slanted account of the struggle to get the bill through Congress.

54. Item No. 216, *Public Papers . . . Truman, 1949,* 485; Phillips, *Truman Presidency,* 270. See also Acheson, *Present at the Creation,* 313.
55. Item No. 225, *Public Papers . . . Truman, 1949,* 500. The act is Public Law 329 (63 *Stat.* 714). A description of the principles involved in the act as passed and as amended in 1950 can be found in *Major Problems of United States Foreign Policy,* 121, 172–73.
56. Truman to Acheson, November 23, 1949, RG165, USA, Plans and Operations 092, Case 66/5, National Archives. The secretary of state's authority and the terms of administering the act were formalized by Truman in Executive Order 10099, January 27, 1950 (3 *C.F.R.,* 1949–53 Comp., 295). See also Item No. 22, *Public Papers . . . Truman, 1950,* 131–32.
57. *American Military History,* 543.
58. Truman described the negotiations leading to this agreement in his *Memoirs,* II, 252–57. See also William T. R. Fox and Annette B. Fox, *NATO and the Range of American Choice* (New York: Columbia University Press, 1967), 14–15.
59. Truman to Eisenhower, October 19, December 19, 1950, in PF/DDE, Truman folder (2), Eisenhower Papers; Truman, *Memoirs,* II, 257. See also Fox and Fox, *NATO and the Range of American Choice,* 15. Phillips, "Truman at 75," 107.
60. Truman, *Memoirs,* II, 260–61; *Truman Speaks,* 14–15.
61. The recommendations to Truman have been examined at length in Chapter V.
62. Lilienthal, *Atomic Energy Years,* 624.
63. Hammond, "NSC-68," pp. 290–92. See also Schwarz, *American Strategy,* 135. Another factor leading to this assessment was the loss of mainland China to the Communist forces late in 1949. However, the prime motive appears to have been the Soviet atomic bomb. See O'Connor, "Harry S. Truman: New Dimensions of Powers," 32.
64. Hammond, "NSC-68," pp. 304–305.
65. *Ibid.,* 306–307; Phillips, *Truman Presidency,* 307.
66. Paige, *Korean Decision,* 59; Hammond, "NSC-68," p. 306. For a general outline of the document see Acheson, *Present at the Creation,* 374–76.
67. Hammond, "NSC-68," p. 330.
68. *Ibid.,* 363. See also O'Connor, "Harry S. Truman: New Dimensions of Power," 32.

CHAPTER 10

1. Quoted in Robert Alan Aurthur, "The Wit and Sass of Harry S. Truman," *Esquire,* LXXVI (August, 1971), 66.
2. Roy E. Appleman, *South to the Naktong, North to the Yalu, June–November, 1950* (Washington: U.S. Government Printing Office, 1961), 1.
3. Walter G. Hermes, *Truce Tent and Fighting Front* (Washington: U.S. Government Printing Office), 3.
4. Leopold, *Growth of American Foreign Policy,* 271; William L. Langer (ed.), *An Encyclopedia of World History* (Boston: Houghton Mifflin, 1952), 886–87; Matthew B. Ridgway, *The Korean War* (Garden City, N.Y.: Doubleday, 1967), 5–6.
5. U.S. Department of State, *United States Policy in the Korean Crisis,*

Publication No. 3922, Far Eastern Series 34 (Washington: U.S. Government Printing Office, 1950), ix. See also, Hermes, *Truce Tent and Fighting Front*, 4.

6. Martin Lichterman, "To the Yalu and Back," in Harold Stein (ed.), *American Civil-Military Decisions: A Book of Case Studies* (Tuscaloosa: University of Alabama Press, 1963), 576. See also Truman, *Memoirs*, II, 317; Trumbull Higgins, *Korea and the Fall of MacArthur: A Précis in Limited War* (New York: Oxford University Press, 1960), 5.

7. Hermes, *Truce Tent and Fighting Front*, 4–5; Lichterman, "To the Yalu and Back," 576; Truman, *Memoirs*, I, 445, II, 317. For the background of events which led to the selection of the 38th parallel as a dividing line, see Appleman, *South to the Naktong*, 2–3.

8. Because of Soviet intransigence in the European settlements, Truman had decided that he "would not allow the Russians any part in the control of Japan." On the way back from Potsdam he decided to give complete authority over Japan to MacArthur. Truman, *Memoirs*, I, 412, 432–33. See also Item No. 100, *Public Papers . . . Truman, 1945*, 216; Lichterman, "To the Yalu and Back," 576.

9. Lichterman, "To the Yalu and Back," 576; Hermes, *Truce Tent and Fighting Front*, 4–5; *United States Policy in the Korean Crisis*, ix.

10. Lichterman, "To the Yalu and Back," 576–77. Dr. Syngman Rhee, long a Korean nationalist leader, and soon to be president of his country, had wired Truman on August 22, imploring him to intervene rapidly in order to insure a "united, democratic, independent Korea." Rhee to Truman, August 22, 1945, OF, 471 Misc., in Truman Papers.

11. Item No. 136, *Public Papers . . . Truman, 1945*, 324–25. Truman's statement was actually written by Dean Acheson, then acting secretary of state. See Acheson to Truman, September 14, 1945, OF, 471 (1945–48), in Truman Papers.

12. Truman, *Memoirs*, II, 317–19.

13. *United States Policy in the Korean Crisis*, x; Truman, *Memoirs*, II, 318–20.

14. Pauley to the President, June 22, 1946, RG107, OSA, 091 Korea (1946–47), National Archives.

15. Truman to Pauley, July 16, 1946, *ibid.*

16. Truman to Patterson, August 12, Patterson to Truman, August 29, 1946, RG107, OSA (Patterson), 091 Korea, National Archives. "Facts on Korean Military Aid Debunking the '$200 charge.' " Unsigned Study, Files of David D. Lloyd, Speech on Korean War Situation, September 1, 1950, in Truman Papers.

17. Benjamin F. Taylor (Memorandum for Record), May 13, 1947, RG165, USA, 091-Korea, National Archives; Truman, *Memoirs*, II, 322. Truman met with General Hodge for the first time in a conference at the White House in February, arranged by Secretary of War Patterson. See Patterson to Truman, February 19, 1947, OF, 471 (1945–48), in Truman Papers.

18. Forrestal to Marshall, September 26, 1947, OF, 1285 (1952–53), in Truman Papers.

19. *Ibid.* See also John W. Spanier, *The Truman-MacArthur Controversy and the Korean War* (New York: W. W. Norton, 1965), 16–19.

20. Spanier, *Truman-MacArthur Controversy*, 17; Steinberg, *Man from Missouri*, 375; Higgins, *Korea and the Fall of MacArthur*, 7.

21. Truman, *Memoirs*, II, 324. See also *Korea, 1945 to 1948: A Report on*

Political Developments and Economic Resources with Selected Documents (New York: Greenwood, 1969), 47–48.

22. Leopold, *Growth of American Foreign Policy*, 678; *Korea, 1945 to 1948*, 47–48.
23. *Korea, 1945 to 1948*, 6–7. See also Truman, *Memoirs*, II, 324–25.
24. Text of the main provision of the resolution is quoted in *Korea, 1945 to 1948*, 9.
25. Kim to Truman, November 18, 1947, OF, 471 (1945–48), in Truman Papers.
26. *Far East Hearings*, Pt. 5, p. 3362.
27. *Korea, 1945 to 1948*, 19–20, 100–101; Truman, *Memoirs*, II, 327–28. Muccio began an exemplary period of service as U.S. representative to Korea with this appointment. Rhee was quite pleased with him. Less than a month after the appointment, Rhee told Truman that, "Muccio has already proved himself a genuine friend of Korea." Rhee to Truman, September 8, 1948, OF, 471 (1945–48), in Truman Papers.
28. Truman to Hodge, August 15, 1948, OF, 471, in Truman Papers; Truman, *Memoirs*, II, 328. In a countermove, the Soviet officials ordered an election on August 25, thus creating the "Democratic People's Republic of Korea" with Kim Il Sung as president. This government, which was immediately recognized by the Soviet Union, claimed it had jurisdiction over *all* of Korea. Thus there were two governments on the Korean peninsula, both claiming they spoke for all of Korea. As Richard Leopold observed, "The outlook for peaceful coexistence was dim." *Growth of American Foreign Policy*, 678.
29. Ridgway, *Korean War*, 7; Truman, *Memoirs*, II, 328.
30. *Korea, 1945 to 1948*, 22; Hermes, *Truce Tent and Fighting Front*, 8.
31. Item No. 1, *Public Papers . . . Truman, 1949*, 1. See also Ray T. Maddocks to Chief of Staff (Bradley), December 23, 1948, RG165, USA, 091 Korea, National Archives.
32. Appleman, *South to the Naktong*, 5; Truman, *Memoirs*, II, 329; Hermes, *Truce Tent and Fighting Front*, 8; *Far East Hearings*, Pt. 3, pp. 2008, 2112–13, Pt. 4, pp. 2576, 2596, Pt. 5, pp. 3362, 3571.
33. Spanier, *Truman-MacArthur Controversy*, 20; Truman, *Memoirs*, II, 329; Paige, *Korean Decision* 70. Two weeks prior to the attack on South Korea, Ambassador Muccio informed the State Department that the North Korean forces had a great superiority in aircraft, heavy artillery, and tanks, which would "provide North Korea with a margin of victory in the event of a fullscale invasion of the Republic." Muccio's report is quoted in *Far East Hearings*, Pt. 2, pp. 1052–53.
34. Acheson, *Present at the Creation*, 356–57.
35. *Ibid.*, 356–57; Spanier, *Truman-MacArthur Controversy*, 20; Paige, *Korean Decision*, 67–68. Warren, *President as World Leader*, 337. For similar opinions, see Higgins, *Korea and the Fall of MacArthur*, 14–15; Paige, *Korean Decision*, 333–34; Rees, *Age of Containment*, 38; Luvacs, *History of the Cold War*, 89.
36. Truman, *Memoirs*, II, 331.
37. *Far East Hearings*, Pt. 3, p. 1991. Courtney Whitney, *MacArthur: His Rendezvous with History* (New York: Knopf, 1956), 320.
38. Truman, *Memoirs*, II, 331; *Far East Hearings*, Pt. 3, p. 2113. Admiral Roscoe H. Hillenkoetter, director of the CIA, told a Senate committee the

day after the attack that his agency had been reporting North Korean troop movements for months and could not understand why the "receiving agencies" had failed to properly evaluate this information. New York *Times*, June 27, 1950.

39. Item No. 159, *Public Papers . . . Truman, 1950*, 465. See also New York *Times*, June 10, 11, 1950. Albert L. Warner, "How the Korea Decision Was Made," *Harper's Magazine*, CCII (June, 1951), 99.

40. Doc. No. 1, cable, Muccio to the State Department, June 25, 1950, *United States Policy in the Korean Crisis*, 11. Seoul and Washington are separated by seven thousand miles and the International Date Line. Korean time is fourteen hours ahead of Washington. Thus, Muccio's cable arrived in Washington at 9:26 P.M., June 24, but it was then late morning of the next day (June 25), in Seoul. Truman, *Memoirs*, II, 331–32.

41. Paige, *Korean Decision*, 101–102; Warner, "How Korea Decision Was Made," 101; Doc. No. 2, Deputy Representative of the United States [Ernest A. Gross] to the Secretary-General [Lie], June 25, 1950, *United States Policy in the Korean Crisis*, 11–12. See also Glenn D. Paige, (ed.), *1950: Truman's Decision, The United States Enters the Korean War* (New York: Chelsea House, 1970), 55–56. Truman wrote an interesting note to Acheson about a month later. In part, it reads: "Your initiative in immediately calling the Security Council of the U.S. on Saturday night and notifying me was the key to what followed afterwards. Had you not acted promptly in that direction *we would have had to go into Korea alone*." Truman to Acheson, July 19, 1950, in Acheson, *Present at the Creation*, 415. Emphasis supplied.

42. Doc. No. 3, United Nations Commission on Korea to Secretary-General, June 25, 1950, *United States Policy in the Korean Crisis*, 12. Among American scholars, D. F. Fleming seems alone in suggesting the possibility that the fighting began as a North Korean reprisal for a South Korean attack. *The Cold War*, II, 598–600. On June 26, the Communist-oriented *Daily Worker* (N.Y.) had made the same charge. See New York *Times*, June 27, 1950. A Soviet diplomatic note to the United States on June 29 took the same position. See Doc. No. 95, *United States Policy in the Korean Crisis*, 64.

43. Doc. No. 4, Statement by U.S. Deputy Representative to the Security Council, June 25, 1950, *United States Policy in the Korean Crisis*, 13–15. Text of statement also appears in *Far East Hearings*, Pt. 5, pp. 3365–68.

44. New York *Times*, June 26, 1950; Beverly Smith, "Why We Went to War in Korea," *Saturday Evening Post*, CCXXIV (November 10, 1951), 76. See also U.S. Department of State, *United States Policy in the Korean Conflict: July, 1950–February, 1951*, Publication No. 4263. Far Eastern Series 44 (Washington: U.S. Government Printing Office, 1951), 46. The UN resolution of June 25 is printed in *Far East Hearings*, Pt. 5, pp. 3368–69.

45. Truman, *Memoirs*, II, 332; Margaret Truman, *Harry S. Truman* (New York: Morrow, 1973), 456–57.

46. Smith, "Why We Went to War in Korea," 76; Truman, *Memoirs*, II, 333; Warner, "How Korea Decision Was Made," 101.

47. Paige, *Korean Decision*, 126. The Truman family lived at Blair House, across the street from the White House from November, 1948, to March, 1952, while extensive renovation was underway on the White House. The conferees were Secretary Acheson, Undersecretary James Webb, Deputy

314 Notes to pages 167 to 170

Undersecretary Dean Rusk, Assistant Undersecretary John Hickerson, and Ambassador-at-Large Phillip Jessup from the State Department. Defense was represented by Secretary Johnson, Secretary of the Army Frank Pace, Secretary of the Navy Francis Matthews, Secretary of the Air Force Thomas Finletter, and from the Joint Chiefs of Staff, Generals Omar Bradley, J. Lawton Collins, Hoyt Vandenberg, and Admiral Forrest Sherman. Acheson, *Present at the Creation*, 406.

48. Acheson, *Present at the Creation*, 406. See also Truman, *Memoirs*, II, 334; Paige, *Korean Decision*, 127.
49. Truman, *Memoirs*, II, 335; Louis Johnson testimony, *Far East Hearings*, Pt. 4, p. 2580; Acheson, *Present at the Creation*, 406. For a detailed description of the first Blair House meeting, see Paige, *Korean Decision*, 125–41.
50. Bradley testimony, *Far East Hearings*, Pt. 2, p. 933; Vandenberg testimony, *ibid.*, p. 1475; Johnson testimony, *ibid.*, Pt. 4, p. 2573; Appendix K, *ibid.*, Pt. 5, p. 3192.
51. Truman, *Memoirs*, II, 334; Acheson, *Present at the Creation*, 406; New York *Times*, June 26, 1950; T. R. Fehrenbach, *This Kind of War: A Study in Unpreparedness* (New York: Macmillan, 1963), 80–81; J. Lawton Collins, *War in Peacetime: The History and Lessons of Korea* (Boston: Houghton Mifflin, 1969), 15.
52. Truman, *Memoirs*, II, 334.
53. Press Release No. 2444, Statement by the President, June 26, 1950, copy in MacArthur Hearings, Tannenwald Papers.
54. Paige, *Korean Decision*, 145–46.
55. H. Nam Kung to the President, June 26, 1950, OF, 471 Misc. (1948–53), in Truman Papers; *United States Policy in the Korean Crisis*, 2, 17; Truman, *Memoirs*, II, 336–37; New York *Times*, June 27, 1950.
56. Truman, *Memoirs*, II, 337; Acheson, *Present at the Creation*, 407; New York *Times*, June 27, 1950; Smith, "Why We Went to War in Korea," 80.
57. Acheson, *Present at the Creation*, 407–408; Johnson testimony, *Far East Hearings*, Pt. 4, p. 2581; Warner, "How the Korea Decision Was Made," 103.
58. Paige, *Korean Decision*, 165–66, 173–74; Truman, *Memoirs*, II, 337. It was Secretary Johnson's recollection that neither he nor anyone else from the Defense Department specifically approved or disapproved of military involvement in Korea during the meeting. See his testimony in *Far East Hearings*, Pt. 4, pp. 2581, 2584. Acheson has said that, "The recommendations met with general favor, including Louis Johnson's." *Present at the Creation*, 408.
59. Quoted in Smith, "Why We Went to War in Korea," 80.
60. The following persons were on the list: Vice-President Alben Barkley, Speaker Sam Rayburn, Senators Scott Lucas, Tom Connally, Alexander Wiley, Alexander Smith, Walter George, Elbert Thomas, Millard Tydings, Styles Bridges, and Congressmen John McCormack, John Kee, Charles Easton, Carl Vinson, Dewey Short. See Murphy to Matthew Connelly, June 27, 1950, Lloyd Files, Korea folder, in Truman Papers. Mike Mansfield, who was not on the list, did attend. Barkley and George, who were out of town, did not.
61. Truman, *Memoirs*, II, 338; Acheson, *Present at the Creation*, 408; Paige, *Korean Decision*, 187.

62. Truman, *Memoirs*, II, 338. See also Acheson, *Present at the Creation*, 409. A diplomatic note to the Soviet Union, dated June 27, 1950, asked that the Kremlin disavow any responsibility for the North Korean invasion and also that it use its influence to convince the North Koreans to withdraw their forces immediately. The USSR responded on June 29, saying that the fighting was brought on by South Korean border raids, so the responsibility rested with them, "and upon those who stand behind their back." The Soviets refused to intercede, since this, they said, would constitute interference in the internal affairs of Korea and such an act would not be consonant with Soviet principles. See Docs. No. 94, 95, *United States Policy in the Korean Crisis*, 63–64; New York *Times*, June 28, 1950.

63. Acheson, *Present at the Creation*, 409; Truman, *Memoirs*, II, 338; *Far East Hearings*, Pt. 3, p. 1779, Pt. 4, p. 2609.

64. Smith, "Why We Went to War in Korea," 82; *Far East Hearings*, Pt. 3, pp. 1779–80, 2021, Pt. 4, p. 2592.

65. Hoare, "Truman," 191–92. *Far East Hearings*, Pt. 3, p. 2014–15.

66. A copy of the original release, dated June 27, 1950, is in MacArthur Hearings, Tannenwald Papers. See also Item No. 173, *Public Papers . . . Truman, 1950*, 492; Doc. No. 9, *United States Policy in the Korean Crisis*, 18; New York *Times*, June 28, 1950.

67. New York *Times*, June 28, 1950. The *Herald Tribune* is quoted in Eric F. Goldman, *The Crucial Decade—And After: America, 1945–1960* (New York: Random House, 1959), 159. Goldman said that the letters and telegrams were ten-to-one in favor of the president's action. An internal White House memorandum was not as generous. It noted that letters were running approximately ten to one in favor, but a combined total of letters and telegrams showed that 775 approved, 278 were opposed, and 125 were described as "miscellaneous in nature," for an average of approximately three-to-one favoring Truman's decision. See "W. J. H." (William J. Hopkins, White House Executive Clerk) to Charles Ross (Press Secretary), June 29, 1950, OF, 471-B, Korean Emergency, in Truman Papers. Governer Dewey is quoted in New York *Times*, June 28, 1950. His telegram and Truman's reply are printed as Item No. 175, *Public Papers . . . Truman, 1950*, 496; *Christian Science Monitor*, June 29, 1950.

68. New York *Times*, June 28, 1950; Warner, "How Korea Decision Was Made," 104.

69. Paige, *Korean Decision*, 196; New York *Times*, June 28, 1950.

70. *Far East Hearings*, Pt. 5, p. 3211ff. Taft's speech and a rebuttal by Senator Paul Douglas (Dem., Ill.), are excerpted in Doc. No. 28, "Senate Debate of the Commander in Chief's Authority," John P. Roche and Leonard W. Levy (eds.), *The Presidency* (New York: Harcourt, Brace and World, 1964), 199–205.

71. Text of the memorandum appears twice in the *Far East Hearings*, Pt. 5, pp. 3198–3204, 3373–81. It is also published in *Background Information on the Use of United States Armed Forces in Foreign Countries*, Appendix I, 49–54.

72. New York *Times*, June 29, 1950. The Korean Army—less than 100,000 strong—had no combat aircraft, tanks, or heavy artillery and few antitank weapons. The ROK navy was a farcical flotilla, consisting mainly of light patrol craft of World War II vintage. See Hanson W. Baldwin, *ibid.*, June 27, 1950.

73. Doc. No. 15, Statement, Austin to the Security Council, June 27, 1950, *United States Policy in the Korean Crisis*, 23–24. See also *Far East Hearings*, Pt. 5, pp. 3370–71.

74. Doc. No. 16, Security Council Resolution, June 27, 1950, *United States Policy in the Korean Crisis*, 24. See also New York *Times*, June 28, 1950; Allen Guttmann (ed.), *Korea and the Theory of Limited War* (Boston: Heath, 1967), 2–3. In the voting, Yugoslavia cast the dissenting vote and India and Egypt abstained. India approved two days later. The Soviet Union was absent as it had been since a boycott begun in January, 1950.

75. Lichterman, "To the Yalu and Back," 580–81. For a view dissenting from that expressed here, see I. F. Stone, *The Hidden History of the Korean War* (New York: Monthly Review Press, 1952), 75.

76. New York *Times*, June 29, 1950; Warner, "How Korea Decision Was Made," 104–105.

77. Truman, *Memoirs*, II, 340; Acheson, *Present at the Creation*, 411.

78. Truman, *Memoirs*, II, 340–41. See also McLellan and Reuss, "Foreign and Military Policies." 75.

79. Truman, *Memoirs*, II, 340–41; Paige, *Korean Decision*, 223–24. See also Acheson, *Present at the Creation*, 411.

80. Appleman, *South to the Naktong*, 44. According to United Press reports from London, Soviet and North Korean radio broadcasts charged, on June 29, that U.S. B-29's were bombing Pyongyang, North Korea. Washington denied these reports. New York *Times*, June 30, 1950; Collins, *War in Peacetime*, 18–19; Lichterman, "To the Yalu and Back," 581; Whitney, *MacArthur*, 326; Lichterman, "To the Yalu and Back," 581.

81. New York *Times*, June 30, 1950. See also Smith, "Why We Went to War in Korea," 86; Fehrenbach, *This Kind of War*, 86.

82. Item No. 179, *Public Papers . . . Truman, 1950*, 504–505. In a press conference on July 13, a reporter asked Truman if he would still call the Korean fighting a "police action." His reply was, "Yes, it is still a police action." Item No. 191, *Public Papers . . . Truman, 1950*, 522; Truman to Harry I. Schwimmer, July 12, 1950, OF, 471-B, Korean Emergency, in Truman Papers.

83. Paige, *Korean Decision*, 245; Truman, *Memoirs*, II, 341; Collins, *War in Peacetime*, 19–20.

84. Truman, *Memoirs*, 341–42. See also Acheson, *Present at the Creation*, 411–12; Alexander L. George, "American Policy-Making and the North Korean Aggression," in Guttman (ed.), *Korea and the Theory of Limited War*, 73.

85. Docs. No. 89, 90, Chinese Embassy to Department of State, June 29, 30, 1950, *United States Policy in the Korean Crisis*, 56–60.

86. Truman, *Memoirs*, II, 342; Acheson, *Present at the Creation*, 412. See also Paige, *Korean Decision*, 249. General MacArthur did not want the Formosan troops when they were originally offered. See Bradley's testimony, *Far East Hearings*, Pt. 1, p. 652; Truman, *Memoirs*, II, 348.

87. MacArthur, *Reminiscences*, 334.

88. *Ibid.*, 334.

89. Truman, *Memoirs*, II, 343; New York *Times*, July 1, 1950; Richard H. Rovere and Arthur M. Schlesinger, Jr., *The General and the President and the Future of American Foreign Policy* (New York: Farrar, Straus and Young, 1951), 106; Smith, "Why We Went to War in Korea," 88.

90. Truman, *Memoirs*, II, 343. See also Acheson, *Present at the Creation*, 412;

Spanier, *Truman-MacArthur Controversy*, 33. For text of the State Department note declining the Nationalist Chinese offer, see Doc. No. 91, *United States Policy in the Korean Crisis*, 60–61.

91. Truman, *Memoirs*, II, 343; Collins, *War in Peacetime*, 23; Acheson, *Present at the Creation*, 412. For an interesting speculative analysis of the thinking of the policy-makers at this meeting, see George, "American Policy-Making," 74–75.

92. Smith, "Why We Went to War in Korea," 88; Acheson, *Present at the Creation*, 413; Paige, *Korean Decision*, 262.

93. Paige, *Korean Decision*, 262. For the text of Ambassador Austin's statement to the Security Council later the same day explaining the American action, see Doc. No. 18, *United States Policy in the Korean Crisis*, 25–27.

94. Smith, "Why We Went to War in Korea," 88; Acheson, *Present at the Creation*, 413; Paige, *Korean Decision*, 262–63; Truman, *Harry S. Truman*, 470.

95. White House Press Release No. 2454, June 30, 1950, copy in MacArthur Hearings, Tannenwald Papers; Paige, *Korean Decision*, 263–64.

96. Truman, *Memoirs*, II, 464. General Bradley, testifying in 1951, demonstrated complete accord with Truman's sentiments. Asked why the United States intervened, he said that everyone was in agreement that this was an act of aggression that had to be met. *Far East Hearings*, Pt. 2, p. 890. Similar views were expressed by General Vandenberg. See *ibid.*, Pt. 2, p. 1490.

97. Osgood, *Limited War*, 167. D. F. Fleming would agree with Osgood, adding that the failure of the Truman Doctrine in China endangered Truman's European policy as well as his political base in America. Thus, he could not afford another defeat in Asia. *The Cold War*, II, 602–603.

98. Cited in Paige, *Korean Decision*, 45, 289, 304–305, 310–11. In the poll 15 percent disagreed and 12 percent had no opinion. Roper. *You and Your Leaders*, 415. In 1952, Truman told a reporter that the decision to intervene was backed by "almost" 90 percent of the American people. Edward T. Folliard, Washington *Post*, December 27, 1952.

99. New York *Herald-Tribune*, December 27, 1952; Lichterman, "To the Yalu and Back," 579; Hoare, "Truman," 190–91.

100. Acheson, *Present at the Creation*, 413–15. Merlo Pusey has written that Truman's failure to obtain congressional approval for the Korean intervention violated the United Nations Participation Act and stands as a precedent which imperils democracy and impedes establishment of a sound system of collective security. See Pusey, *The Way We Go to War* (Boston: Houghton Mifflin, 1969), 79–85 *passim*. Raymond G. O'Connor considered Truman's refusal to secure a declaration of war from Congress to be "among the innovations" made by the president during the Korean War. See O'Connor, "Harry S. Truman: New Dimensions of Power," 73. Senator Richard B. Russell said (in 1962) that if the administration had requested congressional approval *after* the first troops went in, "it would have been granted unanimously." Quoted in Pusey, *Way We Go To War*, 111.

Chapter 11

1. Truman, quoted in Smith, "Why We Went to War in Korea," 80.
2. Truman, *Memoirs*, II, 344; Hoare, "Truman," 194; Hermes, *Truce Tent*

and Fighting Front, 53–56. When military activity had scaled down considerably, Truman cut the briefings to three per week.

3. Hoare, "Truman," 199. During most of the Korean War the following men constituted the civilian-military hierarchy of the Pentagon: George C. Marshall, secretary of defense; Frank Pace, Jr., secretary of the army; Francis P. Matthews, secretary of the navy; Thomas K. Finletter, secretary of the air force; General Omar N. Bradley, chairman, Joint Chiefs of Staff; General J. Lawton Collins, army chief of staff; General Hoyt S. Vandenberg, air force chief of staff; Admiral Forrest P. Sherman died of a heart attack on July 22, 1951, and was replaced by Admiral William M. Fechteler as chief of naval operations.

4. George M. Elsey to Charles S. Murphy, July 7, 1950, OF, 471-B—Korean Emergency, in Truman Papers.

5. White House Press Release, July 8, 1950, copy in Tannenwald Papers. See also Item No. 189, *Public Papers . . . Truman, 1950*, 520; Doc. No. 100, *United States Policy in the Korean Crisis*, 100; *Far East Hearings*, Pt. 5, pp. 3372–73.

6. Hoare, "Truman," 194–95; *Far East Hearings*, Pt. 1, p. 10.

7. MacArthur to Department of the Army, July 7, 1950, quoted in Appleman, *South to the Naktong*, 118; Truman, *Memoirs*, II, 344.

8. MacArthur to JCS, July 9, 1950, quoted in Appleman, *South to the Naktong*, 119; Collins to the Commander in Chief, July 16, 1950, OF, 471-B - Korean Emergency, in Truman Papers.

9. MacArthur to Truman, July 19, 1950, in Lloyd Files, Message to Congress and Speech re Korea, July 19, 1950, Truman Library, hereinafter cited as Lloyd Files.

10. Truman, *Memoirs*, II, 345; MacArthur, *Reminiscences*, 337.

11. Acheson, *Present at the Creation*, 420–21.

12. Hammond, "NSC-68," 351; Acheson, *Present at the Creation*, 421.

13. Item No. 193, *Public Papers . . . Truman, 1950*, 532; Dulles to the President, July 20, 1950, OF, 471-B—Korean Emergency (June–July, 1950), in Truman Papers.

14. Collins testimony, *Far East Hearings*, Pt. 2, p. 1309; Acheson, *Present at the Creation*, 421. For an excellent description of the relationship of NSC-68 to rearmament, see Hammond, "NSC-68," 351–55, 358–59. The myriad changes in troop levels and supplemental budgetary increments brought on by Korea are detailed in Schilling, "Politics of National Defense," 211–13. See also Bernardo and Bacon, *American Military Policy*, 485–86; Fehrenbach, *This Kind of War*, 163–64; "Louis Johnson's Testimony Before Armed Services Subcommittee on Appropriations, House of Representatives, July 25, 1950," in *Far East Hearings*, Pt. 5, Appendix AA, 3250–55.

15. Truman to Eleanor Roosevelt, August 22, 1950, OF, 471-B—Korean Emergency, in Truman Papers.

16. Appleman, *South to the Naktong*, 68–72, 113–14. See also Millis, *Arms and Men*, 294–95.

17. MacArthur, *Reminiscences*, 336; Bernardo and Bacon, *American Military Policy*, 486; Truman, *Memoirs*, II, 347. As of September 30, 1950, the U.S. Army had 103,601 personnel committed in Korea. They had sustained 24,172 casualties by September 30, with 5,145 of that total having been killed in action. See Appleman, *South to the Naktong*, 605–606.

18. CINCFE to Department of the Army, July 7, 1950, quoted in Appleman, *South to the Naktong*, 118.
19. Quoted in Higgins, *Korea and the Fall of MacArthur*, 44. See also *American Military History*, 553; MacArthur, *Reminiscences*, 346.
20. MacArthur, *Reminiscences*, 346–47. See also Truman, *Memoirs*, II, 347–48.
21. MacArthur, *Reminiscences*, 348; *American Military History*, 553; Appleman, *South to the Naktong*, 493.
22. MacArthur, *Reminiscences*, 349–50; Collins, *War in Peacetime*, 125–26. See also Willoughby and Chamberlain, *MacArthur*, 370–72.
23. Truman, *Memoirs*, II, 358. Secretary Johnson was the only Washington official to openly back the Inchon plan from the outset. See his testimony, *Far East Hearings*, Pt. 4, pp. 2618, 2661. JCS to CINCFE, August 28, 1950, quoted in Appleman, *South to the Naktong*, 494.
24. *American Military History*, 555. The North Koreans probably knew that an amphibious assault was imminent, but were uncertain of the site. Appleman, *South to the Naktong*, 487, says it was generally known among UN forces that such a landing was planned for mid-September. Dean Acheson claims that the Inchon landing was nicknamed, "Operation Common Knowledge" in Japan. He also says that Communist spies learned of the invasion plans through a security leak, but were unable to contact their North Korean counterparts. *Present at the Creation*, 448. Out of a force of some 100,000, approximately 30,000 escaped into North Korea, disorganized and without their support equipment. See Lichterman, "To the Yalu and Back," 584.
25. Quoted in MacArthur, *Reminiscences*, 356; Truman to MacArthur, September 29, 1950, OF, 471-B—Korean Emergency (August–November, 1950), in Truman Papers.
26. Hoare, "Truman," 196–97. See also, O'Connor, "Harry S. Truman; New Dimensions of Power," 69; Johnson testimony, *Far East Hearings*, Pt. 4, pp. 2618, 2624, 2625; In his *Memoirs*, Truman does not discuss Johnson's dismissal at all.
27. Johnson to Truman, Truman to Johnson, September 12, 1950, OF, 1285, in Truman Papers. See Johnson's remarks before the American Bar Association on his last full day in office, September 18, 1950, Office of Public Information, Department of Defense, Press Release No. 177-50S, copy in OF, 1285, in Truman Papers.
28. Truman to Millard E. Tydings, September 13, 1950, Office of Public Information, Department of Defense, Press Release No. 177-50S, copy in Truman Papers; "A Bill . . . to Appoint General of the Army George C. Marshall to the Office of Secretary of Defense," (64 *Stat.* 853). See also Item No. 246, *Public Papers . . . Truman, 1950*, 633–34.
29. Quoted in *American Military History*, 556; D. F. Fleming, who described the crossing of the 38th parallel as a "monumental error" and a "plain invitation to disaster," has estimated that a total of five million casualties (both sides, military and civilian), resulted from the fighting in Korea, with two million of these dead. Of all casualties, according to Fleming, four fifths were sustained after the liberation of South Korea. *The Cold War*, II, 655–56. See also Hermes, *Truce Tent and Fighting Front*, 10.
30. Acheson, *Present at the Creation*, 451; Truman, *Memoirs*, II, 359.
31. JCS to MacArthur, September 15, 1950, in *Far East Hearings*, Pt. 1, p. 718.

32. Item No. 253, Item No. 258, *Public Papers . . . Truman, 1950,* 644, 658, 659. See also Stone, *Hidden History of Korean War,* 108–109; Spanier, *Truman-MacArthur Controversy,* 100–101.
33. Quoted in MacArthur, *Reminiscences,* 458. For a paraphrased text of the directive see Acheson, *Present at the Creation,* 452–53. See also Truman, *Memoirs,* II, 360–62; Lichterman, "To the Yalu and Back," 585–87.
34. Acheson, *Present at the Creation,* 453; Acheson testimony, *Far East Hearings,* Pt. 3, pp. 1943–44, 2258.
35. MacArthur, *Reminiscences,* 358; *Far East Hearings,* Pt. 1, p. 719; Acheson, *Present at the Creation,* 453. General Collins admitted that he and the other joint chiefs, "somewhat overawed by the success of Inchon," recommended approval of MacArthur's plan without having received any details. See his *War in Peacetime,* 158.
36. Doc. No. 9, Resolution Adopted by the General Assembly, October 7, 1950, *United States Policy in the Korean Conflict,* 17–18. Acheson, *Present at the Creation,* 454.
37. Rhee to the president, quoted in cable, Truman to Acheson, October 1, 1950, OF, 471-B - Korean Emergency, in Truman Papers. Those present at the meeting were the Korean ambassador, John M. Chang; the vicechairman of the Korean National Assembly, T. S. Chang; the Korean foreign minister, Gen C. Limb; President Truman; and Acting Chief of Protocol R. D. Muir. See Muir, Memorandum of Conversation, October 11, 1950, OF, 471 (1949–50), in Truman Papers.
38. *United States Foreign Policy in the Korean Conflict,* Appendix III, 50.
39. Appleman, *South to the Naktong,* 612, 623–30 *passim;* Esposito (ed.), *West Point Atlas,* II, Sec. 3, Map Plate No. 7; Lichterman, "To the Yalu and Back," 572. Early in October the JCS warned MacArthur that if "major Chinese units" intervened in Korea, he was to resist only so long as he had a reasonable chance to win. He was also warned not to attack Chinese territory without prior approval. JCS to CINCFE, October 9, 1950, in *Far East Hearings,* Pt. 1, p. 720.
40. Item No. 264, *Public Papers . . . Truman, 1950,* 665–66. See also New York *Times,* October 10, 1950. Truman, *Memoirs,* II, 362–63.
41. Acheson, *Present at the Creation,* 456; Bradley testimony, *Far East Hearings,* Pt. 2, p. 1115; Marshall testimony, *Far East Hearings,* Pt. 1, p. 439; Item No. 269, *Public Papers . . . Truman, 1950,* 673.
42. Spanier, *Truman-MacArthur Controversy,* 111–12; Stone, *Hidden History of the Korean War,* 139–40.
43. Stone, *Hidden History of the Korean War,* 140. On October 19, the U.S. acknowledged responsibility for the attack and offered to make restitution. Spanier, *Truman-MacArthur Controversy,* 111.
44. MacArthur, *Reminiscences,* 361. See also Spanier, *Truman-MacArthur Controversy,* 104. Truman, *Memoirs,* II, 365.
45. Whitney, *MacArthur,* 387. This is partially borne out by the record of the general meeting at Wake Island, wherein Truman is recorded as saying that he had already talked at length with MacArthur about the Philippines. He also said there was no need to discuss Formosa, since that subject had been fully "discussed with MacArthur and that they were in full accord." U.S. Senate, Committees on Armed Services and Foreign Relations, *Substance of Statements Made at Wake Island Conferences on October 15, 1950,* compiled by Omar N. Bradley, 82nd Cong., 1st Sess. (Washing-

ton: U.S. Government Printing Office, 1951), 7–8. See also MacArthur testimony, *Far East Hearings*, Pt. 1, p. 41. Truman, *Memoirs*, II, 364–65;
Spanier, *Truman-MacArthur Controversy*, 105.
46. The principal figures in attendance at this meeting, in addition to Truman
and MacArthur, were General Bradley, Ambassador Muccio, Ambassador-
at-Large Jessup, Assistant Secretary Dean Rusk, Army Secretary Pace,
W. Averell Harriman, and Admiral Arthur Radford, commander of the
U.S. Pacific Fleet. *Substance of Statements Made at Wake Island*, 1. This
document was the cause of much controversy later. It was based on notes
of the meeting taken by Bradley, Jessup, Harriman, Rusk, and two staff
officers, also present. In addition, they draw from a reasonably full steno-
graphic record taken unofficially by Jessup's secretary, Vernice Anderson,
who was waiting in an adjoining room to type out a communiqué on the
meeting. MacArthur and his aide, General Whitney, have claimed that
Truman's press secretary, Charles Ross, had cautioned them that no notes
were to be taken during the conference. See MacArthur, *Reminiscences*,
361; Whitney, *MacArthur*, 381–92. For other commentary on these notes,
see Truman, *Memoirs*, II, 365; Acheson, *Present at the Creation*, 456; *Far
East Hearings*, Pt. 1, pp. 27–29, 683–84, Pt. 2, pp. 926–28, 979–80.
47. *Substance of Statements Made at Wake Island*, 3, 6. During the 1951 hearings on his dismissal, MacArthur reaffirmed this statement, adding that it
was correct up to that time. See his testimony, *Far East Hearings*, Pt. 1, p.
213. See also Truman, *Memoirs*, II, 365–66.
48. *Substance of Statements Made at Wake Island*, 5. See also Truman, *Memoirs*, II, 366; MacArthur, *Reminiscences*, 362; Fehrenbach, *This Kind of
War*, 277. MacArthur later stated that the views he expressed on the possibility of intervention had been qualified beforehand as pure speculation,
based on an entirely military point of view towards a question that was
basically political.
49. Item No. 268, *Public Papers . . . Truman, 1950*, 672; Item No. 269, October
17, 1950, *ibid.*, 673. See also New York *Times*, October 16, 1950.
50. MacArthur to JCS, October 21, 1950, quoted in *Far East Hearings*, Pt. 1, p.
720. Truman's cable is quoted in MacArthur, *Reminiscences*, 364.
51. *Far East Hearings*, Pt. 2, pp. 1216–17, 1240.
52. MacArthur to JCS, October 25, 1950, quoted in *ibid.*, Pt. 1, p. 721, Pt. 2,
p. 1241; Collins, *War in Peacetime*, 180–81. See also Lichterman, "To the
Yalu and Back," 600–601; Appleman, *South to the Naktong*, 670–71.
53. *Far East Hearings*, Pt. 1, p. 718; Bradley testimony, *ibid.*, Pt. 2, pp. 938–39;
Acheson testimony, *ibid.*, Pt. 3, pp. 2100–101; Johnson testimony, *ibid.*, Pt.
4, pp. 2621–22; MacArthur, *Reminiscences*, 358; Ridgway, *Korean War*, 45.
54. Spanier, *Truman-MacArthur Controversy*, 85; Acheson Testimony, *Far
East Hearings*, Pt. 3, p. 1833. See also Acheson, *Present at the Creation*,
452; Truman, *Memoirs*, II, 361–62; Rovere and Schlesinger, *The General
and the President*, 147. The authors of the latter work disagree with the
generally accepted view that the Chinese Communists intervened because
U.S. forces crossed the 38th parallel. (See pp. 147–51) They are supported
in part by Willoughby and Chamberlain, who believe that North Korea had
assurances of Chinese military support prior to the outset of the war. See
MacArthur, 380.
55. JCS to CINCFE, October 9, 1950, quoted in Truman, *Memoirs*, II, 362.
Message also appears in *Far East Hearings*, Pt. 1, p. 720. See also Richard

E. Neustadt, *Presidential Power: The Politics of Leadership* (New York: New American Library, 1964), 132–33.

56. Lichterman, "To the Yalu and Back," 593, 596; MacArthur testimony, *Far East Hearings*, Pt. 1, pp. 18–19, 84; MacArthur, *Reminiscences*, 359.

57. Truman, *Memoirs*, II, 372, 373; New York *Times*, October 22, 1950; Ridgway, *Korean War*, 51; Millis, *Arms and Men*, 296. See also Acheson testimony, *Far East Hearings*, Pt. 3, p. 1833.

58. Quoted in Truman, *Memoirs*, II, 373. See also Acheson testimony, *Far East Hearings*, Pt. 3, p. 1833; New York *Times*, November 6, 1950.

59. Acheson, *Present at the Creation*, 463; Truman, *Memoirs*, II, 373–74; Collins, *War in Peacetime*, 200. Acheson, Truman, and Collins all state that the Pentagon copy of MacArthur's orders was sent by General Stratemeyer to Washington, not by MacArthur, thus implying that the latter sought a *fait accompli*. However, the official Army history of the wars says that the JCS, "received from MacArthur a radio report of the order." See Appleman, *South to the Naktong*, 715. MacArthur's *Reminiscences* (p. 368), sheds no light on who sent a copy of the orders to Washington, but the general does acknowledge that there was a danger of accidentally bombing Manchuria. He leaves the impression that the risk was no longer important, since some Chinese forces had become involved in the fighting.

60. Truman, *Memoirs*, II, 374–75; Acheson, *Present at the Creation*, 463–64; Collins, *War in Peacetime*, 200–201.

61. JCS to MacArthur, November 5, 1950, quoted in MacArthur testimony, *Far East Hearings*, Pt. 1, p. 20; Major General Emmett O'Donnell testimony, *ibid.*, Pt. 4, p. 3090.

62. MacArthur to JCS, November 6, 1950 (November 7 in Tokyo), in Truman, *Memoirs*, II, 375. General Collins has described as "extraordinary" MacArthur's request that the matter be brought directly to the president. *War in Peacetime*, 201.

63. Truman, *Memoirs*, II, 375–76. MacArthur later testified that it was his "violent protest" which caused rescinding of the countermand. See *Far East Hearings*, Pt. 1, p. 20. Quoted in Truman, *Memoirs*, II, 376. See also Bradley testimony, *Far East Hearings*, Pt. 2, p. 741; Acheson, *Present at the Creation*, 464; Collins, *War in Peacetime*. Within a few days the bridges were knocked out. However, less than two weeks later the Yalu was frozen over, allowing the passage of even the heaviest military equipment. See Lichterman, "To the Yalu and Back," 604.

64. Quoted in Truman, *Memoirs*, II, 377. See also *Far East Hearings*, Pt. 3, p. 1834.

65. Truman, *Memoirs*, II, 376, 378; Lichterman, "To the Yalu and Back," 606.

66. MacArthur testimony, *Far East Hearings*, Pt. 1, p. 12; MacArthur to JCS, November 7, 1950, quoted in Truman, *Memoirs*, II, 377.

67. *Far East Hearings*, Pt. 2, pp. 887–88, 1388, Pt. 3, pp. 1722–24; Lichterman, "To the Yalu and Back," 604. For text of letter, see *Far East Hearings*, Pt. 3, p. 1928. Those governments, aside from the U.S. and Korea, contributing military forces to the fighting by mid-November, 1950, were Australia, Belgium, Canada, France, Netherlands, New Zealand, Philippines, Thailand, Turkey, and the United Kingdom.

68. Acheson testimony, *Far East Hearings*, Pt. 3, pp. 1722–24, 1735–36. Tru-

man said that the "hot pursuit" inquiries were submitted to the nations concerned with his approval. *Memoirs*, II, 382.
69. Truman, *Memoirs*, II, 377–78.
70. Lichterman, "To the Yalu and Back," 605. General Ridgway agreed that the UN forces enjoyed a privileged sanctuary, "without which the Korea War could have been a far more tragic story." *Korean War*, 75. See also Morton H. Halperin, "The Limiting Process in the Korean War," in Guttmann (ed.), *Korea and the Theory of Limited War*, 92–106 *passim*.
71. Truman, *Memoirs*, II, 378; Collins, *War in Peacetime*, 206.
72. Truman, *Memoirs*, II, 378–80. See also Neustadt, *Presidential Power*, 134–37; Acheson, *Present at the Creation*, 465–66.
73. Ridgway, *Korean War*, 60; Appleman, *South to the Naktong*, 770; Esposito (ed.), *West Point Atlas*, II, Sec. 3, Map Plate No. 9, Regarding this undetected infiltration, Senator Leverett Saltonstall asked Acheson, "They really fooled us when it comes right down to it, didn't they?" Acheson replied: "Yes, sir." *Far East Hearings*, Pt. 3, p. 1835.
74. Doc. No. 13, Joint Resolution in the Security Council, November 10, 1950, *United States Policy in the Korean Conflict*, 22–23; Item No. 287, *Public Papers . . . Truman, 1950*, 711–12.
75. Quoted in Ridgway, *Korean War*, 59. MacArthur, *Reminiscences*, 171–72, 365–66; Acheson, *Present at the Creation*, 467.
76. New York *Times*, November 24, 25, 1950; MacArthur, *Reminiscences*, 372; Ridgway, *Korean War*, 60; Truman, *Memoirs*, II, 381.
77. New York *Times*, November 25, 1950; Lichterman, "To the Yalu and Back," 610; MacArthur, *Reminiscences*, 374.
78. Truman is quoted in Hersey, "Profiles," Pt. 2, p. 52; MacArthur is quoted in Acheson, *Present at the Creation*, 469.

CHAPTER 12

1. Truman, *Memoirs*, II, 415–16.
2. *Ibid.*, 385–86; Acheson, *Present at the Creation*, 469.
3. Truman, *Memoirs*, II, 386–87; Acheson, *Present at the Creation*, 469, 471. While MacArthur continuously requested authority to bomb Manchuria and blockade the China coast, he never requested that his ground forces be used to invade mainland China. In his testimony in 1951 he characterized such a suggestion as "utterly reckless" and "ridiculous." *Far East Hearings*, Pt. 1, pp. 29, 43.
4. JCS to MacArthur, November 29, 1950, in Truman, *Memoirs*, II, 385. See also MacArthur, *Reminiscences*, 375–76.
5. Rovere and Schlesinger, *The General and the President*, 152. See also Spanier, *Truman-MacArthur Controversy*, 133. Army Chief of Staff Collins testified that the advance by MacArthur was not a "reconnaissance in force," but a full-scale offensive designed to destroy the remaining NKPA forces. *Far East Hearings*, Pt. 5, p. 3495. MacArthur described his offensive as a "reconnaissance" in a letter to Frank W. Boykin, December 13, 1950, OF, 471-B - Korean Emergency, in Truman Papers.
6. MacArthur testimony, *Far East Hearings*, Pt. 1, p. 21.
7. Quoted in Hersey, "Profiles," Pt. 1, p. 43.
8. MacArthur to JCS (and reply), November 30, 1950, in *Far East Hearings*,

Pt. 2, pp. 1145–46; Esposito (ed.), *West Point Atlas*, II, Sec. 3, Map Plate No. 9.

9. Item No. 295, *Public Papers . . . Truman, 1950*, 724–25.
10. *Ibid.*
11. *Ibid.*, 727.
12. *Ibid.*
13. Item No. 203, *ibid.*, 562.
14. White House Press Release, November 30, 1950, copy in OF, 471-B - Korean Emergency, Truman Papers. British Prime Minister Clement Atlee flew to Washington on December 4 to receive personal reassurances from Truman respecting atomic policy. For accounts of their conversations, see Truman, *Memoirs*, II, 396–413; Acheson, *Present at the Creation*, 483–84; "President's Communiqué of December 8, 1950, Regarding His Conferences with Prime Minister Atlee," *Far East Hearings*, Pt. 5, Appendix G, 3501–504; Item No. 301, *Public Papers . . . Truman, 1950*, 738–40.
15. Item No. 296, *Public Papers . . . Truman, 1950*, 728–31. Truman signed the Second Supplemental Appropriation Act of 1951 (64 *Stat.* 1223), on January 6, 1951.
16. Truman, *Memoirs*, II, 390–91; Acheson, *Present at the Creation*, 473–74.
17. MacArthur to JCS, December 3, 1950, quoted in Truman, *Memoirs*, II, 391–93. See also Gavin Long, *MacArthur as Military Commander* (New York: Van Nostrand, Reinhold, 1969), 216.
18. Collins, *War in Peacetime*, 229. Lovett is quoted in Acheson, *Present at the Creation*, 474.
19. Quoted in Ridgway, *Korean War*, 62.
20. Truman, *Memoirs*, II, 393. Truman said that all his military advisers told him that holding the beachheads would be impossible. He said he wanted them to try anyway. See *ibid.*, 399.
21. Acheson, *Present at the Creation*, 475–76; Collins, *War in Peacetime*, 229; Truman, *Memoirs*, II, 393.
22. Collins, *War in Peacetime*, 232–33.
23. Truman, *Memoirs*, II, 415. In an interview on December 1, for example, MacArthur said that prohibition against striking at Manchurian bases was a terrible handicap "without precedent in military history." Quoted in Acheson, *Present at the Creation*, 471–72. See also, *Far East Hearings*, Pt. 1, 342, 570–71.
24. Earl Cocke, Jr. to Truman, December 6, 1950, OF, 471-B - Korean Emergency, in Truman Papers.
25. Brooks Hays, Walter Judd, Kenneth Keating, *et al.*, to the president, December 5, 1950, *ibid.*
26. Joseph R. McCarthy to Truman, December 2, 1950, *ibid.*
27. Memorandum of conversation, John F. Simmons, December 6, 1950, OF, 471, in Truman Papers.
28. P. H. Shinicky to Truman, December 5, 1950, in OF, 471-B - Korean Emergency, Truman Papers.
29. Hillman (ed.), *Mr. President*, 143. Secretary of Defense Marshall agreed with Truman on the seriousness of conditions. In a speech on December 8 he described the U.S. military situation as "more grave" than it had been in 1942. Payne, *Marshall Story*, 313–14.
30. Truman, *Memoirs*, II, 417–18; Lichterman, "To the Yalu and Back," 618.

31. File Memorandum, December 25, 1950, OF, 471-B, in Truman Papers.
32. *United States Policy in the Korean Conflict*, 52.
33. New York *Times*, June 28, 1950. See also ["E.B.S."] to Charles S. Murphy, July 17, 1950, in White House Files, Murphy Papers.
34. Truman, *Memoirs*, II, 417–27. See also Item No. 302, *Public Papers* . . . *Truman, 1950*, 741.
35. John Hersey, "Profiles—Mr. President," Pt. 5, "A Weighing of Words," *New Yorker* (May 5, 1951), 39.
36. Item No. 303, *Public Papers* . . . *Truman, 1950*, 741–46. See also *Far East Hearings*, Pt. 5, pp. 3514–20.
37. A full description of the legislative acts placed in force by the national emergency declaration can be found in J. Howard McGrath to Symington, December 18, 1950, RG340, S/AF, 031.1, National Archives.
38. (64 *Stat.* 1257). Truman requested this additional grant of power in identical letters, dated December 18, addressed to the president of the Senate and the speaker of the House. See Item No. 307, *Public Papers* . . . *Truman, 1950*, 749–50.
39. Ridgway, *Korean War*, 79, 81–83, 100–101; MacArthur, *Reminiscences*, 383; MacArthur testimony, *Far East Hearings*, Pt. 1, p. 150. The Eighth Army line extended from the Imjin River on the west coast, through Yongpyong and Huachon, to Yangyang on the east. Collins, *War in Peacetime*, 235–37.
40. Acheson, *Present at the Creation*, 514, 755. For text of the JCS message to MacArthur, see *Far East Hearings*, Pt. 2, pp. 1464, 1618, Pt. 3, pp. 2179–80, 2223–26, 2244–45.
41. Lichterman "To the Yalu and Back," 620.
42. MacArthur, *Reminiscences*, 378–80. See also Acheson, *Present at the Creation*, 514–15; Walter Millis, "Truman and MacArthur," in Guttmann (ed.), *Korea and the Theory of Limited War*.
43. JCS to CINCFE, January 9, 1951, in *Far East Hearings*, Pt. 1, pp. 332–33, Pt. 2, pp. 1322, 1599–1600. Defense Secretary Marshall testified that MacArthur's proposals would, in his judgment, not have brought a quick decision in Korea, but would have created a hazardous condition, if not world war. See *ibid.*, Pt. 1, p. 369. For an examination of military and diplomatic objections to MacArthur's specific proposals, see Ridgway, *Korean War*, 146–48.
44. JCS to CINCFE, January 4, 1951, copy in Tannenwald Papers.
45. Rhee to Truman, transmitted in letter, John M. Chang to Truman, January 10, 1951, OF, 471-B - Korean Emergency, in Truman Papers. See also Acheson to the president, February 9, 1951, Truman to Rhee, February 10, 1951, *ibid.*
46. MacArthur to JCS, January 10, 1951, in *Far East Hearings*, Pt. 2, p. 906.
47. Acheson, *Present at the Creation*, 515; Sherman testimony, *Far East Hearings*, Pt. 2, pp. 1600–601. Truman, *Memoirs*, II, 434.
48. JCS to CINCFE, January 12, 1951, in *Far East Hearings*, Pt. 2, pp. 737–38, 907, 1414–15.
49. Truman to MacArthur, January 13, 1951, *ibid.*, Pt. 1, pp. 503–505.
50. MacArthur, *Reminiscences*, 382.
51. Marshall testimony, *Far East Hearings*, Pt. 1, pp. 324, 335–36, 703; Bradley testimony, *ibid.*, Pt. 2, p. 907.
52. MacArthur's four proposals, as stated in his message of December 30 to

the JCS called for: (1) air and naval attacks against Chinese military bases and industrial plants; (2) naval blockade of Chinese coastline; (3) acceptance of Nationalist Chinese volunteers; (4) allowing Formosa to attack mainland China. See MacArthur, *Reminiscences*, 378–80; MacArthur testimony, *Far East Hearings*, Pt. 1, pp. 13–16. Some of the other proposed courses of action remain classified, but several have become public record through congressional testimony. Among them were: (1) continue the bombing of military targets in Korea; (2) send a military training mission and increase MDAP aid to Formosa; (3) remove restrictions on air reconnaissance of China's coastal areas and of Manchuria; (4) continue and intensify economic blockade of trade with China; (5) stabilize military positions in Korea or evacuate to Japan; (6) press for the UN to brand Communist China as an aggressor. MacArthur's suggested air and naval attacks on China, while included in the sixteen proposals, were made contingent upon China attacking American forces someplace other than Korea. Marshall testimony, *Far East Hearings*, Pt. 1, pp. 333–34, 340. As for (6) above, on February 4, 1951, the General Assembly passed a resolution denouncing the People's Republic of China as an aggressor in Korea. Doc. No. 28, *United States Policy in the Korean Conflict*, 37.
53. *Far East Hearings*, Pt. 1, pp. 329, 335–36, 505–506, Pt. 2, pp. 736–37, 1321–22, 1531–33; Acheson, *Present at the Creation*, 516.
54. Collins testimony, *Far East Hearings*, Pt. 2, pp. 1210–11, 1227–28; Vandenberg testimony, *ibid.*, 1472–73; Collins, *War in Peacetime*, 251–55; *American Military History*, 561.
55. Collins, *War in Peacetime*, 253–55; Truman, *Memoirs*, II, 436–47. See also Marshall testimony, *Far East Hearings*, Pt. 1, pp. 324, 332; Collins testimony, *ibid.*, Pt. 2, p. 1211; Acheson, *Present at the Creation*, 516; Higgins, *Korea and the Fall of MacArthur*, 98.
56. Esposito (ed.), *West Point Atlas*, II, Sec. 3, Map Plate No. 11; Collins, *War in Peacetime*, 257–58; Hermes, *Truce Tent and Fighting Front*, 12–13.
57. Collins, *War in Peacetime*, 258–62; Ridgway, *Korean War*, 107–112; Esposito (ed.), *West Point Atlas*, II, Sec. 3, Map Plate No. 11.
58. MacArthur, *Reminiscences*, 384–85.
59. Rhee to the president, March 26, 1951, OF, 471, in Truman Papers.
60. Collins, *War in Peacetime*, 262–64. General Collins felt Marshall should not have consulted the army, navy and air secretaries: "So far as I know, this was the first time that a question of major military significance was referred to the service secretaries for comment. It would have been unfortunate if they had been consulted regularly on such matters, because this would have tended to interpose them between the JCS and the secretary of defense, which was not contemplated by the National Defense Act of 1947, as amended in 1949." *Ibid.*, 265n.
61. Pace, Kimball, and Finletter to Marshall, February 24, 1951, RG330, OSD, CD 092 (Korea), National Archives.
62. Collins, *War in Peacetime*, 265–66. JCS reasoning can be seen in General James H. Burns's commentary to Deputy Secretary of Defense Lovett on the State Department Draft Memorandum, February 26, 1951, RG330, OSD, CD 092 (Korea), National Archives.
63. JCS to CINCFE, March 20, 1951, printed in *Far East Hearings*, Pt. 1, pp. 343, 346; Pt. 5, pp. 3180, 3541. For discussion of this document during

the investigation of MacArthur's recall, see *ibid.*, Pt. 2, pp. 1007–1008, 1021–23, 1142–43, Pt. 3, pp. 1915–16, 2184.
64. MacArthur, *Reminiscences*, 387; Ridgway, *Korean War*, 116. See also Lichterman, "To the Yalu and Back," 629. On March 28 the secretary of defense announced that crossing of the 38th parallel was only a tactical decision. Truman confirmed this in a press conference on the twenty-ninth. See Item No. 63, *Public Papers . . . Truman, 1951*, 203, 205–206.
65. MacArthur, *Reminiscences*, 387; Acheson, *Present at the Creation*, 519.
66. Truman, *Memoirs*, II, 442; MacArthur, *Reminiscences*, 387–88. See also Lichterman, "To the Yalu and Back," 628; Fehrenbach, *This Kind of War*, 412–13; Marshall testimony, *Far East Hearings*, Pt. 1, pp. 344, 346; Bradley testimony, *ibid.*, Pt. 2, p. 899. Text of proposed statement is in Truman, *Memoirs*, II, 439–40. Although Truman's statement gives lip service to the objective of a unified Korea, the principle expressed throughout is status quo antebellum.
67. JCS to CINCFE, March 24, 1951, in *Far East Hearings*, Pt. 1, p. 407, Pt. 5, pp. 3181–82, 3542; Acheson, *Present at the Creation*, 519; Truman, *Memoirs* II, 443.
68. Quoted in Truman, *Memoirs*, II, 445–46. See also Collins, *War in Peacetime*, 281; *Far East Hearings*, Pt. 1, p. 412.
69. Item No. 77, *Public Papers . . . Truman, 1951*, 222. The dismissal of General MacArthur is the subject of the next chapter.
70. Marshall to Ridgway, April 11, 1951, OF, 584, Dismissal, in Truman Papers; Pace to the President, May 21, 1951, OF, 1285-B, in Truman Papers; Ridgway, *Korean War*, 162, 169.
71. Lichterman, "To the Yalu and Back," 629; *American Military History*, 564–65; Esposito, (ed.), *West Point Atlas*, II, Sec. 3, Map Plate Nos. 13, 14; Hermes, *Truce Tent and Fighting Front*, 73–75.
72. Truman, *Memoirs*, II, 455–56. See also Acheson, *Present at the Creation*, 529.
73. Truman, *Memoirs*, II, 455–56; Acheson, *Present at the Creation*, 532–33; Hermes, *Truce Tent and Fighting Front*, 15.
74. JCS to Ridgway, June 29, 1951, quoted in Truman, *Memoirs*, II, 458. See also Millis, *Arms and Men*, 300; Hermes, *Truce Tent and Fighting Front*, 16–17.
75. Truman, *Memoirs*, II, 459.
76. *Ibid.*, 462; Mark W. Clark, *From the Danube to the Yalu* (New York: Harpers, 1954), 30.
77. Hermes, *Truce Tent and Fighting Front*, 130, 331; Truman to Lovett, January 9, 1952, RG330, OSD, CD 091.3, National Archives.
78. Roper, *You and Your Leaders*, 163–64.
79. Memorandum for the Record, Robert A. Lovett, September 15, 1952, USA, Office of the Chief of Staff, 091-Korea, National Archives.
80. Transcript, White House Meeting, September 24, 1952, *ibid.*
81. New York *Times*, October 25, 1952. In a press conference on December 11, 1952, Truman described Eisenhower's announcement that he would go to Korea as "a piece of demagoguery" which Eisenhower was obliged to carry through on after the election. Item No. 345, *Public Papers . . . Truman, 1952–53*, 1075. Truman repeated the charge of demagoguery against Eisenhower in interviews held late in December. See New York

Times, December 27, 1952; Washington *Post*, December 27, 1952.
82. Truman to Eisenhower (and reply), August 13, 14, Truman to Eisenhower, August 16, 1952, in Truman, *Memoirs*, II, 512–13.
83. Truman to Patterson, August 2, 1946, OSW (211), AG031.1, National Archives. See also, Patterson to Eisenhower, August 23, 1946, PF/DDE, Patterson folder, Eisenhower to Truman, January 22, 1948, August 17, 1949, Truman to Eisenhower, January 23, 1948 PF/DDE, Truman folder (1), all in Eisenhower Papers.
84. These several communications are all printed in Truman, *Memoirs*, II, 505–10. See also Corwin and Koenig, *Presidency Today*, 128–29.
85. Truman to secretary of state, *et al.*, December 31, 1952, Murphy Files, Correspondence and General File, in Truman Papers; Lovett to the president, January 3, 1953, RG330, OSD, 031.1, National Archives.
86. MacArthur, *Reminiscences*, 363; Whitney, *MacArthur*, 389; Truman, *Memoirs*, II, 187.
87. Quoted in Neustadt, *Presidential Power*, 22.
88. Walter Lippman, New York *Herald-Tribune*, August 24, 1956. See also Warren, *President as World Leader*, 345.

CHAPTER 13

1. Quoted in Phillips, "Truman at 75," 107.
2. See, for example, *Far East Hearings*, Pt. 1, pp. 27–28, 283–84, 499–50; MacArthur, *Reminiscences*, 393. Truman made an extended statement on civil supremacy in his *Memoirs*, II, 444–45.
3. The quotation from Livy is purported to be the views of Lucius Aemilius Paulus, a Roman general (c. 168 B.C.), see Rovere and Schlesinger, *The General and the President*, 120–21.
4. Whitney, *MacArthur*, 326; *Far East Hearings*, Pt. 1, pp. 535–36; Appleman, *South to the Naktong*, 44.
5. Statement of Generalissimo Chiang Kai-shek, August 2, 1950, in *Far East Hearings*, Pt. 5, pp. 3338–84; Truman, *Memoirs*, II, 353–54; Collins, *War in Peacetime*, 272–73. For MacArthur's statement regarding his trip to Formosa, see New York *Times*, August 1, 1950. See also a further statement attributed to a "reliable source," *ibid.*, August 6, 1950. MacArthur is quoted from Harriman's report to the president, in Truman, *Memoirs*, II, 349–53. For MacArthur's statement regarding Harriman's visit, see his *Reminiscences*, 340–41. See also Spanier, *Truman-MacArthur Controversy*, 70–72; Neustadt, *Presidential Power*, 24.
6. Truman, *Memoirs*, II, 354; New York *Times*, August 29, 1950.
7. Truman, *Memoirs*, II, 354–55; MacArthur, *Reminiscences*, 341–42. For text of the letter, Austin to Trygve Lie, August 25, 1950, see *Far East Hearings*, Pt. 5, pp. 3473–74. I. F. Stone felt that MacArthur, through means like the VFW message, deliberately tried to start a world war. See *Hidden History of the Korean War*, 92. On the other hand, General Whitney claimed that MacArthur always felt that his message "innocently ran afoul" of a State Department scheme to turn Formosa over to the Communists. *MacArthur*, 381.
8. Acheson, *Present at the Creation*, 423; Truman, *Memoirs*, II, 359.
9. Johnson to MacArthur, August 26, 1950, in *Far East Hearings*, Pt. 5, p. 3480; New York *Herald-Tribune*, August 29, 1950; Truman, *Memoirs*, II, 355–56.
10. Truman, *Memoirs*, II, 356.

11. Truman to MacArthur, August 29, 1950, OF, 584-MacArthur's Proposed VFW Message, in Truman Papers. Truman to Austin, August 27, 1950, in Tannenwald Papers.
12. Item No. 345, *Public Papers . . . Truman, 1952–53*, 1074. Truman had made an earlier reference to MacArthur's misjudgment (at Wake Island) in a Jefferson-Jackson Day address, April 14, 1951. See MacArthur Chronology, entry for October 15, 1950, Tannenwald Papers.
13. Item No. 345, *Public Papers . . . Truman, 1952–53*, 1074.
14. Item No. 268, *ibid.*, 672; Item No. 269, *ibid.*, 673; Item No. 270, *ibid.*, 679.
15. MacArthur Testimony, *Far East Hearings*, Pt. 1, p. 41. See also Fleming, *The Cold War*, II, 618.
16. Collins Testimony, *Far East Hearings*, Pt. 2, pp. 1216–17, 1228–31, 1240; Collins, *War in Peacetime*, 200; Ridgway, *Korean War*, 61; Acheson, *Present at the Creation*, 463; Truman, *Memoirs*, II, p. 373–74. In 1951 Admiral Sherman of the JCS testified: "Throughout this period the conduct of affairs was made difficult by a lack of responsiveness to the obvious intentions of the directives which were transmitted out there and a tendency to debate and to criticize." *Far East Hearings*, Pt. 2, p. 1630. See also Bradley testimony, 1146.
17. MacArthur to Ray Henle, November 28, 1950, quoted in Washington *Post*, November 29, 1950.
18. MacArthur to Arthur Krock, November 30, 1950, in New York *Times*, November 30, 1950.
19. *Ibid.*, December 2, 1950; *Far East Hearings*, Pt. 5, pp. 3532–33. See also Collins, *War in Peacetime*, 279. For a list of all restrictions placed upon the conduct of military operations in Korea, see Marshall to Richard B. Russell, May 23, 1951, printed in *Far East Hearings*, Pt. 5, Appendix K, 3192–93.
20. MacArthur to Hugh Baille, December 1, 1950, in New York *Herald-Tribune*, December 2, 1950.
21. Washington *Post*, December 3, 1950. MacArthur communicated similar messages to Barry Faris, International News Service and Ward Price of the London *Daily Mail*. See Spanier, *Truman-MacArthur Controversy*, 149.
22. These four themes in MacArthur's statements were identified and elaborated upon by Spanier, *Truman-MacArthur Controversy*, 149–50. Truman wrote that while he was disturbed that he and MacArthur were so far apart in their viewpoints, "It was always proper and appropriate for him to advance his opinion to his Commander in Chief. If he had gone no farther than that, I would never have felt compelled to relieve him." *Memoirs*, II, 416. For MacArthur's own exposition on the second and third points, see MacArthur to Frank W. Boykin, December 13, 1950, OF, 471-B - Korean Emergency, in Truman Papers.
23. Truman's memorandum was transmitted verbatim to MacArthur in JCS to CINCFE, December 6, 1950, OF, 584–MacArthur's Dismissal, in Truman Papers.
24. *Ibid.* See also New York *Herald-Tribune*, April 12, 1951; *Far East Hearings*, Pt. 5, p. 3536.
25. *Far East Hearings*, Pt. 2, p. 889. MacArthur's view was that he had been "muzzled" by "anonymous sources high in government circles," who were propagandizing against him. See *Reminiscences*, 385.
26. Truman, *Memoirs*, II, 384.

27. New York *Herald-Tribune*, February 7, 1951.
28. New York *Times*, February 14, 1951. Secretary Marshall later testified that this statement did not, in his judgment, comply with the December 6, 1950, directive of the president. *Far East Hearings*, Pt. 1, p. 475.
29. Clark, *Danube to the Yalu*, 25–26.
30. New York *Times*, March 8, 1951.
31. Acheson, *Present at the Creation*, 518; *Far East Hearings*, Pt. 1, p. 476.
32. JCS to CINCFE, March 20, 1951, copy in MacArthur Hearings, Tannenwald Papers; New York *Times*, March 24, 1951.
33. M. J. McDermott (statement), March 24, 1951, in OF, 584, Truman Papers.
34. Truman, *Memoirs*, II, 442. See also Hoare, "Truman," 203. JCS to CINCFE, March 24, 1951, copy in MacArthur Hearings, Tannenwald Papers.
35. MacArthur testimony, *Far East Hearings*, Pt. 1, p. 72.
36. Spanier, *Truman-MacArthur Controversy*, 201. Two of MacArthur's biographers have made much the same claim. See Whitney, *MacArthur*, 467–68; Hunt, *Untold Story of Douglas MacArthur*, 507–10.
37. MacArthur Testimony, *Far East Hearings*, Pt. 1, pp. 46–47, 113; Martin to MacArthur (and reply), March 8, 20, 1951, *ibid.*, Pt. 5, pp. 3182, 3543–44; MacArthur, *Reminiscences*, 386.
38. Truman, *Memoirs*, II, 446–47. For other participants' opinions in testimony on the Martin letter, see *Far East Hearings*, Pt. 1, pp. 113–15, 380, 445–47, 572–73, 581–82.
39. Truman, *Memoirs*, II, 442, 448.
40. Acheson, *Present at the Creation*, 520; Acheson Testimony, *Far East Hearings*, Pt. 3, pp. 1733, 1751, 1910.
41. Truman, *Memoirs*, II, 447; Acheson, *Present at the Creation*, 521; Acheson testimony, *Far East Hearings*, Pt. 3, pp. 1751, 1776–77, 1979–80; Bradley testimony, *ibid.*, Pt. 2, pp. 1047. During the hearings, General Bradley, under question by Senator Alexander Wiley (R., Wis.), refused to divulge what was said by any persons present at the meetings with the president regarding MacArthur's dismissal: "In my position as an adviser, one of the military advisers to the President . . . if I have to publicize my recommendations and my discussions . . . my value as an adviser is ruined." *Ibid.*, Pt. 2, p. 763. Chairman Richard Russell (Dem., Ga.), ruled that Bradley was justified in holding that his talks with Truman constituted a privileged communication and were not, therefore, in contempt of Congress. Russell's ruling was appealed, and a lengthy debate ensued lasting two days, occupying over one hundred pages of the hearings' record. The senators argued at length over the principle of the separation of powers, investigative powers of Congress, the relationship of the military to the commander in chief, and numerous other related questions. In the end, the chair was sustained, eighteen to eight, on a bipartisan vote. Four Republicans voted with the majority, and two Democrats, J. William Fulbright (Ark.), Guy M. Gillette (Iowa), voted with the minority. See *Far East Hearings*, Pt. 2, pp. 762–872. Truman later had high praise for Bradley's refusal to testify to conversations held with him as commander in chief, believing it to involve a basic question as to the validity of the separation of powers principle. See Truman, *Memoirs*, II, 452–53.
42. Truman, *Memoirs*, II, 448; Acheson, *Present at the Creation*, 521–22; Marshall testimony, *Far East Hearings*, Pt. 1, pp. 345, 420; Bradley testi-

mony, *ibid.*, Pt. 2, p. 1047; Acheson testimony, *ibid.*, Pt. 3, pp. 1751–52, 1911.
43. Bradley testimony, *Far East Hearings*, Pt. 2, pp. 878–81; Collins testimony, *ibid.*, 1215–16. The reasons that the joint chiefs gave for agreeing in the dismissal were examined at great length by the members of the committee. Perhaps this was because MacArthur had repeatedly insisted that he and the JCS were in total accord. See MacArthur testimony, *Far East Hearings*, Pt. 1, p. 283.
44. Truman, *Memoirs*, II, 448; Acheson, *Present at the Creation*, 522; Marshall testimony, *Far East Hearings*, Pt. 1, pp. 345, 420–21, also Acheson Testimony, Pt. 3, pp. 1752, 1911. After his presidency, Truman said Mac-Arthur would never have been relieved if the Joint Chiefs of Staff were in control of policy. *Truman Speaks*, 24.
45. Truman, *Memoirs*, II, 448–49; Acheson, *Present at the Creation*, 522–23. A full description of the press "leak" can be found in Phillips, *Truman Presidency*, 342–43. For detailed testimony dealing with the method of relief, see *Far East Hearings*, Pt. 1, pp. 345–46, 348–49, 418–19, 519–20, 686, Pt. 2, pp. 746–47; Pt. 3, p. 1777.
46. Truman, *Memoirs*, II, 449. See also Item No. 77, *Public Papers . . . Truman, 1951*, 222–23. The documents released to accompany this statement were copies of the president's directive of December 6, 1950, the JCS messages of March 20, 24, 1951, MacArthur's statement of March 24, and MacArthur's letter to Congressman Joseph Martin. See also *Washington Post*, April 12, 1951.
47. Item No. 77, *Public Papers . . . Truman, 1951*, 222; Truman, *Memoirs*, II, 449.
48. Item No. 78, *Public Papers . . . Truman, 1951*, 223–27.
49. MacArthur, *Reminiscences*, 392, 395. See also MacArthur testimony, *Far East Hearings*, Pt. 1, p. 26; Whitney, *MacArthur*, 417; Long, *MacArthur as Military Commander*, 222. Quoted in Willoughby and Chamberlain, *MacArthur*, 423.
50. Spanier, *Truman-MacArthur Controversy*, 211; Lukacs, *History of the Cold War*, 94n.
51. Quoted in Eldorous L. Dayton, *Give 'em Hell Harry: An Informal Biography of the Terrible Tempered Mr. T.* (New York: Devin-Adair, 1956), 201. A report of a public opinion poll taken at the end of June, 1951, showed Republicans to be very "solid" in their support of MacArthur in the dispute with Truman. Democrats were "evenly divided" in their support, according to a White House memorandum, Lloyd to Murphy, *et al.* (undated) MacArthur Firing, in Lloyd Files.
52. Richard H. Rovere, *Senator Joe McCarthy* (New York: World, 1959), 12. See also Lafeber, *America, Russia, and the Cold War*, 120; Spanier, *Truman-MacArthur Controversy*, 212–13; Rovere and Schlesinger, *The General and the President*, 12–13.
53. Krock, *In the Nation*, 186.
54. Margeurite Mondlock to William Hopkins, May 8, 1951, OF, 584-Mac-Arthur's Dismissal, President's Action in Relieving General MacArthur (folder 2), in Truman Papers.
55. This figure is a compilation of data contained in numerous file memoranda from the weeks just after MacArthur's relief. *Ibid.*
56. Elmo Roper and Louis Harris, "The Press and the Great Debate: A Survey

of Correspondents in the Truman-MacArthur Controversy," *Saturday Review of Literature*, XXXIV (July 14, 1951), 6ff.

57. MacArthur, *Reminiscences*, 400; Rovere and Schlesinger, *The General and the President*, 11.

58. MacArthur, Address to Joint Meeting of the Congress, April, 1951, in *Far East Hearings*, Pt. 5, pp. 3553–58.

59. Rovere and Schlesinger, *The General and the President*, 11.

60. Truman to unidentified correspondent, April 10, 1951, quoted in Hillman (ed.), *Mr. President*, 33.

61. MacArthur Testimony, *Far East Hearings*, Pt. 1, pp. 27–28, 197, 282–84, 289, 308. An embarassing typographical error (or Freudian slip) at one point in his testimony records MacArthur as saying: "I have *not* carried out every directive that I have ever received." See *ibid.*, 30.

62. *Ibid.*, 45, 289.

63. Quoted in Neustadt, *Presidential Power*, 124–125. See also Dahl, *Pluralist Democracy*, 105.

64. Item No. 101, *Public Papers . . . Truman, 1950*, 523. In another press conference following MacArthur's removal, Truman said that the decision to send UN forces up to the Yalu was, "a matter of tactics in the field, and is the responsibility of the field commander. I never interfere with the field commander in any of their maneuvers." Item No. 95, *ibid.* (*1951*), 264.

65. *Far East Hearings*, Pt. 1, p. 45.

66. MacArthur, *Reminiscences*, 392–93; *Far East Hearings*, Pt. 1, pp. 99–100.

67. Quoted in Ridgway, *Korean War*, 233.

68. DOD Release No. 72–51S, "Address by General Omar Bradley, Chairman of the Joint Chiefs of Staff to the National Association of Radio and Television Broadcasters, April 17, 1951," copy in White House files, Korean Documents (folder 2), Truman Library.

69. Statement on the Relief of General MacArthur, April 19, 1951, *ibid.*

70. Truman to Harriman, April 24, 1951, PF/DDE, Truman folder (2), in Eisenhower Papers; Item No. 95, *Public Papers . . . Truman, 1951*, 261–62. Truman had privately expressed the belief that justification for his firing MacArthur would emerge in the congressional hearing. Writing in late April to a New Jersey legislator, Truman had first expressed this conviction. See Truman to Robert G. Hendrickson, April 27, 1951, OF, 584-MacArthur Dismissal, President's Action in Relieving General Douglas MacArthur of His Commands (folder 2), in Truman Papers.

71. Item No. 96, *Public Papers . . . Truman, 1951*, 265–69 *passim*. See also New York *Herald-Tribune*, May 8, 1951; Washington *Post*, May 8, 1951.

72. *Far East Hearings*, Pt. 1, p. 325. Emphasis supplied. See also, Payne, *Marshall Story*, 319–20. The other important army commanders of the period were in substantial agreement with Marshall. For example, see Bradley testimony, *Far East Hearings*, Pt. 2, pp. 752–53, 1041–44, Collins Testimony, 1194–95; Ridgway, *Korean War*, 141–42, 152–53.

73. Quoted in Higgins, *Korea and the Fall of MacArthur*, 25.

74. Hoare, "Truman," 199–200.

75. Truman, *Memoirs*, II, 443; T. Harry Williams, "The Macs and the Ikes, America's Two Military Traditions," *American Mercury*, LXXV (October, 1952), 37; Higgins, *Korea and the Fall of MacArthur*, 40. Another commentary on the parallels between McClellan and MacArthur is in Ridgway, *Korean War*, 152, 261.

76. MacArthur was denied permission to bomb Racin, a North Korean port near the Soviet border. In August, 1951, Ridgway was allowed to strike this target. Hermes, *Truce Tent and Fighting Front*, 107–108. In June, 1952, Truman lifted the ban on bombing dams and hydroelectric plants on the Yalu. *Ibid.*, 319–22. In July, 1952, Truman allowed the bombing of Pyongyang, which had previously been off-limits. *Ibid.*, 324; O'Connor, "Harry S. Truman, New Dimensions of Power," 72.
77. Truman to Colgate W. Darden, April 14, 1951, OF, 584-MacArthur's Dismissal, President's Action in Relieving General Douglas MacArthur of His Commands (folder 2), in Truman Papers; Truman to Michael U. DeVita, April 27, 1951, *ibid.*
78. *Truman Speaks*, 97.
79. Quoted in Phillips, *Truman Presidency*, 350.
80. Truman to Albert, April 17, 1951, OF, 584-MacArthur's Dismissal (folder 2), in Truman Papers; Truman to (Mrs.) W. Coleman Branton, April 19, 1951, *ibid*; Truman to A. E. Augustine, April 23, 1951, *ibid*. This file contains many other letters in which Truman emphasized that he acted from a compulsive sense of duty. The same reasoning is repeated in his *Memoirs*, II, 444–45.
81. Truman to Eisenhower, April 12, 1951, PF/DDE, Truman folder (2), in Eisenhower Papers.

CHAPTER 14

1. Truman to John T. Carlton, April 17, 1951, OF, 584, President's Action in Relieving General Douglas MacArthur of His Commands (folder 2), in Truman Papers.
2. Rossiter, *American Presidency*, 116.
3. Quoted in Hersey, "Profiles," Pt. 5, p. 52.
4. Truman, *Memoirs*, II, 473.
5. Item No. 92, *Public Papers . . . Truman, 1948*, 247.
6. Entry, September 25, 1947, in Millis (ed.), *Forrestal Diaries*, 319–20.
7. Quoted in Hillman (ed.), *Mr. President*, 11.
8. Fairman, "President as Commander-in-Chief," 145. Among the other presidential "jobs" Truman described at various times are chief executive, party leader, legislator, social head of state, and chief diplomat.
9. For a detailed examination of the functional role of the President under the unification act (1947), see Fairman, "President as Commander-in-Chief," 145–61.
10. Item No. 238, *Public Papers . . . Truman, 1950*, 622.
11. Item No. 37, *ibid.* (1951), 154.
12. Williams, *Americans at War*, 142–43; Hoare, "Truman," 183–84; Elmer Davis, "Harry S. Truman and the Verdict of History," *The Reporter* (February 3, 1953), 18.
13. Acheson testimony, *Far East Hearings*, Pt. 3, pp. 1729, 1734–35, 1782, 2256–57. Generals Marshall and Bradley testified to the same effect, see *ibid.*, Pt. 1, p. 570, Pt. 2, pp. 937–38.
14. Spanier, *Truman-MacArthur Controversy*, 259–60.
15. Truman, *Memoirs*, II, p. x. See also McLellan and Reuss, "Foreign and Military Policies," 34; Osgood, *Limited War*, 169; Halperin, "Limiting Process in the Korean War," 97.
16. Spanier, *Truman-MacArthur Controversy*, 2.

17. James, *Contemporary Presidency*, 161. In his last annual message to Congress, January 7, 1953, Truman emphasized this change in warfare. He said that nuclear war was "not a possible policy for rational men." Item No. 366, *Public Papers . . . Truman, 1952–53*, 1125.
18. O'Connor, "Harry S. Truman: New Dimensions of Power," 59.
19. Rossiter, *American Presidency*, 119.
20. Item No. 98, *Public Papers . . . Truman, 1952–53*, 270. See also New York *Times*, December 27, 1952.
21. Item No. 2, *Public Papers . . . Truman, 1945*, 6.

List of Sources

ARCHIVES

Dwight D. Eisenhower Library. Abilene, Kansas.
   Dwight D. Eisenhower Papers
Harry S. Truman Library. Independence, Missouri.
   Clark Clifford Papers
   David Lloyd Files
   Charles Murphy Papers
   Samuel Rosenman Papers
   Harold D. Smith Diary (copy; original in Franklin D. Roosevelt Library)
   Theodore Tannenwald Papers
   Harry S. Truman Papers
   James E. Webb Papers
Historical Records Division, Chief of Naval Operations. Navy Yard, Washington, D.C.
National Archives. Washington, D.C.

GOVERNMENT PUBLICATIONS

Appleman, Roy E. *South to the Naktong, North to the Yalu, June-November, 1950.* Washington: Office of the Chief of Military History, Department of the Army, 1961.
Fowler, Henry H. *War Powers of the President.* Washington: Industrial College of the Armed Forces, 1948.
Hermes, Walter G. *Truce Tent and Fighting Front.* Washington: Office of the Chief of Military History, Department of the Army, 1966.
Lee, Ulysses. *The Employment of Negro Troops.* Washington: Office of the Chief of Military History, Department of the Army, 1966.
Pogue, Forrest C. *The Supreme Command.* Washington: Government Printing Office, 1954.
Public Papers of the Presidents of the United States, Harry S. Truman: Containing the Public Messages, Speeches, and Statements of the President. 8 vols. Washington: Government Printing Office, 1961–1966.

335

U.S. House of Representatives. *Basic Elements of the Unification of the War and Navy Departments.* Document No. 56. 80th Cong., 1st Sess.

——. *National Security Act of 1947: Communication from the President Transmitting a Draft of a Proposed Bill Entitled National Security Act of 1947.* Document No. 149. 80th Cong., 1st Sess.

——. *The Powers of the President as Commander in Chief of the Army and Navy of the United States.* Edited by Dorothy Schaffter and Dorothy M. Mathews. 84th Cong., 2nd Sess. Washington: Government Printing Office, 1956.

——. *Universal Military Training.* Report No. 857. 79th Cong., 1st Sess.

——. Committee on Foreign Affairs. *Background Information on the Use of United States Armed Forces in Foreign Countries.* Report No. 127. 82nd Cong., 1st Sess.

U.S. Senate, Committee on Armed Services. *National Defense Establishment: Unification of the Armed Services. Hearings before the Committee on Armed Services, United States Senate.* 80th Cong., 1st Sess., on S. 758; 3 pts. Washington: Government Printing Office, 1947.

——. Committee on Armed Services and Committee on Foreign Relations. *Military Situation in the Far East. Hearings before the Committee on Armed Services and the Committee on Foreign Relations, United States Senate.* 82nd Cong., 1st Sess., 5 pts. Washington: Government Printing Office, 1951.

——. *Powers of the President to Send the Armed Forces Outside the United States.* Committee Print. 82nd Cong., 1st Sess. Washington: Government Printing Office, 1951.

——. *Substance of Statements Made at Wake Island Conference on October 15, 1950.* Compiled by Omar N. Bradley. 82nd Cong., 1st Sess. Washington: Government Printing Office, 1951.

——. Committee on Foreign Relations. *A Decade of Foreign Policy: Basic Documents, 1941–1949.* 81st Cong., 2nd Sess. Washington: Government Printing Office, 1950.

——. *War Powers Legislation: Hearings before the Committee on Foreign Relations on S. 731, S.J. Res. 18 and S.J. Res. 59.* 92nd Cong., 1st Sess., 1972.

——. Committee on Government Operations, Subcommittee on National Security and International Operations. *The Atlantic Alliance. Hearings before the Subcommittee on National Security and International Operations of the Committee on Government Operations, United States Senate.* 89th Cong., 2nd Sess. Washington: Government Printing Office, 1966.

——. *The Atlantic Alliance—Basic Issues: A Study.* Committee Print. 89th Cong., 2nd Sess. Washington: Government Printing Office, 1966.

U.S. Department of the Army, Office of the Chief of Military History. *American Military History.* Washington: Government Printing Office, 1969.

U.S. Departments of the Army and Air Force. *Joint Army and Air Force Bulletin.* Washington: Government Printing Office, 1945–.

U.S. Department of State. *Foreign Relations of the United States, Diplomatic Papers: The Conference of Berlin (Potsdam), 1945.* 2 vols. Washington: Government Printing Office, 1960.

————. *Foreign Relations of the United States, Diplomatic Papers: The Conferences at Malta and Yalta, 1945.* Washington: Government Printing Office, 1955.

————. *United States Policy in the Korean Conflict: July, 1950–February, 1951.* Publication No. 4263. Far Eastern Series 44. Washington: Government Printing Office, 1951.

————. *United States Policy in the Korean Crisis.* Publication No. 3922. Far Eastern Series 34. Washington: Government Printing Office, 1950.

U.S. President's Committee on Civil Rights. *To Secure These Rights: A Report of the President's Committee on Civil Rights.* Washington: Government Printing Office, 1947.

U.S. Department of War. "General Principles of National Military Policy to Govern Preparation of Post–War Plans: Extracts from Directives by General George C. Marshall, Chief of Staff," War Department Circular No. 347 (August 25, 1944).

U.S. Departments of War and Navy. "The War and Navy Departments' Views on Universal Military Training." Washington: Government Printing Office, ca. 1945.

NEWSPAPERS

Baltimore *Sun.*
New York *Herald-Tribune.*
New York *Times.*
Washington *Post.*

ARTICLES

Aurthur, Robert Alan. "The Wit and Sass of Harry S. Truman," *Esquire,* LXXVI (August, 1971), 62–67, 115–18.

Baldwin, Hanson W. "The Military Move In," *Harper's Magazine,* CXCV (December, 1947), 481–89.

Baumer, William H. "National Security Organization," *The Military Engineer,* XL (March, 1948), 5.

Bernstein, Barton J. "The Ambiguous Legacy: The Truman Administration and Civil Rights," *Politics and Policies of the Truman Administration.* Barton J. Bernstein, ed. Chicago: Quadrangle Books, 1970.

Brant, Irving. "Harry S. Truman-I," *New Republic,* CXII (April 30, 1945), 577–79.

————. "Harry S. Truman-II," *New Republic,* CXII (May 7, 1945), 635–38.

Cornwell, Elmer E., Jr. "The Truman Presidency," *The Truman Period as a Research Field.* Richard S. Kirkendall, ed. Columbia: University of Missouri Press, 1967. Pp. 213–55.

Cousins, Norman K., and Thomas K. Finletter. "A Beginning for Sanity," *Saturday Review of Literature*, XXIX (June 15, 1946), 6–8.

Davis, Elmer. "Harry S. Truman and the Verdict of History," *The Reporter* (February 3, 1953), 17–22.

Emerson, William R. "F.D.R.," *The Ultimate Decision: The President as Commander in Chief*. Ernest R. May, ed. New York: George Braziller, 1960. Pp. 135–77.

Fairman, Charles. "The President as Commander-in-Chief," *Journal of Politics*, XI (February, 1949), 145–70.

Fischer, John. "Mr. Truman's Politburo," *Harper's Magazine*, CCII (June, 1951), 29–36.

Fleming, D. F. "America's Responsibility," *The Cold War—Who is to Blame?* Brian Tierney, Donald Kagan, L. Pearce Williams, eds. New York: Random House, 1967. Pp. 4–17.

Foley, Edward H., Jr. "Some Aspects of the Constitutional Powers of the President," *American Bar Association Journal*, XXVII (August, 1941), 485–90.

George, Alexander L. "American Policy-Making and the North Korean Aggression," *Korea and the Theory of Limited War*. Allen Guttmann, ed. Boston: D. C. Heath, 1967. Pp. 66–79.

Halperin, Morton H. "The Limiting Process in the Korean War," *Korea and the Theory of Limited War*. Allen Guttmann, ed. Boston: D. C. Heath, 1967. Pp. 91–106.

Hammond, Paul Y. "NSC-68: Prologue to Rearmament," *Strategy, Politics, and Defense Budgets*. Warner R. Schilling, Paul Y. Hammond, and Glenn H. Snyder, eds. New York: Columbia University Press, 1962. Pp. 271–378.

———. "Super Carriers and B-36 Bombers: Appropriations, Strategy and Politics," *American Civil-Military Decisions: A Book of Case Studies*. Harold Stein, ed. Tuscaloosa: University of Alabama Press, 1963. Pp. 465–564.

Hersey, John. "Profiles—Mr. President, Pt. 1, Quite a Head of Steam," *New Yorker*, XXVII (April 7, 1951), 42–56.

———. "Profiles—Mr. President, Pt. 2, Ten O'Clock Meeting," *New Yorker*, XXVII (April 14, 1951), 38–55.

———. "Profiles—Mr. President, Pt. 3, Forty-Eight Hours," *New Yorker*, XXVII (April 21, 1951), 35–61.

———. "Profiles—Mr. President, Pt. 5, A Weighing of Words," *New Yorker*, XXVII (May 5, 1951), 36–53.

Hoare, Wilber W., Jr. "Truman," *The Ultimate Decision: The President as Commander in Chief*. Ernest R. May, ed. New York: George Braziller, 1960. Pp. 181–210.

Kenworthy, E. W. "Taps for Jim Crow in the Services," *New York Times Magazine* (June 11, 1950), 12–13, 24–27.

Lee, R. Alton. "The Army 'Mutiny' of 1946," *Journal of American History*, LIII (December, 1966), 555–71.

Leopold, Richard W. "The United States in World Affairs, 1941–1968," *Interpreting American History: Conversations with Historians.* Vol. II. John A. Garraty, ed. New York: Macmillan Company, 1970. Pp. 223–46.

Lichterman, Martin. "To the Yalu and Back," *American Civil-Military Decisions: A Book of Case Studies.* Harold Stein, ed. Tuscalooosa: University of Alabama Press, 1963. Pp. 569–639.

Matloff, Maurice. "Rooosevelt as War Leader," *American History: Recent Interpretations, Book II, Since 1865.* 2nd ed. Abraham S. Eisenstadt, ed. New York: Thomas Y. Crowell Company, 1961. Pp. 418–35.

May, Ernest R. "The Development of Political Military Consultation in the United States," *Political Science Quarterly,* LXX (June, 1955), 161–80.

———. "The President Shall be Commander in Chief," *The Ultimate Decision: The President as Commander in Chief.* Ernest R. May, ed. New York: George Braziller, 1960. Pp. 3–19.

McClure, Arthur F., and Donna Costigan, "The Truman Vice Presidency: Constructive Apprenticeship or Brief Interlude?" *Missouri Historical Review,* LXV (April, 1971), 318–41.

McLellan, David S., and John W. Reuss. "Foreign and Military Policies," *The Truman Period as a Research Field.* Richard S. Kirkendall, ed. Columbia: University of Missouri Press, 1967. Pp. 15–85.

Millis, Walter. "Truman and MacArthur," *Korea and the Theory of Limited War.* Allen Guttmann, ed. Boston: D. C. Heath, 1967. Pp. 44–51.

Morton, Louis, "The Decision to Use the Atomic Bomb," *Command Decisions.* Kent R. Greenfield, ed. Washington: Government Printing Office, 1960. Pp. 493–518.

O'Connor, Raymond G. "Harry S. Truman: New Dimensions of Power," *Powers of the President in Foreign Affairs, 1945–1965.* Edgar E. Robinson *et al.,* eds. San Francisco: The Commonwealth Club of California, 1966. Pp. 17–76.

Phillips, Cabell, "Truman at 75," *New York Times Magazine* (May 3, 1959), 12, 106–109.

Roper, Elmo and Louis Harris. "The Press and the Great Debate: A Survey of Correspondents in the Truman-MacArthur Controversy," *Saturday Review of Literature,* XXXIV (July 14, 1951), 6–9, 29–31.

Schilling, Warner R. "The H-Bomb Decision: How to Decide Without Actually Choosing," *Political Science Quarterly,* LXXVI (March, 1961), 24–46.

———. "The Politics of National Defense: Fiscal 1950," *Strategy, Politics, and Defense Budgets.* Warner R. Schilling, Paul Y. Hammond and Glenn H. Snyder, eds. New York: Columbia University Press, 1962, Pp. 1–266.

Smith, Beverly. "Why We Went to War in Korea," *Saturday Evening Post,* CCXXIV (November 10, 1951), 22 23, 76ff.

Truman, Harry S. "Our Armed Forces MUST be Unified," *Collier's*, XCIV (August 26, 1944), 16, 63–64.

Warner, Albert L. "How the Korea Decision Was Made," *Harper's Magazine*, CCII (June, 1951) 99–106.

White, Leonard D. "Polk," *The Ultimate Decision: The President as Commander in Chief*. Ernest R. May, ed. New York: George Braziller, 1960. Pp. 57–75.

Williams, T. Harry. "The Macs and the Ikes, America's Two Military Traditions," *American Mercury*, LXXV (October, 1952), 32–39.

BOOKS

Acheson, Dean. *Present at the Creation: My Years in the State Department*. New York: W. W. Norton, 1969.

Adler, Selig. *The Uncertain Giant: 1921–1941, American Foreign Policy Between the Wars*. Toronto: Collier-Macmillan, 1965.

Alperovitz, Gar. *Atomic Diplomacy: Hiroshima and Potsdam. The Use of the Atomic Bomb and the American Confrontation with Soviet Power*. New York: Simon and Schuster, 1965.

Ambrose, Stephen E. *Eisenhower and Berlin, 1945: The Decision to Halt at the Elbe*. New York: W. W. Norton, 1967.

Baldwin, Hanson W. *Great Mistakes of the War*. New York: Collins-Knowlton-Wing, 1950.

Baruch, Bernard M. *Baruch: The Public Years*. New York: Holt, Rinehart and Winston, 1960.

Basler, Roy P. (ed.). *The Collected Works of Abraham Lincoln*. 8 vols. New Brunswick, N.J.: Rutgers University Press, 1953–55.

Berdahl, Clarence A. *War Powers of the Executive in the United States*. Urbana, Ill.: University of Illinois, 1920.

Berman, William C. *The Politics of Civil Rights in the Truman Administration*. Columbus: Ohio State University Press, 1970.

Bernardo, C. Joseph, and Eugene H. Bacon. *American Military Policy: Its Development Since 1775*. 2nd ed. Harrisburg, Pa.: Stackpole, 1961.

Bernstein, Barton J., and Allen J. Matusow (eds.). *The Truman Administration: A Documentary History*. New York: Harper and Row, 1966.

Binkley, Wilfred E. *President and Congress*. 3rd. rev. ed. New York: Random House, 1962.

Blackett, P. M. S. *Fear, War and the Bomb*. New York: McGraw-Hill, 1948.

Buchanan, A. Russell. *The United States and World War II*, 2 vols. New York: Harper and Row, 1964.

Burns, James MacGregor. *Presidential Government: The Crucible of Leadership*. Boston: Houghton Mifflin, 1966.

———. *Roosevelt: The Soldier of Freedom*. New York: Harcourt, Brace, Jovanovich, 1970.

Byrnes, James F. *Speaking Frankly*. New York: Harper, 1947.

Churchill, Winston S. *The Second World War*, Vol. VI, *Triumph and Tragedy*. 6 vols. Boston: Houghton Mifflin, 1953.

Clark, Mark W. *From the Danube to the Yalu*. New York: Harper, 1954.

Collins, J. Lawton. *War in Peacetime: The History and Lessons of Korea*. Boston: Houghton Mifflin, 1969.

Compton, Arthur H. *Atomic Quest: A Personal Narrative*. New York: Oxford University Press, 1956.

Corwin, Edward S. *The President: Office and Powers, 1787–1957*. New York: New York University Press, 1957.

Corwin, Edward S., and Louis W. Koenig. *The Presidency Today*. New York: New York University Press, 1956.

Crabb, Cecil V., Jr. *American Foreign Policy in the Nuclear Age: Principles, Problems, and Prospects*. Evanston, Ill. Row, Peterson, 1960.

Current, Richard N. *Secretary Stimson: A Study in Statecraft*. New Brunswick, N.J.: Rutgers University Press, 1954.

Dahl, Robert A. *Pluralist Democracy in the United States: Conflict and Consensus*. Chicago: Rand, McNally, 1967.

Dalfiume, Richard M. *Desegregation of the U.S. Armed Forces: Fighting on Two Fronts, 1939–1953*. Columbia: University of Missouri Press, 1969.

Daniels, Jonathan. *The Man of Independence*. Philadelphia: Lippincott, 1950.

Davison, W. Phillips. *The Berlin Blockade: A Study in Cold War Politics*. Princeton, N.J.: Princeton University Press, 1958.

Dayton, Eldorous L. *Give 'em Hell Harry: An Informal Biography of the Terrible Tempered Mr. T*. New York: Devin-Adair, 1956.

DeConde, Alexander. *A History of American Foreign Policy*. New York: Scribner, 1963.

Dunning, William A. *Truth in History and Other Essays*. New York: Columbia University Press, 1937.

Dupuy, R. Ernest, and Trevor N. Dupuy. *Military Heritage of America*. New York: McGraw-Hill, 1956.

Ekirch, Arthur A., Jr. *The Civilian and the Military: A History of the American Antimilitarist Tradition*. New York: Oxford University Press, 1956.

Esposito, Vincent J. (ed.). *The West Point Atlas of American Wars*. 2 vols. New York: Praeger, 1959.

Fehrenbach, T. R. *This Kind of War: A Study in Unpreparedness*. New York: Macmillan, 1963.

Feis, Herbert. *Between War and Peace: The Potsdam Conference*. Princeton, N.J.: Princeton University Press, 1960.

———. *Contest Over Japan*. New York: Norton, 1967.

———. *Japan Subdued: The Atomic Bomb and the End of the War in the Pacific*. Princeton, N.J.: Princeton University Press, 1961.

Fishel, Leslie H., Jr., and Benjamin Quarles (eds.). *The Black American:*

A Brief Documentary History. Glenview, Ill.: Scott, Foresman, 1970.

Fleming, D. F. *The Cold War and Its Origins, 1917–1960*. 2 vols. Garden City, N.Y.: Doubleday, 1961.

Fox, William T. R., and Annette B. Fox. *NATO and the Range of American Choice*. New York: Columbia University Press, 1967.

Gardner, Lloyd C. *Architects of Illusion: Men and Ideas in American Foreign Policy, 1941–1949*. Chicago: Quadrangle, 1970.

Goldman, Eric F. *The Crucial Decade—and After: American, 1945–1960*. New York: Random House, 1960.

Guttmann, Allen (ed.). *Korea and the Theory of Limited War*. Boston: Heath, 1967.

Hammond, Paul Y. *Organizing for Defense: The American Military Establishment in the Twentieth Century*. Princeton, N.J.: Princeton University Press, 1961.

Hewlett, Richard G., and Oscar E. Anderson, Jr. *A History of the United States Atomic Energy Commission*, Vol. I, *The New World, 1939–1946*. University Park: Pennsylvania State University Press, 1962.

Hewlett, Richard G., and Francis Duncan. *A History of the United States Atomic Energy Commission*, Vol. II, *Atomic Shield, 1947–1952*. University Park: Pennsylvania State University Press, 1969.

Higgins, Trumbull. *Korea and the Fall of MacArthur: A Précis in Limited War*. New York: Oxford University Press, 1960.

Hillman, William (ed.). *Mr. President: The First Publication from the Personal Diaries, Private Letters, Papers and Revealing Interviews of Harry S. Truman, Thirty-Second President of the United States of America*. New York: Farrar, Strauss and Young, 1952.

Hofstadter, Richard. *The American Political Tradition and the Men Who Made It*. New York: Vintage Books, 1954.

The Hoover Commission Report on Organization of the Executive Branch of the Government. New York: McGraw-Hill, 1949.

Hunt, Frazier. *The Untold Story of Douglas MacArthur*. New York: Devin-Adair, 1954.

Jackson, Henry M. (ed.). *The Atlantic Alliance: Jackson Subcommittee Hearings and Findings*. New York: Praeger, 1967.

———— (ed.). *The National Security Council: Jackson Subcommittee Papers on Policy-Making at the Presidential Level*. New York: Praeger, 1965.

James, Dorothy B. *The Contemporary Presidency*. New York: Pegasus, 1969.

Kaplan, Lawrence S. (ed.). *NATO and the Policy of Containment*. Lexington, Mass.: Heath, 1968.

Kennan, George F. *Memoirs, 1925–1950*. Boston: Little, Brown, 1967.

Koenig, Louis W. (ed.). *The Truman Administration: Its Principles and Practices*. New York: New York University Press, 1956.

Korea, 1945 to 1948: A Report on Political Developments and Economic

Resources with Selected Documents. New York: Greenwood Press, 1969.

Krock, Arthur. *In the Nation: 1932–1966.* New York: McGraw-Hill, 1966.

———. *Memoirs: Sixty Years on the Firing Line.* New York: Funk and Wagnalls, 1968.

LaFeber, Walter. *America, Russia, and the Cold War, 1945–1966.* New York: John Wiley and Sons, 1967.

Lamont, Lansing. *Day of Trinity.* New York: Antheneum, 1965.

Langer, William L. (ed.). *An Encyclopedia of World History.* Boston: Houghton Mifflin, 1952.

Leahy, William. *I Was There.* New York: McGraw-Hill, 1950.

Leopold, Richard. *The Growth of American Foreign Policy.* New York: Alfred A. Knopf, 1962.

Lilienthal, David E. *The Journals of David E. Lilienthal,* Vol. II, *The Atomic Energy Years, 1945–1950.* New York: Harper and Row, 1964.

Long, Gavin. *MacArthur as Military Commander.* New York: Van Nostrand Reinhold, 1969.

Lukacs, John. *A History of the Cold War.* Rev. ed. Garden City, N.Y.: Doubleday, 1962.

MacArthur, Douglas. *Reminiscences: General of the Army Douglas MacArthur.* New York: McGraw-Hill, 1964.

Major Problems of United States Foreign Policy, 1951–1952. Washington: Brookings Institution, 1951.

Millis, Walter. *Arms and Men: A Study of American Military History.* New York: New American Library, 1956.

——— (ed.). *American Military Thought.* New York: Bobbs-Merrill, 1966.

——— (ed.). *The Forrestal Diaries.* New York: Viking Press, 1951.

Morison, Elting E. *Turmoil and Tradition: A Study of the Life and Times of Henry L. Stimson.* Boston: Houghton Mifflin, 1960.

Neumann, William L. *After Victory: Churchill, Roosevelt, Stalin, and the Making of the Peace.* New York: Harper and Row, 1969.

Neustadt, Richard E. *Presidential Power: The Politics of Leadership.* New York: New American Library, 1964.

Osgood, Robert E. *Limited War: The Challenge to American Strategy.* Chicago: University of Chicago Press, 1957.

Paige, Glenn D. *The Korean Decision, June 24–30, 1950.* New York: The Free Press, 1968.

——— (ed.). *1950: Truman's Decision, the United States Enters the Korean War.* New York: Chelsea House, 1970.

Payne, Robert. *The Marshall Story: A Biography of General George C. Marshall.* New York: Prentice-Hall, 1951.

Phillips, Cabell. *The Truman Presidency: The History of a Triumphant Succession.* New York: Macmillan, 1966.

Pusev, Merlo J. *The Way We Go To War.* Boston: Houghton Mifflin, 1969.

Rees, David. *The Age of Containment: The Cold War, 1945–1965.* New York: St. Martin's Press, 1967.

Ridgway, Matthew B. *The Korean War.* Garden City, N.Y.: Doubleday, 1967.

Roche, John P. *The Quest for the Dream: The Development of Civil Rights and Human Relations in Modern America.* Chicago: Quadrangle Books, 1968.

Roche, John P., and Leonard W. Levy (eds.). *The Presidency.* New York: Harcourt, Brace and World, 1964.

Rogow, Arnold A. *Victim of Duty: A Study of James Forrestal.* London: Rupert Hart-Davis, 1966.

Roper, Elmo. *You and Your Leaders: Their Actions and Your Reactions, 1936–1956.* New York: William Morrow, 1957.

Rossiter, Clinton. *The American Presidency.* New York: New American Library of World Literature, 1956.

―――. *The Supreme Court and the Commander in Chief.* Ithaca, N.Y.: Cornell University Press, 1951.

―――― (ed.). *The Federalist Papers.* New York: New American Library of World Literature, 1961.

Rostow, W. W. *The United States in the World Arena: An Essay in Recent History.* New York: Harper and Brothers, 1960.

Rovere, Richard H. *Senator Joe McCarthy.* Cleveland: World Publishing, 1959.

Rovere, Richard H., and Arthur M. Schlesinger, Jr. *The General and the President and the Future of American Foreign Policy.* New York: Farrar, Straus and Young, 1951.

Ryan, Cornelius. *The Last Battle.* New York: Simon and Schuster, 1966.

Schlesinger, Arthur M., Jr. *The Age of Roosevelt,* Vol. II, *The Coming of the New Deal.* Boston: Houghton Mifflin, 1959.

Schwarz, Urs. *American Strategy: A New Perspective, The Growth of Politico-Military Thinking in the United States.* Garden City, N.Y.: Doubleday, 1967.

Singletary, Otis A. *The Mexican War.* Chicago: University of Chicago Press, 1960.

Smith, Louis. *American Democracy and Military Power: A Study of the Military Power in the United States.* Chicago: University of Chicago Press, 1951.

Spanier, John W. *American Foreign Policy Since World War II.* 2nd rev. ed. New York: Frederick A. Praeger, 1965.

―――. *The Truman-MacArthur Controversy and the Korean War.* New York: W. W. Norton, 1965.

Steinberg, Alfred. *The Man from Missouri: The Life and Times of Harry S. Truman.* New York: G. P. Putnam's Sons, 1962.

Stillman, Richard J. *Integration of the Negro in the U.S. Armed Forces.* New York: Frederick A. Praeger, 1961.

Stimson, Henry L. and McGeorge Bundy. *On Active Service in Peace and War.* New York: Harper and Brothers, 1947, 1948.

Stone, I. F. *The Hidden History of the Korean War.* New York: Monthly Review Press, 1952.

Truman, Harry S. *Memoirs*, Vol. I, *Years of Decision.* Garden City, N.Y.: Doubleday, 1955.

———. *Memoirs*, Vol. II, *Years of Trial and Hope.* Garden City, N.Y.: Doubleday, 1956.

———. *Mr. Citizen.* New York: Popular Library, 1961.

Truman, Margaret. *Harry S. Truman.* New York: William Morrow, 1973.

Truman Speaks. New York: Columbia University Press, 1960.

Vandenberg, Arthur H., Jr. (ed.). *The Private Papers of Senator Vandenberg.* Boston: Houghton Mifflin, 1952.

Warren, Sidney. *The President as World Leader.* Philadelphia: J. B. Lippincott, 1964.

Watson, Richard L., Jr. (ed.). *The United States in the Contemporary World, 1945–1962.* New York: The Free Press, 1965.

Weigley, Russell F. *Towards an American Army: Military Thought from Washington to Marshall.* New York: Columbia University Press, 1962.

Whitney, Courtney. *MacArthur: His Rendezvous with History.* New York: Alfred A. Knopf, 1956.

Williams, T. Harry. *Americans at War: The Development of the American Military System*, Rev. ed. New York: Colliers, 1962.

———. *Lincoln and His Generals.* New York: Alfred A. Knopf, 1952.

Williams, William Appleman. *The Tragedy of American Diplomacy.* New York: World Publishing, 1962.

——— (ed.). *The Shaping of American Diplomacy: Readings and Documents in American Foreign Relations, 1750–1955.* Chicago: Rand McNally, 1956.

Willoughby, Charles A. and John Chamberlain. *MacArthur, 1941–1965.* New York: McGraw-Hill, 1954.

Wilson, Charles (Lord Moran). *Churchill: Taken From the Diaries of Lord Moran: The Struggle for Survival, 1940–1965.* Boston: Houghton Mifflin, 1966.

Wiltz, John E. *From Isolation to War, 1931–1941.* New York: Crowell, 1968.

Index

Acheson, Dean: and atomic energy, 66, 67 68; and Russo-Turkish confrontation, 127; and Greek-Turkish aid, 129–30; and Mutual Defense Assistance Program, 149–50; and SHAPE, 150; "Perimeter" speech of, 163–64, 238; and Korean War, 165–71 *passim*, 179, 196, 222, 231, 235; justifies Korean intervention, 172; and MacArthur, 199, 205, 225, 232, 233, 250, 253, 254; on Red China entering war, 203–204; requests "national emergency" declaration, 218; McCarthy attacks, 219; mentioned, 77, 187, 188, 218, 234, 244, 252

Advisory Commission on Universal Training, 84–85

Air Force: seventy air-group program of, 121–24; requests aircraft for Berlin airlift, 139, 145; mentioned, 90–92, 108, 123. *See also* Symington, Stuart

Air Policy Commission, 120–21

Alamorgordo, N.M., 51

Alaska, 139

Albania, 129

Albert, Carl, 263

Aleutian Islands, 163

American Labor Party, 173

American Legion, 251

Antung, China, 205

Armed Services Committee. *See* House (or Senate) Armed Services Committee

Army Air Force: bombing raids on Japan, 28–29; and unification, 96; mentioned, 116

Army, Department of the: racial reforms in, 90–92; and Berlin Blockade, 139–45 *passim*; and Mutual Defense Program, 150; and military aid to Korea (1888), 154; mentioned, 108, 122, 123

Arnold, Henry H.: on unification, 96; mentioned, 54, 58

Atlee, Clement, 218, 219

Atomic bomb: use of, on Japan, 44, 45, 48, 51–56 *passim*; successful testing of, 45, 51; FDR discusses, 46; Truman informed of, 46–48; dissent over, 49–50; and "second-bomb" strategy, 56–58; public reaction to, 59; Truman's second thoughts on, 61; use of, in Korea, 215; as deterrent factor, 268. *See also* Atomic energy; Interim Committee; Manhattan Project

Atomic energy: nuclear policy on, 64, 142–43; postwar tests of, 75–76; and "air-atomic reaction," 119, 127; custody question of, 142; and thermonuclear crash program, 151–52

Atomic Energy Act of 1946, pp. 74–75, 269

Atomic Energy Commission: creation of, 70; and Atomic Energy Act, 71–74; and Military Liaison Committee, 73; crash program of, 76–78; and

166–68; meets re offer of Formosan troops, 180; meets re forces in Korea, 180–81; and Soviet Union, 187–88; Truman ousts Johnson as secretary of, 193–94; and North Korean invasion plans, 197; on chances of Red China entering war, 204–205; and Yalu bridge-bombing order, 205–206; "hot pursuit" policy of, 208; Truman asks $16.8 billion increase for, 216; and MacArthur's December 3, 1950, message, 217; recommends cease-fire, 232; mentioned, 89, 168, 230

Demobilization: point system of, 116; problems of, 116; plans for, 117; causes protest demonstrations, 118; causes letter-writing campaign, 118; Truman's statement on, 118; armed forces after, 119

Democratic National Committee, 90

Denfeld, Louis: opposes cancellation of supercarrier, 125–26; in revolt of the admirals, 126; removed from CNO post by Truman, 126

Desegregation of armed forces, 268

Dewey, Thomas E., 25

Division of Military Application, 74

Doenitz, Karl, 34

Dresden, 58

East Germany, 145

Eberstadt, Ferdinand, 95, 99

Eberstadt Committee, 95,110

Eden, Anthony, 29

Egypt, 175

Eighth Army: pushes NKPA to 38th parallel, 192; advances on North Korea, 198; captures Pyongyang, 202; contacts CCF elements, 211–12; splits from Tenth Corps, 214; in critical position, 217; establishes line north of 38th parallel, 221; First and Ninth Corps of, advance, 229; mentioned, 187, 190, 197, 217

Eisenhower, Dwight D.: shifts allied advance from Berlin, 31–32; accepts German surrender, 35; and unification, 99; assumes NATO command, 150–51, 236; breaks with Truman, 238; receives CIA reports,

238; goes to Korea, 239; ends Korean War, 240; Truman's respect for diminished, 241; receives letter from Truman re MacArthur, 263; mentioned, 21, 34, 58, 81, 105, 119, 126, 128, 137, 259, 261

Elbe River, 31, 35

England. *See* Great Britain

Eniwetok Atoll, 75

Europe: and nuclear-weapons planes, 143; Berlin affects U.S. policy toward, 143; and Cold War, 147; mentioned, 176, 207

European Recovery Act, 133

Executive Order 9877: on changes in military organization, 111

Executive Order 9980: on fair employment policies, 90

Executive Order 9981: on reform in military racial policies, 90

Far East: surrender of Japanese in, 155–56; defensive perimeter of, 163–64

Far East Command: warns of North Korean buildup, 164; mentioned, 165–66, 184

Farrell, Thomas, 76

Federal Bureau of Investigation, 89

Federalist Papers, 3–4

F–80, fighter aircraft, 199–200

Finletter, Thomas K.: rejects second advance over 38th parallel, 231; mentioned, 120, 176

Finland, 147

Fire bombs. *See* Incendiary bombs

First Marine Division, 212

Fitzhugh, Gilbert, 114

509th Composite Group, 20th Air Force, 54

Formosa: MacArthur visits, 242; MacArthur's post–Wake Island view on, 246; mentioned, 163, 243, 251

Forrestal, James: assesses Truman Committee, 23; on Japanese surrender terms, 61; on nuclear weapons policy, 66, 142–43; on racial reforms in military, 91–92; and unification, 93–113 *passim*; named Secretary of Defense, 108, 113–14; death of, 114; on demobilization,